Block Island — The Land

Land meets the sea dramatically, two hours after the great landslide of April 10, 2001

Overleaf:

View of the bluffs two hours after the great landslide of April 10, 2001, just west of Lakeside Drive.

The event — unprecedented in the recorded history of Block Island or the State of Rhode Island — occurred in the front yard of a newly constructed summer rental house. This crumbling of the bluffs laid a swath of land up to 30 feet high along a 250-foot stretch of otherwise flat beach; a loss to Block Island approximately 1,000 times larger than usual incidents of erosion. In only three days the portion of the landslide that impertinently jutted into the sea, washed away. (See closeup photo, page 263.)

BLOCK ISLAND
The Land

---

by Robert M. Downie

Book Nook Press

Block Island, Rhode Island

Published by Book Nook Press
Block Island, Rhode Island 02807

Designed by A. Frederick Clarke
Composition by AptArt Publishing Co., East Greenwich, RI 02818

Printed on archival paper in United States of America.

Library of Congress Cataloging-in-Publication Data:

Downie, Robert M.
Block Island—The Land/Robert M. Downie
Includes Index.
1. History–Block Island, RI
2. Description–Block Island, RI
3. Photographs–Block Island, RI
I. Title
974.58 Dow-2

ISBN: 0-9658983-2-6

SRP $29.95

For other information about Block Island, see the companion volume
Block Island – The Sea, comprised of additional photographs and stories.

Cover Photo: View from Beacon Hill Road showing one of the Island's two windmills, 1884
(see page 208 for full photograph)

CONTENTS

1870 map

Boundaries are shown for Block Island's five school districts of the 1800s and early 1900s. (See Chapter 11).

Roads in the southern half of the Island radiated like fingers from the old Center. Throughout the tourist boom-years of the 1870s and 80s, sections of public roads were created to link the ends of the fingers, forming the familiar circular route of today. (See map on opposite page)

Block Island — 2001

Paved roads are shown solid; major dirt roads are dashed.

For other Block Island maps see:

- 1635 Dutch map, southern New England — pages 126-127
- 1661 Settlers' survey map — page 60
- 1886 (southwest) portion of "stonewall map" — pages 62-63
- 1900 (New Harbor/Old Harbor) horse car route — page 161
- 1909 (Beach Ave. & Center Rd.) Central House — page 88
- 1940s World War II "fields of fire" — page 11
- 1989 Nathan Mott Park & airport — page 57
- 1999 (southwest) Greenway path — page 250
- 2001 conservation land — page 253

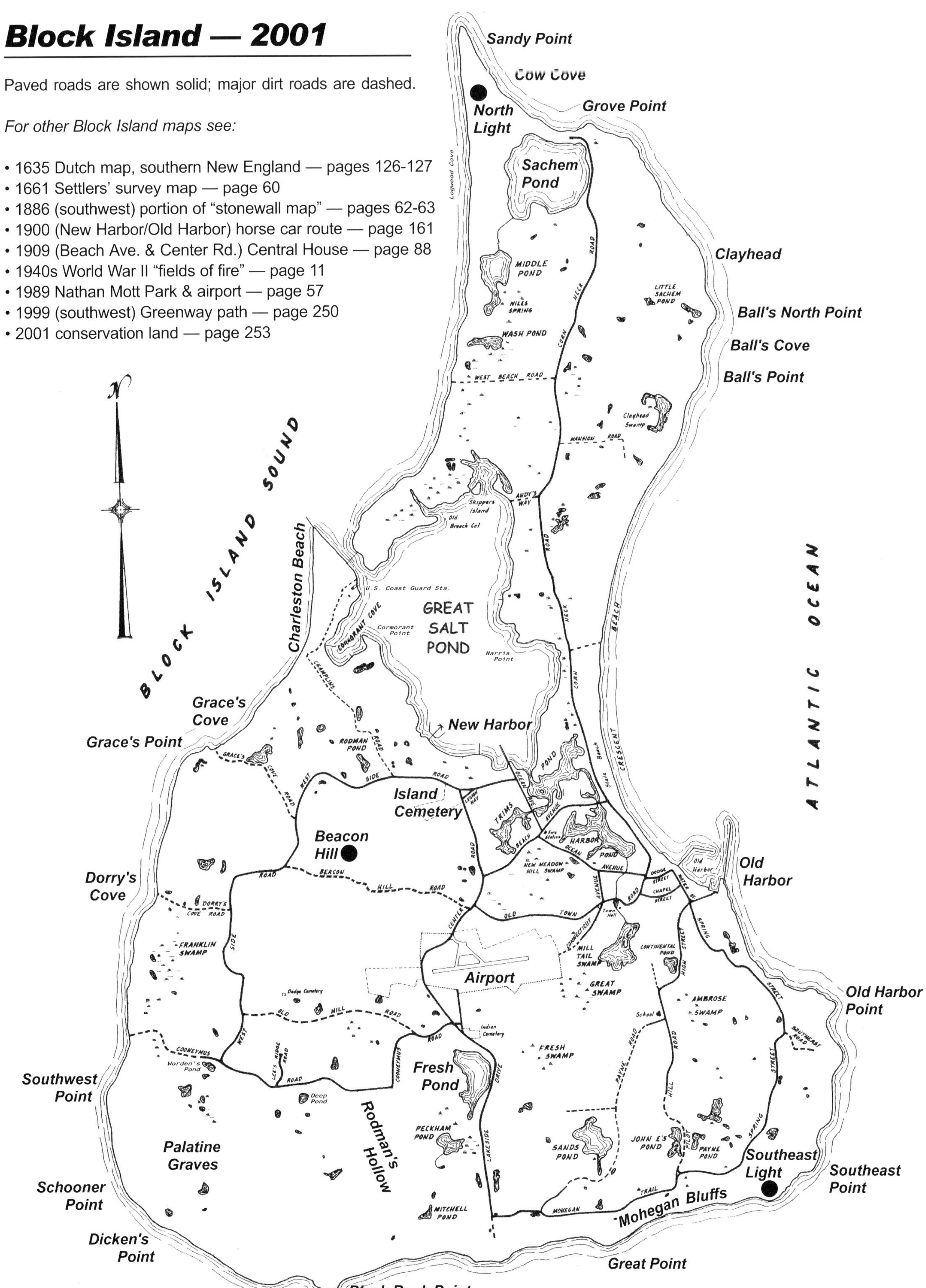

Changes soon to happen at New Harbor:
• on the promontory called Job's Hill between the two docks (Champlin's on the left and Payne's on the right), a third marina was built in the late 1960s: the Block Island Boat Basin.

Aerial View of New Harbor and Old Harbor, October 6, 1963

Changes soon to happen at Old Harbor:

- between the two breakwaters, a new T-shaped dock was built in 1965 for the ferry, and half of the sand dunes and beach were paved for a parking lot.
- the 360-foot Ocean View Hotel (south of the large breakwater, below) burned on July 6, 1966 — see Chapter 3 — leaving the 150-foot Spring House (further to the south, below) as the Island's largest hotel.

BLOCK ISLAND
The Land

Dedicated to everyone
who loves Block Island

Block Island is unique, being more distant from land — from the mainland or from other islands — than any other town along the 1,800-mile eastern coast of the United States.

Adding to the isolation, Block Island is farther from the state capital than any community in Rhode Island — and is the smallest town in the smallest state in the country.

What is it like living on an island, a real island: one besieged by waves, wind, fog, and spray — in the best of conditions separated from the mainland by an hour's boat trip, and in the worst, by a wait of several days?

Non-islanders cannot know, especially those from communities with large schools, and those used to shopping, without batting an eyelash, at the nearest mall. But sometimes one may attempt to comprehend, or at least recognize he doesn't understand, as a state official did in 1942, near the start of World War II, saying after his visit to Block Island:

> *"They're pretty well organized ... There's no doubt but what they have a different problem from that of any community on the mainland and they're handling it."*

CHAPTER 1

World War II — The Furthest Island

Fourth of July Parade, 1991

Left to right — Tony Gutierrez, Walter McDonough, Dan Oneiu, Adrian Mitchell.

The spirit of Block Island strides onward during each Fourth of July parade, particularly in the yearly evocation by these fine gentlemen of the famous image *The Spirit of '76* — a painting of Revolutionary marchers by artist Archibald Willard, made for the nation's 100th anniversary in 1876.

Parades were held on Block Island in 1961 (for the 300th anniversary of the arrival of settlers from Massachusetts), in 1972 (the 300th anniversary of the charter of the Town of New Shoreham), and in 1976 (200th anniversary of the United States). In 1986 the Fourth of July parade became an annual event (see photo on page 9).

IN JANUARY 1942, just a month after the United States declared war on Germany, state officials in Rhode Island questioned whether residents of Block Island should be evacuated to the mainland.

The state was not kidding.

Everyone knew of the experiences of the past two years: Europe had been overrun by the Nazi blitzkrieg, cities and civilians had been bombed indiscriminately. The conquered residents, those not sent to concentration camps, walked a tightrope between obeying the Germans explicitly on the one extreme, or aiding neighbors and friends in the underground resistance, on the other. Each civilian of the occupied countries remained continually at risk of arbitrary, retaliatory killings by the Germans.

The English — bombed night and day and under threat of invasion — separated many of their children from obliging parents, sending the young ones for safety to Ireland, and even 3000 miles away to North America.

Americans knew that the Channel Islands, English possessions located just off the coast of France, had been occupied by the Germans in June 1940. The Islands' civilians were to be captives until Germany's final surrender in May 1945. For those five years it was simply too risky and unnecessary for the Allies — who bypassed the Channel Islands while liberating the rest of France — to root out the German soldiers stationed there.

Block Island, at a little more than eight miles from the closest part of the mainland, is at a greater distance from other land — from the mainland or from other islands — than any other town along the Atlantic coast of the United States.

In early 1942 that coast was suddenly under the guns and torpedoes of German U-boats, which were to sink 600 ships in just the first six months after America entered the war — equal to three million tons, or half the tonnage of American merchant ships afloat. Most of the sinkings occurred in waters supposedly defended by U.S. Navy and Army Air Forces.

The Germans weren't kidding either, and they were just beginning.

Block Islanders had been through this twice before, in the American Revolution in the 1770s and in the War of 1812. During each conflict the Island was — as both the English and Americans knew — at the complete mercy of British ships.

In August 1775, four months after the opening battles at Concord and Lexington, 30 minutemen were ordered to Block Island by the Rhode Island General Assembly. The next month the General Assembly voted that the sheep and lambs should be removed from the Island — a decision the Islanders agreed with — to prevent the British from using Block Island as a food supply. In November, General George Washington ordered the cattle also taken from Block Island, as he similarly demanded for nearby Fisher's Island, the Elizabeth Islands and Martha's Vineyard.

Then, in December, the troops stationed on Block Island were told to leave by General Washington, and an emissary from the state visited to "earnestly exhort the inhabitants of New Shoreham to remove off from the Island." But most Islanders stayed. The British did come ashore, on and off at will, leaving the residents in limbo for six years until England's defeat at the battle of Yorktown, Virginia, in 1781.

During the War of 1812 — a generation later — Block Island, helpless once more, was proclaimed neutral at the outset. British men-of-war anchored off the northern end of Corn Neck, refilling their casks at Middle Pond and Sachem Pond. They used another pond as well, at present-day Old Harbor — that pond was later filled, and in 1882 the Empire Theatre was built on its site. Respecting the neutrality, the British purchased produce from the Islanders and even aided in building a meeting house for the residents in 1814 — its former site at the cemetery, a flattened area to the east of the paved driveway's crest, is still obvious, being filled with gravestones of a later time (see photo on bottom of page 43).

With mutual respect still possible between antagonists, the War of 1812 was vastly safer than the wars of the 1900s.

At the end of that bleak January month in 1942 when state defense officials visited Block Island, the Islanders spoke in unison. They were not leaving, their outlook echoing the basic rationale used after the cattle and sheep were removed during the Revolution.

"There ain't a thing here any enemy would wantta get a hold of, so fur as I can see," said George S. Sheffield, a farmer, and chairman of the local defense council. Tall and thin with greyed hair topped by a leather fisherman's cap, he looked in a photograph of 1942 more like a stiff-upper-lipped Britisher who might at any moment shoulder a wooden rifle to practice for the defense of his village.

At the* Island Light & Power Company, *1942

Police Chief George S. Sheffield, who served as head of the Island defense council, shows how an air raid warning would be sounded at the Island's electric light plant.

The 671 residents were already feeling the effects of the war in that first month of the year. The entire Island's ration for tires in January 1942 was one auto tire — for about 250 cars — and six truck tires. For the following month it was to be one auto tire and just one truck tire.

And yet that July the Islanders turned in 12 tons of discarded tires in a statewide rubber drive — plucked from farms where thrifty farmers used them for tying down haystacks or tethering grazing animals, and from boats and pilings where they had served as fenders. The per capita rate of 35 pounds for each resident was the highest in Rhode Island.

The meeting with state defense officials on January 27, 1942, to decide the Island's future took place at the National Hotel over two antique parlor tables. The Island's defense leaders, most in their 50s and 60s, came in one-by-one, wearing the workaday clothes of overalls, hip boots, and windbreakers — nearly a dozen, including one woman.

Said a *Providence Journal* writer who was present:

"Whenever evacuation was mentioned, they cast beady eyes out of windows toward the blue water on whose crest rode the ships of the fishing fleet. Brown and white sails were hoisted against the clearing sky to dry, while owners or helpers shoveled or scrapped snow from decks or cockpits."

The reporter explained how the meeting at the National progressed:

"[The state officials] who worked on a survey of evacuation preferences among the Island's population explained that no effort had been made [by Islanders] to list the race or religion of the residents. These facts have been gathered in other parts of the state to guide evacuation officials in properly placing evacuees in receiving areas. But on Block Island they feel these things are a man's own business — or a woman's. 'We just take people the way we find them,' they said. Besides, the survey revealed that nobody wanted to be evacuated. Nobody at all. On the mainland, the voluntary evacuees in so-called danger areas run from 60 to 85 percent of those canvassed."

As the meeting continued, the *Journal's* writer became amused, admiringly so, of the down-to-earth Islanders' stance and their matter-of-fact answers to mainland defense officials who had no conception of just how different an Island eight miles at sea — and 15 miles from the nearest harbor — really was.

The Island's local defense council, for instance, could not find jobs for the 112 Islanders who had signed up. Block Island did not, as did the mainland, need auxiliary firemen and policemen — just one air raid warden, to check that lights were not visible at night, would be fine.

It was explained to state officials that there were already 68 volunteer firemen for only one piece of apparatus — and the Coast Guard patrolled the beaches night and day, while the Army watched for enemy planes and ships from eight cement lookout towers disguised as silos and farmhouses.

In case of a night air raid, said Joseph Pennington, operator of the Island's electric generating plant and member of the Block Island defense council, "a switch could be pulled in 15 seconds" that would darken most of the Island.

Why, the mainlanders asked, was the Island's warning center — which was connected by phone to a district center in Newport on the mainland — located at the

Providence Journal

BUY DEF[I]
AND

[...]DENCE, THURSDAY, JANUARY 29, 1942

—"COME HELL, HIGH WATER OR GERMANS"—

"The Spirit of Block Island"

In 1942, the Islanders' bravura at the prospect of a possible German landing was applauded by the *Providence Journal* in words and pictures, including this resolute embodiment of confidence and resolve.

Island's power plant? Because that was the only building manned 24 hours a day. And why 15 seconds to pull a switch? Because that was how long "it takes for a man to walk from the office of the Island Light plant to the master switch in the power plant room."

Pennington, "standing there in the hotel parlor in his hip boots, denim overalls and gray shirt," noted that if all lights were extinguished, the Island would still not be hidden: "From the air the Island itself is a dead giveaway against the water, even on dark nights."

He further added, in reference to the often-revised air raid precautions on the mainland that: "If we'd been right up on our air raid warden's work, it looks like we'd have done about three different things three different ways and then we'd have to start all over again."

With that reminder the state officials moved onto another subject, their main mission: discussion of possible evacuation of the 671 residents. The Germans "might want the Island as a bridgehead" they said. The Islanders countered: the mainland was too close for that to be practical — the Island was within easy range of the Naval Air Station at Charlestown and the massive 16-inch gun emplacements at Point Judith.

The state officials, still concerned for the Islanders' welfare, "played a trump card."

"How about a shortage of food — if the Island were cut off?"

To which they were out-trumped by Pennington, who — although it was still a few years before the availability of television and two full decades before President John F. Kennedy became a master of television's political use — seemed to be talking in perfect sound bites:

"I'd rather scrape for my little girl here than have her somewhere I don't know. We're liable to run away from bombs here and have our children hit by automobiles over on the mainland. They're not used to having traffic."

Newspaper editorial cartoons, 1942

Noted illustrator Paule Loring depicted for readers of the *Providence Journal* the philosophical musings of Block Islander Joseph Pennington, who suggested that during an emergency, food would be easier to find on Block Island than on the mainland.

Near Black Rock on southwest corner of Block Island, ca. 1945

A stark remnant of World War II, one of eight cement lookout towers built on Block Island for spotting enemy aircraft and ships, stands out like a sore thumb in an open pasture above the Atlantic.

In an attempt at camouflage, many of the towers were designed to resemble farm houses or silos.

After the war, this tower at Lewis Farm, together with another just out of view to the left, were demolished with dynamite by the land owner.

As for food supply, Pennington referred first to the main thoroughfare of the state's capital city, Providence, and second to a wooded rural town in northern Rhode Island, shooting back politely to the state officials: "You can't dig clams in Westminster Street and you can't get lobsters in Scituate."

You see, to the Islander "evacuation" meant "running away."

The next day, on January 28, 1942, the House of Representatives of Rhode Island passed a resolution congratulating the Islanders for their "patriotic fortitude." The resolution was introduced by Representative Taylor of Newport who wished to commend "a splendid instance of the inflexible spirit that made Rhode Island." He added:

"At last some people have been found in Rhode Island who are not afraid — a spirit I would like to see more generally distributed through the state."

Block Island — the most physically isolated town on the Atlantic coast, then and now — is different, thank goodness. And some of the Islanders are too.

The Eastern Sea Frontier

In those first few months of **1942** the United States almost lost the war for the allies, not by the staggering loss of military ships when Japan bombed Pearl Harbor, but by the ongoing slaughter of merchant vessels in the Atlantic by Germany. America was so unprepared and untrained, that desperate England — although fearing a Nazi invasion on her own shores — felt compelled to send a fleet of converted trawlers and another fleet of corvettes to aid in the defense of the East Coast of the United States against German subs. While hundreds of merchant ships were being destroyed in American waters, the first sinking of a U-boat off the United States did not occur until May 1942 — five months after America joined the war.

A massive reorganizing of American efforts ensued, part of which, as vast organizations are wont to do, was an invention of nomenclature. The waters off the eastern coast of the United States were designated the Eastern Sea Frontier — the last official frontier in America was NOT the deserts and plains of the West in the 1880s, but the wild, unknown and more deadly Atlantic Ocean of the early 1940s.

Every possible effort had to be made to defend this frontier. That spring Captain Vincent Astor, a millionaire yachtsmen and member of the U.S. Naval Reserve, was sent to ports along the coast to see if fishermen would volunteer to carry special radios to report U-boat sightings back to shore. The first place he stopped was Block Island, where Islanders remembered well what occurred in World War I when a German U-boat sank an entire fishing fleet off Georges Bank. Captain Albert Sanchez, owner of what many considered the finest Block Island fishing boat ever, the schooner STARBUCK, was shelled into submission trying to escape — but he was the only captain to bring back his ship's papers and flag.

A few days after his Block Island visit, Captain Astor reported to superiors that he had found 20 competent and eager Island fishermen, adding:

"The loyalty of the men is unquestionable, and I am inclined to think that they have a good fighting spirit too. Some of them come from families who have lived on the island for generations. One of the leading ones with whom I had a talk told me that he not only would report on an enemy submarine, but would trail it and chase it until he had been shot full of holes and sunk."

These fishermen were later awarded certificates from the United States Navy — signed by Captain Astor and also by Admiral Leary, Commander of the Eastern Sea Frontier — stating:

"Be it known that this Certificate from the Eastern Sea Frontier is awarded to... in recognition of his patriotic services as a Confidential Observer in Atlantic Waters during World War II."

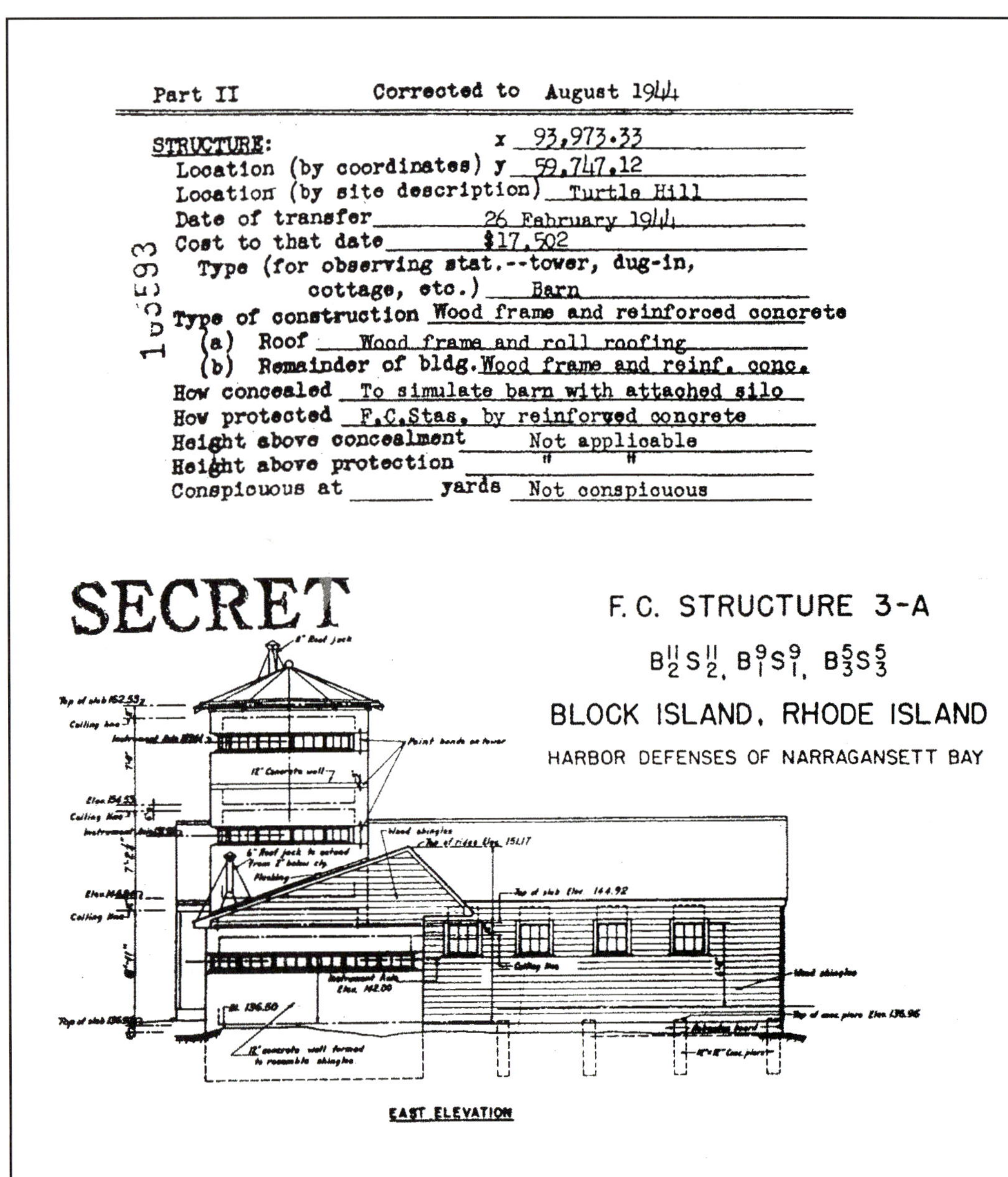

Part II Corrected to August 1944

STRUCTURE: x 93,973.33
Location (by coordinates) y 59,747.12
Location (by site description) Turtle Hill
Date of transfer 26 February 1944
Cost to that date $17,502
Type (for observing stat.--tower, dug-in, cottage, etc.) Barn
Type of construction Wood frame and reinforced concrete
(a) Roof Wood frame and roll roofing
(b) Remainder of bldg. Wood frame and reinf. conc.
How concealed To simulate barn with attached silo
How protected F.C.Stas. by reinforced concrete
Height above concealment Not applicable
Height above protection " "
Conspicuous at ______ yards Not conspicuous

1u3593

SECRET

F. C. STRUCTURE 3-A

$B^{11}_{2}S^{11}_{2}$, $B^{9}_{1}S^{9}_{1}$, $B^{5}_{3}S^{5}_{3}$

BLOCK ISLAND, RHODE ISLAND

HARBOR DEFENSES OF NARRAGANSETT BAY

EAST ELEVATION

World War II report for Spring Street lookout tower, 1944

No longer a "SECRET," this report shows the design of the "wood-frame and reinforced concrete" structure built off Spring Street shortly after the war began, to be used by mainland artillery for "Fire Control."

The three-story building was concealed and disguised "to simulate barn with attached silo" and therefore was considered "not conspicuous."

The building is now a private home, as are the three other remaining towers: on Pilot Hill Road, Corn Neck Road and Beacon Hill.

(See plans for Beacon Hill lookout tower on page 169.)

From a little harbor — came the improbable

THERE WAS A LOT OF ENTHUSIASTIC TALK during World War II, staving off one's own fears no doubt. Ultimately someone would have to do the job. And they did.

Ninety-five Block Islanders fought World War II. As any such group of Americans might, they had planes and ships on which they served shot from underneath them, while traversing the globe from the swamps of Munda on New Georgia island in the southwest Pacific — to the D-day beaches of Normandy, France.

Amongst those in the Navy, Coast Guard, Army, and Army Air Force, the Islanders were lucky, losing only one killed, Albert Gooley — drowned when his torpedoed destroyer sank in December 1944.

Statistical chances of injury functioned more truly in the dangerous merchant marine. The handful of Islanders who sailed the oceans in that capacity lost three ships amongst them — all torpedoed — with one more Islander drowning.

But the mathematical curve went skittering wildly off the chart in another regard. Of the four Block Island men serving in the merchant marine at the start of World War II, two became master sea captains with unlimited licenses, each being the youngest American at the time ever to rise to that supreme position — one, Capt. John Robinson Lewis, in 1943 at the age of 25 — followed, most improbably, by the other, Capt. Evan Dodge, in 1944 at the age of 24.

Each of the two master captains had learned his basic skills growing up on the fishing fleet of Old Harbor — anchored just on the other side of the windows from the National Hotel's antique parlor tables.

As Humphrey Bogart might have said in the World War II movie *Casablanca*, "Of all the little harbors, in all the towns, in all the world..."

Fourth of July Parade, Water Street, 1991

Phelan Real Estate on left, Bare Necessities in middle, Book Nook on right. (See photo on page 2.)

View from concrete lookout tower at the Maze on Corn Neck — gazing southerly toward Old Harbor, 1968

The taller of the two adjacent concrete towers at the Maze, February 1972

The two World War II towers at the Maze, constructed on the highest point of Corn Neck, were blown up by the landowner in February 1976, putting an end to one of the Island's most remarkable views.

A new tower, of wood, should be built on the spot.

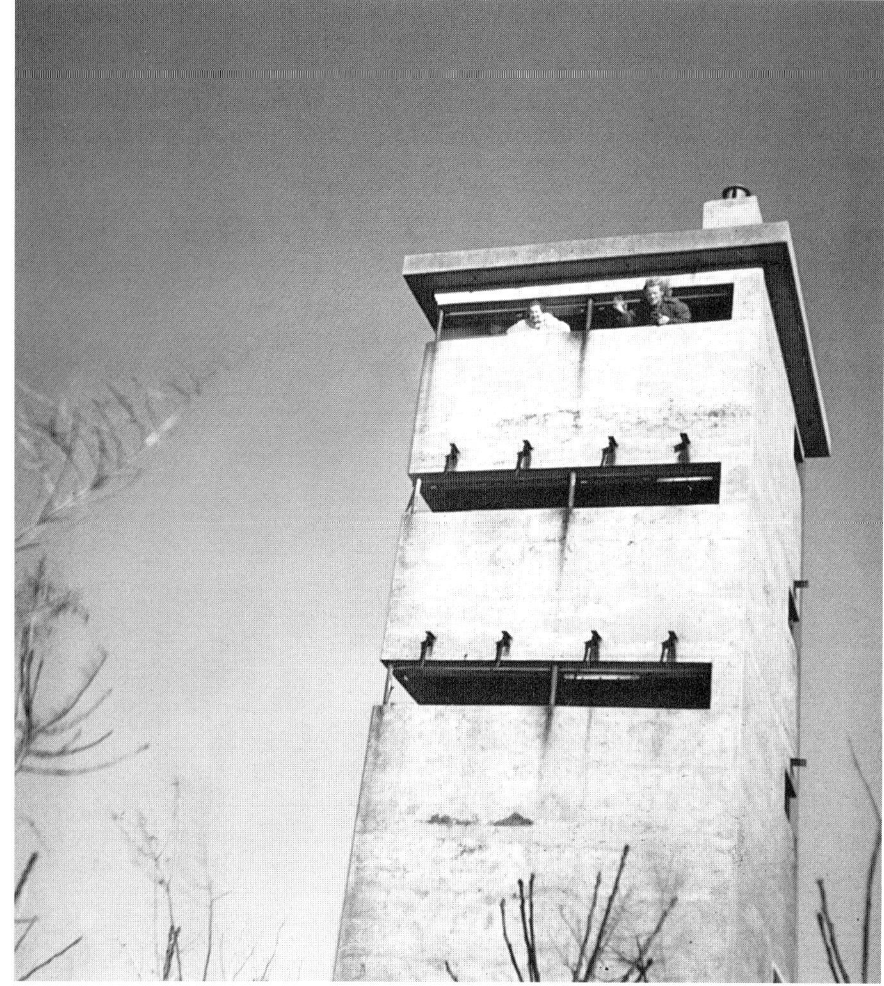

Drawing of Fields of Fire over ocean

Artillery coverage of Block Island and the surrounding waters was achieved by the installation of 16" naval guns at "Ft. Greene" (see map), located a mile from the present-day ferry terminal at Pt. Judith, Rhode Island.

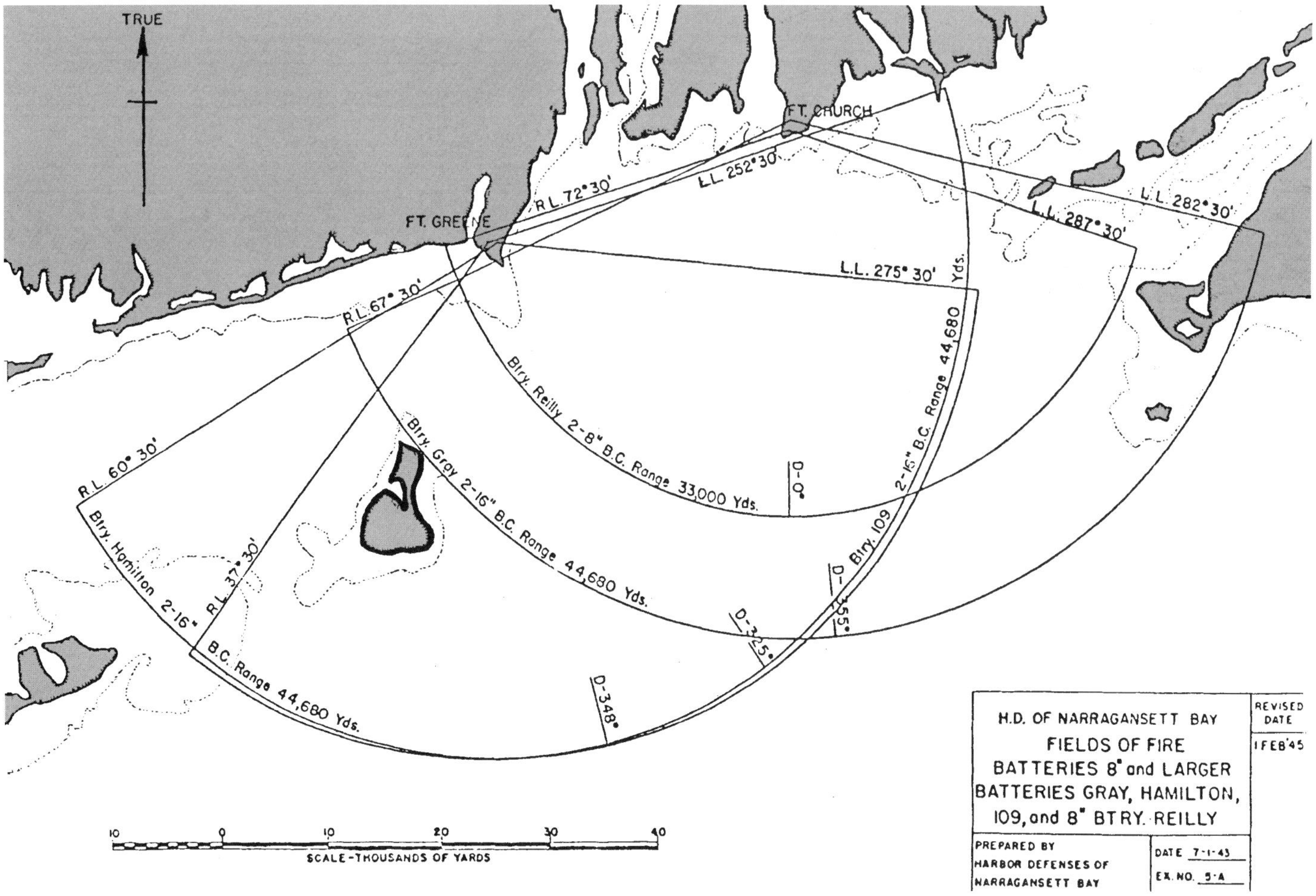
TRUE
FT. CHURCH
FT. GREENE
R.L. 72°30'
L.L. 252°30'
L.L. 287°30'
L.L. 282°30'
L.L. 275° 30'
R.L. 67° 30'
R.L. 60° 30'
R.L. 37° 30'
Btry. Reilly 2-8" B.C. Range 33,000 Yds.
2-16" B.C. Range 44,680 Yds.
Btry. Gray 2-16" B.C. Range 44,680 Yds.
Btry. Hamilton 2-16" B.C. Range 44,680 Yds.
Btry. 109
D-0°
D-355°
D-325°
D-348°
10 0 10 20 30 40
SCALE-THOUSANDS OF YARDS
H.D. OF NARRAGANSETT BAY
FIELDS OF FIRE
BATTERIES 8" and LARGER
BATTERIES GRAY, HAMILTON, 109, and 8" BTRY. REILLY
REVISED DATE
1 FEB '45
PREPARED BY HARBOR DEFENSES OF NARRAGANSETT BAY
DATE 7-1-43
EX. NO. 5-A

The earliest photograph, summer 1873

This first photograph of Block Island was made by Joshua Appleby Williams, a Newport commercial photographer, while standing at the corner where the Surf and National hotels were later built. One half of the stereoscopic image is enlarged above. The stereoview was sold to tourists for many years — eventually as a poorly re-copied card bearing the facetious caption "Block Island Express," part of an economically priced series named *American Scenery.*

Note the curve of the ox-cart tracks in the road. The Atlantic Ocean is to the left, out of view. On the right, in front of the nose of the ox, the dirt of Water Street wends by the shore. Beyond the bed of the cart can be seen masts at Pole Harbor where Islanders tied up their small *double ender* sailboats, now the site of the ferry parking lot.

That August of 1873, the enormous Ocean View Hotel was begun by Nicholas Ball on the hill behind the ox-cart driver. Just over the middle of the ox stands the largest building in this view of Old Harbor; owned also by Ball, the building served as the post office (see text, page 107) and as a grand country store, but it burned to the ground on September 20, 1873. The present-day post office, opened in December, 1996, overlaps the foundation site of the post office destroyed 123 years earlier.

CHAPTER 2

The First Photographs of Block Island

BLOCK ISLAND WAS BACKWARDS. People said so, one well-traveled visitor from the mainland writing in 1856:

"The present inhabitants purport to number in all about fifteen hundred souls, and with very few exceptions are a race of hardy fishermen and sea-faring men. In what is called worldly wisdom they are perhaps fifty years behind the present progressive age."

Amongst various other peculiarities before the late 1800s, Block Island had no harbor, which forced all boats to be small enough that they could be pulled by oxen onto a beach — and for warmth in winter, the inhabitants dug peat from swamps to burn in their fireplaces. When an Islander did get to the mainland — to sell fish and farm products, and purchase wares — he was easily identifiable: by his characteristic boat and the distinctive aroma of peat smoke that hung in his clothes.

That writer of 1856 was enchanted by the place, though. With curiosity piqued, he suffered the fate of many a visitor since — becoming hooked:

"Of all the islands that lie off the coast of the United States, the most interesting, to my mind, is Block Island."

And he liked the people:

"They are temperate in their habits, and not addicted to the vanity of dancing and other nightly fandango doings which are so common among the poorer classes of all countries ... The stranger there, by lounging around the fish-houses with the fisherman, has a capital chance to hear them spin their uncouth but pleasant yarns."

Uncouth, or otherwise, how much we are poorer that no one preserved those stories — of life on the same roads, fields and beaches where we now live 150 years later.

Not only are we prevented by a lack of word descriptions from forming a detailed mental picture of that old Block Island culture, but more surprisingly, we cannot even view that Island in photographs. From 1839 when discovery of the photographic process was announced to the world, more than 30 years were to pass before a camera was used to make an image of the Island.

During that three-decade span, photography recorded much of the planet. America's transcontinental railroad was completed in the 1860s — and photographed. A telegraph cable from Massachusetts to Europe was laid under the Atlantic Ocean in the 1860s — and photographed. Entire wars were chronicled, such as the Crimean in the 1850s, and, in the 1860s, the American Civil War, when Matthew Brady and his assistants made 3,500 images under the worst conditions.

Photographic galleries spread from large cities to small towns, catering to thousands of collectors of a new fad: the three-dimensional stereoview. Because books, newspapers and magazines were then incapable of reproducing photographs, the stereoview had a duel attraction: as well as enjoying the novelty of a fantastic optical trick, viewers could, for the first time in their lives, see realistic images of distant places — knowing, with a certainty those of us living today cannot realize,

View of Dodge Street, looking west, 1875

This image was taken from the same spot as the 1873 stereoview of the ox-cart on page 12 — to view the length of Dodge Street, the photographer turned ninety degrees to his right, placing the harbor and ocean at his back. The photograph was reproduced as an etching in *Harper's Magazine*, July 1876 — but with a ubiquitous Island ox-cart drawn in. The only building still standing is the white house on Calico Hill in the distant center — it is the house that gazes down on the present-day Historical Society.

None of the four houses visible on Dodge Street — three on the left and one on the right — survived to the present. The house in the left foreground was removed in 1888 to make room for the National Hotel. The next house on the left lasted until the 1970s, when it was demolished to build the Island Free Library.

The house seeming to protrude into the road on the right, owned by Richard Dodge (1834-1895), was declared to be a nuisance to traffic, and was torn down in 1898 when the road was widened. The Blue Dory Inn was built on the site that same year by Richard's son, Burnal H. Dodge (1871-1939). Richard's mother, known as Elizabeth "Aunt Betsey" Dodge (1796-1883) gained considerable renown as a weaver.

Passersby could stand on the street looking through her window, watching as — according to the lengthy story of Aunt Betsey on pages 328-330 of Rev. Samuel Livermore's 1877 history of the Island — she worked with her "old-fashioned treadles, harnesses, shuttle, lathe, and beams of her loom."

Besides her industrious nature, Livermore observed, she was "one of the best talking Yankee women we ever met." If only *we* could pass further into this stereoview, beyond the trick of the three dimensions, into a fourth.

When viewed as a three-dimensional stereoview, the stonewalls, buildings, and the man on the right will seem to leap out from this view. Once the knack is achieved — of making the left eye look only at the left-hand image, and the right eye look at the right-hand one — many individuals can simply stare at a stereo-photograph on a flat page, such as this image, and see the photo in startling 3-D. Others may need to use one of the traditional handheld stereoviewers, which force the eyes to accomplish the same task. However you do it, stereoviews are fascinating to experience in the manner originally intended.

that they had little chance of ever seeing those locations in person. Eagerly competing photographers, traveling to remote parts of the earth, brought back pictures to a public that could not be satisfied.

In the late 1860s a New Englander could buy souvenir stereoviews of London and other European cities — or of forests, rivers, mountains and Indians thousands of miles away in the American West — but no one could buy, or had ever even seen, a photograph of Block Island.

The photographers had all missed Block Island.

It would not be until 1873 that a camera made a representation of the Island. The *Providence Evening Bulletin* reported the event simply enough in August 1873: that several artists were taking stereoscopic images from desirable standpoints. One of the stereoviews from that summer has come down to us, of a man and an oxcart in the road — the earliest known photograph of Block Island (see page 12).

How could a generation of entrepreneurs record most of the known world except here? The answer has three parts:

— the common method of photography until the 1870s used glass plate negatives that had to be soaked in a chemical, used while wet, then dipped immediately in other chemicals to be developed;

— photographers would have found it daunting to transport their equipment 20-25 miles across the sea from the nearest ports — Stonington in Connecticut, or Newport in Rhode Island — in one of the Islanders' small undecked *double ender* fishing boats, land on a beach exposed to waves, and wade ashore carrying bottles, glass plates, a wooden camera, and enough other supplies to create a darkroom;

— not many people cared, or even knew about Block Island.

Much of that changed when the breakwater at Old Harbor was begun in 1870. In September 1872, the first vessel was able to unload — it carried a cargo of coal. By the next summer a dock was constructed for steamers to land a more valuable cargo — tourists — and the Block Island boom began.

The First Photograph, summer 1873

THE FIRST KNOWN PHOTOGRAPH of Block Island (page12) was a stereoview taken at the corner where the Surf and National hotels now stand. They had not yet been built — nor had the majestic Ocean View Hotel, which was begun later in 1873 on a vacant hill in the distance.

The background is particularly secondary in this view, however, since the subject of the photograph was one of the giant ox-carts that Islanders then depended on. The ox-cart on land, and the *double ender* boat on water — the basic vehicles of life here — each uncouth in the eyes of mainlanders, and therefore, ironically, of some interest.

Soon after, in November 1873, a daguerreotype saloon — a business that often made indoor portraits of stern-faced sitters — was reported in operation near the breakwater at Old Harbor. No doubt there were many such studio portraits made on the mainland of Block Islanders before 1873, still tucked away perhaps in a very few Island attics and closets — unnamed, undated, and forgotten — but no photograph of the Island itself is known to be earlier than the stereoview of 1873.

Joshua Appleby Williams (1818-1892) of Newport, Rhode Island

THE MAKER OF BLOCK ISLAND'S FIRST PHOTOGRAPHS was a professional, Joshua Appleby Williams, who practiced his craft in Newport from the 1850s to the late 1880s. Between 1873 and 1876 Williams made at least thirteen stereoviews of Block Island. Because no other photographs are known to have been made by anyone else until 1877 — each of his 125-year-old stereoviews is the earliest depiction of that image's particular subject.

Three of J. A. Williams' views — of Dodge Street, the North Light, and the Southeast Light — were used to create etchings published by *Harper's Magazine* in July 1876, illustrating an article that made Block Island known, quite suddenly, throughout the country (see pages 14, 18, 19, 30).

Two other stereoviews by J. A. Williams show *double enders* in Old Harbor: at the dock inside the new basin, and nearby on the beach of the ancient Pole Harbor (below, and on opposite page). During the next 20 years, *double enders* were replaced by deeper-draft vessels — just as, with improved roads, the use of oxcarts gave way to horse-drawn wagons.

Other early photographers

BETWEEN 1877 AND THE 1940S, more than a half-dozen other photographers lugged their cameras off the ferry, successfully chronicling the Island for the tourist trade. **Thomas Lewis** came from Cambridgeport, Massachusetts, in 1877 to make at least 15 views. The **Hacker Photo Co.** of Providence, Rhode Island, arrived later in the 1870s, soon selling its business and negatives to **W. R. Carr & Co.**, also of Providence, who likewise sold out quickly to a fellow citizen, the prolific **H. Q. Morton**, who was to dominate photography on Block Island throughout the 1880s and 90s (see photo, top of page 180). Photographers of minimal activity on the Island about 1880 were **Theodore F. Chase** of Providence, and **Webster's Photographic Studio** of Norwich, Connecticut.

Only two Islanders took up the profession: **Orlando F. Willis** (1857-1927) for a

The new breakwater, 1875

Barber's Restaurant on the right, specializing in 50-cent shore dinners, opened in the summer of 1875 and evolved into the famous Ballard's Inn of this century that was walloped by hurricanes in 1938 and 1954, completely destroyed by fire in July 1986, then rebuilt from the sand up. See Barber's ad, page 124 and Ballard's photo, page 151.

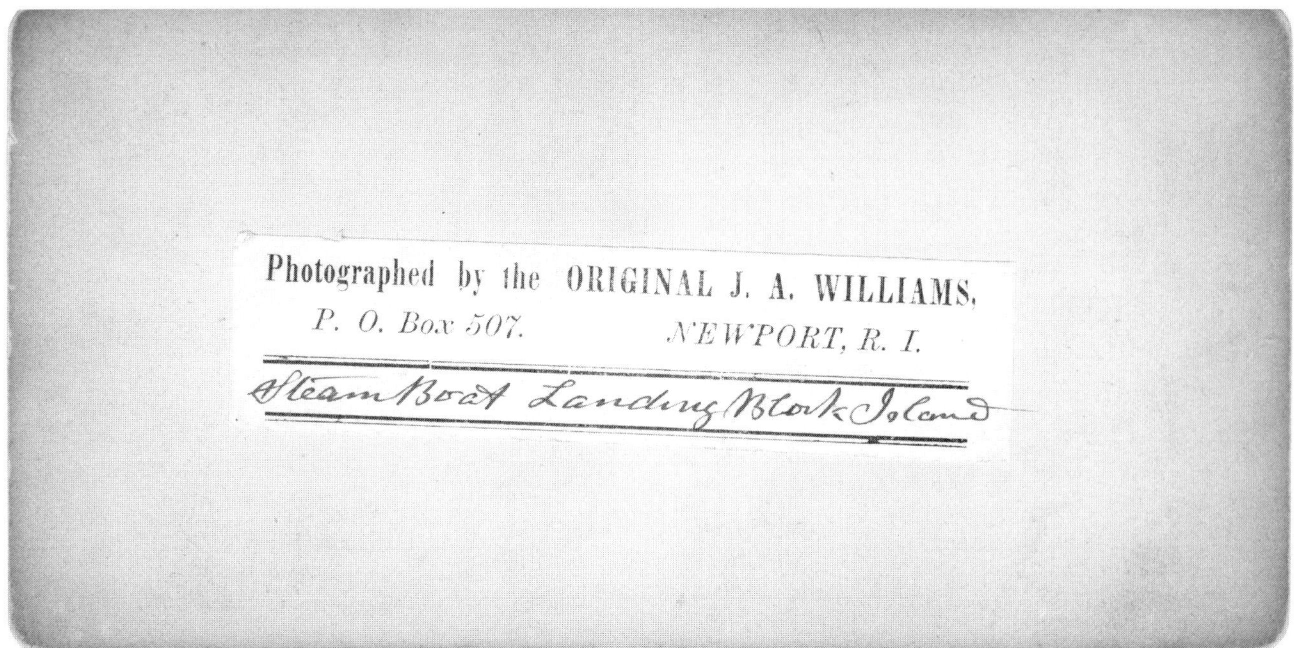

very short time beginning in July 1880, making at least five different stereoviews — and **Richmond "Adelbert" Negus** (1877-1938), an eager practitioner from about 1915 to the mid-1920s (see pages 196, 197).

During the five decades after 1920, the Island went from boom to bust, two-thirds of the population leaving by 1950. The once-proud buildings were stripped of their newness by the elements, their fancy gingerbread decorations peeled off by impoverished owners rather than repaired.

Everyone still has a chance to make their own historic photographs. The present-day landscape is sure to change every dozen months, on an Island booming again, nonstop for the past 30 years.

For photographers of the early 1900s — see Chapter 20, pages 190-199

The bluffs, 1876

Three-dimensional photography is the only way to appreciate fully the elusive glory of the earth's features, such as the Mohegan Bluffs shown here. In 3-D, the sinuous beauty of this precipitous 150-foot-high clay sculpture is revealed.

Pole Harbor and eight of the Islanders' double enders, 1876

Before the Old Harbor breakwater was built in the 1870s, nearby Pole Harbor was the most often used refuge for the Islanders' small *double enders*. The seeming helter-skelter of oak pilings were actually arranged in rows, forming berths that could be sold by one Islander to another, as was the berth for the RAINBOW in 1853 and duly recorded in the town deed books.

Four *double enders* are on the left, the largest nearly obscuring one behind it, and three *double enders* are visible on the right — the furthest to the right having both sails up. Note on the left the half-barrels and four-legged workbench.

The North Light, 1875

As with other of J. A. Williams' stereoviews of Block Island, this is the earliest photograph of the North Light. The building, built in 1867 and still standing, is the fourth North Light constructed at the Island's northern tip, called Sandy Point. An etching made from this image, and reproduced in the July 1876 issue of *Harper's Magazine*, included the bonus of a man and a woman drawn into the foreground, and another person added to the dunes on the right.

The Southeast Lighthouse, 1875

The earliest photograph of the Southeast Lighthouse is this stereoview. Lit on February 1, 1875, the National Landmark building was visited by President Grant in August that same year, and by President Clinton in 1997 (see photos, page 128, 129).

For the July 1876 issue of *Harper's Magazine,* an etching was made based on the photo — faithful to the original except for a party of relaxed people drawn in the foreground.

THE NEW LIGHT-HOUSE ON MOHEGAN BLUFF.

The Harbor windmill, when located off Old Town Road, 1876

(See Chapter 22 for other views of the Island's two windmills)

Ocean View Hotel, July 6, 1966

The Island's largest hotel burned to the ground in 2½ hours on a foggy summer evening.

CHAPTER 3

The Ghost of a Grand Hotel

The spirit of Block Island's most famous hotel, burned to the ground in 1966, still stalks the bluff above Old Harbor

THE YEAR IS 1890. AN OLD MAN IS SEATED in the luxury of a Pullman Palace car headed west for a reunion of the 'Forty-Niners. As the wheels clack over the tracks, the old man's mind ranges backward over the years of his life, to the golden days of his youth in the dirt of the California Gold Rush of 1849, where a generation of determined young men gathered — hard work and fate deciding who amongst the 100,000 would help carry the country forward for the rest of the 1800s. The winners would find wealth, and Nicholas Ball was one of them.

Back to a time when the headland on Block Island looking over Old Harbor was vacant — where now, in 1890, his beloved Ocean View stood as the largest hotel in southern New England, a meeting place for the nation's elite: supreme court justices, senators, governors, captains of industry.

Three decades after the Ocean View Hotel burned to the ground in 1966, present day Block Islanders are deciding the fate of that same headland, once more vacant, that looks over Old Harbor and the sea. They do so with a remembrance of what once stood there, of who built it, and of what the grand hotel had meant to Islanders and visitors.

Nicholas Ball was the youngest of 11 children raised in a small cottage that stood south of Great Salt Pond. To the east could be seen the Atlantic Ocean and passing ships. He began sailing for a wage at the age of nine and a half, continuing his schooling part-time for four months each winter. By October 1849, at the age of 20, he had worked his way from cabin boy to first mate and was familiar with harbors in Scotland and France, and from Maine to the Caribbean.

That month, as a shareholder of the brig GENERAL COBB, Nicholas left Block Island on a six-month sailing trip to the Gold Rush, arriving in San Francisco by way of Cape Horn in May 1850.

In the harsh world of the California frontier he opted for digging gold at a slow and steady pace, after a year packing up his earnings and heading back to Block Island for the summer of 1851. He later wrote of his return home: "In a few weeks, dreams of California and its wealth so far overcame home ties, that October 23 found me leaving once more, bound for the land of gold."

But not before marrying and — in October of 1851, just before heading west again — making a remarkable land purchase. In an era when most property transactions were in the hundreds of dollars, Nicholas spent $4,800 for about 40 acres around the Island's most popular landing spot. There was no breakwater or protected harbor at that time, only beaches to drag small boats up from the reach of the waves. The purchase was for mostly vacant land, but it comprised what is now nearly half the village of Old Harbor: the land along the shore from the Spring House to present-day Chapel Street. He had made a fellow Islander wealthy by this transaction, but Nicholas was off to California for more funds.

Nicholas Ball, 1888

The second time at the Gold Rush, Nicholas was twice as smart. He became a sailing captain — his first claim to that title — and part owner of a small coastal vessel transporting wood and supplies to feed San Francisco Bay's insatiable needs. With the inflated prices of the gold frenzy, he came back to Block Island after two years, in October 1853, having earned twice as much money shipping freight, as he had made on his first trip digging gold.

Throughout the 1850s from the hills near Sacramento there poured forth such driven men, with gold to fuel their dreams. Most would return eastward, changing villages and cities for generations to come, but few if any would have the impact on their hometown that Nicholas Ball had on Block Island.

His start was unpretentious. He became a storekeeper on the Island and a politician representing his town at the state level. Over the next twenty years Nicholas was elected a representative twice and a senator 12 times.

And he took up a quest that had begun when the first white settlers arrived in the 1660s: to make a harbor on Block Island. Two hundred years of efforts had proved futile, but singlehandedly Nicholas convinced politicians in Washington, D.C. that a breakwater built at Block Island — where ships numbering in the hundreds had gone aground — would serve the nation's interests.

In 1870 the breakwater was begun by army engineers — built in front of the land Nicholas Ball had purchased 20 years earlier. He began his own construction in 1873, of a modest-sized hotel which opened for summer of the following year.

The *Providence Evening Bulletin* of June 9, 1874, reported the occasion:

"Last Saturday evening, May 30, the Ocean View Hotel was illuminated with gas, from cellar to cupola, the new gas works and fixtures having been just completed. Three years ago such a sight was not even dreamed of by the quiet fishers of this little island, yet here we have, right on Block Island, a large, commodious, first-class hotel, located upon its eastern bluffs, only 250 feet from the breaking surf of the broad, blue

"The Rocker" from* Voyages of Nicholas Ball *— extract from the text:

"We came down on the Bar from the mountains, and formed a company of seven to work on the sand bank . . . Two went to Sacramento to buy oxen and a scraper, and found on their return Thursday afternoon that the rest of us had washed out $120.

"All worked Friday, Saturday, Monday, Tuesday, and Wednesday, scraping sand from a strip of land twenty feet wide extending from the base of the hill to the river, digging up roots and bushes, and heaping stones to be thrown into the holes from which dirt would be removed later to rocker and pan.

"Having cleared our lead by Thursday noon, we began systematic washing."

Ocean View Hotel

Stage 2, 1876, length of facade = 97'

Atlantic; surrounded by broad cool piazzas, and smooth, grassy lawns; finished with large, high sleeping apartments, parlors, halls, billiard-room and barbershop; well supplied with water, and every room lighted with gas, in fact a first-class hotel in all its appointments."

The hotel — due to the breakwater that allowed steamers to land tourists — was such a raging success that its prosperity, enthusiasm and fame spilled across the adjacent fields creating a boomtown around Old Harbor. During the next ten years, nearby landowners built their own hotels and stores. Nicholas created small building lots near the shore selling them to farmers and storekeepers who proceeded to erect half of present-day Old Harbor — the other half that he did not own, north of Chapel Street, grew just as fast.

Each year after the summer season ended, the hotels were expanded with additions. The demand could not be met, as mainland newspapers observed:

July 1877 — "The increasing popularity of excursions to Block Island is evidenced in the additional steamboat travel and enlarged hotel accommodations afforded on the island. Of late, the latter business has quadrupled, there being now nearly a dozen public houses for the accommodation of guests.

"The principal and prominent hotel, the Ocean View, has experienced the necessity for an enlargement, and under the competent management of Hon. Nicholas Ball, gives comfort and pleasure to hundreds of transient and permanent boarders, while the other hotels, also delightfully situated at neighboring points, find considerable patronage."

September 1878 — "The season of '78, now very near its close, has been an exceedingly prosperous one at Block Island, and it is unmistakably evident that the place is rapidly increasing in popularity ... It was considered a pretty good day when seven or eight hundred or perhaps a thousand excursionists would arrive, but when they pour in to the extraordinary number of twenty-two hundred on one steamer, as was the case on one day this season, landlords begin to look about and see if there isn't a need of enlargement."

August 1879 — "The Ocean View Hotel was visited, and I found it almost doubled in size from last season ... In all its details it is the equal to any of the hotels of Newport, Long Branch, Coney Island, or other watering places. But nature has here attractions that none of the other places can boast of."

Three of the eight stages of the Ocean View Hotel

Nothing captured more expressively the explosive growth of the Island as a tourist attraction in the late 1800s than the mushrooming of the Ocean View Hotel from 40 to 210 rooms in just the seven years between 1876 and 1883, as shown in the images at left.

But as great as that Victorian-era building boom was, it occurred only near the two harbors, leaving 90% of the Island untouched in a quiet pristineness for all to enjoy.

The ongoing boom from the 1970s to the 1990s, however — consisting mainly of hundreds and hundreds of summer houses — has impacted the entirety of Block Island's landscape.

Stage 4, 1878, length of facade = 127'

Stage 5, 1879, length of facade = 181'

Stage 8, 1883, length of facade = 335'

A bridge extends to the nearby annex. Known as the Shamrock Inn in the 1900s, the annex was torn down in the mid-1970s.

March 1880 — "Perhaps in no country town of the State has there been more activity among builders during the past winter."

June 1880 — "There never have been half so many people on the island at this season of the year as at the present time ... We cannot escape the conclusion that Block Island bids fair to be the watering place of this coast."

July 1883 — "Since Sept 1st, 1882, there has been landed upon the shores of Block Island more than 2,000,000 feet of lumber, most of which has been built into hotels and other buildings intended for summer use."

The *New York Times* printed lengthy columns about the Ocean View Hotel, including a half page account titled "King Ball."

The last major addition built onto the Ocean View occurred in 1883. In eight stages over ten years the length had increased from 97 feet to 335 feet, with verandas extending much further. The building boasted electric lights, steam heat, stock market reports via telegraph, a music hall and orchestra, piazzas one third of a mile in length, accommodations for nearly six hundred guests, a house physician, fresh and salt water hot baths, steam laundry, library, art studio, fresh vegetables from the hotel's own farm, and the highest prices on the Island.

Nicholas Ball continued lobbying the federal government for improvements to Block Island, being successful in 1872 with the construction of the Island's first life-saving station (at Cooneymus Road), in 1874 with a second life-saving station (at Old Harbor), in 1875 with the magnificent Southeast Lighthouse, and in 1880 with an underwater telegraph cable to the mainland.

President Grant stopped at the Ocean View in 1875 while visiting the new Southeast Light, led on his tour by Nicholas Ball.

From across the Northeast region, and from the hot South and the Midwest, visitors poured onto Block Island each summer, the very elite usually staying at the Ocean View: Vice-presidents Thomas Hendricks and Schuyler Colfax; senators; representatives; ambassadors; governors; so many U.S. Supreme Court Justices that they once held a hearing on the Island; circus promoter P.T. Barnum, who came for weeks at a time; explorer General Adolphus Greeley, who was once closer to the North Pole than anyone else; financier Russell Sage whose money created the college of that name; John Jacob Astor, who was amongst the famous to perish on the Titanic; and Philip Armour, who, after a successful career in meat packing, begun at the Gold Rush, would die with a fortune of $50,000,000.

Ocean View Hotel and Old Harbor, 1883

The Ocean View Hotel utterly dominated the village of Old Harbor and the surrounding area — as shown by this view from Crescent Beach, taken shortly after the building had reached its final size.

The best way to appreciate the size of the sprawling Ocean View is to realize that the front facade alone was more than twice the length of the largest hotel now on Block Island: the Spring House. (See aerial photograph at front of book, page XI.)

Ocean View Hotel and Water Street, 1882

None of the buildings — whether small or large — in this photograph exist today, except for the life-saving station (with dark roof, just of right of center in photograph), which was moved to Mystic Seaport museum in 1968.

The large squarish structure just to the right of the life-saving station was a blacksmith shop, torn down in the early 1900s. Since the mid-1960s, the site has been occupied by the Sullivan Real Estate building.

The area shown as water and beach, except for a portion in the foreground, is now the paved parking lot for the ferry.

In this view the Ocean View Hotel had not yet reached its final length — that occured in the spring of 1883 when the left wing was extended 50 feet.

The 1890 trip back to the Pacific with fellow members of the Society of California Pioneers was a time of closure for Nicholas Ball. The next year his 312-page account of that five-week cross-country reunion, *The Pioneers of '49* was published in Boston.

In 1891 he printed a pamphlet about his family's genealogy, detailing all the Balls who had lived on the Island since the first one arrived in the 1670s.

His children now managed the Ocean View Hotel.

From September 1891 to May 1892, Nicholas and his wife traveled on an excursion around the world, going again to San Francisco, but this time to come home, heading westward across the Pacific — the ultimate closure for a sailor.

Other volumes, privately bound in limited numbers, were written by Nicholas detailing the behind-the-scenes work needed to secure federal funding for the breakwater, life-saving stations, telegraph cable and Southeast Lighthouse.

In 1895 he published his most noteworthy effort, *Voyages of Nicholas Ball*. Although slim, being only 40 pages, the gold-embossed hardbound rarity is invaluable for the contents. Nicholas listed the dates, destinations, earnings and other details for each of his seagoing trips as a youth, including all the lumber-carrying ventures in California. He also printed his daily mining record, the amount of gold washed out, and his dealings with various partners — these are the raw basics, the nuggets of reality, omitted from most Gold Rush books.

The end came the next year at the age of 67. After a week of heart and stomach problems, Nicholas Ball died on July 31, 1896, at his hotel overlooking the Atlantic, leaving two ocean views worthy of preservation — the sweeping panorama of the sea and the material substance of the grand hotel.

- *For an interior view of the Ocean View Hotel — see page 31*
- *For photograph of Nicholas Ball's gravestone — see page 50*
- *For photographs taken from the Ocean View Hotel cupola — see pages 110 & 111*
- *For brochures and engravings of the Ocean View Hotel — see pages 125 & 184*

Ruins of Ocean View Hotel, twenty-five years after the fire, 1991

Floor plan of the Ocean View Hotel, superimposed with hash marks |||||||||||||||| showing some of the prominent present-day foundation walls

The ruins of the Ocean View Hotel could be saved and transformed into a sunken garden, with walkways winding through the 127-year-old granite walls — a park to remember how Block Island's present economy began, a place of beauty that residents and visitors would seek out. The Ocean View Hotel has not survived, but the ocean view can. Towards that purpose, in May 2000 a small, graceful gazebo was dedicated on the site.

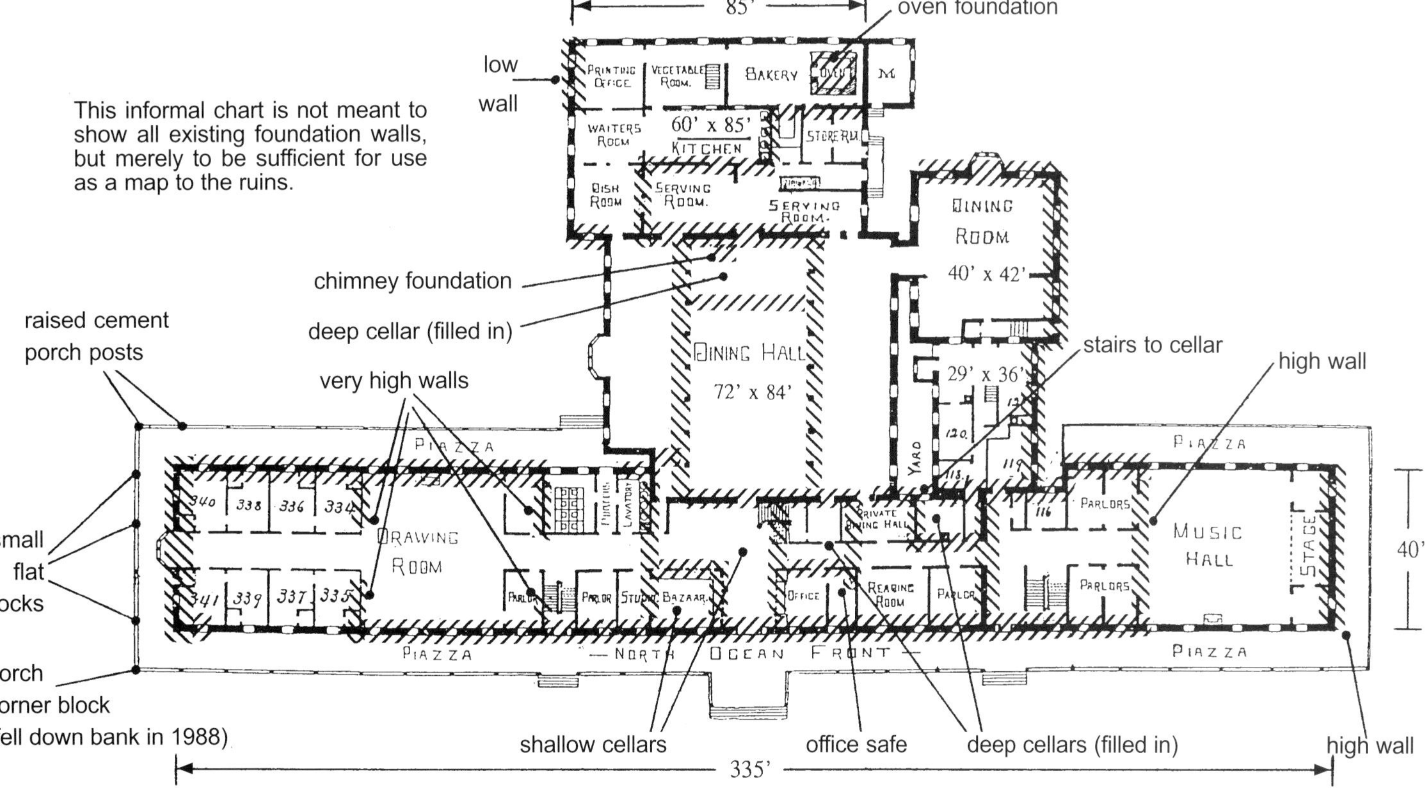

CHAPTER 4

Ume Tsuda

In 1875, on her way to changing the world, a 10-year-old Japanese girl visits the Ocean View Hotel on Block Island

Ume Tsuda, ca. 1875

Ume Tsuda (on left), with two of the five children sent from Japan to learn American customs — about the time she visited Block Island in August 1875, at the age of 10.

MASAKO OWADA, AGE 29, EDUCATED at Harvard and Oxford, walked into the woods of Tokyo's Imperial Palace in June 1993 to marry Crown Prince Naruhito — becoming next-in-line to be Empress of Japan. Formidably talented, well-accomplished in diplomatic and business circles, the worldly Masako was following the small footsteps of a remarkable 10-year-old Japanese girl who visited Block Island in 1875.

That child, Ume Tsuda, would grow up to become a leader of women's education in Japan, helping to transform her country from a feudal society into a modern one. While on her late-August trip to Block Island more than a century and a quarter ago, the precocious youngster was noticed by a reporter for the *Providence Journal*, who fashioned in words an engaging and perceptive portrait (see page 31).

In 1872 Ume was sent to the United States to do precisely what she managed to accomplish — to become educated in Western culture, with the understanding that she would return to her homeland as an adult and help lead her people out of centuries of isolation. The men of Japan who sent the tiny child on such a mighty challenge succeeded completely, even more than some may have wished.

This calculated endeavor was the result of the "Meiji Restoration" of 1868, when liberal-minded Japanese gained power and immersed their country in a crash course to embrace the ways of Europe and the United States: in agriculture, industry, political reform, the adoption of Christianity, and the discovery of educational methods needed to enlighten Japan's close-minded population, which had long been ruled by military dictatorship.

Ume Tsuda (1864-1929) was the youngest of the first five girls sent to study in America, celebrating her seventh birthday while crossing the Pacific Ocean. Fortune placed Ume in the care of Charles and Adeline Lanman, allowing her, for nearly 11 years, to mature in a well-to-do American home located in the Georgetown section of Washington, D.C.

Besides having been Daniel Webster's secretary in the 1840s — writing that famous politician's biography after Webster died in 1852 — Lanman was a well-traveled artist, wrote more than 30 books, and corresponded with notables of his era such as Henry Wadsworth Longfellow, William Cullen Bryant, Horace Greeley, Charles Dickens and Washington Irving.

Lanman discovered Block Island in the 1850s — two full decades before tourists came to the resort en masse. Many of his Block Island paintings were lent by a mainland collector to the Island Free Library in 1976, part of a temporary exhibit honoring the Bicentennial of the United States. A few of Lanman's artistic works can still be found in Island homes, saved by families from the time of his many visits during the late 1800s.

The culture, Christianity, and emphasis on public service that were part of the Lanmans' world left their mark on the girl in their care. Returning to Japan in late 1882, Ume found herself overly educated in a country that had by then made a reactionary reversal in goals. Nearly three years elapsed before she was appointed to be a teacher

168 HARPER'S NEW MONTHLY MAGAZINE.

BLOCK ISLAND.

By CHARLES LANMAN.

MOHEGAN BLUFF.

Mohegan Bluffs, ca. 1875

Harper's Magazine published this etching of Block Island's majestic Mohegan Bluffs in 1876 as part of an extensive article by Charles Lanman describing the Island.

The view is based on a painting by Lanman, possibly made during the same 1875 visit when the Lanmans brought their young protege, Ume Tsuda, to the Ocean View Hotel. Not only were the natural beauties of this emerging resort portrayed in *Harper's*, but so were the fascinating customs of the Island's inhabitants, who were, themselves, still rooted in a much earlier time.

Several images based on Lanman's artistic work were used in the story — other etchings in the same article were made from the photographs of J. A. Williams (see pages 14, 18, 19).

in a government school. Having forgotten the Japanese language — and possessing values different from those around her — Ume wrote numerous long letters to Mrs. Lanman while trying to adjust to a now alien culture. The voluminous correspondence lasted until Mrs. Lanman's death in 1914.

Ume's second stay in the United States — from 1889 to 1892 — was spent mainly at Bryn Mawr College in Pennsylvania, and only aggravated her dissatisfaction with the elementary teaching methods, and the red tape, of her government school job in Japan. Realizing the limitations of Japanese men's vision of women's education, which was geared to the training of "good wives and wise mothers" (sound familiar?), Ume resigned in 1900 after fifteen years' service to open her own school — the first private Japanese school to offer higher education to women. Later named Tsuda College in her honer, the institution to this day remains one of the bastions of women's learning in Japan.

In 1984, several hundred of Ume's letters were discovered in the main building of Tsuda College. Spanning the years 1882 to 1911, they are vivid testimony to the young woman's struggle with her strange fate, her sense of mission, and her dedication to the improvement of her countrywomen's status through education. Excerpts from many of the letters were published in 1991 in *The Attic Letters*, edited by Yoshiko Furuki.

Also published in 1991, and authored by Furuki, was *The White Plum, A Biography of Ume Tsuda, Pioneer in The Higher Education of Japanese Women*. The white plum, which blooms in the last harsh days of winter, is Ume's namesake — an appropriate choice, given her own resilience.

In her later years, Ume was not only an honored, influential educator in her own land, but also a cultural ambassador who met and exchanged correspondence with leading figures of her day, including Theodore Roosevelt, Charles Dickens, Helen Keller, and Florence Nightingale.

In the 1870s Block Island was itself feverishly busy embracing a wider world — transforming in only a few years from an isolated fishing and farming community, into a crossroads for visitors, both notable and ordinary, from across the palette of American society.

As testified by the newspaper report of Ume's brief visit to the Island in 1875, ignorant prejudice did not exist when the various cultures met at the Ocean View Hotel — only a wondrous appreciation of the differences, and similarities, of people.

Tsuda College, up-to-date as ever, has an Internet site: www.tsuda.ac.jp/

The college's motto: **"Empowering Women Since 1900: TSUDA."**

The following glimpse of a future heroine of Japanese culture, who was then just 10 years old, appeared in the Providence Journal, *August 24, 1875. The writer, identified only as E. M. C., was another guest at Block Island's Ocean View Hotel.*

Although these comments might express the admiration that all parents have at some point toward their own children, one must wonder how many other great personages, when young, inspired unabashed and prophetic praise from casual onlookers.

The Ocean View Hotel's special guest

Beautiful children abound here, and we could draw many pleasing pen-pictures as we watch them swinging in the hammock, wandering on the beach, playing in the lawn, or busy with their games around the house.

One little girl among them is an object of unique interest, for she is a Japanese sent to this country to be educated for a teacher.

She is the youngest of the five girls sent out by the Japanese government at the same time for the same purpose, and consigned on their arrival to the care of Mr. Charles Lanman, the American Secretary of the Japanese Legation at Washington, who with his wife and foreign ward is spending his summer vacation at this hotel.

Two of these girls have returned to Japan, two are being educated in New Haven, while little Ume Tsuda has had the rare good fortune to find judicious care and parental devotion in Mr. Lanman's family.

She is a very sweet and interesting little girl, and is now ten years old, having been in the country for three years. She is wonderfully docile and tractable, speaks English perfectly and possesses an intelligence, power of acquisition and retention remarkable for her years.

She is very anxious to become thoroughly educated, so that she can teach the Japanese girls, is an ardent patriot, and talks as intelligently and wisely of her country and its institutions as if many years had written their impress on her thoughtful brow.

She has the complexion, hair and marked features of her race, is small in stature, quick and graceful in her movements, and attractive from the naive unconsciousness and quiet dignity of her whole demeanor.

With an intelligence beyond her years, and an earnest desire to improve every opportunity for obtaining knowledge, are mingled the sweet innocence and careless ease of childhood, while she is as eager for play as for books, and is apparently uninjured by the attention she receives.

The little Ume has fallen into loving hands, and if her life and health are spared, bids fair to reward the faithful care of her American friends, become a blessing to the native land she loves so dearly, and a source of pride and affection to the dear mother and father who willingly gave up their darling child to be educated on a foreign shore for the good of the Japanese women of the future.

A parlor of the Ocean View Hotel

Large ceiling brackets, as shown flanking the fireplace, where used throughout the many public rooms on the first floor of the Ocean View Hotel.

The construction method suggests the hefty knee-braces used for support under the decks of wooden ships.

The full-rigged ship, a model of one Nicholas Ball sailed on, was given to the Block Island Historical Society in the 1940s — no objects were saved from the hotel when the Ocean View burned on July 6, 1966 (see photo, page 20).

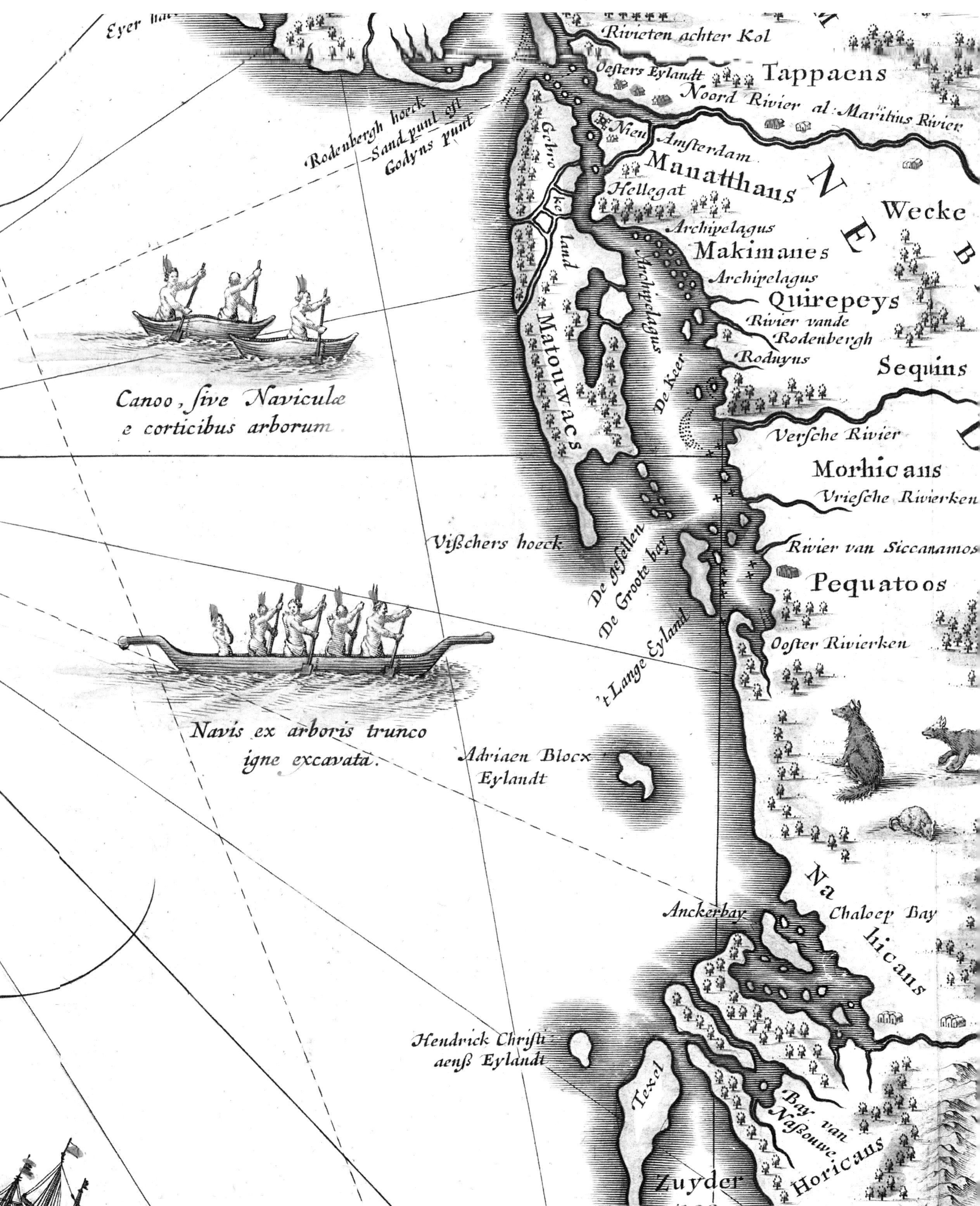
Rivieten achter Kol
Oesters Eylandt
Tappaens
Noord Rivier al: Maritius Rivier
Rodenbergh hoeck
Sand punt oft
Godyns punt
Nieu Amsterdam
Manatthans
Hellegat
Gebroken land
Wecke
Archipelagus
Makimanes
Archipelagus
Quirepeys
Rivier vande Rodenbergh
Roduyns
Sequins
Matouwacs
De Keer
Canoo, sive Naviculæ e corticibus arborum
Versche Rivier
Morhicans
Vriesche Rivierken
Vißchers hoeck
De Gesellen
De Groote bay
Rivier van Siccanamos
Pequatoos
't Lange Eylandt
Ooster Rivierken
Navis ex arboris trunco igne excavata.
Adriaen Blocx Eylandt
Anckerbay
Chaloep Bay
Nahicans
Hendrick Christiaenß Eylandt
Texel
Bay van Naßouwe
Horicans
Zuyder

CHAPTER 5

"We discovered an Island…"

We discovered an island triangular in form, distant ten leagues from the continent … full of hills, covered with trees, much populated judging by the continuous fires along all the surrounding shore which we saw they made …

This is the most beautiful people and the most civilized in customs that we have found in this navigation. They excel us in size: they are of bronze color, the face sharply cut, the hair long and black, upon which they bestow the greatest study in adorning it: the eyes black and alert, the bearing kind and gentle …

Giovanni da Verrazano,
Explorer for the King of France,
April 1524

WITH THIS DESCRIPTION OF BLOCK ISLAND and the tribe of Narragansett Indians, of which the local Manisseans were part, Europeans for the first time became aware of the people that for unknown centuries had called Block Island part of their homeland.

For 90 more years the Island that Verrazano mentioned remained unnoted by other Europeans until the Dutch fur trader and explorer, Adrian Block, came upon it again in 1614, giving the land his own name.

A map showing his discovery of Long Island Sound with the newly named "Adriaen Blocx Eylandt" — the first printed map to show canoes and North American fauna — was published in Holland in 1635. The two canoes, filled with Indians, are depicted in the vicinity of Block Island — one a "Navis ex arboris trunco igne excavata" or *boat made from a tree trunk hollowed by fire*; and another a "Canoo, sive Navicule e corticibus arborum" or *canoe boat made of tree bark*.

The inland forests of New England are filled with drawings of deer, bear, otter, and beaver — the same species that organized archaeological excavations, first undertaken in the 1890s, have uncovered on Block Island.

Ancient shellheaps of the local Manisseans contain the bones of animals and other spoils of the Indians' meals. In one of the nicer laws of chemistry, the alkaline of the shells conveniently neutralizes the decaying effects of the acidic soil, and bones that normally would soon disintegrate, are instead preserved for centuries.

Two types of native canoes, near "Adriaen Blocx Eylandt"

This map is sideways. North is at the right. Narragansett Bay in Rhode Island is at the bottom, Manhatten and Long Island in New York State are at the top.

Two canoes made from the bark of trees (in Latin: *corticibus arborum*) are shown at the top, while at the bottom is a larger canoe, dug out with the use of fire *(igne excavata)* from the trunk of a tree *(arboris trunco)*.

This map was made by the Blaeu family of Holland in 1635, based on the original handwritten chart from Adrian Block's 1614 expedition. See more of this map on pages 126-127 of the color section.

The shellheaps, often called middens, are still scattered about the Great Salt Pond. Some have been catalogued, some are unexplored, and some are dug up by unthinking "collectors" who in their clandestine activities remove the arrowheads, stone tools, pottery and animal bones, destroying forever the priceless story hidden in the earth. Several artifacts recovered during archaeological excavations sponsored by the Block Island Historical Society in the late 1980s and early 1990s are 3,000 years old. By determining types of food eaten at a site, the past use of that location can be identified as seasonal or year-round. Almost all of the explored sites were seasonal, used only during the summer, perhaps by Indian visitors from the mainland.

From the shallows of Great Salt Pond, the Indians found a varied diet of shellfish, including oysters, scallops, soft-shelled clams, quahogs, boat-shells, mussels, and black sea-snails.

Abundant food was also supplied by the open ocean, as indicated by the remains of blackfish whales, harbor seals, gray seals, harp seals, cod, black sea bass, striped bass, bluefish, angler fish, sturgeon, tautog, and mackerel.

Amongst the birds consumed were crows, bald eagles, Canada geese, red-breasted mergansers, double-crested cormorants, herring gulls, common loons, red-shouldered hawks, great horned owls, green winged teals, and razor-billed auks.

The Indians — as they were called by both those who admired them and those who resented them — lived and loved. And as with many tribes through the eons and across the earth's surface, they were not always at peace with each other.

We do not know in their own writings how they lived, or what their thoughts were from day-to-day, but the Narragansett tribe's great friend amongst the Europeans, Roger Williams, did write of them. Williams was the founder of the colony of Rhode Island, settled in response to his persecution by the Puritans of Massachusetts, from whom he fled.

In 1643 Williams wrote his astonishing *A Key into the Language of America*, chronicling the Indians' habits, both good and bad, in a book that is a cross between a dictionary and an encyclopedia (see pages 38 and 39). For 50 years Williams learned their language, living amongst them at times, protecting them from his own culture when he could.

Of the common foundation of mankind's virtues, it is sufficient to choose from amongst the 32 chapters of *A Key*, the following words that Williams used to describe the Indians:

"In this respect they are remarkably free and courteous, to invite all Strangers in; and if any come to them upon any occasion, they request them to come in, if they come not in of themselves."

Whatever life was like for the Indians of Block Island, their world changed forever one summer day in 1636.

Sixteen years had passed since the Pilgrims settled in Massachusetts. A white trader, John Oldham — a man not even well liked by fellow Englishmen — had been killed on his own boat off the shore of Block Island. When the Manisseans were held to blame, men from Massachusetts came to punish this previously untouched Island. The three-day venting of hatred — not unlike that still practiced by governments around the globe in the 1990s — began when nearly 100 men aboard five small vessels approached the gently sloping Crescent Beach, landing and advancing inland, seeking their prey in the finely planted fields of Corn Neck. Most inhabitants found safety amidst the Island's remote swamps.

One of the armored soldiers, Captain John Underhill, wrote of this:

"The cause of our war against the Block Islanders, was for taking away the life of one Master John Oldham, who made it his common course to trade amongst the Indians ...

"Coming to anchor before the island, we espied an Indian walking by the shore in a desolate manner, as though he had received intelligence of our coming ...

"Myself with others rode with a shallop, made towards the shore, having in the boat a dozen armed soldiers. Drawing near to the place of landing, the number that rose from behind the barricado were between fifty or sixty able fighting men, men as straight as arrows, very tall, and of active bodies, having their arrows notched. They

Beaver

From Blaeu's 1635 New England map

In 1524 Verrazano gave the name *Luisa* to Block Island honoring the King of France's mother.

In 1614 Adrian Block named the Island for himself.

But the fairest name of all was given by the natives: *Manisses,* which means *God's Little Island.*

A KEY into the
LANGUAGE
OF
AMERICA:

drew near to the water side, and let fly at the soldiers, as though they had meant to have made an end of us all in a moment. They shot a young gentleman in the neck through a collar, for stiffness as if it had been an oaken board, and entered his flesh a good depth. Myself received an arrow through my coat sleeve, a second against my helmet on the forehead ...

"The arrows flying thick about us, we made haste to the shore; but the surf of the sea being great, hindered us, so as we could scarce discharge a musket, but were forced to make haste to land.

"Drawing near the shore through the strength of wind, and the hollowness of the sea, we durst not adventure to run ashore, but were forced to wade up to the middle; but once having got up off our legs, we gave fire upon them. They finding our bullets to outreach their arrows, they fled before us.

"In the meanwhile Colonel Endicott made to the shore, and some of this number also repulsed him at his landing, but hurt none. We thought they would stand it out with us, but they perceiving we were in earnest, fled; and left their wigwams, or houses, and provision to the use of our soldiers ...

Otter

From Blaeu's 1635 map of New England.

"The next day we set upon our march, the Indians being retired into swamps, so as we could not find them. We burnt and spoiled both houses and corn in great abundance; but they kept themselves in obscurity. Captain Turner stepping aside to a swamp, met with some few Indians, and charged upon them, changing some few bullets for arrows. Himself received a shot upon the breast of his corselet, as if it had been pushed with a pike, and if he had not had it on, he had lost his life.

"Having spent that day in burning and spoiling the island, we took up the quarter for that night. About midnight myself went out with ten men about two miles from our quarter, and discovered the most eminent plantation they had in the island, where was much corn, many wigwams, and great heaps of mats, but fearing less we should make an alarm by setting fire on them, we left them as we found them, and peaceably departed to our quarter; and the next morning with forty men marched up to the same plantation, burnt their houses, cut down their corn, destroyed some of their dogs instead of men, which they left in their wigwams.

"Passing on toward the water side to embark our soldiers, we met with several famous wigwams, with great heaps of pleasant corn ready shelled; but not able to bring it away, we did thro their mats upon it, and set fire and burnt it. Many well-wrought mats our soldiers brought from thence, and several delightful baskets. We being divided into two parts, the rest of the body met with no less, I suppose, than ourselves did ... we spent our time, and could no more advantage ourselves than we had already done, and having slain some fourteen, and maimed others, we embarked ourselves."

AND SO BY A DREADFUL IRONY, the best insight into the life of the Manissean Indians was left to future generations by an enemy soldier who helped end that life forever.

A second expedition from Massachusetts in August 1637 exacted a tribute of 100 fathoms (600 feet, or the length of two football fields) of "wampompeague," the quahog beads drilled and strung by Indians for use in trade. Payments of wampum over the next several years kept Block Island Indians in a kind of absentee servitude.

Two deer

In the forests of New England as depicted on Blaeu's 1635 map, are shown several animals whose bones have been excavated from Block Island's Indian shellheaps, such as: deer, otter, bear, and beaver.

In 1658, Block Island was deeded by the Massachusetts government to four important men of that colony, amongst them John Endicott, the leader of the 1636 invasion, who had since become governor of Massachusetts Bay Colony. The four quickly sold their gift to a group of others who wished to form a settlement on the Island by turning the land into plantations. In 1661 a surveyor drew a map showing which portions each of the 16 would own.

A seventeenth part was drawn out for the settlers' minister. No land was left for the 300 or so Indians who still, of course, lived where they had always lived.

Much as we would like to know what became of them, no clear description of their condition has come down to us. Those Indians who stayed seem to have assumed a role between servant and slave. Many probably left, unable to reconcile the enormous change — while others might have actually stayed partly because of it. If curiosity were to overcome all other emotions, there may have been an interest in some minds to understand the strange European culture with its mysterious implements and different realms of knowledge.

Two Indian villages, with wigwams

The wigwams of northeastern American Indians differed from the tepees constructed in the western portions of the continent. Whether hut-shaped, as shown in these two villages, or dome-shaped, the wigwams' skeletons were formed of bent saplings and covered with woven mats.

Evidence of such wigwams — stained soil in the shape of pointed post bottoms — has been found on Block Island near the northern shore of Great Salt Pond, as well as south of the pond at the extensive Fort Island site.

From Blaeu's 1635 map of New England.

But the relationship clearly was not equal. If any of the Block Island settlers shared the awe felt by Verrazano and Roger Williams in discovering fellow beings of a different mold, they did not write about it. But then again, the individual settlers left no written accounts of *any* of their private feelings — all that exists are the bare facts of the official town records.

An inventory made in 1684 of the estate of the deceased Tormut Rose, one of the original 16 settlers, lists amongst his possessions "one Endan man," valued at 12 English pounds. The same amount of value was assigned to "5 ackurs upland & medow."

The Indians were not specifically forced off the Island but were treated with some degree of benevolence — albeit, of course, by an authoritarian rule which they had no ability to change in a democratic manner.

In 1684, John and William Dodge rented land for seven years from John Rodman with the understanding that:

"The said Rodman shall erect and build upon the said land one house of 16 feet wide and 26 feet long ... and ... the said Dodges shall have the liberty to plant one Indian family upon the said land."

Their subservience to the settlers, or to a particular settler, is revealed by the manner they were referred to:

"Febry. 21th, 1693 ... upon great suspicion of the Engens stealing of sheep by reason one of their own company made complaint against them, the several accused persons ... confessed and the several persons ordered to pay the several sums following as a fine *(in pounds, shillings & pence)*:

	lb: s: d
Harry, old Neds son	*0:05:00*
Samson, Thomas Mithels man	*0:10:00*
Jeofry, Joshua Raymond man	*0:10:00*
Gorg, Mr. Sands servent, Neds son	*0:05:00*
Mr. Nathaniell Nyles men and Willtom son	*1:02:00*
Pishags	*0:10:00*

As well as punishing the Indians, the laws also offered a degree of protection. Special rules were created, however, just to govern them — this theory of "separate rules" being a kind of discrimination not banned in the United States until the 1950s and 60s during the Civil Rights Movement.

In 1709 a decree stated:

"No Indian nor Negro servants shall walk abroad after nine a Clock at night without his master or mistress leave, and if said servants or slaves shall be found or taken from home after nine A Clock at night by the Constable or any freeholder of said Town and brought to the Wardens or Warden, shall be taken and stript and receive ten lashes on his or her naked back."

Some of the rules governing Indians seem mysterious today, such as being barred from keeping dogs in 1719 — or the following:

"At a Town meeting held July 12th, 1685:

"It was concluded that no Indian or Indians shall dig up any land for getting of ground unless that they are to lay it level forthwith and to lay the sward upward and if any Indian be found digging and not laying it level shall pay forthwith ten shillings."

Were the Indians attempting to plow the land to grow corn? Or find edible roots underground? Or dig worms for fishing?

The 1730 census listed 250 whites and 20 "Indians" on Block Island. Also noted were 20 "Negroes" who had been brought to the Island to live as outright slaves, a practice popular throughout all of Rhode Island.

By 1790 the State of Rhode Island's census ceased using the categories of "Indians" and "Negroes" — but that year 47 "slaves" were listed on Block Island.

For the 1850 census the state used the term "colored" for nonwhites, of whom Block Island counted 44. This new category was created for two reasons: (1) although the Civil War that was to free all slaves in the United States was 11 years in the future, slavery had already been outlawed in Rhode Island for the past several decades, and (2) for more than 100 years Indians and Negroes throughout the state had tended to mingle into one culture.

The last Manissean Indian died in 1886. His name, Isaac Church, is still attached to Isaac's Corner, the intersection of roads at the northern end of Fresh Pond. The vacant field where Isaac's residence once stood is just south of the intersection, near the pond, and is now part of conservation land. The so-called Indian cemetery — which an 1876 booklet mentions was "for negroes" and "devoid of headstones" — is 100 yards to the northeast on the opposite side of Lakeside Drive.

In another paradox of history, the sentiments expressed by a Block Islander in a newspaper account shortly after Isaac's death, echo the enraptured appreciation of Verrazano 350 years earlier when the two cultures had first met:

"We now come to the last of the Manisseans, 'Uncle Isaac' as he was called by everybody. We know him well. He died in 1886.

"He was a full blooded Indian. His straight black hair; his high cheek bones; his tall and stately carriage, and many other peculiarities denoted his Indian descent.

"His stately manners, his polite and graceful bow; his distinct 'yes sir' and 'no sir', would lead anyone to infer that he was probably a descendant of some former warlike sachem. We remember his appearance long after he had passed his three score and ten years.

"He seemed like some lofty chieftain.

"Uncle Isaac gained a never to be forgotten distinction by always being present at funerals. No matter what the weather might be, or how far he had to walk, Uncle Isaac was sure to be there, always dressed in his best suit, wearing a high silk hat, and carrying his ancient Indian cane. He followed many of his townsmen to their last resting place.

"When at last he bid adieu to earth there were many assembled to pay their last tribute of respect to the 'last of the Manisses' — last Block Island Indian."

With their passing on Block Island and throughout other parts of North America, a belated, more widely held respect developed for the Indian and his culture.

This wonder was expressed long ago in a short essay, the *History of Block Island*, by Henry T. Beckwith, secretary of the Rhode Island Historical Society, who wrote in 1857:

"An Indian chief, whose name I do not remember, was once asked how the Indians knew that there was a Great Spirit. He arose, pointed to the mountains, the sea, the woods, and the fields, and sat down. We wish, that with all our boasted civilization, we were as much impressed with these works of the Almighty. We should not witness the enormous, and in the great majority of cases, needless destruction of natural beauty that is going on around us, and it would be better for us in many respects."

In America, appreciation for the near vanished culture of the Indians grew during the 1970s and 80s — but Native Americans often remained on reservations voluntarily, not intermingling in awe with the good aspects to be found amongst other cultures around the world.

And with the rise of Indian gambling casinos in the 1990s — created by a federal loophole, opened further by several judges — the unfortunate stereotypical views of 'good and bad guys' inculcated by many of Hollywood's early movies, and the reality of drunken reservation dwellers, may find an equally bad replacement in the concept of 'Casino Native Americans,' who will be resented for casting aside mankind's nobler thoughts and catering to the baser instincts of all the earth's tribes.

The new Native Americans, although professing to serve a need, are inculcating a vice. They may well be regarded by history with the same disdain we feel for white residents of the United States who, in the 1800s, sold liquor to susceptible Indians.

The best way to envision the manner in which Block Island's Manissean Indians lived, is to study the Narragansett Indian tribe on the mainland with whom they were associated — and to accomplish that task one should peruse Roger Williams' 1643 book:

A Key into the Language of America.

There is no evidence Roger Williams ever visited Block Island. But in 1636, he interceded with Massachusetts authorities on behalf of Island Indians to discover which specific individuals had murdered John Oldham, a trader whose body was found aboard his ship.

The Indians had no written language. When Williams translated their words into English, he wrote the Indian pronunciation in phonetic syllables. Note that his spelling of English words varies from modern English. The following extracts, many of which would have related to Indian life on Block Island, are from a reprint of Roger Williams' book made in 1936.

excerpts from:

A Key into the Language of America

by Roger Williams, 1643

Chapter II — Of Eating and Entertainment:

Whomsoever commeth in when they are eating, they offer them to eat of that which they have, though but little enough prepar'd for themselves. If any provision of fish or flesh come in, they make their neighbours partakers with them.

If any stranger come in, they presently give him to eate of what they have; many a time, and at all times of the night — as I have fallen in travell upon their houses — when nothing hath been ready, have themselves and their wives, risen to prepare me some refreshing.

Cowàump? = Have you enough?
Nowâump. = I have enough.

Chapter IV — Of their Numbers:

Having no letters nor arts, 'tis admirable how quick they are in casting up great numbers, with the helpe of graines of Corne, instead of Europes pens or counters.

Nquitte mittànnug = 1,000
Piuckque mittánnug = 10,000
Nquit pausuckóemittànnug = 100,000

Chapter VII — Of Parts of Body:

Nature knowes no difference between Europe and Americans in blood, birth, bodies, &c. God having of one blood made all mankind.

Wunnícheke = hand
Mohcônt = leg
Wussète = foot
Cummínakese = You are strong.

Chapter XI — Of Travell:

These thick Woods and Swamps are the Refuges for Women and children in Warre, whil'st the men fight ...

They are joyfull in meeting of any in travell, and will strike fire either with stones or sticks, to take Tobacco, and discourse a little together.

Míshoon hómwock = They goe or come by water.
Awanick payánchick = Who come there?
Tocekétuck = Let us wade.

A KEY into the
LANGUAGE
OF
AMERICA:
OR,
An help to the *Language* of the *Natives*
in that part of AMERICA, called
NEW-ENGLAND.
Together, with briefe *Obſervations* of the Cuſtomes, Manners and Worſhips, *&c.* of the
aforeſaid *Natives*, in Peace and Warre,
in Life and Death.

BY ROGER WILLIAMS
of *Providence* in *New-England.*

LONDON,
Printed by *Gregory Dexter*, 1643.

Portion of title page from Roger Williams' 1643 book

Chapter XIV — Of the Winds:

This [Southwest wind] is the pleasingest, warmest wind in the Climate, most desired of the Indians, making faire weather ordinarily; and therefore they have a Tradition, that to the Southwest, which they call Sowwaníu, the gods chiefly dwell; and hither the soules of all their Great and Good men and women goe.

Pìtch Sowwánishen = It will be Southwest.

Chapter XV — Of Fowle:

The Indians having abundance of these sorts of Foule [geese, swans, brants, ducks] take great pains to kill any of them with their Bow and Arrowes; and are marvellous desirous of our English Guns, powder and shot — though they are wisely and generally denied by the English ...

These [cormorants] they take in the night time, where they are asleepe on rocks, off at Sea, and bring in at break of day great store of them.

Kítsuog = Cormorants

Yo aquéchmock = There they swim

This [laying nets] they do on shore, and catch many fowle upon the plaines, feeding under okes [oak trees] upon akrons [acorns], as Geese, Turkies, Cranes, and others, &c.

Nipponamouôog = I lay nets for them

Chapter XIX — Of Fish and Fishing:

Poquaûhock [quahaug] ... a little thick shell-fish, which the Indians wade deepe and dive for, and after they have eaten the meat there — in those that are good — they breake out of the shell, about halfe an inch of a blacke part of it, of which they make their Suckauhock, or black money, which is to them pretious.

The Natives take exceeding great paines in their fishing, especially in watching their seasons by night; so that frequently they lay their naked bodies many a cold night on the cold shoare about a fire of two or three sticks, and oft in the night search their Nets; and sometimes goe in and stay longer in frozen water.

Hoquaùn = Hooke

Peewâsicks = Little hookes

Maúmacocks = Great hookes

Npunnouwaûmen = I goe to search my nets

Chapter XXII — Of their Government:

I could never discerne that excesse of scandalous sins amonst them, which Europe aboundeth with. Drunkennesse and gluttony, generally they know not what sinnes they be; and although they have not so much to restraine them — both in respect of knowledge of God and Lawes of men — as the English have, yet a man shall never heare of such crimes amongst them of robberies, murthers, adulteries, &c. as amongst the English.

Neen pitch-nnadsíttamen = I will inquire into it.

Chapter XXIV — Of their Warres:

I once travelled — in a place conceived dangerous — with a great Prince, and his Queene and Children in company, with a Guard of neere two hundred; twentie, or thirtie fires were made every night for the Guard — the Prince and Queene in the midst — and Sentinells by course, as exact as in Europe; and when we travelled through a place where ambushes were suspected to lie, a speciall Guard, like unto a Life-guard, compassed — some neerer, some farther off — the King and Queen, my selfe and some English with me.

Askwhítteass = Keep watch.

Askwhitteâchick = The Guard.

Askwhitteaûg = It is the Guard.

Table of Contents from Roger Williams' 1643 book

The TABLE.

Headstone and footstone for Susanna Littlefield, who died in 1820

CHAPTER 6

The Resting Ground

Block Island's cemetery

IN THE EARLY 1880S, 52 were counted in the Block Island cemetery. Tall or short, tilting or straight, perfect or broken — they were the only gravestones with inscriptions earlier than 1805.

That was Edward Harris' joy in the summer of 1883 — a self-appointed vacation task to record the written words still visible on the Island grave markers of the 1600s and 1700s. Published later that year in a limited edition of 100 hardbound copies, the small book, titled *Block Island Epitaphs*, was as elegantly lettered as the stones themselves.

The oldest grave found in 1883, and one still well-preserved, was that of Margaret Guthry — or, as spelled in 1687, the year she died, "Margret Gvtry" (see photo below and on page 132 of the color section).

Other stones have not fared as well in the harsh winds, and freezes and thaws, typical of a Block Island winter. None of the words on the headstone of Matthia Rock, who died in 1755, are visible today, yet they were in 1883. The only way to tell now where 16-year-old Matthia was buried in early November by his melancholy parents, William and Katharine, is from his second marker — the smaller footstone — which still bears the initials "M. R." If not for that cryptic clue, the location of his remains would be lost forever, his once mourned marker becoming another anonymous piece of rough stone on the mowed hillside. Nothing else of Matthia Rock is known — not even of the most meager triviality.

Graves, being one's final resting place, formerly were marked by both a headstone and a footstone — similar in concept to the headboard and footboard of a bed. The headstone contained the rester's name, pertinent dates and sometimes an epitaph, while the smaller footstone bore only the name or initials of the deceased. Comparison to a bed is evident when viewing the two Island gravestones of Susanna Littlefield who died in 1820 (see photo on left).

When the white settlers arrived on Block Island in 1661, they choose a slope overlooking Great Salt Pond for their community cemetery. Below the hill, bordering the pond, the settlers laid out individual house lots — these are now the flat fields along West Side Road, stretching eastward from the cemetery toward present-day New Harbor's small assemblage of restaurants (Dead Eye Dick's, Smuggler's Cove) and marinas (Payne's Dock, the Hog Pen).

Island's oldest gravestone, 1687

The town that was envisioned in this area by the early settlers never materialized. The harbor channel they dug by hand into Great Salt Pond during the 1680s soon filled with sand — and the pond would not become a harbor for another 200 years, when a permanent channel was finally dredged in 1895 with state and federal help. During the 1700s and 1800s, the town center evolved instead at a nearby inland crossroads, now marked by two old grindstones on Center Road near the airport.

But the cemetery on the hill, overlooking the beautiful inland waters and the ocean beyond, flourished. As each century passed, the graves spilled down the slope, filling it. Today the cemetery spreads ever further on the plateau beyond the hilltop.

In 1814, during the War of 1812, when the undefensible Island remained neutral as it had during the Revolution in the 1770s, Commodore Hardy of the British blockading squadron assisted the Islanders in building a new meetinghouse at the cemetery — where the Baptist minister could preach regularly each Sunday. Located near the top of the hill, next to the main dirt driveway, the meetinghouse was moved in the late 1850s to the Center crossroads where it served as the town hall, and secondarily as the high school — until burning mysteriously to the ground on Halloween night, 1923 (see photo below).

In the late 1800s, the meetinghouse's former site at the cemetery was filled with new gravestones made of marble or granite. This site, a small flat rise bordered by curbing, is easily discernable, intruding amongst the colonial-era markers carved from grey slate or brown sandstone (see photo on lower right).

Old Town Hall at the Center, ca. 1905

Compare to photo on page 144 — and to a later photo, showing an addition, on page 98.

Bulldozing new roads in cemetery, 1992

The old town hall once stood in the foreground, near the driveway, 1994

After the placement of Margaret Guthry's upright sandstone marker in 1687 — and two nearby horizontal sandstone slabs in 1695 and 1708 to honor members of the Island's once prevalent Sands family — few sandstone markers were erected in the Island cemetery until the late 1700s.

Slate, instead, was the favored material for gravestones of that century.

Usually incised into the top portion was one of several typical images used throughout English colonies in America.

Fortunately for squeamish present-day Island visitors who walk this hill, the "winged skulls" that are widespread at some mainland cemeteries are absent here — Block Islanders felt no need to display the bony heads, made more hideous by enlarged eye sockets over bared teeth — although they did not mind the feathered wings sprouting from where ears should be.

Simon Ray Littlefield, died 1780; slate stone carved by John Stevens of Newport

Chosen instead were the benign full faces of cherubs, oval-shaped with sparsely drawn facial features — the enormous wings representing the flight of the soul.

These flatly rendered heads were Christian symbols, leftovers from medieval Europe when towns often centered their activity around religion — where death came by abrupt mysterious disease; where few could read or write, or see any form of art or image; where no books existed, nor computers nor movies. When a walk through the cemetery could be the major visual experience of one's village life.

Templates of symbolic faces were kept by gravestone carvers, many such craftsmen becoming distinctive by their own style. In Newport, Rhode Island, one prominent family of carvers carried the name "John Stevens" through three successive generations, from the late 1600s to the early 1800s. Their fame has remained to this day, their stones still to be found from New England south to the Carolinas.

On Block Island, work by the Stevens' family dominates the wing-faced slate stones — the carver's identity apparent by the occasional initials "J. S." at the bottom of a marker, as well as by the border design, the features of the carved faces, and the distinctive refinement of the lettering.

The slate stone of Hannah Rose, who died in 1791, displays an unusual winged face turned slightly to the side, rather than in the familiar full frontal view. The angle of perspective is represented in the wings, one being dramatically smaller than the other (see photo on right).

This identical image can be found in a churchyard nearly a thousand miles away on the 1787 gravestone of Christiana Knox in Charleston, South Carolina — a city in which two Newport carvers lived briefly: John Bull, who carved in the manner of the Stevens' family, and John Stevens III.

Hannah Rose, died 1791; slate stone carved by John Stevens of Newport

Horizontal sandstone graves of James Sands and his son, Edward Sands

HERE LYES IN
TVRRED T̄E BODY
OF M^{R} IĀMES SĀNDS
SENIOVR ADED 73
YEĀRS DEPĀRTED
THIS LIFE MĀRCH
THE 13 1695

HERE LYETH INTERRED
THE BODY OF CAPT^{N}
EDWARD SANDS WHO
DEPARTED THIS LIFE JVNE
Y^{e} 14 1708 IN Y^{e} [illeg.]
YEARE OF HIS AGE

Epitaphs as transcribed in Edward Harris' 1883 book

At least one other carved face can be found on Block Island and also at the graveyard in Charleston, South Carolina.

The winged head, which looks straight at the viewer, is on the 1761 slate gravestone of Mercy Littlefield. Her southern twin is on the stone of Robert Stedman, who died in 1766.

The two finely rendered images feature a distinctive hairstyle and ominously hidden pupils — probably the work of John Stevens II or his brother William — see photo at right, and a photo of the entire winged face on page 133.

Stone of Mercy Littlefield, carved in 1761

Sandstone marker for William Greffeth, drowned 1755

The nearly blank face, enveloped by two drooping wings, seems vaguely like an Egyptian pharaoh. The eyes are the smallest to be found on any Block Island effigy of a soul.

In the 1790s, the Island cemetery took on a new, post-Revolution look, when markers from Connecticut's sandstone quarries were imported in greater numbers.

One was erected in 1791 in memory of Samuel Gruman who lived in Norwalk, Connecticut, drowned near Long Island. His body washed ashore, presumably, at Block Island, where he was soon buried next to a gravestone supplied by his hometown relatives.

Edward Ball's sandstone marker of 1796 bears a striking admonition found in other New England graveyards (see photo on right):

As you pass by pray cast an eye,
As you are now so once was I,
As I am now so must you be,
Prepare for death and follow me.

Sandstone marker for Edward Ball 2nd, died 1796

A few plain slate stones were used after 1800, but the winged faces had lost favor. The United States was swept up in the European neoclassical rage, fostered by rediscovery of sculptures from the ancient Greek and Roman empires. Weeping willows now became a fashionable figure to carve near a gravestone's curving top (see photo at lower right).

But as the 1800s progressed, brown sandstone gave way to white marble markers, many of which maintained the classic "tombstone" shape of the early slate stones, while incorporating more ornate edges and a greater variety of symbols and poetic epitaphs.

By the mid-1800s, marble was the Island favorite, with carved decorations of crosses, crowns, flowers, ribbons, and hands — but relatively few of the classical "willow and urn" motifs so often used at mainland cemeteries.

Sandstone marker for Mrs Caty Mott, died 1814

Marble gravestone for Capt. Gideon Dodge, died 1871

Anchor motif on granite obelisk

Since the 1660s, individual Block Islanders had usually acquired a strong knowledge of the sea, becoming masters of their own local fishing boats, or captains of mainland ships that sailed the world's oceans. The slate gravestones of the 1700s used the terms "Mr." and "Esq." — making few references to seafaring — but in the 1800s the marble stones often bore the title of "Capt." or "Captain." Anchors, symbolic for many men from this seagirt town — and innately cross-shap ed — adorn stones in this period.

After the Civil War in the 1860s, a fourth type of stone material became popular: granite, which remains to this day the preferred choice for graves.

With the change to granite, the old type of short, nearly two-dimensional tombstone gave way to every conceivable type of three-dimensional tower, spire and turret, often rising in levels like a wedding cake. Rather than ethereal symbols relative to the universe as a whole, objects specific to the life of the departed person decorate many such graves.

Granite gravestone for Capt. Francis Willis and his wife, Hannah

Marble gravestone, Lydia Mott, died 1877 at age 35

We miss thee when the morning dawns,

We miss thee when the night returns;

We miss thee here, we miss thee there,

Lydia we miss thee everywhere.

A general guide to gravestone ages:

time period	*material*	*color*	*shape*	*some carved symbols*
The 1700s	SLATE	dark grey	short, 2-dimensional	winged faces
Early-1800s	SANDSTONE	brown	short, 2-dimensional	winged faces, willow trees
Mid-1800s	MARBLE	white	short, 2-dimensional	willows, crosses, anchors
Late-1800s to present	GRANITE	light grey	tall, 3-dimensional	almost anything

Marble gravestone of Charles W. Willis, died 1892

Charles W. Willis, owner of the Surf Hotel, died in 1892. Two years later his family erected a monument described at the time as:

"... far surpassing anything yet erected on the Island. The base six feet long by four wide, upon which rests the second piece, carved with the family name and the emblems of the Odd Fellow and American Mechanics of which the late Mr. Willis was a member. The die with the family record has pillars in bas-relief on the four corners. This is surmounted by a handsomely carved dome, upon which is a life-size bust of Mr. Willis ... by the finest sculptor in the State. The monument is built of the best Italian marble, the design an original one, which was planned by the family, is executed in every detail in a most tasteful and artistic manner."

Charles W. Willis continues to be the only person with a bust at the cemetery.

Bust of Charles W. Willis

Granite gravestone of Nicholas Ball, died 1896

With Mr. Willis as a precedent, the 1896 tombstone of Nicholas Ball — owner of the Island's largest hotel, the Ocean View — is carved with an *anchor* for his youthful seafaring days, a *pick and shovel* for his gold-digging in California, and a *book* for his writing talents; all surmounted by a highly polished, black granite *globe* of the earth denoting a trip made around the world in his later years.

From that great era of Block Island prosperity there are grand obelisks whose purpose is to memorialize the dozen-or-so most prevalent Island surnames of the 1800s.

But most old Island families are so intertwined, that one surname or another hardly matters. Though those early names now form a minority of the Island's population — and some Islanders are preserved only in Edward Harris's 1883 book of the earliest graves — the blood of the old Islanders, sometimes under newer names, will not die out.

• *See etching of Nicholas Ball — page 22*

Ball, showing Europe and Africa

In the cemetery near the crest of the hill, six to twelve-foot tall monoliths have been built during the past century. At night they lumber about, as would figures on a chessboard, bumping into each other, teeter-tottering over territory we are not keen to claim, forming from habit the social orders their honorees once knew in life. By morning the stones' ageless positions are assumed once more. Listen on a calm night — lie on the hill — and hear the wave-like rumble around you.

Nathan Mott Park, looking west from Center Road, 1957

For this view in 1957, the photographer stood on Center Road with the airport runway behind him. To the left of the sign, two rough stone posts flank the ancient lane that led to the 1600s homestead of John and Margaret Rathbun. The lane is now overgrown with brush and tall evergreens, but the unmarked location of the former homestead, in the hills beyond, can be approached by a Greenway entrance 300 feet to the right (or north) on Center Road.

This sign is long gone. Four years after the photograph was made, 13 acres of the land in the foreground was taken by the state when the airport property was expanded for runway lights (see map page 57).

After Lucretia Mott Ball, a direct descendent of John and Margaret Rathbone, left the land to the public in her 1941 will, there was a flurry of activity by Islanders in response — such as the planting of the Enchanted Forest on the horizon (flush with the right side of the sign), and the planting of a border of maple trees at 20-foot intervals along the southern boundary (next to Old Mill Road) and along the western border — these large trees are easily seen today.

The Nathan Mott Park was the first effort at public land use on Block Island since the settlers of 1661 laid aside their Common Land, most of which later became private, including, even, the Minister's Lot on Corn Neck which, in the mid-1960s, was the site of the Island's first housing development (see photo, page 244).

The Nathan Mott Park was named for Lucretia Mott Ball's father at her request, given to the public at her request, and contained within its boundaries the house site of her distant ancestor, John Rathbun, from whom nearly all Rathbuns, Rathbones, and Rathburns in the country are descended.

Yet the Nathan Mott Park was so neglected by trustees in the 1970s and 80s, that in late 1989 this land also nearly became the site of a housing development and was actually subdivided, despite the obvious prescence of the park's trees. Salvation occurred in the nick of time, snatched from the illegal proceedings after several tense Island meetings — yet with the loss of 3.35 acres in the northeast corner near today's Greenway entrance.

CHAPTER 7

The Rathbun family

All From Two

'buns, 'bones, and 'burns

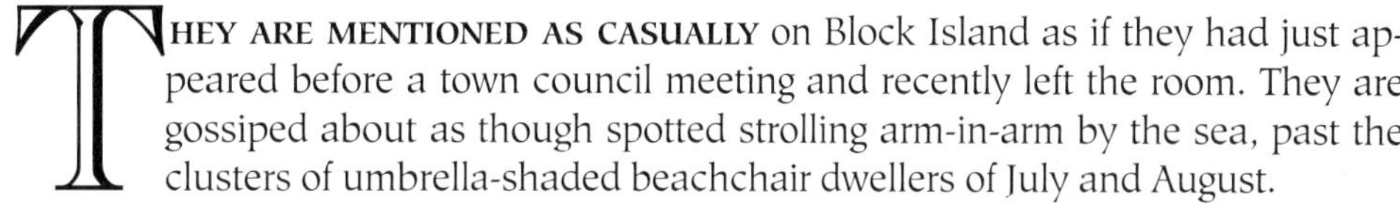

THEY ARE MENTIONED AS CASUALLY on Block Island as if they had just appeared before a town council meeting and recently left the room. They are gossiped about as though spotted strolling arm-in-arm by the sea, past the clusters of umbrella-shaded beachchair dwellers of July and August.

They are John and Margaret to those in the know — but no one has seen the couple and there are no pictures, drawings or photos of them. They exist only in words, on fragile paper — penned again, printed again, Xeroxed into immortality.

They might have been forgotten. But they left a further legacy. They left people — descendants, more accurately. And ten or so generations later, some of those offspring journey every few years to Block Island — to a reunion — to steal glances at themselves and find in their faces the common denominator that was John and Margaret Rathbun, settlers of Block Island in 1661.

Led by their uncommon rallier during the 1980s and 90s, Frank Rathbun, a former newspaperman and congressional aide from Virginia, the Rathbuns may have developed into the largest family association in America. Nearly all the Rathbuns, Rathbones and Rathburns in the country are descended from John and Margaret Rathbun of Block Island — and, as editor and publisher of the quarterly magazine *The Rathbun-Rathbone-Rathburn Family Historian*, Frank Rathbun tried to embrace them all.

The first Block Island visit of the Rathbun Family, in July 1983, was also the first national reunion of the association. During the group's visit to the Island in September 1989, nearly 200 cousins from 29 states paid homage to their common roots.

The 1993 gathering honored the 250th anniversary of the Rathbun Family Bible, published at the Clarendon Press in Oxford, England, in 1725, and first inscribed with family births, marriages, and deaths by John and Margaret's son, Samuel, on September 4, 1743 — the Rathbuns timed their reunion of 1993 to the exact day.

Block Island, claimed by the Massachusetts government in the early 1600s, was granted in 1658 to four influential men from that colony, John Endicott (former governor), Richard Bellingham (former governor), Daniel Dennison (a major-general, who rewrote the Massachusetts laws in 1658 and was given 1/4 of Block Island as compensation) and William Hawthorne (a major). Their gift was sold in 1660 to a group of 12 purchasers led by John Alcock — a doctor and a Harvard graduate of the class of 1646. The purchasers intended to — in the words of the early colonists — "plant" Block Island by creating a town sustained by farming and fishing.

By 1661 when the settlement began, the owners of Block Island had grown to 16. This was a profit-making venture — for many just an investment — and only seven of the 16 landowners actually moved to Block Island.

The other nine purchasers were absentee landlords who sent workers to farm the land as tenants — of those nine workers, four were former Scottish prisoners of war,

The Rathbun family memorial, erected at the cemetery in 1983

The first annual reunion of the Rathbun Family Association was held on Block Island, July 23, 1983. Contributions from more than 225 descendants and their families paid for this memorial marker, erected near the crest of the cemetery hill.

captured by the English forces of Oliver Cromwell in the battles of Dunbar (1650) and Worcester (1651), and sold to become indentured servants in the New World for a prescribed number of years.

Almost immediately the Island's land began to change hands — amongst the settlers and with new arrivals from the mainland — a continuing process to this day.

John Rathbun — from Lancashire England, as were others who settled Block Island — was among the first purchasers in 1660, and one of the seven landowners who moved to the Island the following year.

John and his wife Margaret were successful here — he appointed often as one of the Island's representatives to the Rhode Island General Assembly, while Margaret raised a family of eight children who reached a prominence of their own. John also owned a home in Newport, as well as a share in that town's prospering wharf, but he was always considered a Block Islander, and it is here where his family of five sons and three daughters were raised. Each of the sons had between eight and 11 children, for a total of 47 offspring of whom 21 were males. — a good start for the Rathbun Family Association.

Most of the children and grandchildren moved to the mainland, pursuing the dream of the American West shared by Europeans in the New World. Other Block Islanders continued this exodus during successive centuries, right to the present time.

But the large size of families during that era — which would tend to make local land harder to acquire and therefore more precious — was not the only factor influencing a person's choice to emigrate.

For instance, when land and homes were available cheaply in the 1940s and 50s, many residents of Block Island left anyway — even those who *had* land on Block Island left, leaving deserted, boarded-up homes behind them.

Conversely, after the Island's real estate prices began escalating faster than the mainland's in the 1960s and land became very valuable, Islanders who already had land, willingly sold out — as they continue to do. Ultimately, in other words, the price or the availability of land is not the primary factor determining whether or not a person will remain on Block Island.

The Rathbun family's land holdings on Block Island changed during several succeeding generations. By the early part of the 1900s the land containing the original homestead site (just west of today's airport) was owned by Lucretia Mott Ball (1866-1941), inherited through her great-grandmother Catherine Rathbun (1768-1824).

Other Rathbun heirs lived in the vicinity, including:

— to the west, at the present-day duPont family home (plat 16, lot 71) on Beacon Hill Rd: the home of Catherine's son, Abraham Rathbone Mott (1806-1867);

— and to the south, embracing the northern end of Fresh Pond: where there now exists the 1950s house called Smilin' Through (plat 11, lot 1), a replica of the 250-year-old gambrel-roofed house of Walter Rathbone Mott (1800-1882), another of Catherine's sons (see photos of house on pages 222-225).

Lucretia Mott Ball (see photo on page 202) also inherited the family bible of Catherine's great-grandfather, Samuel Rathbun (1672-1757), the youngest son of John and Margaret Rathbun. When Lucretia died on March 11, 1941, her will influenced Block Island in several major ways (see page 206), two of them being the stipulations:

(1) that "my farm on Block Island known as the 'Nathan Mott Farm' [after her father] shall be converted into a public park to be named the 'Nathan Mott Park' for the use, enjoyment and benefits of the residents of Block Island and visitors thereto ... to be forever maintained as a public park as aforesaid," and

(2) that "such items of my personal property as shall be of historical or genealogical interest or shall be of value as antiques and art objects shall not be sold ... but shall be given to such museums or historical collections as ... seems most fitting, giving preference to institutions located in the state of Rhode Island ..."

The 77-acre Nathan Mott Farm did become the present-day Nathan Mott Park, through which Greenway paths exist for the public — but on three occasions incursions were made into the land, shrinking the park to only 39 acres.

In 1949 the state took the eastern 21 acres to be filled and flattened for the new airport runway (see map on page 57).

In 1961 the state took 13 acres to the west of the paved road, to be left undeveloped but used for approach-path lights.

And in 1990 the town council, acting as Probate Court for the ill-handled estate, gave 3.35 acres on the northern boundary to the Harbor Baptist Church at the church's insistent request.

But the site of the original Rathbun homestead, although not precisely discernable, is preserved within the remaining parkland.

The second benefit to the community of Lucretia Mott Ball's will was the creation of the Block Island Historical Society, formed by friends after her death to ensure that her fine collection of antique furniture and heirlooms — which she had bequeathed to the public — did not leave the Island.

Her bible, *The Rathbun Bible*, is housed in the Society's safe. The earliest date inscribed in the book is the 1672 birth of her great-great-great-great grandfather, Samuel Rathbun; the last date is Lucretia's birth in 1887.

The gathering of the Rathbuns on Block Island in 1993 was to honor the occasion 250 years earlier, on September 4, 1743, when Samuel had taken pen in hand and entered the first family statistics in his bible.

Also to be remembered, though, is Samuel's wife Patience (1669-1747) — because those descended from this couple are indebted equally to Patience's forebears. Her father, John Coggeshall the 4th (1618-1708) was born in Essex Co., England, but became Rhode Island's Deputy-Governor. And his father, John the 3rd (1601-1684), arrived in Boston in June 1632, was a founder of Newport in March 1638, and became President of the Colony of Rhode Island in 1647. He in turn was descended from John Coggeshall of London, noted for building an almshouse for the poor at Halstead, England, in 1553, with his coat-of-arms over the door. But this seems to be another story, perhaps for the Coggeshalls.

A more encompassing thought — a theory derived from archaeological and genetic research in the 1980s — is that we are all descended from one particular woman, dubbed "Eve" by archaeologists, who lived in Africa eons ago. All other lines of humans died off — including any of "Eve's" brothers, sisters, or distant cousins, as well as any separate families of humans that evolved independently elsewhere on the planet.

We are literally one family — all from the same two.

The "Rathbun Rathbone Rathburn" *Family Historian*

THE MAGAZINE *Rathbun-Rathbone-Rathburn Family Historian* takes the reader on a whirlwind adventure of American life, from the present to the past, from the fringes of insignificant events to the center of great ones.

One oft-told story is the family's connection to the life of Abraham Lincoln, from his birth — brought into the world by a midwife who later married a Rathbone — to his death. The following is excerpted from an article in the issue of April 1991:

Our family's final Lincoln connection came on April 14, 1865, when the president was assassinated by John Wilkes Booth at Ford's Theater in Washington, D.C.

Lincoln and his wife were accompanied to the theater on that tragic evening by Major Henry Reed Rathbone [7th generation of Rathbone's] and Rathbone's fiancee and stepsister, Clara Harris.

Clara's father was Senator Ira Harris of New York, one of Lincoln's most loyal supporters in Congress.

Major Rathbone had served as an infantry captain during the early years of the Civil War, and had won a battlefield promotion to major. In 1864, he was assigned to the provost-marshall's office in Washington, where he and Clara were frequent guests at the White House.

At Ford's Theater, about an hour into the play "Our American Cousin," Booth made his way to the rear of the presidential box, slipped inside unseen by anyone, and bolted the door. From a distance of only a few feet, he fired his derringer into the back of Lincoln's head.

Major Rathbone immediately leaped to his feet and ran toward Booth, who slashed at him with a large hunting knife. Rathbone parried the blow with his left arm, and suffered a lone, deep gash which began spurting blood.

Booth, said Rathbone in later testimony, "sprang toward the front of the box. I rushed after him, but only succeeded in catching his clothes as he leaped over the railing."

By interfering with Booth's leap, Rathbone had thrown the assassin off balance, so that he broke one of his ankles as he hit the stage floor.

Rathbone shouted out, "Stop that man!," then turned to the president, who had slumped into a coma. The major then unbolted the door with some difficulty due to his wounded arm, and permitted an Army surgeon to enter, forbidding anyone else to enter the box. He tried to accompany the president as he was carried across the street to a boarding house, but collapsed from loss of blood and was taken home.

Lincoln died several hours later.

The Family Moves West (1720-1850)

Rathbun family magazine, July 1985

Although most of the stories contributed to the family magazine chronicle anecdotes and history from around the country, the family's beginnings on Block Island in 1661 — with John and Margaret Rathbun — are well-covered, such as these facts from the July 1985 issue:

John and Margaret lived briefly in Massachusetts, then spent almost all the rest of their lives on Block Island. Two of their sons and most of their grandsons moved to the mainland, to towns on or near the coastline in Rhode Island and Connecticut. The next two generations moved further inland — to western Massachusetts and Connecticut, Vermont and New York. Successive generations continued the drive westward ... across the entire breadth of America in the next 150 years ...

John and Margaret gave farms on Block Island to all [five] of their sons and at least one of their daughters, and family tradition relates that this was done to encourage all of them to remain on the island. This was not to be ...

Three of John and Margaret's sons — John Jr., Thomas and Samuel — remained on the island and died there. The other two left about 1725 — William to Westerly and Joseph to Exeter, both in Rhode Island ...

Most of their children and grandchildren were born there [on Block Island] and many were married there, but only one of their grandsons was to die there ... Samuel Jr. ...

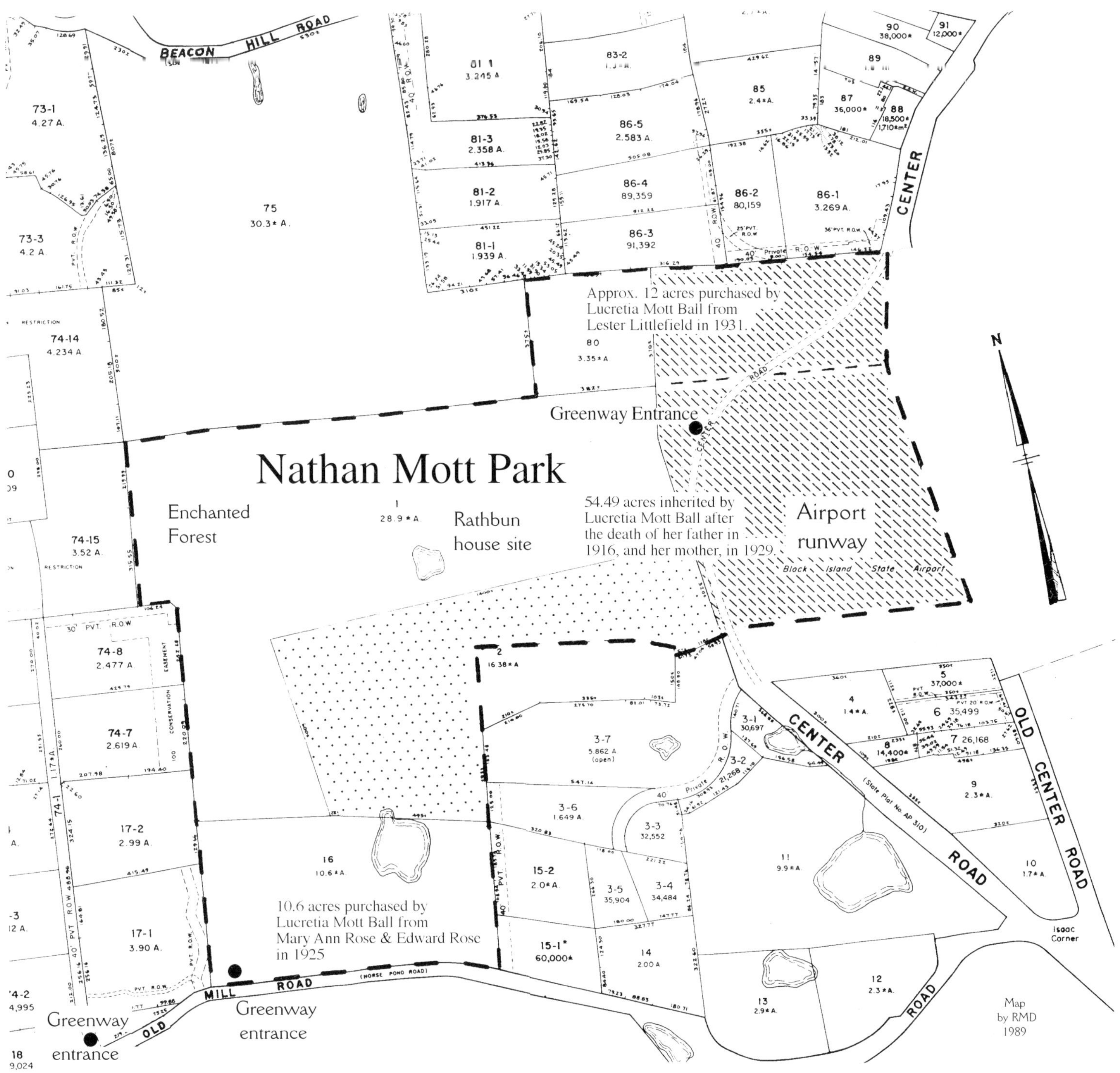

Nathan Mott Park — donated by Lucretia Mott Ball in 1941

Map showing area of John Rathbun's homestead in late 1600s

The farm property of Lucretia Mott Ball at the time of her death in 1941 is shown within the dark dashed lines. She left the land to the public, but large sections were twice usurped for use by the state airport: the slashed area in 1949; and the dotted area in 1961.

Compare the curve of the new Center Road as shown on this map, to an aerial photograph of that road on page 236.

Trees were planted in the northwest corner of the Nathan Mott Park in the early 1940s by Earl Dodge, and the resultant woods have long been known as The Enchanted Forest. The homestead of Lucretia's ancestors, John and Margaret Rathbun, was near the center of the park, just to the right of the smaller pond.

Bold Dashed Border
Delineates the 77.09 acres of Lucretia Mott Ball's land at the time of her death on March 11, 1941.

Shaded Area
Represents the 21.04 acres of Lucretia Mott Ball's land taken for the State Airport in 1949.

Shaded Area
Represents the 13.2 acres of Lucretia Mott Ball's land taken for the State Airport in 1961.

The Block Islanders of 1661

The first 16 settlers were NOT the same as the first 16 landowners.

Only seven of the first settlers were landowners — see dotted lines below.

Four of the first settlers were former Scottish prisoners of war, captured by the English.

Names of early Islanders are sometimes spelled differently in Island records than in the records of mainland towns that the settlers came from, or later moved away to.

	16 landowners *(as named on 1661 Settlers' map)*	**16 settlers** *(left in a boat from Taunton, Massachusetts, to settle Block Island)*		
		SPELLING of NAMES by G. Andrews Moriarty (from mainland records) — in 1920 & 1951 articles	**SPELLING of NAMES by Samuel Livermore (from BI town records) — in his 1877 book**	
		John Acres	John Ackurs	1
1	John Alcock			
		William Barker	Wm. Barker	2
		William Billings	William Billings	3
2	Richard Billings			
		William Cahoone or *Colquhon*	Wm. Cahoone [a Scottish ex-prisoner]	4
3	Samuel Dearing	.... Samuel Dearing	Samuel Dering	5
		Tristram Dodge	Trustaram Dodge	6
4	Richard Ellis			
5	Thomas Faxon	.... Thomas Faxon	Thomas Faxun [he preceded settlers, with surveyor]	7
6	Peter George			
7	John Glover			
		David Kimball	David Kimball	8
8	John Rathbone	.... John Rathbone	John Rathbone	9
9	Simon Ray	.... Simon Ray	Simon Ray	10
10	Tormut Rose .... [given land in 1662]	.... Tormut Rose .... or *Dermot Ross*	Thormut Rose [a Scottish ex-prisoner]	11
11	James Sands [arrived shortly after first settlers, became their leader]			
12	Thomas Terry	.... Thomas Terry	Thomas Terry	12
		William Tosh or *McIntosh*	Wm. Tosh [a Scottish ex-prisoner]	13
13	Edward Vose	.... Edward Vose	Edward Vorse	14
		Nicholas White	Nicholas White	15
14	Philip Wharton			
		Duncan McWilliams or *McWilliamson*	Duncan Williamson [a Scottish ex-prisoner]	16
15	Hugh Williams			
16	Nathaniel Winsley			

The spellings of names in **columns one & two** are from:

- ***The Scotch Prisoners at Block Island***, by G. Andrews Moriarty; in the Jan.1920 *Collections of the Rhode Island Historical Society*
- ***Notes on Block Islanders of Seventeenth Century***, by G. A. Moriarty; in the July 1951 *New England Historical and Genealogical Register*

The spellings of names in **column three** are from:

- ***History of Block Island***, by Samuel Livermore, 1877 (reprinted 1961)

Settlers' Rock

Block Island's much-fabled "original 16 settlers" are not the same individuals as the original 16 landowners. All of their names, however, from both groups, are on the bronze plaque attached to Settlers' Rock, the rough granite monument at the Island's northern end, erected in 1911 for the 250th anniversary of the settlers' arrival at Cow Cove.

Most historians in the late 1800s and early 1900s who pondered the circumstances of the settlers' arrival on Block Island, have surmised they probably landed on the Island in early 1662 — not in 1661 — but the monument was rededicated with another plaque in 1961, and about 1970 a small local hotel changed its name from the Florida House to the 1661 Inn, further cementing the popularity of that date.

Settlers' Rock, and the sweep of Sandy Point's dunes in the distance crowned by the North Light, are a favorite culmination of year-round tours by Islanders, as well as summer trips by bicyclists — demonstrated here during a photo-shoot for the periodical *Barbara* in June 1965.

Settlers' Rock and North Light, June 1965

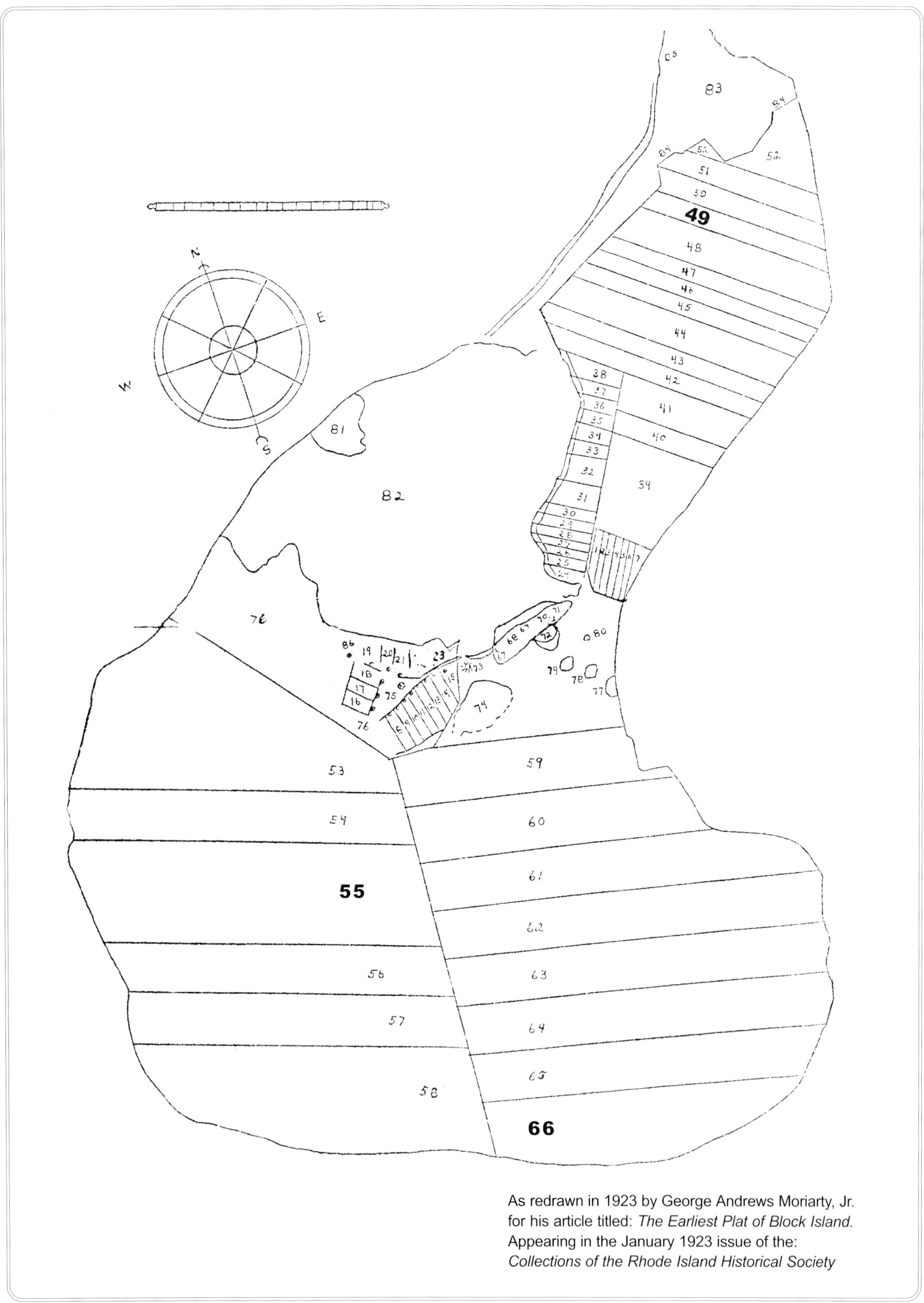

As redrawn in 1923 by George Andrews Moriarty, Jr. for his article titled: *The Earliest Plat of Block Island.* Appearing in the January 1923 issue of the: *Collections of the Rhode Island Historical Society*

On the southern shore of Great Salt Pond the first settlers of 1661 divided the land into small house lots in hopes of establishing a town. Out-of-view on the left, they established the Island Cemetery, and out-of-view on the right was their refuge on Fort Island. But Great Salt Pond could not be successfully kept open to the sea, and the town envisioned in these fields never materialized. Finally, in 1895, the channel in the distance was dredged with state and federal funds, creating New Harbor — a fine port, but no threat to the by then well-established village of Old Harbor.

Visible on the right is the Narragansett Inn, built in 1912. Three marinas for summertime boaters line the shore (from left): Champlin's Marina, Block Island Boat Basin, and Payne's Dock. Directly at the bottom-center is the foundation of the Crown Hotel built in 1906, and burned accidentally in 1940 (see brochure, page 188).

Where the town should have been — New Harbor ca. 1972

The fields escaped large-scale residential development plans for more than 300 years but succumbed in the end. In the left half of the immediate foreground, there now exists the spiderweb-like development called Trim's Ridge, built in the late 1970s — the Island's first condominiums, and a sign of what developers would strive to build during the next two decades wherever their investment backers, lawyers, expert zoning witnesses — and obliging Island politicians and landowners — would allow them.

◄Settlers' Map of 1661

John Rathbun, as did other settlers, received two lots on Block Island — a large one in the south, and a medium one in the north on Corn Neck. Rathbun's share comprised about 1/16th of the Island — or about 1/18th to be more precise, since a large portion of the Island was set aside as Common Land, and a much smaller area preserved for rental purposes to support a minister (the Minister's Lot on Corn Neck Road, see photos on pages 230, 232, 244).

The largest of the original Rathbun lots (area # 66, on lower right of the accompanying Settlers' Map) included the land where the Southeast Light stands, and extended westerly along Mohegan Trail to the corner by the "painted rock" (see photo page 129). At this intersection the dirt Snake Hole Road comes up from the sea, becoming the paved Lakeside Drive, which heads north following the original "Great Road" laid out by the settlers. This original road runs from the sea at the southern end of Block Island by Snake Hole, to the sea at the northern end near Sandy Point — splitting the Island lengthwise into two halves.

A medium size Rathbun lot was near the northern end of the Great Road, on Corn Neck (#49 on the Settlers' Map), extending from the Atlantic on the east, across the road to the dunes on the west bordering Block Island Sound — the dunes themselves were originally common land, and still are. This former Rathbun land now comprises, on the east: part of the Clayhead Nature trail, donated to the public by the Latham family in the 1980s — and on the west, part of the private overgrown fields near the top of Bush Hill, from whence a magnificent panorama of Rhode Island and Connecticut unfolds along Corn Neck Road.

Common Land was laid out for the settlers around the Great Salt Pond (#82) in the Island's center and consisted of areas #59, #76, # 81 (now the Beane property on the northern side of the channel's entrance), #83 (Sachem Pond), #84, and #85 (Sandy Point).

The meeting house (#75) was at the present-day Island Cemetery, and the fort (#73) at Fort Island. Between those two structures were laid out small house lots for the settlers — not, though, for the Rathbuns. But the prospective town never developed — those mostly unbuilt lots, along today's West Side Road, are now the fields of the Narragansett Inn, Red Gate Farm, Trim's Ridge, etc.

As the settlers commenced transferring land shortly after their arrival, John Rathbun purchased 58 acres in 1671 and 1674 — this new Rathbun land (#55 on the Settlers' Map) was west of the present-day airport. As late as 1876 the outline of the filled-in cellar of John Rathbun's former "mansion house at Block Island" was visible near "a beautiful spring of water" — but the home's precise site can no longer be identified.

A public Greenway path — its entrance found opposite, and a few hundred feet south of, the airport driveway — now accesses this land. After twists and turns, the main branch eventually follows the remains of an old terraced lane to a secluded, elevated pond — the general location of the Rathbun house (see maps, pages 56, 63).

On Center Road, about 300 feet to the south of the Greenway entrance, can be found the stonewall-lined route (see photo on page 52) that originally accessed the old Rathbun homestead from the Great Road. The overgrown lane runs due west through the present-day evergreen trees and is flanked by rough stone gate posts near its beginning — the lane later intersects, and then coincides with, the Greenway path that leads to the pond.

Due to the severe threat of Lyme Disease on Block Island, do not push through bushes or tall grass. The settlers were wise to clear the land — we have lost it, and the beauty of the earth's contours, to the relentless march of brush, nettles, and thorned bushes.

This section of the paved Center Road, with its perfectly engineered constant-radius curves, was built in 1950 when the state airport was constructed (see aerial photo on page 236). The original Great Road is 700 feet to the eastward, buried under the present runway — but north and south of the airport the ancient, nearly 300-year-old route continues intact (see maps, pages 57, 63).

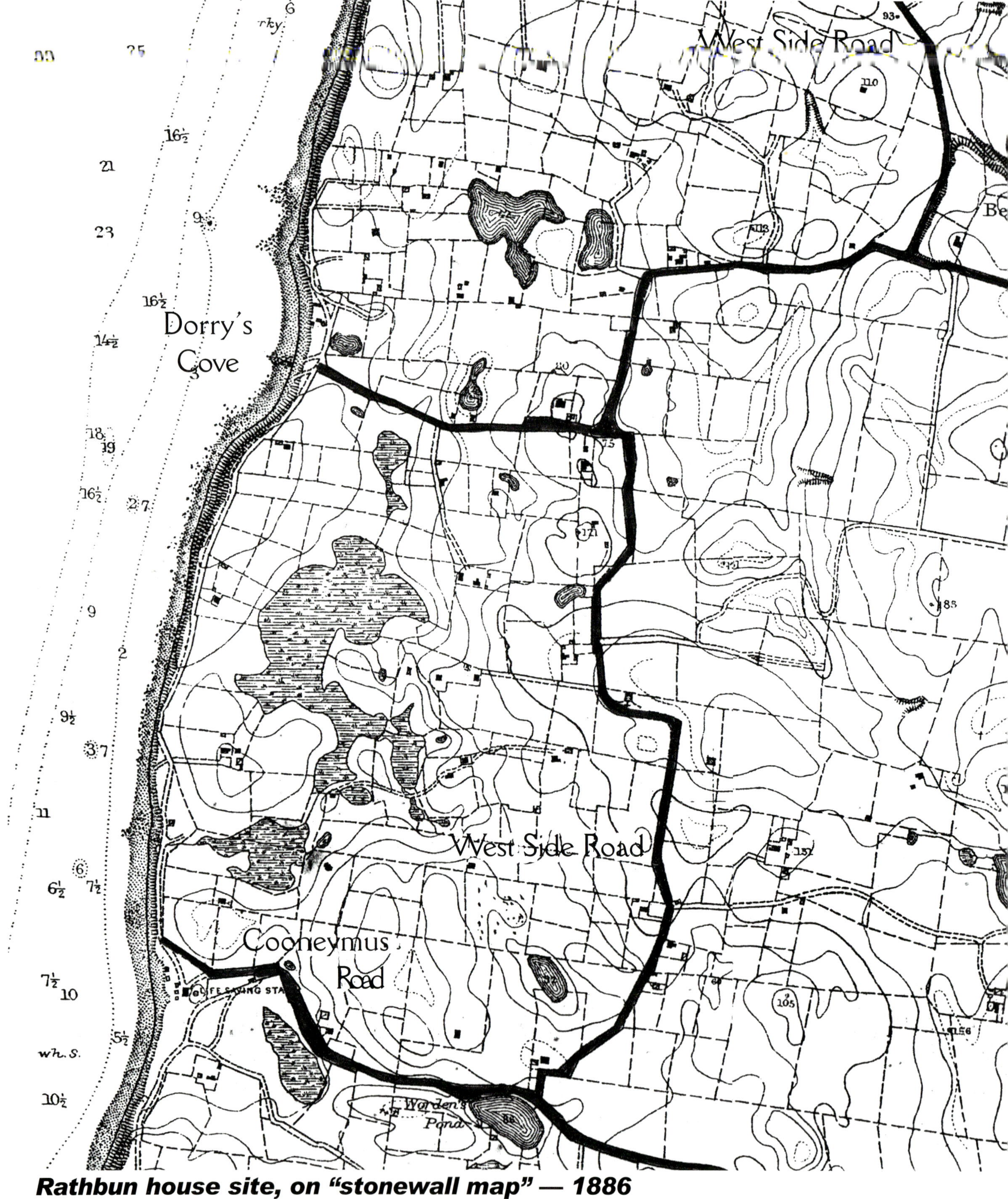

Rathbun house site, on "stonewall map" — 1886

The original lane to the Rathbun house was as straight as an arrow for 1,100 feet — as shown on this map of the Island's roads, stonewalls, houses, and contours, surveyed by the federal government in 1886. (The names of the Rathbun house site and several geographic locations were superimposed on the original map for this book.)

The lane leading to the site of the Rathbone house curves as it approaches a small pond (compare to map, page 57). This 400-foot portion of the lane is part of a present-day Greenway path that leads uphill to the now secluded pond.

On this map, stonewalls are delineated by evenly spaced dashes, and

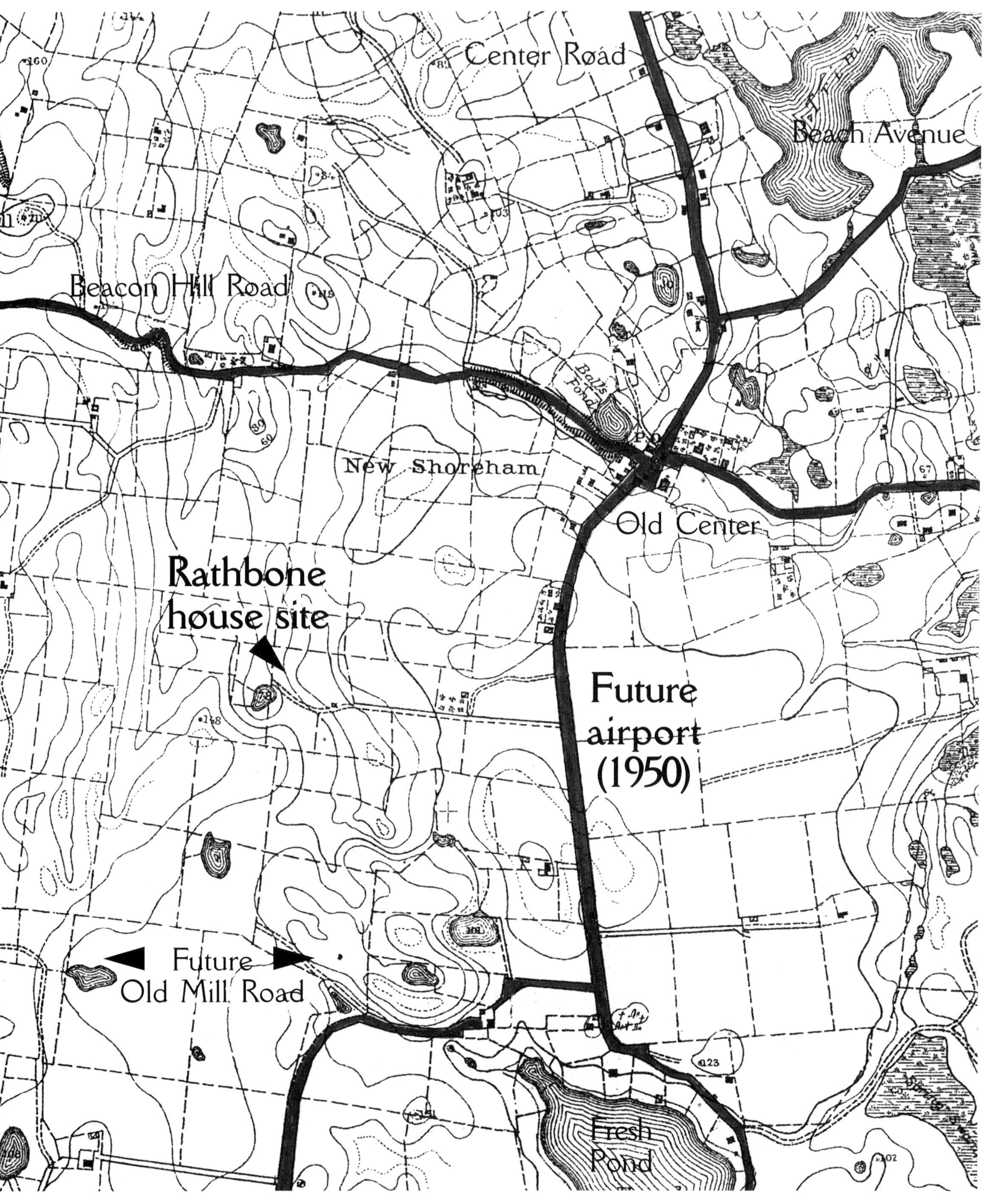

can often be spotted by their straightness. The curved solid lines are contours, each representing a 10-foot change in elevation. Almost all the Island's roads were bordered on each side by stonewalls — even roads in Old Harbor (out-of-sight to the right) such as High Street, Spring Street, Dodge Street, etc., along which walls are now missing.

The few houses of 1886 are represented as small black squares. Those looking for Old Mill Road will not find it, although portions then existed as lanes to houses. The road was cut through a few years later — as a short cut from Fresh Pond to the West Side, and to one of the Island's two windmills (see text and photos, pages 214-215).

Corn husking, Ocean Ave., ca. 1900

Where the electric power plant was built in 1925, and has stood ever since, large fields of corn once flourished. These workers — and a well-dressed onlooker in a straw hat — pause next to the steam engine used to propel corn up a chute to the top of the silo.

For reference, on the right of the photo can be seen two distant houses still in existence — a white one on Beach Avenue owned for a third of a century by the Meyers family (plat 17, lot 13) — and on the extreme right, the mansard-roofed home at the intersection of Beach Ave. and Center Road, once an annex of the Central House (see photo, top of page 214, and map, page 88).

CHAPTER 8

Farming of the past

… when Block Islanders *really* had to live off the land

IN A BROCHURE OF **1914**, the Narragansett Inn's owners boasted of their hotel: "For a back ground it has a beautiful farm owned by the proprietor from which the table is supplied with vegetables, milk, chickens, eggs, etc." That was the heyday of agriculture on Block Island.

Just 25 years later, farming on the Island had nearly disappeared — the victim, as in much of New England, of refrigerated rail cars that brought fresh foods quickly from western states and Florida. The sparse clumps of bayberries that stood as spots of dark foliage in the fields during the 1940s spread in the next 20 years, linking with each other, forming the forests of impenetrable brush that became by the 1970s the new, less friendly, landscape.

The Mott family, proprietors of the Narragansett since it was constructed in 1912 — the last great hotel built on the Island — had been farming for 200 years, since their arrival in the early 1700s. They were the newcomers then.

Within 50 years of the first settlers' arrival in 1661, much of the land was cleared. To ensure success for the resulting agrarian society, rules were created.

Some arrangements were private, governing the relationship between the landowners who remained in Massachusetts, and their workers or tenants on Block Island. In 1672 John Williams rented his Island land for seven years to a "planter," John Gunnill, age 27 — the rent to be paid in "wheat, barley, Indian corn, or porke."

Gunnill also agreed not to:

"cut nor Waste any of the timber … that is upon the said farm, but what shall be for his own firewood and fencing, and necessary building upon the said land."

And he had to:

"leave the fences in as good repaire; as the fence now is with as many posts, Railes & Pallasades as now is upon it, or other fence as good."

A sense of the preciousness of wood on Block Island is evident, landowners fearing renters absconding with the material, just as hotel owners now worry about losing towels to their paying guests.

Other rules, more general in nature, were made to govern all of the Island's farmers.

Pigs were regulated by a decree of the town on November 24, 1676 — making us think how easily the first settlers, being both fair-minded and efficiently practical, would have quickly curbed the mopeds belonging to today's five rental dealers, whose dangerous business has bloodied and broken the bones of more than 1,000 tourists on the Island during recent years:

"It is ordered that all the swine that are now in the Corne Neck be fetched out and … if any swine be found there … any man hath liberty to kill them: but if any break in … the owner is to have notice of it, and if the owner fetch him or them not out in twelve hours after due notice given them, they are to be killed and the person killing of them to be blameless and the owner or owners to lose their swine."

By this edict the settlers were protecting their crops on Corn Neck. They had learned what the corn-planting Indians of the early 1600s had also discovered: this northern half of Block Island contained the largest stretches of fertile soil. The only other large area of such high yielding ground occurs at the Lewis-Dickens farm in the southwest — although nearly all the Island's farmland was improved by fertilization with peat ashes, fish offal, and seaweed.

To protect crops further, the grazing of sheep was restricted on April 8, 1679:

"It is ordered that no sheepe be penned anywhere upon the Island except as it be in the comon penn that is joyning to John Rathbones house lott ... except men that have pastures ... may then at their pleasure penn what they have within their own land."

Predatory pests were also controlled — again in an expeditious manner so competent as to make current town council members, and others of the 1980s and 90s, appear derelict in their duty to rid the Island of deer and the attendant problem of Lyme disease. On April 13, 1686, the town council declared:

"that every man ... above 16 year age should kill 24 black birds the insuing year ... and so many as any man kills more than above [he] shall have [one] pence apiece for each, provided the heads be brought in to the treasurer or warden, and what is wanting of 2 dozen [he] shall pay 2 pence apiece."

Down on the farm, towering horns do not intimidate this young boy, ca. 1910

As the land was continually cleared and cultivated, the community prospered. The farms remained large — in 1756 there were only 45 houses, for 55 to 60 families, or a total population of 378. (There are now about 1,450 houses for 850 year-round residents — 80% of the houses are for summer use only).

By the time of the Revolution — when all the land was farmed and there were, practically speaking, no longer any trees — the Island was famous throughout the colonies for its cattle, sheep, butter and cheese.

About 1800, land began to be converted from pasturage to tillage, and the chief agricultural products became corn, barley and potatoes. In 1819 there were 128 houses and 722 inhabitants.

A state geologist, Dr. Charles Jackson, wrote in his 1840 *Report on the Geological and Agricultural Survey of the State of R.I.*, that:

"Indian corn grows well on Block Island, and the crops vary with the amount of manure used, from 20 to 60 bushel to the acre; the average crop being estimated at 25 bushels.

"In 1831, Mr. Sands tilled 13 acres of land, manured it with a compost of seven tons of seaweeds, mixed with soil. His crop amounted to 387 bushels of corn, equal to 29 and 7/10 bushel to the acre ...

"Rye is an uncertain crop. Barley is said to suffer from 'scalding,' the sun acting upon the rain or dew which covers the stalks of the grain. Grass crops are generally good, and the yield is about one ton to the acre."

An 1857 pamphlet, *The History of Block Island*, by Henry T. Beckwith, echoed the same, adding more:

"The largest crops raised are those of Indian corn and grass, both of which do well: I have never seen finer looking fields of corn anywhere.

"Many thousand bushels of oat, which also are of excellent quality, are raised for the Providence market, and there are other smaller products. The land is also stocked [with animals] quite as heavily as is profitable, and large quantities of poultry are raised.

"The fisheries are important; yet as the majority of the inhabitants are farmers and not fishermen, as many suppose, the income of the fisheries is subordinate in amount to the value of the farm produce. As the landed estates have become so small, many are obliged to combine farming or gardening with fishing ...

"The trade of the Island is carried on principally with Stonington, New London, Providence, and Newport. The Islanders carry over cattle, horses, sheep, hogs, grain, fish, poultry, and eggs; and expend much of the proceeds in articles for home consumption."

Edward H. Champlin, farmer, ca. 1909

Four generations were on the family porch for this photograph.

The prosperous farmer Edward H. Champlin (1823-1911) poses with (from left):

- his daughter Carrie Champlin (1857-1924),
- his granddaughter Florence Ball Madison (child of Edward's other daughter Mary Champlin Ball),
- and his great-grandson Harold Madison.

Edward was the grandson of the first Champlin on Block Island: Nathaniel Champlin (1767-1836). Edward's great-grandson Harold Madison — the baby in the photograph — has great-grandchildren living on Block Island.

That's nine generations total since the time of the American Revolution.

Great Salt Pond, looking NW from near Champlin's Marina, ca. 1900

Below the house in this photograph are grazing cows, and just below that a cornfield. The dirt road known as Champlin's Road (or Coast Guard Road) is 400 feet behind the hill where the photographer stood. Just to the right, out-of-view, is the area where the present-day Champlin's Marina would later be built.

The west side of Great Salt Pond was long the farmland of the Champlin family, since the arrival of Nathaniel Champlin on Block Island in the late 1700s. In 1894, Edward H. Champlin's farm, visible along this shore, consisted of 100 acres — much of it is still in the family.

To visit a neighbor on Block Island then, and until the early 1960s, you didn't need roads — you just walked in a straight line.

The Island of the 1800s, all 5,000 usable acres, was at its land-use peak, saturated with agriculture, every bit of the former forest erased — just one large community farm turned into a rolling checkerboard of weaving stonewalls that determined the ownership and various uses of the fields.

In 1885 the various sizes of the Island's 225 farms were:

Farm size:	# of farms:
1-2 acres	19 farms
3-9 acres	78 farms
10-19 acres	52 farms
20-49 acres	55 farms
50-99 acres	14 farms
100-199 acres	6 farms
200-299 acres	1 farm

In the 1880s and 90s, a Victorian resort was superimposed on this landscape. It affected primarily Old Harbor where steamships could tie up at the new breakwater and new hotels catered to tourists seeking carefree companions and cool summer breezes. Mainland-inspired architecture impacted the rest of the Island very little, and the rolling farmland, sprinkled with the occasional farmhouse, predominated into the mid-1900s.

Although the massive exporting of farm products declined precipitously after 1900, small farms continued during the 1920s and 30s to supply the Island's needs.

The following letter was written in 1923 to a prospective guest by the owner of Willow Grove Farm, a boarding house (plat 2, lot 19-1) located near the end of Corn Neck Road. Care, attention and pride were still in evidence on Block Island:

"June 30, 1923

"My dear Mr. Kirkland:

"In reply to your letter of June 27, beg to advise that Fifteen ($15.00) dollars per week includes both room and board. I can give you a single room.

"I serve good food cooked in the old-fashioned way and plenty of it and enough so that everyone if they do not want to gain will have to diet on their vacation. I do not use any canned goods or baker's goods. All vegetables, milk, eggs, cream, butter and fowl are from the farm. I also serve plenty of sea food.

"The farm is situated on the state road which is the main drive on the Island and about three miles from boat landing ...

"Thanking you for your inquiry and hoping to hear favorably from you, I am,

"Yours truly,

"Mrs. James A. Maxfield"

Potato field on Spring Street, 1883

A view down the driveway of the Spring House hotel shows a potato field (on right) along one of Spring Street's curves.

Five years later on this corner, Mrs. Annie M. Cahill built the "Fern Cottage," which developed into the small hotel known as the Florida House for most of the 1900s, but in the early 1970s was renamed the 1661 Inn.

The white house on the extreme left, dating from the 1700s, was the home of Annie's mother, Matilda Rose (1829-1916). During the last third of the 1900s, the home has been *The White House* of Island lovers, Violette and Joseph V. Connolly.

Block Island Census 1885

NEW SHOREHAM.

TABLE LXIV-12.—AGRICULTURAL PROPERTY AND PRODUCTS.

PROPERTY AND PRODUCTS.	Basis.	Quantity.	Value.
PROPERTY, TOTAL	VALUE	....	$1,115,393
Buildings, land, etc.	*value*	....	*1,030,170*
Buildings	value	....	472,250
Implements	"	....	14,720
Additional capital	"	....	2,650
Farm Land	"	....	540,550
Land acreage	....	*4,578*	....
Land plowed	acres	873	....
" other mowing.	"	1,685	....
" pasture	"	2,020	....
Live stock	*value*	....	*85,223*
Horses	number	209	28,090
Colts	"	7	590
Milch cows	"	351	13,759
Heifers	"	79	1,530
Bulls	"	8	240
Oxen	"	197	12,930
Calves	"	46	535
Sheep	"	1,192	4,858
Lambs	"	1,070	4,967
Swine	"	430	3,942
Dogs	"	85	446
Hens and chickens	"	15,324	7,691
Ducks	"	182	100
Geese	"	852	848
Turkeys	"	3,019	4,697
PRODUCTS, TOTAL	VALUE	....	147,455
Cereals	*value*	....	*12,394*
Barley	bushels.	1,325	1,048
Corn, Indian	"	10,129	8,068
Oats	"	8,544	3,278
Dairy Products	*value*	....	*21,736*
Butter, used	pounds.	23,315	5,829
" sold	"	12,615	3,175
Cheese, used	"	1,425	143
" sold	"	825	92
Milk, used	gallons.	75,690	9,840
" sold	"	17,225	2,575
Cream, used	"	22	35
" sold	"	30	47
Fodders	*value*	....	*38,322*
Fodder corn, green	tons	320	1,272
" dry	"	579	2,942
Hay, English	"	1,781	30,453
" clover	"	10	100
Straw, oat	"	288	2,970
Turnips, fodder	bushels.	1,078	426
Beets, "	"	400	159
Fruit Products	*value*	....	*800*
Apples	bushels.	389	213
Pears	"	16	17
Peaches	"	1	2
Quinces	"	119	249

PRODUCTS.—Con.	Basis.	Quantity.	Value.
Fruit Products, Con.			
Strawberries	quarts	1,853	$264
Blackberries	"	10	1
Raspberries	"	10	1
Currants	bushels.	28	53
Poultry Products	*value*	....	*25,350*
Eggs, used	dozen	13,371	3,075
" sold	"	47,010	10,560
Chickens, used	pounds.	12,100	2,057
" sold	"	12,462	2,010
Ducks, used	"	315	47
" sold	"	47	9
Geese, used	"	1,520	243
" sold	"	4,975	800
Turkeys, used	"	4,219	844
" sold	"	21,865	4,335
Hen and bird manure.	value	....	1,370
Vegetables	*value*	....	*14,226*
Beets	bushels.	1,896	919
Beans, string and shell	"	491	492
" dry	"	163	324
Carrots	"	481	265
Corn, green	dozen	10,221	1,501
Cabbage	heads	4,239	222
Cucumbers	bushels.	648	648
Lettuce	heads	2,340	47
Melons	number	634	56
Onions	bushels.	111	111
Potatoes	"	13,965	7,065
Pumpkins	pounds.	510,100	1,290
Parsnips	bushels.	128	80
Pease, green	"	74	75
" dry	"	7	14
Radishes	bunches	65	3
Rhubarb	pounds.	1,850	41
Squashes	"	4,300	83
Spinach	bushels.	5	3
Tomatoes	"	71	.48
Turnips	"	2,131	939
Peat	*value*	....	*1,545*
Peat, for manure	cords	310	1,545
Other Farm Products.	*value*	....	*33,082*
Animal manure	value	....	7,120
Sea "	"	....	10,932
Slaughtered animals	"	....	13,812
Wool	pounds.	4,806	1,218
Average Product per Acre	*value*	....	*$32.21*
Manures and Fertilizers used	*value*	....	*$19,508*
Manure, animal	value	....	7,120
" hen and bird	"	....	1,370
" sea	"	....	10,932
Fertilizers	"	....	86

In only one lifetime, the farmland disappeared, covered now with naturally occurring bayberries bushes and shad trees; by the taller Japanese black pine, a non-indigenous tree dying away in recent years to the delight of some residents who enjoy more distant ocean views; and by the foundations and multi-windowed walls of summer houses — the reason, beginning 30 years ago, that the pines were planted by irate neighbors who wished to block their view of the new construction. Nearly no one, though, envisioned the Japanese black pine trees self-spreading into mini-forests that would blot out the open character of the landscape which everyone came here to enjoy in the first place.

On an Island whose once-open vistas are now subdivided into a suburbia of small house lots, it is incredible to think of some of the bare statistics from the year 1885: six farms of 100-200 acres, 14 farms of 50-99 acres, and 55 farms of 20-49 acres — and another 170 smaller farms.

Perhaps it is by a natural wisdom that the land attempts to return to forest. Windswept and salt-laden, the plants grow back around the summer homes — like grass growing in the cracks of sidewalks, attempting to hide the unsightly manmade intrusion laid upon the earth.

The lesson on Block Island was "farm it, or lose it."

There are no farms left.

For other striking photographs of farmland see:

- *Nathan Mott Park in 1957 — page 52*
- *peat story — page 76*
- *digging potatoes with ox-team — top of page 122*
- *from Beacon Hill, ca. 1890 — page 165*
- *Lewis-Dickens Farm in 1984 — page 247*
- *leaving school in 1950 — page 261*

For views of farmhouses, see pages 72-73 and:

- *two-chimney house on Old Town Road — page 78*
- *Peleg Champlin house in 1890s & in 2001 — pages 80 & 81*
- *Mitchell Farm in 1996 — bottom of page 141*
- *gambrel-roof house in 1884 on Beacon Hill Road — page 208*
- *gambrel-roof house: Smilin' Through — pages 222-224*
- *Elizabeth Dickens' Cape Cod-style house in 1948 — 258*

Halfway down Beacon Hill Road, looking east, 1916

The caption for this photograph, from a tourist brochure of 1916, reads:

"The Rolling Green and Stone-walled Slopes of Block Island Remind One of Cornwall, Southern England."

The gentle curve in this portion of Beacon Hill Road is still visible, but none of the now overgrown landscape is — preventing any modern-day traveler from seeing this pastoral scene appreciated by earlier generations. Behind the photographer, out of view on the road's left side, is a two-story mansard-roofed home that can be easily located today.

The house on the right under trees — just above the wooden gate — still exists (plat 16, lot 82) — but the clearly visible house (plat 18, lot 72) just to its left, which stood across the road, was torn down in November 1998 (see photo, page 165).

Such destruction of old buildings occurs unexpectedly — without any chance of saving the structures — because town council members during the past 25 years have refused to put any historic restrictions on the overwhelming majority of the Island's most historic old homes.

The New National

Block Island, R. I.

Menu

Dinner

QUEEN OLIVES SWEET MIXED PICKLES CHOW CHOW

Soup

CONSOMME MACEDOINE
MOCK TURTLE AU COGNAC

Fish

BAKED BLOCK ISLAND BLUEFISH A L'ANCHOVIE
POMMES WINDSOR SLICED CUCUMBERS

Entrees

FILET MIGNON A LA RICHELIEU
BAKED SPAGHETTI, ITALIENNE
GATEAUX DES POMMES A LA NATIONAL

Boiled

LEG OF SOUTHDOWN MUTTON, PROVINCALE
FERRIS SUGAR CURED HAM A LA PIQUANT

Roast

SIRLOIN OF BEEF AU JUS
PRIME RIBS OF BEEF, DISH GRAVY
NATIVE GREEN DUCKLING, CRAB APPLE SAUCE

Vegetables

BOILED NEW POTATOES MASHED POTATOES
BOILED SWEET POTATOES NATIVE GREEN PEAS
BERMUDA ONIONS A LA CREME GREEN CORN ON COB

Salad

SLICED TOMATOES PLAIN LETTUCE

Dessert

GREEN APPLE PIE COCOANUT CUSTARD PIE
STEAMED FRUIT PUDDING, MADEIRA SAUCE
COFFEE JELLY WITH WHIPPED CREAM
PEACH ICE CREAM WITH SPONGE CAKE
FLORIDA ORANGES BANANAS
CALIFORNIA PLUMS SNOW APPLES
ICED WATERMELON
SPANISH LAYER RAISINS MIXED NUTS
ROQUEFORT CHEESE
CONNECTICUT CREAM CHEESE
SALTINE CRACKERS
CAFE NOIR DEMI-TASSE

AUGUST 20, 1911

Menu, August 20, 1911 — From "Florida" and "California" to the National Hotel

The demise of farming in New England was inadvertently spelled out in the National Hotel's menu for August 20, 1911, with the words: "FLORIDA ORANGES" and "CALIFORNIA PLUMS." But this writing on the wall — or rather, under their noses — was probably little understood by summer diners.

With the further development of refrigerated rail cars, and the electrification of towns throughout the country, produce could be shipped evermore easily from distant farms — mammoth in size — and kept fresh in one's own kitchen. The first mechanical refrigerator for American homes was marketed in 1916 — by 1920 there were 10,000 refrigerators sold annually; that figure rose in 1925 (the year Block Island was electrified) to 75,000 per year; in 1929 to 800,000 per year; and in 1939 to 3,000,000 each year.

In 1911, though, many of the vegetables on the tables of Island hotels were still from local farms — in addition, of course, to varieties of fish from nearby waters, such as the "Baked Block Island Bluefish a l'anchovie" offered on this menu.

A tourist booklet written by Beatrice Ball — daughter of Ocean View Hotel owner C. C. Ball — touted the Island's farming virtuosity in 1909:

"Vegetables are somewhat later than on the mainland, but when they are ready for use are unrivaled anywhere. The common vegetables are raised in great abundance, and with the list may be mentioned, artichoke, strawberries, tomatoes, mushrooms, etc. The farms supply the hotels in summer with poultry, milk, eggs and fresh vegetables, and supply lamb and veal for the markets. In the fall, butter and cheese are added to the list, and around Thanksgiving time the demand for Block Island turkeys exceeds the supply."

Ocean View Hotel dining room, 1879

After filling up on a hardy dinner of Island produce, hotel guests could wander to the hotel's bazaar, or down the hill to Old Harbor, to buy this souvenir three-dimensional stereoview (one half shown) of their own dining room — a reminder of the carved watermelon that graced each table as a centerpiece, and the folded napkins placed inside the stemmed drinking glasses.

Old Farmhouses Still To Be Seen

Capt. Welcome Dodge house and potato field, Amy Dodge Lane, ca. 1895

The classic, ca. 1840, home of Capt. Welcome Dodge, Sr. (1813 - 1909) still stands on Amy Dodge Lane, but rows of potatoes no longer grow near the front door, as in this view. The $1\frac{3}{4}$ story house was long owned by Welcome's grandson, fabled telephone operator Henry Dodge — and for the last quarter of the 1900s, by Daniel J. Millea, who in 1973 founded the Book Nook store and became the husband of Rosemary Howarth.

Capt. Nathaniel Willis homestead, Corn Neck Road, ca. 1895

Capt. Nathaniel Willis (1821-1891) built his home about 1850 after making several land purchases on the west side of Corn Neck — reportedly paid for with nuggets from his California "Gold Rush" days. His $1\frac{3}{4}$ story house is still in the family, but which members are visible in this photograph is not known. Two of the Captain's sons, Everett and Loren, and his daughter, Mrs. William Littlefield Jr., used part of the farm property to build three houses in a row along Corn Neck Road, just to the north of their parents. Two of the three homes still exist: Loren's, built in 1888, now the Harborview (plat 4, lot 46) — and Everett's, built in 1897, now the Bayside (plat 4, lot 48).

Almanza Littlefield house, Old Town Road, ca. 1890

Although the majority of the stonewalls in this view no longer exist, the home of Almanza Littlefield (1826-1900) can be easily spotted on Old Town Road by its relation to the town hall — which is on this side of the road, 100 yards to the right. The $1\frac{3}{4}$ story construction is typical of houses built on Block Island in the later 1800s. When standing in a room on the second floor, the side wall would come to about one's knees — higher than a $1\frac{1}{2}$ story Cape Cod style house (see below), which have no side walls — but not as high as the full-height walls of a two-story home. More than 40 Cape Cod style houses and 120 $1\frac{3}{4}$ story houses are scattered across Block Island — nearly all built in the 1800s for farmers and fishermen.

For views of other farmhouses, see list on page 70

Mid-1700s house of Nathaniel Littlefield, Mansion Beach, ca. 1920

The Nathaniel Littlefield house, a hospital in the Revolution and still in the original family, is one of the most magnificent seaside farm settings on the Atlantic coast — as nearby vacationers at Mansion Beach, on the Island's northeastern shore, have long agreed (see photo, page 252). Visible in this photograph from the 1920s are rows of onions, corn and myriad other vegetables. Not apparent are the sheep and cows that often grazed the rolling, stonewall-bordered fields — perfectly placed, it always seemed, to pleasure the eye.

Gathering Hay Through The Ages

Oxen pulling hay, ca. 1890

Gathering hay in the late 1800s, as well as the late 1900s, could be a family affair.

A weathered Block Island farmer, pitchfork in hand, guides two oxen pulling a rope to gather hay. Riding the haystack are a young girl, seated — and a man, standing.

Horse pulling hay, ca. 1900 (upper right)

Two small children help weigh down a haystack. As the horse pulls a loop of rope across a field, the pile — and the fun — grow larger.

From the 1870s until the 1960s — when the changes started — this landscape, rising and heaving unfettered into the distance, is what tourists adored about Block Island, and not a few Islanders themselves regret the loss.

Pulling hay, three generations of Spragues, August 1970

Block Island Times founder, Margaret Cabel Self, photographed Adrian "Tiny" Sprague Jr., Adrian Sprague Sr., and 14-year-old "Little Joe" gathering hay in the timeless tradition.

CHAPTER 9

Burning Peat

Winter's warmth from shoveling summer's peat

Barefoot work — ca. 1890

Seneca Sprague (1819-1903) digging peat barefoot — there might be some fun to this, after all.

A TUG HOUSE IS NOT LIKE AN ICE HOUSE, fish house, smoke house, hot house, hen house, outhouse, or boarding house, but in the old days on Block Island every child, woman and man would have been familiar with one — and could not have lived without it.

Since before 1750, when the Island's forests were depleted, until well after 1850, when coal was imported in ever-increasing amounts, Islanders were dependent on these small low buildings, with walls built loosely of stone for the wind to pass through. In them were stored the balls of peat that had been gathered and dried during summer and fall — soon to become the fuel to feed winter fireplaces.

So central were tug houses to existence on the Island that the word "tug" — commonly meaning "to pull with great effort" — was used also by Islanders to name the mucky substance they tugged and shoveled out of the ground. The mixture of old rotted vegetation, often found at the bottom of swamps or ponds, burned after being dried. Elsewhere it was known as peat.

Getting tug was work. It could also be fun — at least in retrospect — according to one old Islander who wrote in the 1890s looking fondly back to former years and the start of the tug season.

First the local swamp was drained by digging ditches to let any standing water run off. A muddy bottom would be left after a few days or weeks. Then, when the mowing season was over, all hands turned out "to tug it for a week or so," but not before one of the Islanders sailed "over to Stonington and returned with many kegs and jugs of the West India wet goods."

A small jug of the rum was taken down to the swamp, everyone took a "hooter," *then* the labor began. The muck was thrown up from the bed "wet and heavy" into a heap, and tramped upon "to knead the stuff so as to ball it." If oxen were available, they were driven through the batch too.

With a sled or wheelbarrow the tug was carried to a south facing hill where the youngsters formed the oozing material into balls about six to eight inches in diameter. "This was done with the naked hands, sleeves pushed up to shoulders. A tugging outfit consisted of shirt and pants, maybe a hat."

The balls were left in the sun and wind to dry, later turned to expose the other side, then stacked like cannon balls two or three feet high. After sufficiently drying, the peat was taken to the tug house for storage throughout the winter months.

Tug was not burned in stoves. Fireplaces with grates were needed, their wide chimneys taking up the smoke. A peat fire was kept burning continually for the entire winter. If the fire "got lost" — as the local vernacular termed it — "someone was started off with a kettle to the nearest house for a 'piece of fire.'"

And so the long winters were spent. On very cold nights the children would be brought down from the upstairs rooms and "placed on the hearthstone with feet toward the fire, and in this way were kept from freezing to death." With wind howling against thin walls, they listened to the harrowing stories of pirate visits long ago.

Two types of chimneys, photographed in 1930s

This Cape Cod style house was owned by William "Smith" Mott (1833-1912) during the late 1800s. He moved the building from Corn Neck to its present location off Old Town Road, near the former Center. The main house has a chimney of large dimensions, a size needed for fireplaces that burned peat or wood. But the ell had a small chimney, just sufficient for the lesser requirements of a coal burning stove.

Newporters, it was said, could tell by the aroma when a Block Islander ventured to that mainland Rhode Island city. But the peculiar smoke of peat got into the clothes of many other New Englanders as well. In the early 1800s, nearly 100 towns in Massachusetts had deposits of peat. The state geologist reported in 1833 that the use of peat for fuel "was rapidly increasing especially in the eastern part of the state where [firewood] fuel is more expensive." Although cords of wood were brought down by boat from the coasts of Maine and Nova Scotia to keep eastern cities warm, peat was still cut from meadows on Cape Cod until the 1860s to be sold in Boston.

Anthracite coal — hard coal, meant to be burned in stoves not fireplaces — was first brought to New England as a fuel in 1828, and to Block Island in the 1840s. But farmers throughout New England, including those on Block Island, did not use coal in great abundance until the 1850s.

In 1875 Islanders dug 544 cords of peat. But the days of peat were numbered, not only was coal easier to use, but Islanders obtained substantial amounts of free coal from shipwrecks — thousands of tons of it — from two and three-masted schooners in the late 1800s, and from wooden barges and steel-hulled steamers during the first four decades of the 1900s.

Tug, however, had two small revivals on Block Island, the first coming in 1935 during the middle of the Depression — a year when coal prices rose sharply. Otto Mitchell and his wife Rosie — she of later taxicab fame — gave tugging a try near Sandy Hill, on their 13-acre farm off Dorry's Cove Road. Thirty years had passed since any peat had been dug on the Island and it required their 68-year-old neighbor, Smith Sprague, to show the Mitchells how to tug.

An area was marked out four feet by 12 feet at the edge of a swamp. They found peat — resembling mud and decayed leaves — nine feet below the surface. Water began draining into the bottom of the pit, hastening the pace of the work. Using an ox-drawn wagon (see photo at right) the shoveled-out peat was taken to an adjacent field. The gooey muck was softened more by patting it with shovels, then rolled into balls and left to dry. Ten days later the peat balls were turned over, and after another ten they were piled in pyramids that allowed air to pass through. After a third 10-day period — 30 days after being dug out — the peat was ready to burn.

The *Providence Bulletin* described the results:

"When first dug, the peat is a bright reddish brown color, which gradually becomes darker, and after a few days, is coal black. Noticeable was the absence of any worms or bugs, and compressed leaves were as perfect in color and shape as though they had just fallen from a tree. Tree roots presented the biggest problem in digging ...

"Mr. Sprague said that five peat bogs, four by 12 feet each, would furnish enough fuel for two houses in a winter. He said that the old-timers always started tugging in summer, when the swamps were dry, avoiding the difficulty of the bog holes filling up before the men finished digging.

"Younger members of Island families are visiting the Mitchell farm every day to watch this process which they have heard their parents and grandparents describe, but never expected to see."

There is no record of the venture passing far beyond the experimental stage. The Islanders' fuel needs in the 1920s and 30s were alleviated to a greater extent by the timely wrecking of several coal-carrying vessels, such as the **Penn** and **Meteor** along the southwestern shore, and the **Putzta** off Clay Head. Chunks of coal from those wrecks, or from others, are still tossed onto the beach during storms.

Peat in the town records

Block Islanders depended on peat in the past to such an extent that a state almanac published in 1853 mentioned the fact in describing the three essential elements of an Islander's existence: "The people are mostly fishermen; they have no harbor, and peat is their only fuel."

The early records of the town reflect this basic life. References to peat permeate the written words of the Islanders, just as the smoke once saturated fibers of their clothing. The right to dig peat, and even the stone tug houses used to store the valuable material, were sufficiently noteworthy to be recorded in the town's deed books.

In 1827, two generations of an Island family decided the future of their home, and their tug house, and recorded the agreement by deed (vol. 8, page 295). Thomas Mitchell purchased ½ acre from his father, Samuel G. Mitchell for $25, "together with that part of my dwelling house which said Thomas does at this time occupy, with his having the privilege of passing in and out of the south door of my dwelling house, also the privilege of my west fireplace and passing up and down the stairs into the west chamber which belongs to that part of the house I have sold him now. I reserve to myself the tug house which is joined onto the west end of my dwelling house with the privilege of moving it when I think proper ..." This old 1½ story Cape Cod style house still stands along a dirt lane that leads off the east side of Corn Neck Road, nearly opposite Andy's Way.

In 1851, when Joshua Rose bought one-half interest in his father's property for $1.00, the land came "with a Dwelling House and peat tug or Barn house thereon Standing" (vol. 12, page 349). The building is now the Hardy Smith House, a bed & breakfast on High Street.

Property purchased by Capt. Solomon Dodge in 1853 came with a "tug house" (vol.12, page 532). Solomon's 2½ story colonial style home still stands off Old Town Road, at Old Harbor, now owned by the Glen family.

Because certain prolific ponds or swamps became famous for their yield of peat, the word "tug" was also used in geographic names. At Mitchell Farm on Corn Neck Road (where the cows are), tug rights were purchased from Hancock Mitchell for $12 in 1816, for use of 1/9 acre of "the great Georging Swamp" — a wetland still known as Georgian Swamp. To increase the size of the farm, 1¼ acres of land were bought a month later from Nathaniel Sands for $20, and another 2/5 acre in 1818 from John Paine for $40 — each parcel was bounded on the north by a "tugswamp" (volume 7; pages 80, 96, and 194).

In 1877, William L. Rose bought 5 acres from his brother, Erastus, bounded on the north by the "New Meadow Hill tug or peat swamp" (vol. 15, page 174). The home that William Rose built, off Old Town Road, is now owned by Capt. John R. Lewis.

But one does not need to delve into obscure records to find evidence of past peat digging. The large pond next to Pilot Hill Road immortalizes the word "tug" quite well — it is named John E's Tug Hole.

Otto Mitchell unloading balls of peat to dry, 1930s

Peleg Champlin house & outbuildings, 1890s

The classic, ca. 1820, 1½ story, Cape Cod style home of Peleg C. Champlin (1800-1880), and his son Weeden (1829-1906), still exists to the southward off Coast Guard Road. Although stone foundations of a few of the many outbuildings still survive, none are now used for their original purpose — see photo at right. This 1890s photograph, though, is not ancient enough to show the family's tug house, a type of building — in that era of coal stoves — whose need had been defunct for several decades.

The late 1970s

PEAT'S LAST HURRAH on Block Island welled up from the nationwide oil-shortage in the 1970s. Electricity bills were already high enough on Block Island — with local fuel costs increased by freight, and then artificially jacked up further by the private Block Island Power Company. The cost of 29 cents per kilowatt-hour was said to be the highest in the nation — a claim that is still made.

An Arab oil embargo just made things worse, leading the Block Island Economic Development Foundation to seek, and win, a $10,000 grant from the U.S. Department of Energy to investigate the peat resources of Block Island. A survey of the Island's ponds, swamps, and wetlands was begun in 1978, directed by Jon Boothroyd of the Department of Geology at the University of Rhode Island.

Another grant, for $19,400, was won in 1979 to "investigate the practical use of peat for domestic heating." Dreams went far beyond those of the Island's old farmers who in centuries past had ventured out to the stone tug house to carry a ball or two of peat back to the fireplace. In the late 1970s an idea evolved to mine peat on Block Island with heavy machinery, using modern technology to convert the wet muck to a gaseous fuel that would directly feed diesel powered generators at the electric plant. As a bonus, solid waste material from the sewer plant would also be turned into a burnable gas.

The price for a peat compactor was $50,000, and for a gasification unit, a few hundred thousand dollars more. Several jobs for Islanders were to be created. The cost per kilowatt-hour for an electric customer, according to one expert, would be reduced from 29 cents to five cents.

The idea might seem as outrageous as a science fiction plot to us now, in the late 1990s, when a relatively simple task — the emergency pumping of drinking water from Fresh Pond during several particularly dry summers — created a major environmental furor.

A cross section of Ambrose Swamp

Ambrose swamp is off High Street, across from the school. This cross section shows a layer of moist swamp material approximately 10 feet deep (white top layer, 300 centimeters high), under which lies a bed of peat 30 feet thick.

Drawing from:
Peat Resources of Block Island, 1979

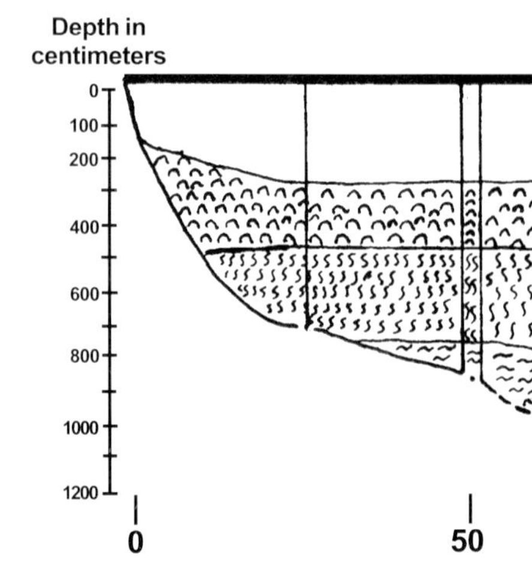

Peleg Champlin house & outbuildings, February 2001

However, the technological aspect of digging for peat is feasible. In Ireland, for instance, 15% of the electricity is created by burning peat at enormous generating plants and small bricks of peat are commonly purchased at the local supermarket to burn for warmth in home fireplaces.

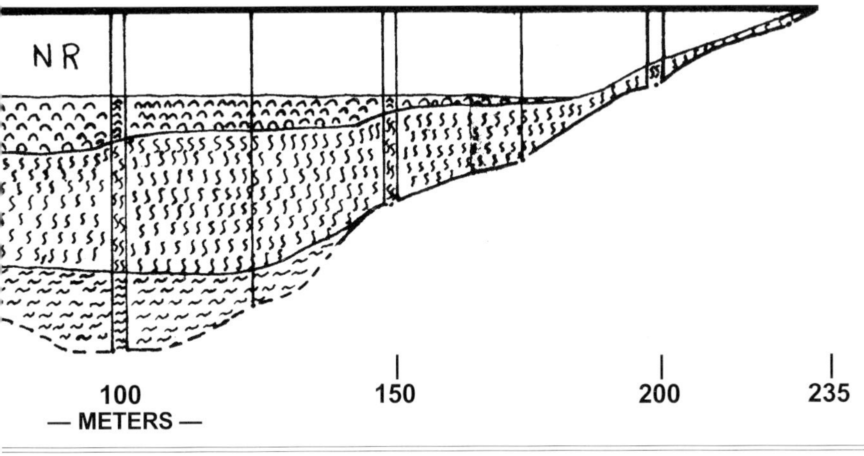

On Block Island, the more difficult issue to fathom and to overcome would be the prospect of mucking around with the wetlands. And how did the Island's Peat Committee address that concern in 1980?:

"Harvesting the peat would restore the bogs to the original condition, open expanses of fresh water, which in turn would enhance our water supply, and provide a natural environmental habitat for wildlife."

A proposal asking for a $1,000,000 to do that was rejected by the U. S. Department of Energy.

The project's high-water mark came in 1980 with the winning of a $90,000 grant from the U.S. Bureau of Mines to conduct additional tests. But the grant was canceled — "rather abruptly" one committee member said — before mining could begin.

The thick, official reports of this enterprise are scarce to find, perhaps they were burned as fuel. But the comprehensive maps that resulted, delineating the location, size and plant characteristics of all the wetlands, remain as an invaluable resource from this last bit of Island tugging ... purse strings.

• *For a description of a highly unusual use of peat at an Island school in the 1830s — see page 94*

• *For a photo of Block Islanders salvaging coal from a shipwreck — see page 259*

Three homemade iceboats on Fresh Pond, with icehouse in background, ca. 1915

While cutting and stacking ice was hard work, sailing on the very same frozen pond was pure fun. Since at least the mid-1870s Block Islanders have enjoyed this sport — although the homemade boats are now likely to sport a multi-striped Sunfish sail, appropriated until the following summer.

Because conditions are not always choice, as in this stunning image, the good winters are ones to remember. This view is toward the east — compare with the 1930 photo on page 91 when the icehouse, with a sagging roof, had been abandoned to history.

CHAPTER 10

Block Island Ice

Danger, work and fun

TO VISITORS ENTRANCED BY BLOCK ISLAND'S equable summer temperatures — elated to escape mainland heat — all the word 'ice' means is a refreshing cube in a drink. But the ice that has played a more major role in the Island's history is decidedly different — bigger than a bread box, for instance.

Much bigger.

Think of an ice cube four times the height of the Empire State Building, its breadth stretching from here across the continent, and thence around the world. It existed — just 15,000 years ago, or so — and was called the last ice sheet. Standing approximately a mile high, the huge mass bulldozed a swath down the length of New England, leveling mountain tops, filling valleys, and pushing a jumbled array of rocks, boulders, and gravel before it.

The glacier stopped here — the seminal event in the Island's history.

So much of the earth's water was tied up in the ice, that the ocean level was 300 feet lower than today — to walk to the beach would have been a 70-mile trip to the south, although canoes or rafts might have made part of the journey on rivers and streams. As the glaciers melted and retreated northward, the ocean rose, forming the Island's basic size 8,000 to 10,000 years ago.

Skip ahead to the winter of 1740-41 and you would have found humans who may have felt the glacier had returned. From December to March there were 30 major snow storms. Narragansett Bay in Rhode Island froze 25 to 30 inches thick. From the mainland the ocean was a sheet of ice as far as the eye could see. People passed regularly back and forth between Newport and Providence — on the ice — and one man was said to have taken his horse and sleigh 250 miles from New York to Cape Cod by traveling just offshore.

For generations the hardy settlers — maintaining themselves through fishing and farming — worked around the ice as best they could. Sometimes it caught up to them.

Readers of the *Providence Evening Bulletin* on February 22, 1877, were regaled by a story of men versus ice, with thrusts and parries worthy of a latter-day boxing story by Ring Lardner, or a Hemingway bullfight. If you consider yourself a good sailor, then imagine performing these several things on the spur of the moment with your 44-foot heavily laden fishing schooner, in a crowded harbor confined by rock breakwaters, after the hull, deck, shrouds, running rigging, and masts had become covered in ice:

"On Monday evening the wind freshened to a strong breeze from the northwest. The schooner HATTIE REBECCA, which had been fishing at some distance from the Island, rounded the breakwater on her return, at about 10 o'clock PM, heavily loaded with ice.

"The main halliards were loosed, but the mainsail would not come down. The schooner was ploughing directly before the wind. Knowing it to be dangerous to run at that rate into the 'Basin', filled as it was with boats, the captain put down the helm and let go the anchor. The anchor dragged.

"Men were sent aloft and the halliards were cut, but the sail kept its place. The schooner was now dangerously near the ragged rocks of the breakwater on which the waves were shattered directly under her lee. Getting headway, the captain attempted to tack, but burdened by the anchor, the boat misstayed, and she fell off on the other course, just in time to clear the breakwater.

"The crew of the Life-Saving Station nearby, seeing her distress, were now coming to aid the schooner. Capt. Dodge, of the HATTIE, not willing to struggle longer at such risk, lowered the other sails, and bore directly into the Basin. A large rope in the course was parted as a cobweb, but the hawser of the NATHAN F. DIXON so deadened her headway that, by the aid of the crew of the Station, the vessel was brought safely to the dock."

Harvesting ice, looking west across Fresh Pond, ca. 1915

Icehouses once existed at three different sites along the shore of Fresh Pond, one on the north shore and two on the east. To fill the buildings, snow was first scrapped off the pond and the surface scored with an iron plow pulled by a horse. The two-inch teeth of a special saw, inserted into a hole used as a starting point, cut the ice along the grid lines.

Each piece was broken off using a pole-like lever called a *spud.* With long-handled *pikes,* the blocks were manipulated down an open channel, hauled up the icehouse ramp, and packed between layers of insulating straw.

Cutting pond ice

WITH THE ADVENT OF TOURISM **in the 1870s**, the need for ice — to preserve meant and fish on the summer tables of hotel guests — was satisfied by long winters hours spent cutting and storing frozen blocks of pond water that could weigh 100 pounds each. At various times from the 1870s to the 1920s, icehouses were located on the shores of more than eight Island ponds, some of which supported two or three of the well-insulated buildings.

When the conditions were right, whether daytime or at night, ice dealers and their dozens of helpers moved great amounts of weight — glacially heavy it seems now. The *Evening Bulletin* related in January 1877:

"On Friday and Saturday last, Hon. Nicholas Ball stored in his icehouse, some two hundred tons of as good ice as was ever obtained on the island, of the thickness of eleven or twelve inches.

"Mr. William C. Sands has stored some one hundred tons of excellent quality.

"Mr. Richmond B. Negus has from ten to fifteen men busily employed each day, and men at work by night in filling his new ice-house, which is estimated to have a capacity of more than 1000 tons.

"The ice is a foot or more in thickness, and is of the best kind. From present indications, it is probable that the island will not need to import ice next summer."

But each year more and more ice was needed — Oct. 31, 1877:

"Mr. William C. Sands has erected a large ice house near a large pond of fine water.

"Mr. R. B. Negus has a large ice house erected last year, and has the foundation laid for another to hold a thousand or two tons."

If enough ice had not been cut in the winter, then it was imported the next summer from Maine in the holds of large coastal schooners. Even for the average householder, a daily need for ice had developed — its power could not be denied — July 24, 1879:

"Every room at the Spring House is engaged, and nearly all are occupied. There are nearly two hundred and fifty at the Ocean View. The proprietors of the smaller houses say that they are fuller than at this time last year ...

"The ice dealers are doing a thriving business. How quickly what seemed as luxury grows to be a necessity when we get accustomed to its use. Before ice was regularly supplied, few private families missed it, but now how hard it would be to do without it."

In the winter of 1882-83, three Islanders harvested ice in mid-January: Cassius C. Ball (whose store is now Ernie's Restaurant in Old Harbor), Lorenzo Littlefield (whose store is now the Old Town Inn), and ice dealer William C. Sands (who owned the

Harvesting ice, looking northwest across Fresh Pond, ca. 1915

These seven men — and one advisor on the left — are using pikes to push ice toward the right side of the photograph where a rope angles into the water, ready to pull the blocks up a ramp for storage in the icehouse.

They are standing on the east shore of Fresh Pond. On the skyline in the far distance, between the second and third men from the right, is the large rock that perches atop a hill across the road from the house known as Smilin' Through.

See other snowny winter photos:
- *cemetery — bottom of page 132*
- *Old Harbor — page 207*
- *Southeast Light — top of page 252*
- *Mansion Beach — bottom of page 252*

former Summit House hotel near Sands Pond; plat 9, lot 10-1). Their progress was reported on January 18:

"C. C. Ball, with a gang of men numbering fifty, is putting in ice in the houses belonging to R. B. Negus. They are working day and night. The ice is six inches thick.

"Wm. C. Sands & Co. have put up 300 tons of ice nine inches thick.

"L. Littlefield has filled his ice houses with 150 tons."

The need for pond ice is remembered as part of the childhood of current Islanders. Electric lines were not strung across Block Island until 1925 when the power plant was built. Although late by most mainland standards, this was still a decade before the New Deal's TVA program brought dams and electricity to towns in Tennessee.

The advent of electric refrigerators on Block Island in the mid-1920s ended the type of mild panic that occurred in the early summer of 1919 — described on July 12 by a *Newport Mercury* news writer not too seriously alarmed:

"Sam Rose, the local postmaster, who in his idle moments conducts the managerial department of the Governor Gorton Farm, in providing for the comfort and enjoyment of the summer guests, is protesting the scarcity of the most necessary seasonable adjunct — ICE.

"Sam says that during the extreme torrid spell just experienced the only cool place on his farm was a picture of George Washington crossing the Delaware, hung in his parlor, adding that during the hot afternoons the guests would assemble in the front room and watch George juggle the ice.

"At the Meadowbrook Farm one of the guests claims that the heat was so intense that the butter was served on the table in ketchup bottles provided with sprinkler tops, while the visitors at Negus Cottage were supplied with paint brushes, the butter being served in individual bowls; printed instructions in the dining room advised the guests to apply a thin coat on biscuits and bread.

"Edgar Willis, proprietor of the Continental Inn, tried a new scheme — cutting the picture of a cake of ice from a newspaper he placed the clipping under a five-pound box of butter before he went to bed in an endeavor to save it."

The Governor Gorton Farm (plat 2, lot 35) near the end of Corn Neck is now a private house, as is Meadowbrook Farm (plat 19, lot 72-4) off Grace's Cove Road. Negus Cottage (plat 6, lot 41) on Connecticut Avenue became the Beachcomber. The Continental Inn (plat 7, lot 90) on High Street retained its name, but its original Victorian-era design was stripped away in the 1970s. They all have refrigerators now.

Hauling ice up the chute, south side of Ocean Avenue, ca. 1912

See other side of building in photo at lower right

"Block Island Ice Co." wagon, ca. 1905

The wagon was built and owned by the Negus family — blacksmiths whose home was the venerable, but much neglected, structure called the *Solviken* (on plat 5, lot 5) just north of the *Beachhead Restaurant*. Before the construction of the electric power plant in 1925, ice was delivered to homes and hotels to keep meat and fish edible. The photograph was made looking south along Center Road — the house on the left, then Ray Littlefield's store, still stands at the corner of Beach Avenue (plat 17, lot 29) — see map, page 88.

Double icehouse on south side of Ocean Avenue, ca. 1912

Ballard's Service Station was built on this site (plat 6, lot 35) about 1930. The Cape Cod style house across the street, in the upper right of this photograph, is on the property known since the 1980s as the *Island Exchange.* From behind the corner of the two ice houses, the distant Hygeia Hotel pokes several rooms of its long length — the grand hotel burned in 1916 and is now the site of the fire station. The house with the tower, also in the distance, has long been owned by artist Sperry Andrews. This is a winter scene, with snow drifted against the distant stone walls.

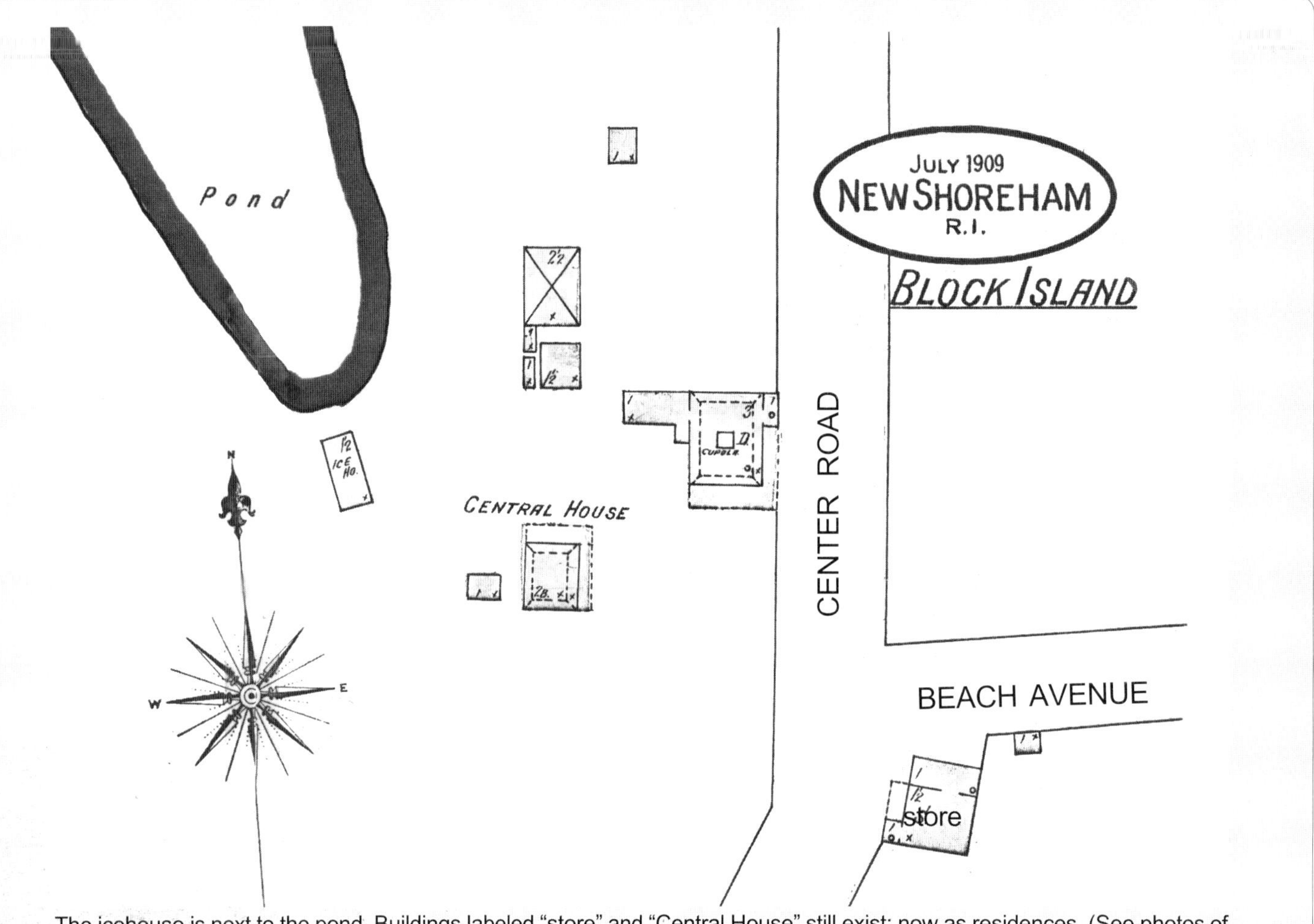

The icehouse is next to the pond. Buildings labeled "store" and "Central House" still exist; now as residences. (See photos of each, top of page 87 and top of page 214.)

Block Island Icehouses

At various times from the 1870s to the 1920s, icehouses were located on the shores of more than eight Island ponds, some of which supported two or three of the enterprises. An incomplete list, for posterity, follows:

- ***John E's Tug Hole*** (named for John E. Millikin); three icehouses: Herbert Millikin, Hamilton A. Mott (owned present-day New Shoreham House), and Delorin A. Mitchell (owned Highland House, now empty field next to Atlantic Inn).
- ***Sand's Pond***; three icehouses: William C. Sands (owned Summit House, next to pond), Ray Littlefield (owned Central House), and C. C. Ball (store owner whose father, Nicholas, owned the Ocean View Hotel).
- ***Pond behind former Central House*** (at junction of Beach & Center Avenues): icehouse of Ray Littlefield (owned Central House) — see map above.
- ***Pond next to former Vaill Hotel*** (near Mohegan Bluffs); hotel's icehouse.
- ***Fresh Pond;*** three icehouses: Lorenzo Littlefield (owned present-day Old Town Inn), the Payne family, and another — see photos, pages 82, 84, 85, 91 (bottom), and 223-224.
- ***Pond next to present-day Ballard's gas station*** *on Ocean Ave.*; icehouse of Harold Littlefield (Ray's son).
- ***Ocean View Hotel & Spring House hotel pond***: icehouses for hotels — see pond in 1963 aerial photo, page x, following Table of Contents.
- ***Harbor Pond*** (fresh water until 1903): icehouses of Richmond Negus, an ice dealer.
- ***Pond near Champlin farm*** (off Coast Guard Road): icehouse of Edward P. Champlin.

Unloading Maine ice at Old Harbor, ca. 1905

When winters were too mild, Block Islanders imported ice from Maine. The large three-masted schooner **A. NEBINGER**, shown tied up at the Old Harbor dock about 1905, has two unloading chutes deployed — one to unload the hold between the foremast and mainmast, and another for the hold between the mainmast and mizzenmast.

In the foreground a brace of horses hauls a wagon filled with ice blocks — looking like giant white ice cubes — up the gently ascending roadway to the Ocean View Hotel, the largest building ever built on Block Island.

Ice manufacturing plant (on left) at Old Harbor, ca. 1930

The newly-built functional-looking square building, located in what is now the ferry parking lot at Old Harbor, seemed to promise Island fishermen future prosperity. But the Great Hurricane of 1938 tossed asunder the cement blocks of the ice plant's walls. On the extreme left is the porch corner of present-day Finn's Restaurant (see photo, page 106), the only building in this photograph that still exists — the fish buildings in the center were torn down in 1965 by the new owner of nearby Ballard's Restaurant (to the right, not in this view; see pages 16, 151). The steamer is the **MOUNT HOPE** at her customary dock, used from 1888 until her last trip in September 1934.

The ice plant, after the 1938 hurricane

The ruination of the ice plant was a blow that struck at the heart of Block Island's fishing industry. Three years later many young Islanders left to fight in World War II, while older ones left to work in war-related jobs on the mainland. After the war, returning Island fishermen attempted to make a living fishing out of Old Harbor, but in a few years the region's fishing prosperity gravitated — with some Block Islanders following along — to the newer facilities at the large port of Point Judith on the mainland.

For some visitors who carefully pick their seasonal forays to Block Island, the land seems permanently fixed in a summer never-never-world — but the north winds of winter descend here.

Whilst summer lingers with a seeming promise of faithfulness, dwell on mere ice cubes if you wish.

But some may find a warm patch of beach instead, and dare to think of the next glacier coming, as surely as each winter does, to cover man's works with detritus hundreds of feet tall, shoved by a 5,000-foot-high wall of ice.

Old Harbor frozen in, winter of 1917-18

The extended cold wave of 1917-18 created the most frigid winter of modern times. On the mainland, Narragansett Bay was covered — and flow ice two to eight feet thick lay around Block Island.

The famed Island ornithologist Elizabeth Dickens (see Chapter 27) — whose farm now forms the basis of the Lewis-Dickens conservation area in the Island's southwest corner — viewed the sea near her house with binoculars on February 6, 1918, recording in her diary:

"I stand on the bluff at Dickens Point at noon and look east, west, south and north with glasses and can't see a drop of water, just one sheet of motionless ice."

The ice boats

THE SAME PONDS THAT WERE THE SCENE of such strenuous work to fill the icehouses, would ring later in the winter with shouts of devoted playing. On Harbor Pond during the mid-1870s, behind the present-day Beachhead restaurant, a fleet of iceboats raced back and forth, idling away winter days — an observer said they were "long remembered by the boys who have there enjoyed so many voyages, capsizings, and wrecks while accompanied by sisters, and other gentle-handed cousins and neighbors." That ended when the channel between Great Salt Pond and the Atlantic Ocean was dug in 1895 — making Harbor Pond salt water.

Winter sailing, and now hockey, is still a rite of passage for year-rounders. It is practiced at the usual locations, such as Fresh Pond, John E's Tug Hole, Sachem Pond, Rodman Pond, and the exquisite little double-jewel nestled in a corner (plat 18, lots 6 & 7) of West Side Road across from the old A-and-A Tea Room.

Six iceboats on Fresh Pond, with icehouse in background, ca. 1930

The icehouse, on the right, with sagging roof and no door, was abandoned when this picture was taken (compare to photo on page 82) — rendered obsolete by the electrification of the Island in 1925. The site of the icehouse has long been the Island's favorite launching point for ice boats. The white house on the right (plat 11, lot 57) was built in the 1880s and survived for more than 100 years, but when the last longtime Island owner died, it was replaced with a summer home by a new owner. The house on the left (plat 11, lot 58) still exists at the pond's northern end. There are six iceboats on the pond. On the left, one is overturned for fine tuning, in front of a rowboat-style ice boat with a gaff mainsail and a jib.

The Center School, 1901

Maude Willis Chase, the teacher, is seated in the middle. To the right, and behind her, is Gertrude Payne, born in 1891 to Abraham Lincoln Payne Sr. and Julia Ann Perry (see full photo on page 101; Gertrude's brother, Abraham Jr., is on the far left).

The one-room Center School, now a private residence, still exists on Center Road, 300 yards south of the cemetery (see more recent photo on page 105).

Also see the 1870 map showing Block Island's five school districts — page VII.

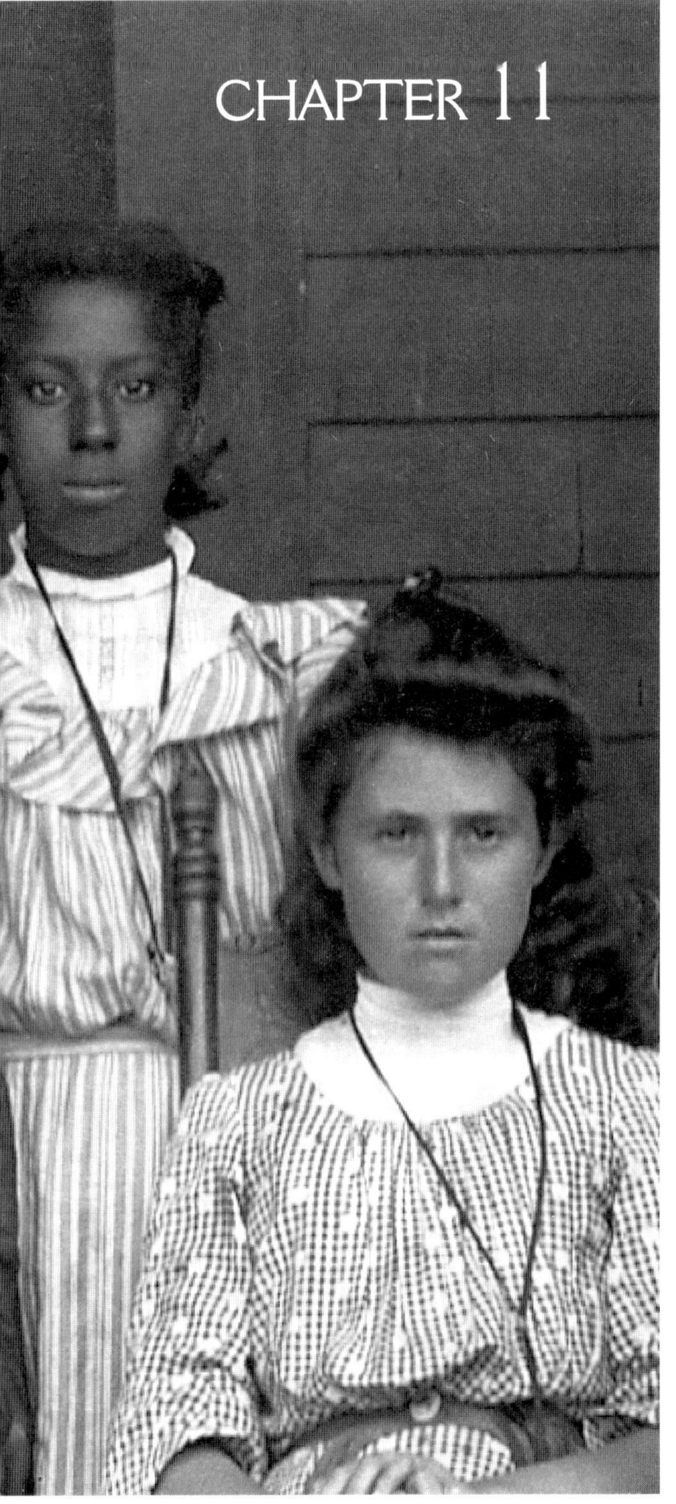

CHAPTER 11

School Days

Squirming in delight, the children recited the end of the famous rhyme about a girl named Mary:

... He followed her to school one day,
That was against the rule;
It made the children laugh and play
To see a lamb at school.

THUS WAS THE ESSENCE OF LIFE so easily rendered to those who could scarcely read or write. The nursery rhyme about Mary and her little lamb was written in 1830 by Sarah Josepha Hale and has been a part of English-speaking childhoods ever since, sublimely teaching the sophisticated dichotomy that the unusual is fun, especially if it breaks someone's rule — and that maybe schools are fun too, because teachers have lots of rules.

The first publication to mention schoolhouses and Block Island in the same breath was an 1819 gazetteer that dutifully reported the Island had no schools. Teaching surely had occurred, though, during the previous 150 years of white settlement, but, as on much of the mainland, at home rather than in separate buildings set aside at public expense.

In 1828 Rhode Island passed a law requiring all towns to finance public schools with local taxes. That year, approximately 100 students attended a single Block Island school at least part of the time. The year was broken into four sessions, with no classes during two *winter* months.

By 1830 about 150 students — from the total population of 1,185 people (1830 census) — were registered at three different schools located in various parts of the Island.

The number of districts — and schools — was increased to five in 1843, with an attendance of 344 children out of the Island's total population of 1,069 (1840 census).

In 1852, from a population of 1,262 (1850 census), 392 students registered. The average daily attendance was only 188 of those students, or 48%, considerably less than the 73% statewide average.

In another regard, however, Block Island was far superior to the rest of the state. The figure of "392 students" on Block Island included virtually every child in the community, meaning that nearly *all* Island children went to school at least part of the year. On the mainland, though, an alarming 33% of Rhode Island school-age children *never* attended school.

The stove lesson — 1830s

IN 1857 THE STATE SCHOOL COMMISSIONER reported the Island had "as good schools as any in the State" — but that did not mean classes always proceeded in a sterile, constrained atmosphere, with eager devotees continually advancing themselves.

A teacher's rule in the popular rhyme about Mary, declared that lambs, even with fleece "white as snow," were unwelcome at school. Perhaps that thought stuck in the minds of young Island boys one day long ago, subliminally stirring them to rebellion in an effort, it seems, to banish *all* whiteness from their school world.

The Neck School, ca. 1910

In 1906, William Payne Lewis (1822-1912) wrote a memoir of his childhood on Block Island during the 1830s. The last of the wooded areas had been cut down a hundred years earlier — and coal would not be imported in large amounts until the 1850s — so Island homes had long been heated by burning peat. During summer months the wet peat, a heavy muck, would be dug from ponds and dried into balls — the resultant product aptly earning the name "tug":

"I well remember the first school I attended. It was in the chamber of a one-story house owned by Robert Dodge and the teacher was Mrs. Hannah Dodge. The next school I attended was in a small room about 14 feet square in a one-story dwelling house owned by Lot Mott.

"One incident that happened at this school I shall always remember. It was in the winter time. The room was heated by a fireplace and tug was used for fuel almost altogether in those days. Boys were mischievous then as well as now. One noontime some of the larger boys unbeknownst to the teacher dug a hole in a lump of tug and put in a charge of powder. It was carried in about time for school to begin and put on the fire. The teacher always sat braced back before the fire to hear the first classes read. About the time the class had begun reading, the fire having reached the powder, there was a tremendous explosion. The teacher came over backwards with a whack, the room was filled with smoke and ashes, and all was confusion. It seemed to us smaller scholars that the end of time had come and I think the teacher was of about that opinion also. Some made their escape through the door and others through the windows and the room was soon cleared.

"Such were the schools in which we got our early training, and teachers compared very well with the schoolrooms. When I had grown to be about ten years old, my father with a number of others built a school-house, the first in the town, down on the town lot, northeast from the Fresh Pond, and named it 'The Washington School-house.'

"At about the same time the people around the harbor, or east side, built a school-house. At that time there was no public money from either State or Town for schools, and no district system.

"But the schools commenced to improve at about this time."

The Neck School, 1904

Of the Island's five one-room schools built in the late 1800s, the Neck School is the only one that no longer exists.

Back Row: Edna Sheffield, Sarah Littlefield, Sarah Sheffield, George Smith, Mary Chase, Ethel Harvey Hayes **(teacher)**, Iva Littlefield, Gladys Littlefield, ? Westcott, ? Westcott, William ? (lived at Sam Rose's)

Middle Row: Viola Littlefield, Annie Sheffield, Phoebe Sheffield

Bottom Row: ? Tourgee (father in Coast Guard), Percy Littlefield, Rodney Tourgee, Lovell Willis (back to left post), Byron Littlefield, Agnes Louisa Littlefield, ? Mitchell, Iola Littlefield, Mary Sheffield, Arlo Littlefield (back to right post), Emerson Mitchell, Winfield Conley, Marguerite Littlefield

(Also see enlargement at lower left.)

Close-up of Neck School

A young Agnes Louise Littlefield sits with authority between Byron Littlefield (left) and an unknown member of the Mitchell family.

(See full photo above.)

Rather than sinking into the pack, William P. Lewis grew to become the Island's leader. As first warden of the town council for nearly 30 years, he rendered decisions — as would a district court judge — in 80 civil and 20 criminal cases, his wisdom based undoubtedly on his youthful observations at Block Island's earliest schools.

THE 1885 CENSUS OF RHODE ISLAND listed Block Island's student attendance at 89.4%, 15th out of Rhode Island's 36 communities. While the Island's rate of attendance had increased dramatically since the 1850s, the rest of the state had also improved.

Block Island, however, placed an admirable second in illiteracy, at 3.2% — behind only Little Compton. Astonishingly, towns such as Warren, Coventry, Lincoln, North Smithfield, Woonsocket, and Warwick averaged more than 20% illiteracy — the definition of illiteracy being those persons "10 years old and upwards who cannot read or who cannot write."

As a state, Rhode Island was 11.2 % illiterate in 1885, a poor 28th out of the 47 states. But at least the situation was not worse — the highest percentage of illiteracy was in the Deep South, where *one-half* of the residents in 10 states could neither read nor write.

The five school districts created in 1843 — each with its own one-room school — remained basically unchanged for eight decades, until the 1920s, shortly before the present school building, appropriately called the Consolidated School, opened in 1933.

To contrast eras, the Island's population surpassed 1,000 residents only in the censuses from 1830 to 1930, and again in 2000 — with a high of 1,320 in 1860.

The population dropped throughout the Depression years of the 1930s — from 1,029 people (1930 census) to 848 (1940 census) — and it kept dropping. When the Consolidated School opened in 1933, there were 157 students in grades one through 12. In 1941, just before the United States entered World War II, only 102 students were enrolled. Three years later, in 1943, with the war draining soldiers and workers away to the mainland, the number of pupils fell further to 58.

Finally, as the fishing industry collapsed and tourism remained moribund, the population fell below 500 during the late 1950s — to 486 (1960 census). The last time there had been so few people on Block Island was two hundred years earlier, during the Revolutionary War.

In the last three decades of the 1900s, the Island's population climbed back to 850 year-round residents — and the school's total number of students averaged about 100.

The following essays, part of a series of assigned compositions, were written in October 1884 by 14-year-old Edna B. Dodge, who lived in the mansard-roofed house still to be found halfway down Beacon Hill Road. Note in *My walk to school* that Edna refers to her home as *"the Island"* — with a capital *"I."*

If not following the many shortcuts that led across the Island's cleared landscape, and which would have cut her journey in half, Edna walked down Beacon Hill Road (see photo, page 70) to Center Road and turned left to go to the one-room Center School, just past the intersection of Beach Avenue. The walk now is vastly different amidst a landscape overgrown with bushes and with more summer houses than year-round ones.

Eleven years later Edna married William S. Mott — a farmer, fisherman, and lifesaver — and continued residing on Beacon Hill Road, outliving by a decade-and-a-half her husband, who died in 1939.

Edna's grades for these compositions were *96* and *94* — penned by her teacher in the upper left corners — each the average of *spelling, punctuation, penmanship,* and *language.*

Spelling — 100
Punctuation — 99
Penmanship — 95
Language — 90
4)384
Average — 96

My walk to school.

Edna B. Dodge.

My walk to school — Oct. 1884

On my walk to school, I can see many different objects such as trees and flowers in bloom, and the birds, and farmers hoeing their fields, and gardens.

I can see many other things such as horses, oxen, sheep, lambs, and hens, and chickens, and I see children out at play, and sometimes see the steamer when she leaves the Island for Newport and Providence.

In the winter, when I walk to school, I can slide on the little ponds in the road, and I see the children slide down hill on their sleds, and see them slide and skate on the pond, and go out sleighing and enjoying themselves in many different ways. And, on washing days, I can see the people hanging out their clothes.

Edna B. Dodge — age14

Cleaning House — Oct. 1884

Cleaning house is a very tiresome job. Some people clean house twice a year in the spring and fall.

In the spring, they take down the stoves, and clean out the closets, and wash the dishes before they put them back, and take up the carpets and put them on the clothesline, and beat the dirt out of them, and wash the floor, before they are put down again, and wash the windows, and clean the paint and paper, or paint the walls, and put up the curtains, and get the room settled again.

In the fall, they do about the same as in the spring, only they put up the sitting room stove, and that is a good job for the men but some don't like to do it. Cleaning house is a very disagreeable job for everything is turned up side down.

Edna B. Dodge — age 14

Block Island in the 1870s

School problems galore, but five new replacement one-room school buildings were built to help solve them

This was a different Island then, where you could turn and turn and see all the ocean horizon, unblocked by trees or shrubs — yet though you could see far, you seldom went there. So distanced by winding rutted roads were these 10 square miles, that five separate school districts were needed.
The trials and tribulations of teachers and students alike, were present in the past, as they are now.

New Shoreham School Superintendent's Report for school year ending April 1, 1871:

District #2 School, on Center Road —

"The summer and winter terms of this district were taught by Miss Mattie E. Ball. Miss Ball distinguished the first term, for the progress which her pupils made in learning. On visiting the school, found her well qualified in learning to teach a public school.

"It is with regret, I have to say, she did not succeed as well in her second term. On visiting the school, found but little interest manifested in study or learning. Government wanting."

District #4 School, on West Side —

"Winter term. This term was taught by Mr. Williams, who possesses good attainments as a teacher; he maintained the order necessary to advance a school in learning; he kept each pupil at his work. The recitations were good, and all questions answered promptly. Not a blot found on any of the writing books. No moving or changing seats even in that small and crowded house of children. In fact, the whole business appertaining to the school moved like the wheels of a clock; and when a wheel moved, the class advanced.

"If Mr. Williams had been favored with a proper schoolhouse, the improvement of the children would have been in proportion to the means he had to work with."

New Shoreham School Superintendent's Report, 1878-1879:

"Good blackboards, out-line maps, globes, etc., if not absolutely essential, are nevertheless such valuable aids to instruction, that they should be furnished by every district without delay ...

"The condition of society for the future, depends largely upon the intelligence and culture of the present generation of school children. I submit to you, then, that a parsimonious, penny-wise, pound-foolish policy with regard to reasonable expenditures for educational purposes is exceedingly unwise ...

"The terms in all districts should commence and close on the same days, thus making the length of the terms uniform"

The five new one-room schools, built in late 1870s:

As years went by, the original school buildings of the 1830s and 40s deteriorated, while the expectations of parents rose — and civilization, even in such a tiny community, wended forward in fits and starts.

The Island prospered in the 1870s due to the new industry of "tourism" — which brought not only money, but increased interaction with people from afar. A worldliness washed the shores bringing new ideas and a resolve to fulfill old aspirations.

In just seven years, all five school buildings were replaced with new ones. Several Islanders living today remember attending these red one-room schools.

Four of the five schools built in the 1870s still exist:

District #1 — *Harbor School* — built in 1877 at Old Harbor on Old Town Road, became the town hall in 1933 and was added onto twice in the 1970s. There briefly existed a small District #6 — but those students merged with District #1 in the late 1870s when the new Harbor School was built.

District #2 — *Center school* — built in 1877 on Center Road by Almanza Littlefield, became a house after 1933. Extensive remodeling in 1992 removed much of the original appearance.

District #3 — *Gully school* — built in the late 1870s, now a private home on Payne Road near the present-day school.

District #4 — *West Side School* — built in 1876, its roof raised from 1½ stories to 1¾ stories in the 1930s to become the parsonage for the West Side Baptist Church. Renovated drastically in recent years into a completely changed structure.

The ***Neck School*** in **District #5,** has disappeared. The site, halfway down Corn Neck Road across from Cottage Farm, is now occupied by a small summer home.

Yet even with these vast improvements, the never-ending concerns felt by most parents continued — from globes and blackboards then, to computer screens now.

Firot Privato High School 1875

THE FIRST HIGH SCHOOL on Block Island, a private one, was begun in the fall of 1875. Students paid $10 apiece — and even so, prominent citizens were called on to subsidize the teacher, Arthur W. Brown of Middletown, Rhode Island, who was the driving force behind the school's establishment. The first term, with 10 students — soon to increase to 16 — began on Monday, November 29, 1875, using rough pine tables set up at the old town hall at the Center (see photos, below and on page 42).

The first 10 high school students on Block Island were:

Adrietta P. Ball, Edith Ball,
Erwin Ball, Schuyler C. Ball,
William T. Dodge, Ray G. Lewis,
Annie L. Mitchell, Hamilton Mott,
Annie Payne, and Addie Smith.

For the second term, well-made tables of ash were procured, along with an organ and a musically inclined assistant, Kate Backus of Ashford, Connecticut.

The private high school continued until 1898, the year Block Island's first public high school was opened. During the last 20 years of its existence, from 1878 to 1898, the private high school was run by Island resident Charles E. Perry, and its location changed several times. But from 1895 to 1898, classes were held at the office of the *Mid-Ocean* newspaper on Water Street — where Perry was also the paper's editor and chief writer. That building still exists, just to the right of the Empire Theatre, functioning in recent years as the Figurehead gift shop (see photo, page 134).

First Public High School — 1898

THE PUBLIC HIGH SCHOOL, begun in October 1898, gave Block Island a small claim to fame — it was the first completely free high school in Rhode Island. While other towns had offered tuition-free high school classes, Block Island was

The old town hall at the Center, May 1921

The Island's town hall was built during the War of 1812 as a church, or "Meeting House," with the help of British sailors (who were supposed to be the enemy, but weren't).

Originally located at the cemetery, the building was moved in the 1850s to the Old Center, leaving no buildings at its former windswept location.

This building also acted as the public high school from 1908 until October 1923, when the structure burned mysteriously on Halloween night (see photo of building without the two small ells, page 42.) On the right is the rear of the Methodist Church, built in 1907 — now the Sassafras bed and breakfast.

Masonic Hall on High Street, 1942

The Masonic Hall filled the role of high school from 1923, when the town hall at the old Center burned, until 1933 when the new school opened further up High Street.

This photo was taken on September 6, 1942, when Islanders — many of whom had helped promote the construction of the new school in 1933 — met in the Masonic Hall to establish the Block Island Historical Society, which was formed that year.

the first town to also provide books and materials at no cost.

Four years later, the first graduating class — the Class of 1902 (see page 100) — received their diplomas from superintendent Ray G. Lewis (1857-1936). He was one of three sons of William P. Lewis, who, since witnessing the exploding ball of peat in the 1830s, had seen a lot of changes in Block Island schools.

Until the present school on High Street was opened in 1933 — encompassing, for the first time since 1830, all students within one building on the Island — the lesser grades continued meeting in the various one-room schools scattered about the Island. Meanwhile, the public high school wrestled with fate's slings and arrows, trying to find a permanent location. Classes for the public high school were held:

- in the Baptist Church at the old Center (behind the millstone monument, near today's airport), until that building was leveled by fire in 1908 — see photo, page 144
- in the town hall at the old Center (diagonally across the intersection from the church), until it also was destroyed by fire, of unknown origin on Halloween night in 1923 — see photos, on left, and pages 42, 144 — and
- at the Masonic Hall on High Street, which in recent years operated as the Block Island Pharmacy — see photo above.

Present High School building on High Street — opened 1933

THE PRESENT PUBLIC SCHOOL was constructed in 1932 and 1933 — see photo, page 103 — on land donated to the town by the Payne family. Although the country was in the midst of the Depression, the construction effort was a community response to years of clear-cut need.

In frugal fashion — which was formerly the way, but is contrary to the approach of the Island's government in the 1990s — the flag pole was made from the mast of the shipwrecked fishing dragger **PETREL**.

For other photographs of early schools see:

- *Private high school building in late 1890s — page 134*
- *Baptist Church and town hall at Center (where high school met) — pages 42, 144*
- *students of 1950 at bird class with Miss Dickens — page 260*
- *students of 1950 leaving new school, crossing fields — page 261*

Block Island Public High School Graduates — 1902-1999

Adapted from a list started by Hattie Hayes Littlefield, a graduate of the Class of 1905
and continued by her niece, Marilyn Littlefield Rose, Class of 1941

1902
Ball, Beatrice
Ball, Clossie
Hayes, Alma

1903
Dodge, Hazel

1904
Champlin, Bella
Sprague, Mattie

1905
Conley, Deborah Rose
Dunn, Cleon Alton
Hayes, Hattie Millikin
Hayes, Mabel Leora
Littlefield, Minnie 'Addie'
Rose, Sarah 'Rebecca'
Smith, Leon Elwood

1906
Champlin, Robert
Dodge, Gladys
Littlefield, Austis
Mott, Elno
Sprague, Adrian
Steadman, Milton

1907
Ball, Pearl
Champlin, Rose
Dodge, Elmer
Dodge, Ralph
Mott, Howard
Mott, Mary
Steadman, Sarah Gladys

1908
(church/school burned)
Gaffett, Florence
Lewis, Clarence
Littlefield, Almeda
Smith, George
Willis, Ruby

1909
Allen, Amanuel
Allen, Eugene
Gaffett, Effie
Hayes, Frances
Littlefield, Gladys
Littlefield, Iva
Madison, Wayne
Rose, Harry
Sheffield, Phebe
Sprague, Scott
Wescott, Bertha
Willis, Lovell

1910
Dodge, Elizabeth
Mitchell, Lenice
Rose, Armenia

1911 ?

1912
Dodge, Ottowell S.
Littlefield, Agnes L.

1913–15 ?

1916
Conley, Ruth
Littlefield, William
Rose, Lillian
Rose, Mildred
White, Caroline

1917
(2-yr. program begun)
Mott, Alzadia
Mott, Merton
Sprague, Arthur

1918
(2-yr. program)
Barber, Sylvia
Clark, Anna
Smith, Thelma

1919
(2-yr. program)
Millikin, Eunice
Payne, Elizabeth
Sprague, Rena

1920
(2-yr. program)
Mott, Venetia
Thomas, Beatrice

1921 ?

1922
(2-yr. program)
Conley, Eleanor
Dodge, Edna
Mitchell, Adrian
Rose, Reginald
Rose, Rheta
Sprague, Ida Frances

1923
(school burned Oct.)
Dunn, Alba
Jaixen, Frances
Littlefield, Thomas
Sanchez, Sadie
Steadman, Linda

1924
(2-yr. program)
Conley, Grace
Heinz, Martha
Milliken, George
Mott, Bernice
Wheeler, Ralph

1925
(eight students were eligible to graduate with 2-yr. diplomas, but exercises were not held because of desire to resume the 4-yr. program)

1926

1927
Conley, Harriet
Littlefield, Dorothy
Northup, Alice
Payne, Harriet
Steadman, Isabelle

1928
Dodge, Edith
Sanchez, Ruth
Smith, Stella
Sprague, Kenneth
Thomas, Madeline

The Class of 1905

Although the usual admonition is *never* to write on photographs, that rule was fortunately broken by Gladys Steadman, whose informality saved for posterity what would have been just one more blank, unknown image of anonymous people. And where did the always smiling, always with a quip, Gladys learn her rebellious ways? She was a graduate of the Class of 1907.

Inset images: from photograph of children at Gully School in 1900.

— see full image on page 105.

The Center School, 1901

People known in this photograph are the teacher Maude Willis Chase; students Gertrude Payne (back row right) — see close-up on page 92 — and her brother Abraham Lincoln Payne Jr. (at left, second row); and Ottowell S. Dodge, sitting on the right side, dressed for the occasion in a bowtie, cap and dark jacket.

1929
Ball, Effie Beatrice
Dickens, Anna
Sanchez, Albert
Sanchez, Edward
Wescott, Clara

1930
Ball, Nicholas Jr.
Fell, Elsie
Rose, Lila

1931
Banks, Mary
Champlin, Russell
Littlefield, Maud
Sprague, Stanley

1932
Jaixen, Hannah
Littlefield, Beatrice
McLarren, Estelle
Northup, Frances
Rose, Harry Jr.
Stinson, Stanley

1933
(new school opens in fall)
Ball, Cassius
Ball, William
Dodge, Annette
Johnson, Lloyd
Stowell, Richard

1934
Gooley, Albert
Lewis, John Robinson
Mitchell, Milton
Payne, Anna
Payne, Frank Jr.
Pierce, Hope
Sprague, Mildred
Thomas, Mary

1935
Champlin, Kathryn
Cyr, Aline
Rose, Virginia
Slate, Claire
Tinker, Thelma

1936
Ball, Bertrand
Grattage, Harold
Littlefield, Eileen
Steadman, Muriel

1937
Burgess, Bergernetta
Conley, Susan
Cyr, Ulric
Sprague, Edith
Steadman, Ruth
Tinker, Frances

1938
Banks, Icy
Cyr, Albea
Cyr, Noella
Dunn, Virginia
Gaffett, Claire
Gaffett, Edna
Mott, Antonette
Murray, Georgette
Slate, Albion

1939
Ball, Marion
Carr, Richard
Dodge, Harold
Mitchell, Beatrice
Rose, Kenneth
White, Brayton
Willis, Hope

1940
Cyr, Raymond
Cyr, Rita
Dodge, Thelma
Douglas, Clara
Jacobsen, Louise
Lewis, William P.
Milliken, Florence
Mott, Julia

1941
Carr, Ruth
Cyr, Cecile
Grimes, Holbrook
Lewis, Norma
Littlefield, Elizabeth
Littlefield, Marilyn
Mott, Harriet
Osterholm, Ellen
Peace, Ruth

1942
Ball, Katherine
Dodge, Elwin
Mitchell, Natalie
Mott, Norma

1943
Dunn, Imogene
Hall, William
Mitchell, Miriam
Mott, Phoebe
Sprague, Ida
Steadman, F. Lloyd

1944
Battey, Emmons
Cyr, Madeline
Dunn, Emily
Littlefield, Caroline
Mott, Albert
Sprague, Annie

1945
Ball, Lewis

1946
Cyr, Arthur

1947
Beebe, Barbara
Blane, Rosemary
Brown, Everett
Conley, Wilfred
Hall, Allen W. III
Littlefield, Edith
Littlefield, Walter

1948
Dodge, Barbara
Grimes, Evaline
Jones, Fred
McConnell, Eleanor
Mitchell, Phyllis
Peterson, Mary Jane

1949
Bodington, Jean
Hall, Edrie
Milliken, Eva
Milliken, Ruth
Sprague, Norman

1950
Brown, Malcolm
Gifford, Priscilla
Westcott, Barbara

1951
Benson, Fred
Conley, Edward
Conley, Richard
Pennington, Barbara
Phillips, Gardner

1952
Battey, Evan
Beebe, Norma
Dodge, S. Willis
Ritzinger, Ellen

1953
Bodington, Roberta
Brain, John
Gaffett, Lewis
Lewis, Mary
Rose, Lawrence

1954
Littlefield, Lester
Mott, James
Sprague, George

1955
Swancott, Betty

1956
Anderson, J. Raymond
Conley, Marceline D.
Cyr, Robert E.
Littlefield, Everett R.
Sheldon, Malcolm S.

1957
(*no graduation* — only senior, Alice Thomas, passed away)

1958
Ball, Ellen C.
Ernst, Alvin W.
Littlefield, Irene
Mott, Alton H.

1959
Ernst, Ellen E.
Rose, Robert E.
Westcott, Robert H.

1960
Champlin, David R.
Heinz, Henry Dennis
Millikin, William E.
Mitchell, Fred C.
Morris, William H.
Phelan, Marcia D.
Sprague, Lillie E.
Vann, Peter

1961
Anderson, David
Mitchell, Adrian
Mitchell, Clifford
Mott, Douglas
Northup, Edward
Phillips, John
Smith, Clifton

1962
Metz, Judith
Vann, Cynthia

1963
Ball, William O. Jr.
Mitchell, Margaret A.
Morris, Mary Anne

1964
Boyle, Gerald F.
Howarth, Frederick J.
Lewis, Keith A.
Rachels, Carol L.
Rachels, Madeline A.
Sprague, Gerald E.

1965
Hill, John E.
Howarth, Rosemary
Lee, Cara L.
Lewis, Nancy J.
Murray, James A.
Northup, Barbara M.
Rice, Cheryl L.
Riley, Stephen L.
Rose, Bernice E.
Slate, Patricia A.

1966
Brooks, Edward W.
Slate, Della B.
Stevens, Gillian D.
Tripler, Linda Diane

1967
Brooks, Gary A.
Conley, Edward A.
Dodge, Nancy L.
McIntire, Sanford E.
Mitchell, James R.
Rose, Marshall H.

1968
Conary, Carolyn B.
Dodge, Carol J.
Donnelly, Michael F.
Smith, Jeanette Deborah
Stevens, Brandon S.
Wagner, Michael J.

1969
Ball, Martha A.
Donnelly, Patricia M.
Douglas, Edward J.
Hall, Georgia I.
Lewis, David S.
McCabe, Elizabeth P.
Ritter, Wayne M.
Rose, Clifford M.
Tillson, Phillip T.
Transue, Andrew R.
White, Russell C.

1970
Collins, James W. IV
McCabe, Thomas F. N.
Millikin, Diana J.
O'Hayer, Thomas F.
Ritter, Rosalind
Tillson, Mark A.

1971
Conley, Grace E.
Inman, Roger E.
Lutton, Lynnette M.
Shelton, Anthony D.
Slate, Leslie D.
Sprague, Carol J.
Transue, Lynlee A.

1972
Batchelder, Richard W.
Fletcher, Belinda G.
Hall, Gail F.
McCabe, Olwyn C.
Smith, Steven C.
Traber, Melissa B.
Wagner, Jeffrey D.

1973
Blane, Peter E.
Brown, Stephen E.
Donnelly, Mary Ann
Hall, Gay Anne
Hauser, Donald D.
Sprague, Catherine L.

1974
Blane, Marianne Brown
Fowler, Sheila A.
Hall, Gary A.
Inman, Dorothy I.
Lime, Neil L.
Littlefield, John H. Jr.
Murray, Jay W.
O'Hayer, Matthew
Rice, Marc J.
Smith, Wesley E.
Sprague, Adrian Joseph
Transue, Marlee E.
Wright, Brian E.

1975
Blane, Christopher J.
Dodge, Charlie S.
Donnelly, Marguerite M.
Gaffett, Kimberly H.
McCabe, Victoria M.
Mitchell, Thomas S.
Wright, Lorna

1976
Chambers, James W.
Fletcher, Andrew B.
Gaffett, Lewis Nathaniel
Gifford, Cheryle J.
Hall, Geoffery S.
Huggins, William P.
Millikin, Sue Ann
Mott, James W.
Riker, Janice C.
Ritter, Georgianna
Smith, Donna M.
Sprague, Cheryl A.

1977
Bertholdt, Kathy M.
Bertholdt, Laurie A.
Hauser, Crystal D.
Littlefield, Amelia L.
McCabe, Timothy J.
Mott, Susan E.
Murray, Mark W.
Ritter, Amy
Sprague, Charlene E.
Sprague, Cynthia M.

1978
Gaffett, Beth
Gifford, Jay F.
Gifford, Lorraine B.
Hall, Gloria (as a junior)
Littlefield, Charon B.
Mott, Kenneth W.

1979
Bannister, Paul G.
Donnelly, Kathleen M.
Joseph, Jeffrey F.
Littlefield, Albert G.
Murray, Deborah Holmes
Salmon, Sally
Shinners, Kelly E.
Vann, Ruth Esther

1980
Battey, Gary M.
Brown, Adam J.
Gleisner, Peter B.
Inman, Tammy Bertholdt
Littlefield, Robert A.
Manley, Abra M.
McCabe, Alexandra H.
Mott, George D.

1981
Battey, Sandra A.
Donnelly, Elizabeth
Holmes, Nelson E. Jr.
Mitchell, Dorothy K.
Mott, Peter

1982
Crabtree, Kenneth J.
Littlefield, Cindy J.
Mitchell, Maureen M.
Shea, Cheryl A.
Smith, Alan M.
Wampler, Kaaren

1983
Hall, Glen W.
Mitchell, Patricia A.

1984
Brain, Bethanie J.
Delvy, Michael
Donnelly, John F.
Halikas, Candy
Hall, Gene A.
Lopez-Quesada, Maria Q.
Sommer, Andrea
Wilder, Kerry

1985
Brain, Cathie L.
Brown, Daniel H.
Ferrara, Karen J.
Gaffett, Heather M.
Gaffett, Kerri H.
Gritman, Kim A.
Larson, Martha (as a junior)
Littlefield, E. Russell
Murphy, Cynthia L.
Vann, Loretta A.

1986
Delvy, Karoline
Goburn, Melissa
Littlefield, Kirk A.
Mazzur, Samantha
Smith, Genevieve M.

1987
Brain, Tabetha
Sargent, Greg
Wilder, Hye-Jin

1988
Brown, Robert D.
Clark, Zena R.
Gonzalez, Jose F.
Schaller, James D.
Todd, Kimberly A.
Winberg, Deirdre E.

1989
DelPadre, Heather G.
Dulac, Danny M.
Heinz, Tracy G.
Pare, Stephen J.

1990
Glen, Matthew W.
Inman, Michele A.
Nyzio, Karen M.
Sprague, Gerald E.

1991
Ernst, Michael D.
Howarth, F. Jason
Ryan, Erik G.

1992
Frageau, Jacqueline S.
Glen, Sabra A.
McAloon, Meredith E.
Szabo, Jonas S.
Tonner, Rachel E.
Tresca, Linda M.
Williams, Sara D.
Zeiller, Robert W. Jr.

1993
Cattera, Sharon
Eckert, Charles J. III
Frageau, Shannelle
Hall, Laura
Inman, Michael R.
Lemoine, Seth
Schaller, Lisa S.
Sprague, Vincent L. C.
Szabo, Jared

1994
Brown, Jeremy H.
Eckert, Daniel P.
Ernst, Geoffrey S.
Ernst, Kevin H.
Lemoi, Joshua R.
Ryan, Jordan M.
Santana, Francisco P.
Santana, Jose

1995
McAloon, Kathleen
Payne, Tristan
Rose, Danielle

1996
Brown, Suzanne
Keogh, Christopher
Tracy, Jason
Walter, Todd

1997
Antadze, Nino
Battey, Nicholas J.
Bendokas, Teresa A.
Brady, Lauren B.
Euglow, David
Millikin, Charles E.
Rondinone, Micah
Santana, Waldyn
Shaw, Ely Milliken
Tripler, Nathaniel

1998
Edwards, Benjamin
Gasper, Steven
Michel, Scott
Ryan, Sean
Swienton, Jonmathew
Swienton, Kristie

1999
Blane, Melanie
Brown, Jess
Closter, Robert
Draper, Kyle
Fowler, Colleen
Lonergan, Meaghan
Millikin, Georgina
Mitchell, Ryan
Mott, Sam
Rose, Morgan

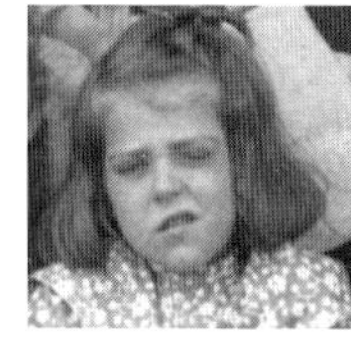

2000
Closter, Jill A.
Dulac, Cyrus G.
Helterline, Daniel Wyatt
Lacoste, Charles A.
Martin, Benjamin J.
Mott, Giles A.
Pike, Melissa N.
Rondinone, Bethany L.
Shaw, Kelsey L.
Sprague, Kate
Sprague, Sarah
Stover, Rebecca C.
Szabo, Jacob G.

2001
Desmaris, Eliza
Draper, Seth
Martin, Alicia
Michel, Laura
Mort, Jeffrey
Savoie, Kara
Stover, Edward

NOTE:
Yearbooks were first published in the mid-1950s. Due to their early printing, well before school ended, several yearbooks have inaccurate listings of graduates. This list eliminates yearbook errors.

The Block Island Consolidated High School, when new in 1933

The Block Island school — with fluctuating enrollments from the 157 pupils on opening day in October 1933, to only 58 students in World War II, and less than a hundred during several succeeding decades — has found a permanent home on High Street.

That was reaffirmed by voters in 1988 when extensive additions were authorized, more than doubling the size of the facility for the grand reopening in September 1989 — including: new classrooms at the rear of the school, a relocated kitchen, a new math and computer room, a library and audiovisual center, and (attached to the right side of the school) a community-oriented gymnasium with a one-room volume never seen on these shores before.

The effort was the culmination of 160 years of improvements urged by many concerned parents, not a few of whom though — as both child and adult — have figuratively blackened several schoolrooms, their overheated words exploding the teacher's stove.

The Gully School, ca. 1915

The one-room Gully School—on Payne Road 300 yards west of the present-day brick school—is now a private residence. The gully is a deep revine that once gave passersby a spectacular panoramic view toward the center of the Island—all the way to Beacon Hill and Great Salt Pond—untill becoming utterly overgrown by tall brush in the mid-1900s. Although located only 100 yards to the right of its namesake building, the gully in nearly invisible today.

Island children, each barefoot, each with a pond lily, ca. 1895

The Gully School, 1900

The "Center" one-room school, 1992

Until renovated in 1992, the Center School was the last intact example of a one-room school on Block Island.

Changes included removal of windows with six panes over six panes, and replacement with windows that were shorter, with one pane over one pane.

The non-historic modifications were made with the unfortunate approval of the Rhode Island Historic Preservation Commission, which monitored the project, the same group who allowed the National Hotel to be drastically altered in 1984.

The eleventh Block Island post office, ca. 1930 — with the fishermen's well

Used as the Island's post office from 1928 to 1962, this building is now famous for housing Ernie's Restaurant, ever popular for breakfast. The grassy area on the right is now the parking lot for the Island's newest post office, opened in December 1996.

The ancient fishermen's well, dating back to at least the early 1800s, is in the center — note the circular stone well, just in front of the car's bumper, and the 35-foot long sweep pole that overarches the entire car, raised high on a 15-foot post serving as the pivot point.

Behind Ernie's, the flat-roofed cement block ice house peaks out, later to be destroyed by the 1938 hurricane (see entire icehouse, page 90). The fish buildings on the right along the dock were torn down in 1965 by the new owner of Ballard's Restaurant, which is out-of-sight to the right. In the distance, the side-wheel steamer **MOUNT HOPE** leaves the harbor under a plume of smoke. The much smaller **SAGAMORE** waits at the town dock on the right — this steamer was the official "U. S. Mail" boat and prominently displayed those words on her bow, which is not visible in this view.

See other photos of the same post office on page 114.

CHAPTER 12

The Mail — Finding the Post Office

13 old Post Offices of the 1830s to 2001

Buildings still exist of six post offices, and photographs of four others

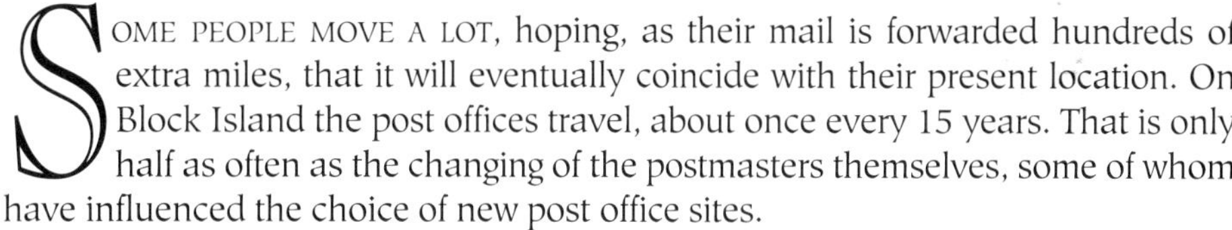

SOME PEOPLE MOVE A LOT, hoping, as their mail is forwarded hundreds of extra miles, that it will eventually coincide with their present location. On Block Island the post offices travel, about once every 15 years. That is only half as often as the changing of the postmasters themselves, some of whom have influenced the choice of new post office sites.

Quite often — in a small town such as Block Island — the location of the post office and the receiving of mail are of less concern than another important aspect of the building: as a place for people to visit each another.

It is not known, however, how that social function played out in 1832 when Block Island's first postmaster, William L. Wright, was appointed, and used his bedroom as the **first post office**.

By the 1850s when two successive Baptist Reverends were postmasters — Charles C. Lewis and Elijah Macomber — other quarters were undoubtedly obtained to sort the mails, but the nature of that office, or of any other possible post office locations in the 1830s, 40s or 50s, is unknown.

What was at least the **third post office** on Block Island, and definitely the **first to be preserved in a photograph**, was the store of Nicholas Ball — he being the Islander who worked diligently acquiring a small fortune at the California Gold Rush of 1849, returning to his hometown to become the main promoter of Block Island's first great tourist influx in the 1870s (see Chapter Three).

Nicholas built a store in 1861 near the shore — the site is the approximate location of the new post office opened in December 1996. During the 1860s, the Ball store was one of just a few buildings located near what was then a sandy shoreline — neither the breakwater nor a town existed, the village instead being located at the old Center near today's airport. The store can be seen indistinctly in the first known photograph of Block Island — made in 1873 (see photo, page 12) — taken a few months before a fire burned the structure to the ground.

A late 1800s account described Nicholas Ball's building as "the palace store of the Island ... It was really one of the largest, finest and best conducted country stores then to be found in New England."

There the postal bag was delivered from the mainland once a week via Block Island's famous sailing *double enders*. The Islanders gathered around in hopes of hearing their names called out by postmaster William L. Millikin, who performed his duty in a ritual that was both a 'mail call' and a weekly social gathering.

When Nicholas's store was destroyed on September 19, 1873, lost also — according to a contemporary record — was "all the material of the Post Office."

A nearby building, called the "Old Post Office" was refurbished. This earlier post office may have been the one used by Reverends Lewis and Macomber in the 1850s, but its location is not known.

In 1876 the old-fashion mail call was stopped when "P. O. Boxes" were installed — today's boxes are new, but the system is fairly old.

The **fourth post office** known to have existed was that of postmaster Charles W. Willis, who replaced William L. Millikin in 1878, and used his store as an office (see photo, top of page 110). The store was located next to Willis' small hotel, the Surf Cottage, later to become the much larger Surf Hotel (see photo, bottom of page 110).

The next year, on November 1, 1879, the official postal name of the Island was changed from "New Shoreham" to "Block Island." This concession to practicality occurred because of the greater renown of the geographic name of Block Island, which refers to the land — as opposed to the political name of "New Shoreham," which refers to the town.

Because the Town of New Shoreham's location, length, width, perimeter, and volume exactly equals that of Block Island — even changing in unison as tides rise and fall — then one of the two names is redundant. "Block" has been used in reference to the Island since 1614, and "New Shoreham" since only 1672 — so the confusion culprit is "New Shoreham."

Meanwhile, winter mail arrival from the mainland increased from once-per-week in the 1830s to thrice-per-week by 1900.

Although mail delivery is now once-a-day year-round, that pace was thoroughly outdone during summers from the late 1800s until at least 1910, when the steamers brought *two* mails to Block Island *each day*.

In 1909, for instance, mail bags were opened at 2:15 p.m. and again at 4:30 p.m.. Some Islanders probably concluded "why leave the post office at all" when the two-hour interval could be easily consumed by a bit of gossiping.

Block Island Postmasters

Postmaster	***Appointment Date***	
William L. Wright	December 13,	1832
Samuel Dunn	July 26,	1837
Alfred Card	June 12,	1841
George Rose	September 23,	1845
Rev. Charles C. Lewis	April 17,	1852
Rev. Elijah Macomber, Jr.	May 17,	1855
Samuel J. Osgood	August 4,	1860
William L. Millikin	June 5,	1861
Charles W. Willis	April 1,	1878
John C. Champlin	July 14,	1888
Alvin H. Sprague	February 8,	1890
Almanza J. Rose	October 27,	1893
Edward S. Payne	January 17,	1898
Ray S. Littlefield	May 9,	1903
Edward S. Payne	June 10,	1908
S. Martin Rose	July 22,	1913
Lenice M. Rose — acting	March 30,	1935
Nicholas Ball	August 27,	1935
Matthew A. Moran — acting	March 31,	1941
Matthew A. Moran	November 18,	1941
Emma L. Gooley — acting	July 31,	1960
Natalie A. Mitchell — acting	June 23,	1961
Natalie A. Mitchell	June 12,	1971
Edrie H. Dodge — officer-in-charge	June 16,	1984
Edrie H. Dodge	August 4,	1984
Charon Littlefield — officer-in-charge	December 3,	1991
Catherine M. Millikin	March 7,	1992
Thomas R. Myers — officer-in-charge	January 4,	1996
Frederick C. Leeder III	April 27,	1996

Searles Ball, plumber, 1960s

Some Items Islanders Found In Their Mail

C. C. Ball's store, 1890s

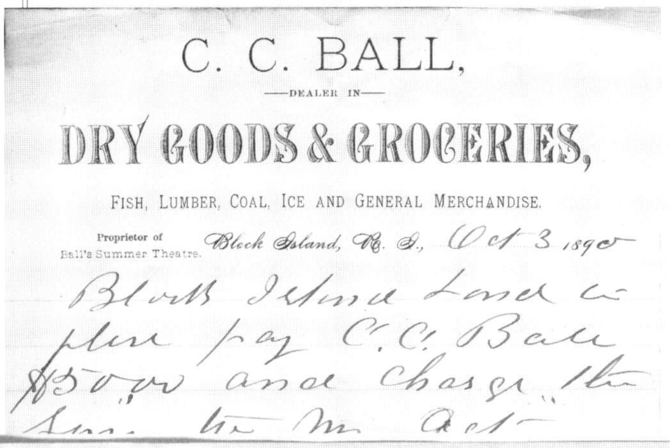

C. C. BALL,

—DEALER IN—

DRY GOODS & GROCERIES,

FISH, LUMBER, COAL, ICE AND GENERAL MERCHANDISE.

Proprietor of Ball's Summer Theatre.

Block Island, R. I., Oct 3, 1890

Block Island Land Co
please pay C. C. Ball
$50.00 and charge the
same to my acct

Mail Call, Mid–1800s

DURING THE MID-1800S the weekly mail arrival was a ritual of unparalleled significance. Dispersal took place at the local general store of Nicholas Ball, a building situated near the site of the present-day post office, which was then at the edge of the shore. The paved parking lot of today's ferry company was open water in the 1860s. The resulting flurry of activity after the arrival of the mail boat was described by one of the Island's visitors:

"Here the mail was opened, and if the visitor waited a few moments he was treated to a unique spectacle. Outside the store a dozen or more saddled and bridled horses were hitched, while two or three open wagons, and half a dozen more ox teams were to be seen. Inside, the people were crowded, waiting for the opening of the one mailbag and the distribution of the few letters and weekly papers. Soon the fun would begin, and the listener would hear something like this: 'Alfred Card,' *Here!* — 'Jonathan Ball,' *Here!* — 'Captain Francis Willis,' *Here!* — and so on to the end of the chapter."

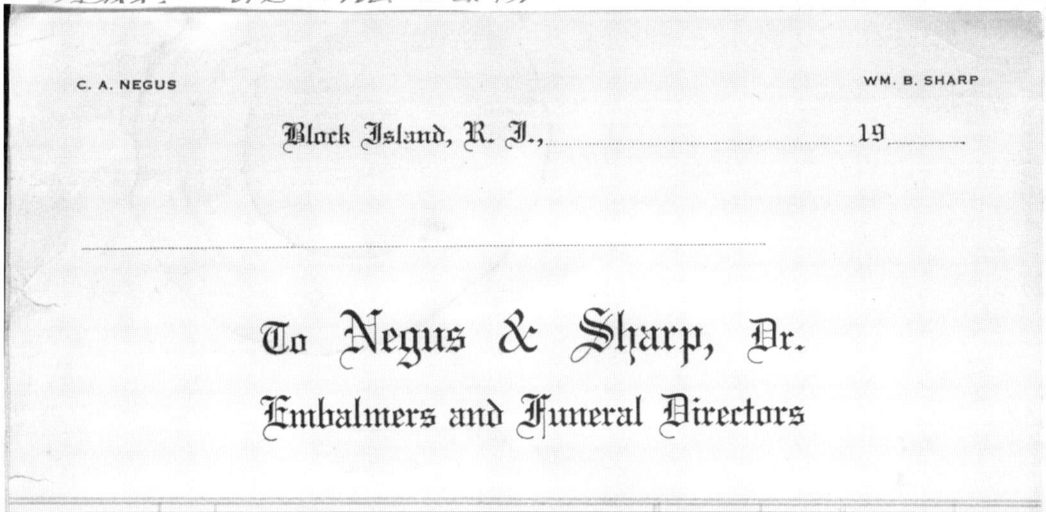

C. A. NEGUS WM. B. SHARP

Block Island, R. I., ... 19......

To Negus & Sharp, Dr.

Embalmers and Funeral Directors

Funeral home, ca. 1915

Ballard's gas station, 1950s

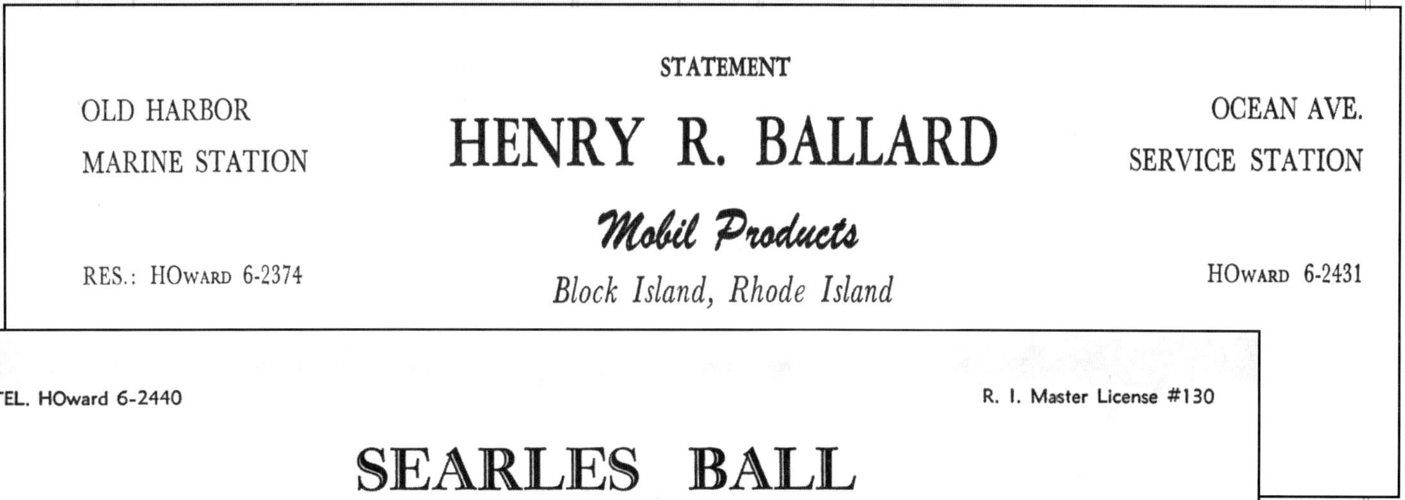

STATEMENT

OLD HARBOR
MARINE STATION

HENRY R. BALLARD

OCEAN AVE.
SERVICE STATION

Mobil Products

RES.: HOWARD 6-2374

Block Island, Rhode Island

HOWARD 6-2431

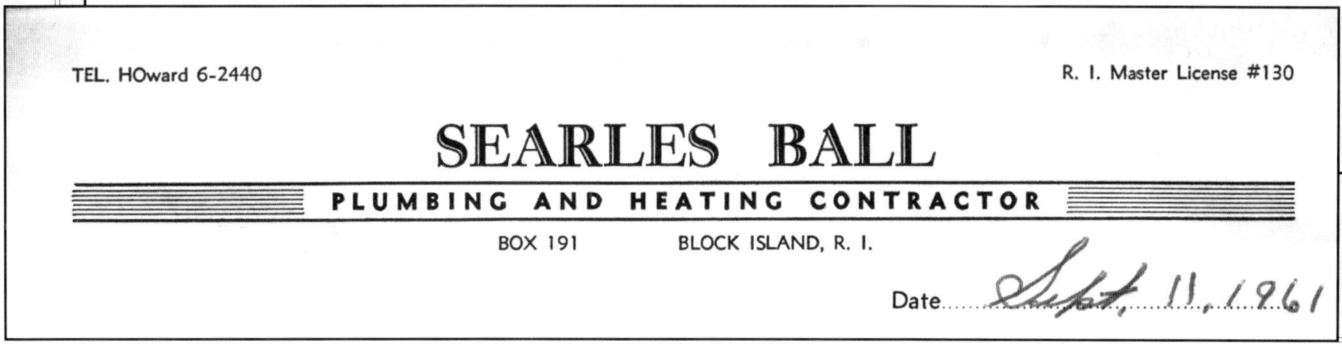

TEL. HOward 6-2440 R. I. Master License #130

SEARLES BALL

PLUMBING AND HEATING CONTRACTOR

BOX 191 BLOCK ISLAND, R. I.

Date Sept. 11, 1961

Third and fourth post offices, next to Surf Cottage, Old Harbor, 1880

The Surf Cottage, in the center next to the water, was owned by Charles W. Willis, postmaster from 1878 to 1888. To the left is Willis's store which served as the location of the Island's fourth post office.

Only two buildings in this photograph still exist: (1) the Surf Cottage, enlarged in 1884 and 1888 to become the present-day Surf Hotel, and (2) in the background next to Crescent Beach the 2 1/2-story blacksmith shop of Richmond Negus, now an unused building called the Solviken, a name lingering from its use as a restaurant in the 1950s and 60s. And rumor has it, one of these two buildings will be torn down with the permission of town officials.

Fifth post office, Surf Hotel, ca. 1888.

The Surf Hotel was briefly the site of the post office, as the dark sign (directly above the two men near the steps) reads. To make room for his three-story Surf Hotel addition in 1884 (center part of hotel, with the impressive cupola), owner and postmaster C. W. Willis moved his store, which also housed the post office, sideways.

Another large section, of four stories (left part of hotel), was added in 1888 — then the old store was demolished, and the post office placed in the new addition.

The Boston Store on the left was erected in 1886 by Richard Dodge and has been known for the past 15 years as "Sheila's" shop.

From 1888 to 1890 the postmaster was John C. Champlin, an Island-born doctor and hotel owner of many talents.

Sixth and seventh post offices, Old Harbor, 1898

This photograph was made from the Ocean View Hotel's roof, as was the photo on the top of page 110.

Hulls of several double ender sailboats rest along the beach — one task of these small vessels, famed for their seaworthiness, was bringing the weekly mail to the Island. After the breakwater and harbor were created in the 1870s, boats capable of unloading passengers and supplies directly onto the beach became obsolete.

Most of the shore area was paved for a ferry parking lot when a new, T-shaped dock was built in 1965 — the same year that the restaurant on the extreme right was torn down (see photos, pages 90, 106).

In the left foreground, two post office buildings are prominently visible, directly across the street from each other:

(1) At the end of the wooden walkway that leads away from the viewer, and with a porch, is the two-story mansard-roofed store of C. C. Ball. The store also served as the post office from 1890 to 1891 under postmaster Alvin Sprague. (The building was later moved across the street, to the right, and from 1928 to 1962 once again housed the post office — see photos, pages 106, top of page 114.)

(2) In the summer of 1891, needing more space for the mail, the post office was moved into another mansard-roofed building owned by C. C. Ball, shown to the right, directly across Water Street. This three-story building was built by Ball as a storehouse in 1884.

There the mail was dispensed by Alvin Sprague until 1893, and by postmaster Almanza Rose until 1898. The structure was removed in the 1950s. In the mid-1970s the vacant foundation was reused for a new two-story store, replete with an attractive mansard roof, in which a gift shop, Strings & Things, happily resides.

Eighth post office, Dodge Street, 1902

Smoke still rises from the ruins in this July 1902 photo taken just after the first National Hotel and four other buildings burned to the ground.

The firemen's hoses are strewn along Dodge Street. Only a short time before, the National Hotel had stood in all its Victorian glory on the foundation to the left — all that remained after the fire was a tall dark chimney.

In this view today, the present-day library is just out of sight to the right and the new National, which opened in 1903, stands on the original hotel's foundation.

The flattened building is a small shop that served briefly as the post office in the mid-1890s. The building was purposely pulled down to prevent the fire from spreading even further.

Ninth post office, ca. 1905 — today's Star Department Store

The small building on the right, which has since been incorporated into the building on the left, was built in 1898 specifically for use by new postmaster Edward S. Payne, who served twice, from 1898-1903 and 1908-1913.

The large building, built in 1883 for H. Q. Morton (compare to photo, top of page 180), was purchased in 1903 by R. Adelbert Negus who immediately extended the bottom floor outward with the glass facade shown above.

In 1912 the facade was extended sideways to the right, across the front of the post office building, and a new post office, now Phelan Real Estate and the Book Nook store, was built further down the road by the Payne family (see photo at top right).

Look at the present-day Star Department Store to see how the top of this former post office was joined to its neighbor (compare this photograph to the aerial view of Water Street on page 239).

Tenth "New Post Office" — postcard, ca. 1912

Frank C. Payne built this building in 1912 on land bought two years earlier — the building has remained in the family ever since (see similar postcard, before the building was built, middle of page 160). At the time, Frank was the assistant postmaster — and his father, Edward, the postmaster. In 1913, S. Martin Rose took over the position, holding it until the year of his death, 1935 — longer than any other tenure.

"Block Island Post Office" — 1925

This building now houses Phelan Real Estate and, since 1973, the Book Nook. Compare to modern photos on pages 2 and 9.

Eleventh post office, now Ernie's Restaurant, 1950

Built across the street as C. C. Ball's store (see photo, top of page 111) and serving also as a post office in 1890 and 1891, this building again boasted the sign of the "U.S. Post Office" department between 1928 and 1962. The first 10-year lease with the government was signed by the owner of the building, Nicholas Ball, son of C. C. Ball.

After scoring higher than six others on a government test in 1935, Nicholas served as postmaster until his death in 1941. He thus found himself employed in the same structure he had worked in as a clerk during his youth, when the building was his father's store on the other side of the street. Nicholas was the first president of the Rhode Island branch of District Postmasters.

Matthew Moran was postmaster in this building from 1941 to 1960, the Island's second longest tenure. Actiing-postmistress Emma Gooley, beginning in 1960, served at this location, the first of a long succession of women to rule the mails/males — until the present postmaster, Frederick C. Leeder, III was appointed in April 1996.

Interior of post office, now Ernie's Restaurant, 1961

Thirteenth (at least) post office, a month before opening in December 1996

Raising the sign, Richard Warfel and Jeff Phillips, November 1996

Twelfth post office, at corner of Ocean Avenue and Corn Neck Road

This location across from the Historical Society (on left) was occupied for an above average time — from 1962 to 1996 — by the flat-roofed, government building that was out-of-place in the midst of Block Island's National Historic District of pitched roofs, gables, cupolas, and gingerbread decoration.

Apparently Postmaster General Arthur E. Summerfield had also not heard of the "Block Island factor" — thought to be a cousin of the Mexican siesta — when he announced that the completion date of the flat-roofed building was July 1, 1960. The post office arrived late by more than two years.

And on the day in August 1962 when the building finally opened, something else was lacking — the mail. A storm had canceled the ferry that morning, leaving the many Islanders who nevertheless came to the new post office with more time to learn their mailbox combinations — and visit each other.

In 1997, after the post office quarters had moved across town, the brick building disappeared — not torn down — but absorbed into a much higher, longer two-story wooden structure built around it.

View of Old Harbor Dock, Block Island — ca. 1905:

Here's where we go catching 'Blue Fish.' It's a great place in summer but in the winter its all froze up and no one lives there. [To Mrs. Josephine B. Dewey, San Francisco, California]

Postcard of side-wheel steamer MOUNT HOPE'S
Providence dock, mailed after a rough fall trip — Oct. 11, 1904:

Here is where we land after a trip to Block Island. It is a welcome sight to those who have had two meals since leaving in the morning — one down and one up. [To Mr. Austin Barney, Natick House, Los Angeles, California]

CHAPTER 13

"This is the only spot on Earth. Moonlight night."

Summer messages on postcards, 1903-1957

THE POSTCARD CRAZE JUST AFTER THE TURN-OF-THE-CENTURY in 1900 flooded this Island resort with pastel images printed on stiff 3½ inch by 5½ inch paper — nearly matching in number, it seems to present-day collectors, the endless waves lapping the beaches.

What did visitors write of so long ago from this picturesque emerald green isle — surrounded often then, as it is now, with the startling blue waters of summer?

Not much.

In the classic postcard age, from 1905 to 1915, nearly a dozen companies created hundreds of different images of Block Island, reproduced in the tens-of-thousands.

From the 1920s to 1940s — matching the decline of tourism itself on the Island — the number and quality of views offered annually for sale was dramatically less.

Although resurgence in the Island's popularity during the last 30 years has been paralleled by the marketing of many new postcards — the modern, shiny, multicolored photographs manufactured since the late 1940s — the present number of different views found in local stores does not approach, even remotely, the heyday of 1910.

The classic age of postcards, though, did not produce classic writing. Banality was the rule, the postcards serving more as a pat on the back or a touch of the arm, than an exchange of substantive ideas.

A string of mundane thoughts written in abrupt non-sentences. No need for verbs. Then or now.

The craze was created in 1898 by a federal Post Office act that allowed a reduced mailing rate for privately printed cards. The same act restricted the postcard buyer, however, to writing messages in a small white strip on the card's front — the rear was solely for the address.

In 1907 postal law changed, allowing messages on half of the back side of postcards, sending postcard addicts into a new frenzy of collecting and mailing.

Some writers took advantage of the increased space, writing finely printed recitations of their entire past week's activities — the kind of message we have all mailed out so diligently, but conversely when received from someone else, hate to decipher.

Many senders continued in the older way — scribing just a few words, written all the larger to make it seem as though the writer must cease for want of space, rather than loss of words or lack of time.

Sometimes purchasers took their Block Island postcards home, to write them at their leisure, or on someone else's time, as did an office worker named Clara:

My dear Bertha

... I liked the postal ever so much ... I remember every place we went to. It doesn't

seem as if I ever could forget, we had such a lovely time. I have been quite busy lately and have sadly neglected my correspondence. I am writing this in the office as the "boss" is away and it is raining and I am so sleepy I just don't feel like working ...
— With love, Clara

Sometimes a bit of the character of Block Island and its long ago visitors is revealed by these old postcards, unexpectedly indicating how times can change — or remain the same.

Sometimes there is nothing to write about, except to write that there is nothing to write about — as this writer did:

April 8, 1914:
Dear Marjorie and Elizabeth, I have just been out on the beach, got some oysters and clams and sat on the rocks and ate them. There is nothing to do, just hang around in the evening. Wish I could get some cards of this place ...
[To Miss Marjorie Shaw, Simsbury, Conn.]

Sometimes imagination or humor is brought to bear, often barely perceptibly — perhaps just an insider's quip, incomprehensible to anyone else.

While some writers really do discuss the weather, and one mailed the quintessential stereotypical message "wish you were here," those authors who declare that the highlights of a Block Island summer are "walking," "picking flowers," "clamming," "the ferry ride," and "home cooking" — as found in the following writings — are not so unsophisticated after all.

Aug. 13, 1903:
This is the only spot on Earth. Moonlight night.
[To Miss Mary McCormack, Hartford, Conn.]

Good tan, and a mystery — Aug. 24, 1904:
We're having the most glorious time here, in and on the water every minute. I'm getting to look just like an Indian. We've been sailing several times. I'm afraid I can't arrange to go to Portland though I should love to. Will tell you why later.
[To Miss Winifred Baker, Wellesley Hills, Mass.]

The Mansion, built in 1888 for the wealthiest woman in the country, burned in 1963, leaving only a stone foundation and a name "Mansion Beach" — July 28, 1906:
Would you be satisfied with life if you owned this place?
—Emma C.
[To Mr. Joel Martin, Irvington, N.J]

Postcard image of the Ocean View Hotel, the Island's largest, which burned in 1966 — Aug. 20, 1907:
Will write this P.M., too busy now. This is the most expensive hotel on the Island. $5 per day.
— With love Edna

A "good" word or two for the Bellevue on High Street — July 9, 1909:
My friend Zoe and I are spending 10 days here at Bellevue House. Fine view. Good board, good room, good bed, good time generally.
—Lovingly Ida
[To Mrs. Mary Seaman, Oxford, Mass.]

At loss for words — Aug. 1909:
Hope you arrived home all right. Having a great time sitting on the beach writing postals this morning. Love to all.
— Alice
[To Miss Cora Hancocks, Valley Falls, RI]

View of a horse car, which ran on rails from Old Harbor to New Harbor — Aug. 13, 1909:
... You should ask for a job as conductor down here. You don't even have to wear a suit and when you go round corners you have to hang on with two hands.
[To Mr. Henry Droney, Milford, Mass.]

Waitress at the National — July 21, 1910:
New National Hotel — Dear Friend — I got your card. Was pleased to hear from you again. I am here as waitress. I came last Thursday. I shall be here about 6 or 7 weeks. The mill I work at is shutting down. Tom Pollic and I had our vacation. We went to New York for a week. We were there when Roosevelt returned. Glad to see you anytime.
— With love to all, Sarah Ellen.

July 26, 1910:
Having a grand time. I am all sunburned. — Kitty
[To Mrs. Allendorf, Hall & Lyon Co., Providence, RI]

Lots of horses — July 12, 1911:
There are 2 or 3 autos down here. I shall be home very soon.
[To Mr. H. P. Richards, New Britain, Conn.]

July 29, 1912:
Dear F — This is a beautiful spot. I wish you could be with me. We are situated on a cliff directly over the ocean. It is so cool that we have to wear wraps constantly. Have not missed a day in bathing. My love to all especially to you.
— Elizabeth
[To Miss Faustina Hurlbrut, Ridgefield, Conn.]

Dandy time at Manisses Hotel, while boyfriend is away — July 16, 1913:
Dear Maude,
I only stayed at Block Island a week because my cousin came and invited me to N.Y. I had a dandy time there, and am having a dandy time here. I called up Loring Pedee last night & he is going to call tonight. I am coming up to see you some Sunday when I get back. We met some dandy fellows at Block Island. My sweetheart is working in Maine. Will see him in September.
— Love from Jenny
[To Miss Maude A. Stanley, Worcester City Hospital, Worcester, Mass.]

A mom happy to get away for awhile, and maybe a bit longer — July 21, 1915:
Dear Edward — It is awfully cold here this morn. Rained last night. There are 27 here now. Have been to pictures both nights. Went to ballgame Monday afternoon. Be a good boy and I will come home Sunday if I can.
— From Mama

A plain postcard, with plain request:

In the completely opposite world of wintertime on Block Island, year-round residents were likely to use pragmatic postal cards with no picture to take up valuable room — such as this one sent by the owner of the 55-acre Governor Gorton Farm near the end of Corn Neck Road.

Most Americans at the time would have known that a "jack" is a male donkey, a "jenny" the female, and "mules" are sterile offspring produced by crossing a male donkey with a female horse.

Jan. 6, 1905:

Gentlemen, kindly send prices of Jacks, Jennys & Mules, about what it would cost to get mules from your place into Rhode Island. Send full particulars. Kindly let me hear from you very early. Name your lowest prices as freight will be a factor.

— Yours, S. Martin Rose,

Box 15, Block Island, R.I.

[To Krekler's Jack Farm, West Elkton, Ohio]

Mohegan Bluffs:

Aug. 10, 1906:

This is where one forgets the trials and tribulations of the strenuous life of the Stenographer.

[To Miss Mary E. Whipple, Providence, R.I.]

Using the new language of the Roaring '20s — July 11, 192?:

Everything 'okey-dokey' here. Weather terrible yesterday, but sunny today. — Virginia & Helen

[To Miss Beatrice Noble, Wethersfield, Conn.]

And what of the daring tourist who ventured here in the off-season? He or she might find themselves in a hostile climate, all alone except for a sense of humor — Oct. 24, 1921:

This is a lovely day ... Wish you were here.

I had the worst time of my life getting here. The wind was blowing 80 miles an hour. I was the only passenger, all alone in the cabin. Sick, you bet, and no one to laugh at me.

[To Miss Grace Holt, Gouldsboro, Maine]

The lamented end of a "perfect" summer in the Roaring 20s; the Mansion during Prohibition advertised dancing, food, and refreshments — Aug. 22, 1926:

Dear Frannie

I received your lovely letter & was glad to hear from you. Am having a perfect time here. Wish you had come over when you were at the pier [in Narragansett, RI].

Only two more weeks & then home & school. Don't you hate the thought of it?

On this card is a "wild time" place.

— Write soon. Oodles of love, Jackie.

Aug. 6, 1933:

Reached here all right. A good place to loaf. Walking is the principle sport. Staying in a house where we have home cooking. Everybody fine. — Dad

[To South Norwalk, Conn.]

Suggestive writing. View of the Mansion is as it looked when new in the 1890s — Aug 19, 1935:

Here's a good place to dance the mambo. Don't forget, I want you to be in good shape to dance the mambo with me when I get back. — Elsie

[To Mr. Herstenberg, Water Street, Quincy, Mass.]

Not prone to seasickness, but forgot the ink bottle — July 15, 1936:

We have a house and it's near a church, a bench, and all the stores. We had a lovely boat trip. The boat went up and down like an elevator and went sideways like a cradle. We are having a lovely time out on the grass. — Love Peggy — P.S. We ran out of ink, so I couldn't finish with ink.

[To Miss Eileen Sheehan, Worcester, Mass.]

From a tourist at boarding house on West Side — July 17, 1941:

West Hillcrest

Dear Aliene,

Every morning we take walks. It's cool for bathing. I hope it warms up so we can go in. We spent yesterday afternoon at the beach. I wonder if things turned out so you could have come just as well. It is certainly peaceful on the Island. We can see the fishing boats and a big expanse of water from the lawn. Here Mrs. Rose the owner does the cooking. There are two waitresses, a laundress, one chambermaid and one handyman. Ten were guests here. Now there are nine. More are coming in Thursday. There are extras for dinners.

Today we tried target practice. Then went in bathing for the first. The water was grand. Robert's new car was delivered Friday. That night he met me at the terminal with it. I wish you could have come. — Sincerely Alma

---

A long way up High Street, near bluffs — Aug. 9, 1943:

We're having a grand time. Found 2 rooms at Pilot Hill House, $^1/_2$ hour walk from beach and to restaurant, after looking all over here. We are just full of dinner at present. — Love Amy

[To Miss Thora Johnson, Providence, RI]

Eager tourist, before Route 95 was built — Aug. 27, 1957:

Greetings! You would have been proud of my auto driving. Made trip in $2^1/_2$ hrs. to ferry in New London in pouring rain. Boat trip a bit rocky, but O.K. Hotel very nice. Expect to enjoy 2-3 days here. Love Kenneth

[To Miss Jane Werckey, Bronx, N.Y.]

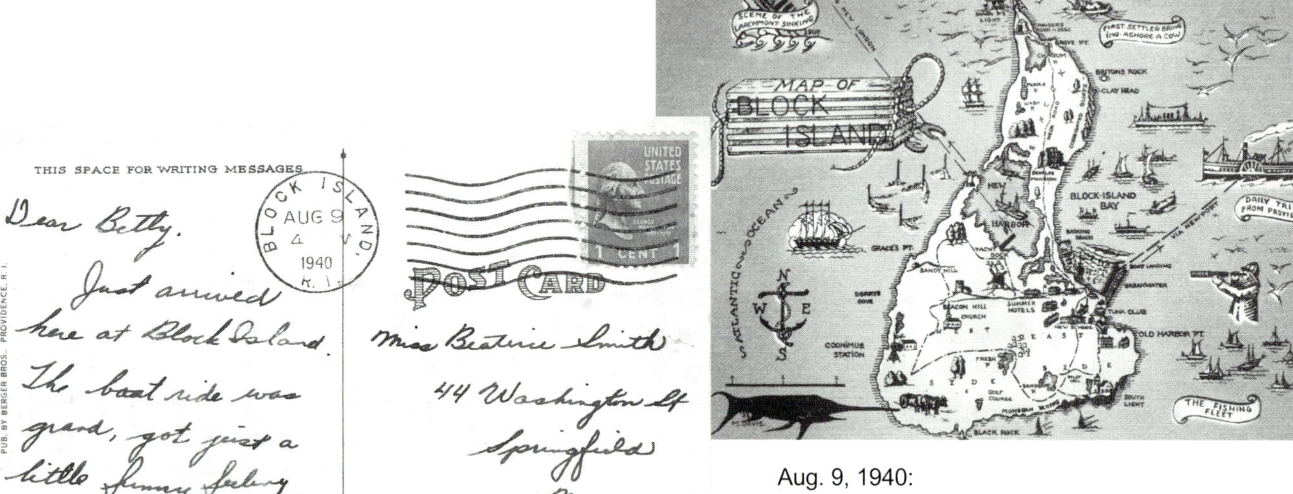

Aug. 9, 1940:

Dear Betty, Just arrived here at Block Island. The boat ride was grand, got just a little funny feeling. — Love Shirley

[To Miss Beatrice Smith, Springfield, Mass.]

On the mainland, electric trolleys had long since replaced horse cars, but the horse car on Block Island, contrary to the deceptive caption on this postcard "Electric Horse Car", was never electrified.
(see similar postcards, pages 152-161).

Summer, ca. 1907:

A view which we don't see very often now is Horse Cars. They race between the two Harbors and during the bathing time they run just to beach & drive through the City(!)

On the "Harbor Village" card you can see them almost in front of the House we stopped at. I only got this as a curiosity of bye gone days. They have just turned the Horses around (in this postcard) & are ready to go back again. So most of the bathers are through their bath.

Suggestive writing. View of Searles Mansion (which burned in 1963) on Mansion Beach

Aug. 31, 1909:

Something besides water here Sully and its good too.

[To Mr. F.A. Sullivan,
c/o United Button Co.,
Springfield, Mass.]

July 22, 1910:

I think you would like it here very much. This morning we picked a large bouquet of pond lilies. We are thinking of staying longer. — May

[To Miss Katherine Clark,
Meriden, Conn.]

Post Card.

BLOCK ISLAND JUL 22 1910

The H. C. Leighton Co., Manufacturers, Portland, Me., U. S. A. (Germany). 30034

This space may be used for Correspondence

I think you would like it here very much. this morning we picked a large bouquet of pond lillies. "May" We are thinking of staying longer.

This space is for Address only

Miss Katherine Clark. No. Fourth St. Meriden. Conn.

Post Card.

PROVIDENCE, R.I. SEP 20 1:30 PM 1910

This space may be used for Correspondence

This space is for Address only

The Hugh C. Leighton Co., Manufacturers, Portland, Me., U. S. A. (Germany). 30020

There is some class to this postal isn't there. Hope to hear from you soon. Anna

Mr. George T. Upper, Bristol, R.I. Gen. Delivery.

Digging potatoes with oxen:

Sept. 20, 1910:

There is some class to this postal isn't there. Hope to hear from you soon. — Anna

[To Mr. George Upper, Bristol, RI]

The Jail, Crescent Beach, in service for about a dozen years:
(see other jail photos, page 150)

Aug. 7, 1914:

Time must be precious or news scarce; which is it? Nellie, what do you think of this place? This is where you'd lodge if you were here. Hurry up and write me a long letter — May

[To Miss Nellie McGuiness, Holliston, Mass.]

The Breakers:

A middling assessment of the boarding house, the Breakers; now a private home on Corn Neck Road near Scotch Beach. The top two windows are marked with X's.

July 12, 1937:

Dear Family — Had a nice trip. We were disappointed with the place we are staying at first, but are used to it now. The beach is right near by and the best one I've ever seen.

The weather is foggy today. Hope it will clear up. The X's on the picture mark our rooms, but they are not so bad as they look.—Love Virginia

[To Worcester, Mass.]

A Glimpse of the old Road and the Wind Mill, Block Island, R. I.

Windmill, Old Mill Road:

(see other views of this windmill, pages 214-215)

July 27, 194-?:

This is the place to come to reduce. We are on a farm almost and have to walk a couple miles each way to get anywhere. One thing it is fine & cool.—Regards, Elsie

[To Miss M. Dickie, Bronx, N.Y.]

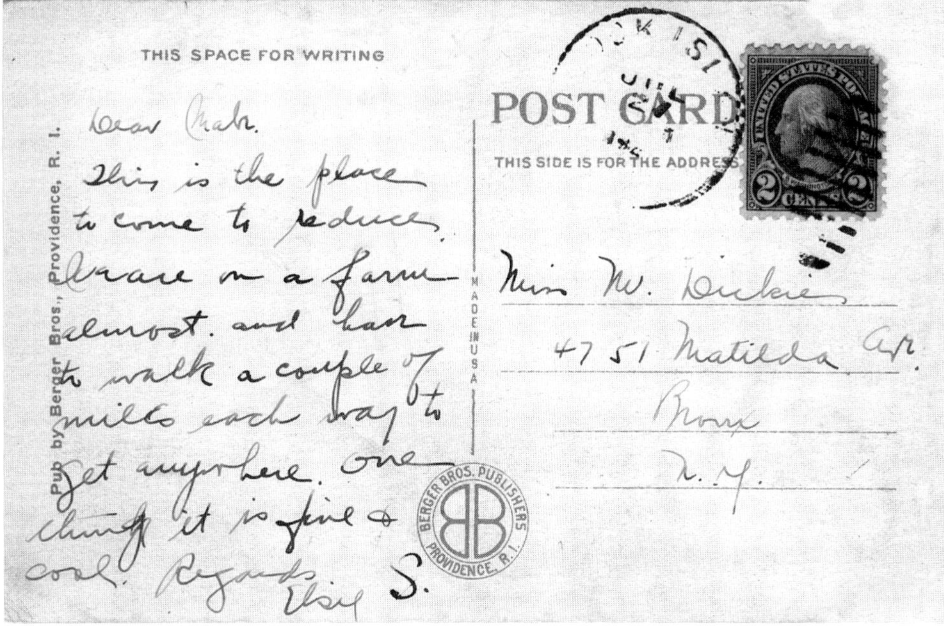
THIS SPACE FOR WRITING

POST CARD

THIS SIDE IS FOR THE ADDRESS

Pub. by Berger Bros., Providence, R. I.

MADE IN U.S.A.

Dear [illegible]

This is the place to come to reduce. We are on a farm almost. and have to walk a couple of miles each way to get anywhere. One thing it is fine & cool. Regards Elsie S.

Miss M. Dickie
4751 Matilda Av.
Bronx
N.Y.

BERGER BROS. PUBLISHERS PROVIDENCE, R.I.

Silk and Paper

Old tourist items

See Chapter 19 for other hotel brochures from the past

Rules and Regulations

Of the Atlantic House.

All Guests of this Hotel without baggage must pay in advance.

Trunks must be ready for Porter at 10.30 a. m. on day of departure.

Guests are requested not to carry the Hotel towels to bathing beach, as towels are furnished at bath houses.

No laundry work must be done in rooms of this Hotel. Patrons wishing such work done will please leave same at office where it will be attended to. Under no condition will guests' laundry be done at Hotel laundry.

The ATLANTIC HOUSE rules — ca. 1910

Called the Norwich House when built in 1878, and now known as the Atlantic Inn, this hotel once distrusted patrons who showed up "without baggage" — they could run away too easily without paying their bill.

The MANISSES HOTEL, logo — 1880s

SHORE DINNER

CONSISTING OF

Clam Chowder, Broiled Fish, Lobster, Roast Beef and Vegetables, Home-Made White and Brown Bread, Tea and Pie or Watermelon,

Only 50 Cents!

On the Landing, First Building at the Left.

M. S. BARBER, - Proprietor.

BLOCK ISLAND
SHORE DINNER HOUSE.

BUKER'S NOVELTY PRESS, PROV. R. I.

"Shore Dinner, 50 Cents" Oval advertisement card — ca. 1880

Barber's Shore Dinner House was renamed Ballard's Inn in 1920 by the Ballard family. The building, much enlarged since the 1870s, burned in June 1986 and was rebuilt for the following summer.

The OCEAN VIEW HOTEL, booklet — 1884

The booklets of the Ocean View Hotel in the 1880s and 90s were the Island's most elaborate. The eclectic motif of this cover was produced by a Boston firm. Note the words "A Summer At Sea" seemingly tucked in on a separate card.

"Block Island Girl" — ca. 1910
Cigarette premium, on silk

Cigarette companies offered lithographed silk panels as premiums from 1900 through the 1920s. In this imaginary image from Zira Cigarettes, nothing — not the lighthouse, the boat, nor the girl — has anything to do with Block Island. In 1910, Turkish and Egyptian cigarettes held 25 percent of the cigarette market — instead of being hand rolled, as were the more expensive brands, the popular and reasonably priced Zira cigarette was produced at a factory in New Jersey owned by the P. Lorillard Company. Other resorts represented by a bathing beauty printed on a silk panel — some produced by other cigarette companies — were Nantucket, Newport, Narragansett Pier, Cape May, and Old Orchard Beach.

Whether with the Block Island Girl of 1910, or the Marlboro Man in advertisements of the 1950s-90s, cigarette companies have been methodically fooling a gullible public since the late 1800s.

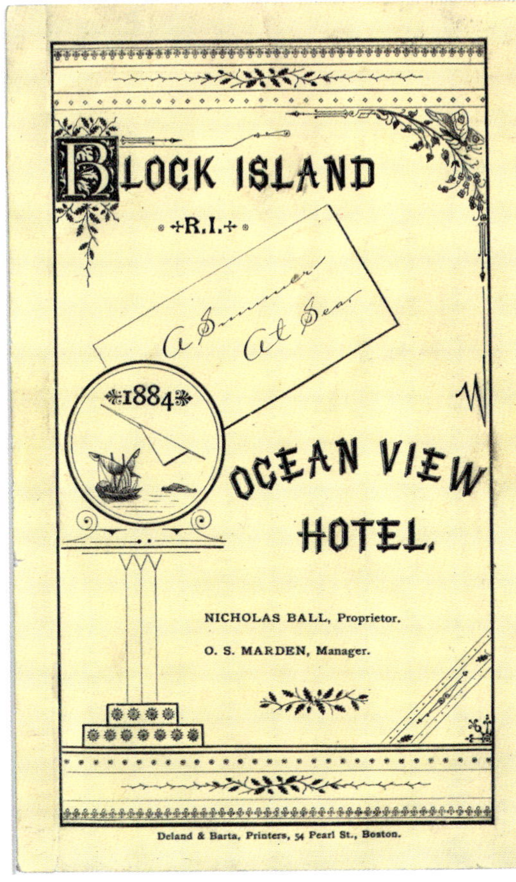

"You can't find me because I'm getting a clam dinner" Postcard — 1906

The writer of this postcard — mailed at Block Island on July 8, 1906 — may well have been at the old Barber's Shore Dinner Hall (see advertisement card, opposite page).

Carriages wait on the left. At right, the tracks for the horse cars curve past the bend by the present-day Sullivan Real Estate office (see other photos of the horse cars, throughout Chapter 16).

Map of New Belgium & New England, showing Adriaen Blocx Eylandt, 1635

North is to the right, not at the traditional top, in this portion of a map printed on handmade paper by the famous Blaeu family of Dutch mapmakers in 1635. This is the earliest printed map to depict canoes and North American fauna. Many geographical details are based on the manuscript map of Adrian Block, made in 1614. On his voyage that year from present-day New York City along the southern shore of Connecticut, Rhode Island and Massachusetts, Block was the first European to discover Long Island Sound.

Two types of watercraft are shown near *Adriaen Blocx Eylandt.* At the top are canoes made from the bark of trees (in Latin: *corticibus arborum*). Below them is a larger canoe, manned by five natives, dug out with the use of fire (*igne excavata*) from the trunk of a tree (*arboris trunco*) — see close-up, page 32.

Block Island, being clearly visible from Montauk Point on Long Island, and from the shores of present-day Connecticut and Rhode Island, was easily accessible to several nearby tribes. Starting from the top, several of the prominent Indian tribes are: the *Manatthaus* (near the town of *Nieu Amstersdam*) for whom the island of Manhattan is named; the *Matouwacs* for whom Montauk Point on Long Island is named; the *Pequatoos,* now the Pequot tribe of eastern Connecticut; and the *Nahicans,* for whom Narragansett Bay in Rhode Island is named.

Below Block Island in this image, the two islands of Martha's Vineyard and Nantucket are erroneously shown as one long, stretched out island (*Texel* & *Vlielant*). At the bottom, Cape Cod's familiar shape — a curled arm — is easily distinguished.

For information about Block Island's Indians, see Chapter 5.

Modus muniendi apud Mahikanenses.
De groote Riuier van Nieu Nederlandt
Magnus fluvius
Novi Belgy
De groote Kraal
Irocoiſienſis
NOVA
BELGICA
ET
ANGLIA
NOVA

Where's Bill?—August 17, 199

Water Street

On August 17, 1997, President William Jefferson Clinton, wife Hillary, and daughter Chelsea visited Block Island, staging a surprise hour-long walk down the full length of Water Street — from the National Hotel to the statue of Rebecca — all to the ecstatic gasps and cheers of ever larger throngs of admirers.

Arkansas Lemonade — August 17, 1997

Each summer young entrepreneurs test the waters of business along the Island's roads — as these youngsters do near Rodman's Hollow — wondering, no doubt, whether they'll attract the attention of the southern-born president, or at least create a photo-op good enough to be published.

"Mr. President, Keep Block Island Green!" The painted rock — August 17, 1997

Block Island's locally famous painted rock received a repainting for President Clinton's visit — the change in the rock's theme occurring in the usual impromptu manner by an unknown artist. The president's announced purpose for his five-hour visit to the Island was to promote conservation of the landscape.

The president near the statue of Rebecca

President Clinton peruses a welcoming banner from *Ben and Jerry's* ice cream store announcing the flavor of the day: *Chubby Hubby.*

Any person in this photo not looking at the president — and there are more than a dozen — is a secret service agent.

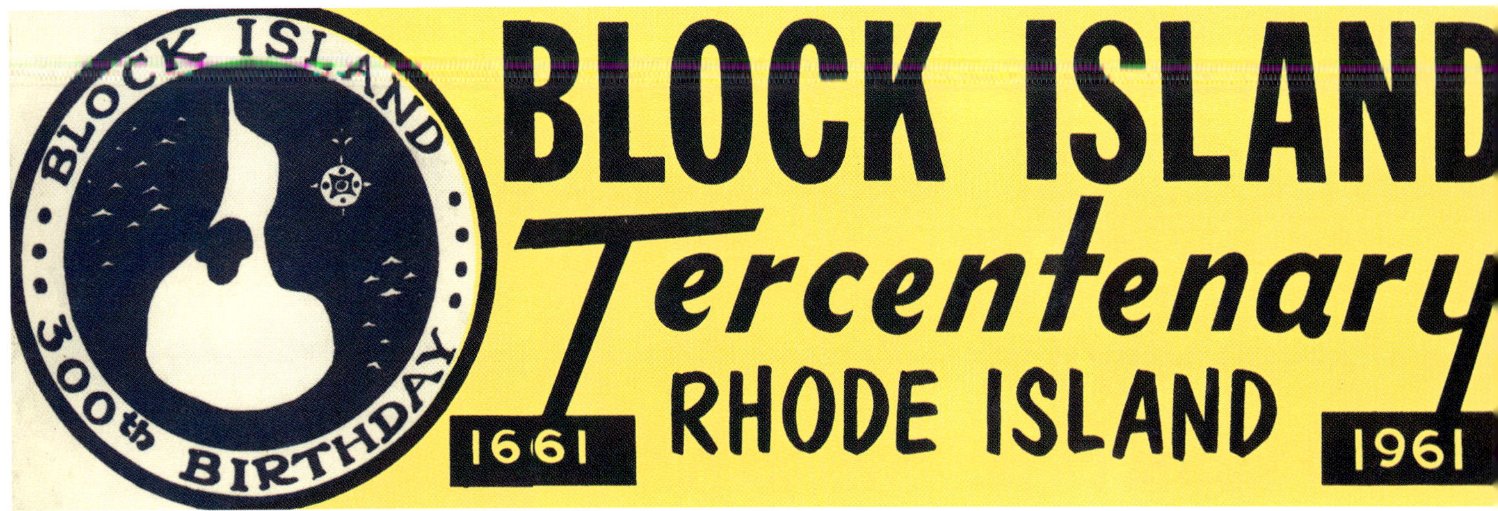

Block Island Tercentenary 1961 — The Island's oldest bumper sticker

The 300th anniversary celebration of the first white settlers' arrival in 1661 produced an output of homegrown publications unmatched in quantity by any other Island event, such as: a commemorative envelope, a 2-inch blue and white decal, a postcard of the 12-foot diameter birthday cake being hauled past the Surf Hotel, a 100-page red-covered history booklet, a program for the June 10th launching of a replica Block Island *double ender* boat, a metal medallion, two souvenir *Block Island Beacon* newspapers, and a bumper sticker — the first one ever printed concerning Block Island.

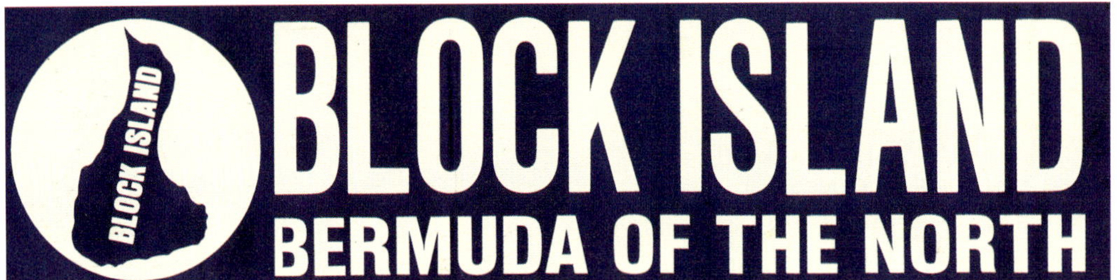

***Block Island — Bermuda of the North*, 1970s**

This term was first used as a tourist lure in the 1880s on the covers of some hotel brochures, leading pundits to forever after ask whether Bermuda has slogans that advertise "Block Island of the South."

***Save Open Space*, by the Block Island Conservancy, 1972**

To help preserve the Island's landscape, and the heart of its people, the phrase "Save Open Space" was used for the Block Island Conservancy's first conservation effort: the rescue of Rodman's Hollow from the thick fingers of contractors and architects. The slogan also mimicked the traditional mariner's cry for help: *S O S*, meaning "Save Our Souls" — a dead-on reminder of what developers would readily cast away.

***Block Island* (showing Southeast Light), 1980s**

The Southeast Lighthouse, moved back from the edge of the 150-foot Mohegan Bluffs in 1993, is often used as a symbol not only of Block Island, but of the entire state.

Bumper Sticker Museum

For other examples, see bumper sticker story, Chapter 24

***Block Island, R.I.* — with Town of New Shoreham Coat-of-Arms, 1980s**

The town's coat-of-arms, while appearing ancient, was formulated only in 1928, one of a series made for Rhode Island by Providence historian Howard M. Chapin. Featured are a *double ender* fishing sailboat; a codfish, which Islanders formerly depended on for a living; and a lion, representing the settlers' English origins. The bumper sticker version differs slightly from the official design, which can be seen on plaques at the Historical Society and on the memorial obelisk at the corner of Water and Dodge Streets. BEWARE OF SOUVENIR FLAGS sold to Block Island tourists in the 1990s that invert these three figures. The *double ender*, codfish and lion should be facing INWARD toward the emblem's center, not outward.

Bethany's Airport Diner, 1990s

An unlikely, but eye-catching, eight-engine seaplane soars past Block Island's North Light. The diner at the airport has been a hit since 1950. See page 229 for another of Bethany's bumper stickers.

Club Soda, 1990s

This refuge at the Highview Inn from the usual tourist scene, has a new name — used since the early 1990s — for a well-established bar that is a fairly short walk, but a distant mindset from the center of Old Harbor.

One of the Last Great Places*, by The Nature Conservancy, *1990s

The nationwide Nature Conservancy first aided the Island in 1972 when the local, and separate, B. I. Conservancy was formed to save Rodman's Hollow from a housing development. With an expanding interest in the Island and the state, the Nature Conservancy opened its first Rhode Island office in 1989 with Block Island's Keith Lang as director. In 1991, the Nature Conservancy designated Block Island one of the Western Hemisphere's 12 "Last Great Places" — often forgotten is that the full name includes the far larger Peconic region of Long Island's eastern end.

For the winter

When the ground was too frozen to dig, temporary storage — provided through this small entrance at the base of the cemetery hill — was needed until the next thaw.

Margaret Guthry — 1687, Block Island's oldest gravestone

The gravestone of Margaret Guthry, who died in 1687, is the oldest on Block Island and the only known work here by John Stanclift — a prolific Connecticut carver of the late 1600s who incised his "A's" with a line across the top, and commonly cut a single step on the left and right sides of the stones.

Margaret's marital circumstance, as wife of the Island's town clerk, Robert Guthry, may have kept her from reposing under an unlettered boulder, as was the fate of many early Islanders.

She will instead be remembered a while longer by words, ever more hidden, in the shadow-darkened lettering of her red sandstone marker.

Gravestone of Mercy Littlefield — 1761

Mercy Littlefield, wife of Caleb Littlefield, died on April 3, 1761, in the 66th year of her age.

See Chapter 6, page 45 for more information about this stone and others.

Passing years — the Island Cemetery

◄ **_Passing years_**

The grey slate stones, the reddish ones made from sandstone, and the white marble markers, pass the centuries relatively unchanged.

Mid-Ocean *newspaper office on Water Street, Old Harbor, ca. 1900*

The ***Mid-Ocean*** has been a landmark near the statue of Rebecca since the early 1890s, one of many 'small' buildings that once lined Dodge Street and Water Street. Although representing the Island's past, and part of two overlapping town and national historic districts, owners tend to tear such structures down. In August 2000 the small shop was moved slightly, to Chapel St., making way for a much larger building with a tower. Also see photos: pages 200 & 207.

CHAPTER 14

People want to know

15 different Block Island newspapers — at least

YOU READ THEM COMPULSIVELY; you need to know. And if you miss an issue from laziness or you're just too tired hearing about other people's problems, then someone will manage to admonish: "Didn't you read about it last week?"

They are the Island's newspapers, for more than a hundred years they have sought to offer facts where there were no facts before — the *Surf, Island Home, Hooter, Ocean View,* and *Crier* — amongst others.

The precursor to the Island's first published paper, and the all-time smallest in circulation, was the ***Block Island Star*** — so ephemeral that each issue's single hand-written copy was recited to its patrons during the winters of 1875-76 and 1876-77.

Addie Smith, the editor, read the *Star* at the Island's largest hall, often to over-flowing crowds. Her words were not lost forever into the night air — many stories were printed in mainland newspapers, preserved for a while longer on earth.

As reported a decade after its demise:

"The *Block Island Star* was then brightly in the ascendant, and would soon have been invested with all the dignity that type can bestow; but the deaths of Misses Smith and Conley, occurring almost simultaneously, caused sudden eclipse to this literary light and removed two of the most highly cultured ladies that have ever adorned Block Island society."

Addie L. Smith died on July 27, 1877, at the age of 19 (see sister's wedding page 143). Mary Louise Conley, a teacher at the East Greenwich seminary on the mainland, died on November 3, 1877, age 39. Each is buried at the Island cemetery.

The same "literary light" has struck many times since, as evidenced during the past 20 years alone, when several newspapers and a plethora of less aspiring works were begun locally. These smaller printings, xeroxes and mimeographs — usually in the form of newsletters — have been published by several groups and individuals, and include these items that had an official name:

- the Chamber of Commerce *Outlook*;
- the League of Women Voters *The Way It Is*;
- the Community Education *Share News*;
- the Writers' Workshop *High Tide*;
- the Harbor Baptist Church *The Harbor Light*;
- the Island Clinic *Medical Fact & Comment*;
- the Resident's Association *Soundings*;
- the Block Island Power Company *Wind Turbine News*;
- various annual Race Week dailies in late June;
- the Mid-Ocean Press's *Mid-Ocean Forum*; and
- the well-designed but strictly promotional *The New Harbor*, a faux newsletter.

Then there are the magazines and booklets, but that's another story.

Each effort spreads the news, or the views, then current. Future historians will have an in-depth — maybe too deep — view of the late 20th century here.

The real newspapers served a broad community from a broad palette, and were intended to have a lengthy publication life — but usually failed after a few years.

H. S. Millikin,
Real Estate Broker,
offers for sale at a bargain
THE HYGEIA HOTEL PROPERTY, INCLUDING COTTAGE.
Also three cottages, all in good condition, and nearly new, also House Lots and Farms on various parts of the Island for sale cheap. Pleased to consult with any one desirous of buying or selling.
Office: Masonic Hall, High Street, Block Island, R. I.
Office Hours from 1 to 7 P. M.

Bills of Fare, ... Invitations, Envelopes, Show Cards, PRINTED AT MID OCEAN OFFICE, Opposite C. C. Ball's Store.

VOLUME VI.—NO. 12. BLOCK ISLAND, R. I., TUESDAY, AUGUST 12, 1890. PRICE 5 CENTS.

DEVOTED TO THE INTERESTS OF BLOCK ISLAND AND ITS DEVELOPMENT AS A SUMMER RESORT.

Almy's

Surf Cottage Hotel Visitors.

Among the prominent guests who have visited this well known house

Ocean View Echoes.

The stones on the bathing beach have been productive of much evil during the past week. Several ladies and gentlemen have suffered

A Pleasing Entertainment.

The guests of the National Hotel have enjoyed their full share of entertainment during the past two weeks. Hops, sleight of hand per-

Mine host Chester Rose, of the Narragansett Hotel, knows how to make it pleasant for his guests, and his well-filled house speaks for itself. On Wednesday evening last the guests were treated to a concert

Redfern
LA IES' TAILOR
NEWPORT

The Mid-Ocean, 1890

The longest running paper is ***The Block Island Times*** begun as a twice-monthly in the summer of 1970, evolving 15 years later into the current year-round weekly, and becoming, in 1988, Block Island's official newspaper of record (meaning legal notices could be accepted). No other Island newspaper has been published for an entire year throughout the winter.

Along the way, three Island newspapers competed head-to-head during the summer of 1903 — while there were several other occasions when two coexisted.

Those summers so rife with printed information contrast with the nearly 50 years previous to the 1960s when no local paper was published — an indication of a low-key era when people did not flock to the Island in droves, and the "news of record" could be passed, as done in former centuries, by word-of-mouth.

In the last three decades of the 19th century, the literary life of Block Island was upheld by Charles E. Perry, a native-born resident and a descendant of the Island's Champlin family (and not to be confused with Dr. Charles F. Perry who came to the Island from the mainland, practicing medicine here for much of the first half of the 1900s).

As a local school teacher and correspondent for the Associated Press, Perry maintained a lifelong interest in reporting Island events. He was the editor of that era's dominant newspaper, the summertime ***Mid-Ocean***, from its inception in 1885 as the weekly ***Block Island Budget***.

Besides events, anecdotes, and lengthy listings of the guests at each of the Island's major hotels, the *Mid-Ocean* sometimes addressed social issues — which pale compared to today's, which seem only to have costly "solutions." In the 1890s, complaints were of dusty roads (buy a horse-pulled sprinkler wagon), more street lights in Old Harbor, and broken planks in the wooden sidewalks along Water, High, and Spring Streets (see pages 147-151).

The *Mid-Ocean* continued to be printed until 1906, by its owner and publisher, *The Newport Mercury*.

In 1901, Perry assumed a short-lived editorship of the ***Block Island Surf***, owned by the Croke Printing Company which also published the *Narragansett Surf*.

Then — against his better judgement as he later declared in writing — Perry edited another new Island paper, the ***Block Island Press***, which began publication on May 2, 1903. Intended to be a year-round weekly, and relying heavily on standard worldwide dispatches and installments of serial novels, the *Press* made it through the next winter but ceased publication in the spring of 1904, before a full year of issues were completed.

The Surf, June 28, 1894

Cover page

Block Island Wireless.

PUBLISHED BY THE PROVIDENCE JOURNAL CO.

One of Two Daily Newspapers in the World Whose News Dispatches Come by Wireless Telegraph.

VOLUME I. NO. 18. BLOCK ISLAND, R. I., JULY 29, 1903. FIVE CENTS.

FOUGHT FOR BREAD.

Many Persons Were Knocked Down and Trampled Upon.

Newark, N. J., July 28.—There was no bread in Newark to-day owing to a strike of Hebrew bakers, who demand a holiday on Sunday.

Hebrews returned from New York with two wagon loads of bread and a crowd of hungry men and women fought for a share of the precious load. Many persons were knocked down and trampled upon and many women were carried fainting from the crowd.

THE INGOMAR WON.

Long Distance Race Between Schooner Yachts.

CLOSING QUOTATIONS.

New York Stocks.

Amalgamated Copper,	41 3-4
American Sugar Refining,	116 1-8
Atchison,	63 3-8
Brooklyn Rapid Transit,	44 1-2
Canadian Pacific,	123
Erie,	29 3-4
Illinois Central,	132 1-8
Louisville and Nashville,	104 1-4
Manhattan Elevated,	132 1-8
Metropolitan,	118
Missouri Pacific,	98 3-4
New York Central,	121 1-4
Norfolk and Western,	63
Pennsylvania,	123 1-2
Reading,	49 3-8
St. Paul,	142 1-4
Southern Pacific,	43 3-4
Southern Railway,	20 7-8
Union Pacific,	75 1-8
United States Steel,	24

Cotton Market.

SENSATION IN CHATTANOOGA.

Remarks of Judge in Whiteside Will Contest the Cause.

Chattanooga, Tenn., July 28.—A sensation was sprung in the Circuit Court today in the Whiteside will contest involving an estate of nearly a million dollars. The jury has been deadlocked more than a week. Judge Allison asked if attempts had been made to unduly influence them and one juror said when he asked for change for a $5 bill at Chattanooga Bank the teller pushed out to him $10 in silver. When he handed back the surplus the teller pushed out another pile. The bank is one of the executors of the Whiteside estate. Attachments for bank officers have been issued.

Season for Big Yachts Ended.

The Wireless, 1903

During the summer of 1903 the weekly *Press* competed not only against the twice-weekly *Mid- Ocean*, but also with another newcomer, the ***Block Island Wireless.***

As the Island's first and only daily, the *Wireless* was a well-funded summer paper published by the Providence Journal Company. Its sole reason for existence was as a high-spirited experiment in the new technology of radio.

Although not quite making history as a world record "first," the masthead of the *Wireless* nevertheless boasted that it was "One of Two Daily Newspapers in the World Whose News Dispatches Come by Wireless Telegraph" — the first such endeavor, on Catalina Island off the California coast, was launched a few months earlier.

Depicted on either side of the masthead were the giant antennae that the *Journal* built at Pt. Judith on the mainland, and near the Southeast Lighthouse on Block Island.

The *Wireless* published 45 issues between July 9 and August 29, creating considerable news about the operation in its parent paper, the *Providence Journal*, and attracting a constant stream of visitors to the press building located northeast of the Southeast Lighthouse. The humble stump of the giant 200-foot antenna mast — the highest structure (above water level) ever erected on Block Island — can be seen next to the former home of John Hapgood, which was the newspaper's headquarters (plat 8, lot 2).

Besides reporting local happenings and the names of hotel guests, the *Wireless*, as did all the early papers, reported world news as well. That summer the Pope's illness and subsequent death, and the third attempt of England's tea baron, Sir Thomas Lipton, to win the America's Cup, provided instant news suitable for the wireless operation.

When lightening rendered the radio system inoperable for two days, the *Wireless* dutifully reported that the world's news was now being received by the Island's underwater telegraph cable — which had been functioning for 21 years — and was slower than radio by only a matter of seconds, but not, obviously, as intriguing.

The Surf, June 28, 1894

Front page

BLOCK ISLAND SURF

An Illustrated Journal, devoted to the interests of the Island and the Entertainment of Visitors during the Summer season

VOL. I. BLOCK ISLAND, R. I., THURSDAY, JUNE 28, 1894. No. 1.

BLOCK ISLAND---ITS LOCATION AND ATTRACTIONS.

BLOCK ISLAND lies out at sea twelve miles from the nearest point of land on the southern coast of Rhode Island, fifteen miles southwest from Point Judith, and about thirty miles from Newport. Being at this distance out at sea, it possesses a climate unequaled at any summer resort. No land breezes can ever reach the Island, and the temperature is so equable that the mercury varies but a few degrees from day to day. The air is always cool and bracing, at the same time having a mildness unknown elsewhere.

The Island is free from all annoyance of mosquitoes. In

THE LANDING.

many respects it is the most perfect summer resort in America. Standing out in a bold, clear cut mass, it is a conspicuous object from any elevated point on the southern coast of Rhode Island, or from the decks of vessels traversing the upper part of Long Island Sound.

It is triangular in shape and is from seven to eight miles long by about three and a half in its widest part. The only harbor on the island is Block Island Bay, an indentation in the coast which affords little shelter, for, although it lies for two miles along the shore, it is not more than half a mile deep and the waves continually beat on its shore in a moderate surf. At the extreme southern end the shore makes a deeper sweep, and here an artificial harbor has been formed by the construction of a government breakwater begun in 1871, costing $265,000 and which is now more than 1,500 ft. in length. The break waterconsists of a huge rough wall of immense blocks of granite piled promiscuously upon each other. The space protected by the breakwater affords good anchorage ground, utilized by fishing vessels at certain seasons of the year. The whole place lies fully in view from the deck of an approaching steamer.

The bathing beach is about three miles long and one of the finest on the coast. Being entirely free from undertow and currents, it is perfectly safe for children. Hundreds of people daily take advantage of the excellent opportunities afforded.

Three main roads lead from the harbor village, and they reach every portion of the island. Northward runs the Neck road leading to Sandy Point and light, a distance in this way of about six miles; directly across the island westward runs Main street, between three and four miles in length, midway passing through the "Centre," the only other village on the island, where the town house and public library are located; Southward High street leads up the hills to the southeastern bluffs and the light-house, a distance of about two miles.

Southward the land slopes upward from the harbor village to a series of high, precipitous bluffs, rising from 100 to more

THE ONLY ONE — OUT EVERY SATURDAY — NEWSY AND BRIGHT — ITS ADVS PAY

BLOCK ISLAND TOPICS

DEVOTED TO THE INTERESTS OF THE ISLAND AND ITS SUMMER VISITORS

VOL. 1, NO. 2 | SATURDAY, JULY 12, 1913 | PRICE FIVE CENTS

THE ISLAND'S SPECIAL ATTRACTIONS FOR SUMMER RECREATION SEEKERS ARE

ITS rare combination of seashore and country atmosphere;

ITS ideal average summer temperature of 74;

ITS cool, sunny days and invigorating pure, salt air;

capacity crowds. The Shinnecock, arriving first, from New York at 7 in the morning, landed a full passenger list of arrivals for extended stays, then steamed over to Montauk Point to bring in a great mass of excursionists from New York and points on Long Island. There was a steady procession from the wharves for what would be several city blocks, after the docking of the various steamboats. And each

The Topics, 1913

The Block Island Fly.

(Official Organ of New Shoreham and the West Side Weeds.)

Edition No. 2 | SEASON 1917 | Edition No. 2

NOTICE

This paper is published by the "FLY PUBLISHING CO., LTD." And through its large staff of correspondents endeavors to publish all the authentic news of the Old-Harbor village and suburbs, including the Bandit Hills of the West Side.

All society news, murders and scandals, including advertisements and marriages should be submitted to any of our reporters whose names appear below:

Kit. Littlefield	Honorary Editor
Venie Willis	Editor-in-Chief
Nick Ball	Chief of Reporters

REPORTERS

New Harbor	Giles Dunn, Jr.
Old Harbor	Wm. P. Lewis
West Side	Phil. Mott
Southeast Heights	Web. Clarke
"Mansion" Meadows	Wm. Littlefield
Clay Head Terrace	Sam Hayes

NEW FRATERNITY

A new fraternal order was formed last week at Hi Willis' Hall. It will be known as the "Ancient Order of Pole Cats." Dell Hull was elected Supreme Squirt and Frank Eccles Vice-Squirt.

The charter is now open. All those desiring to become brother Pole Cats please consult Brother Bert Sprague for blanks.

WEATHER INDICATIONS

Predicted by
TAL. DODGE
(The False Prophet)

To-Night—Beer showers, followed by perpindicular winds.

WANTED

PASTRY COOK—Either a male man or a female woman. Must know how to make "Onion Pie" and "Bean Cake." Apply in person at the Lunatic Asylum.
Owen Mitchell, "Head Loon."

CLASSES NOW FORMING

(Mohigan Hall)
Learn the "Toilet Roll" and the "Death Clinch"
NORMAN DODGE and BONY ROSE
Instructors in Modern Dancing.
Music furnished by
Fred Slate and his Chinese Orchestra.
Phil. Mott, Director.

AWAITING TRIAL

Leon Tabbott and Arlo Littlefield, the two assassins who tried to "shoot up" the Sheriff on the West Beach last winter, will be tried before Judge Millikin next month. The Sheriff says that when they fired at him he was so frightened that he turned a complete somersault, changing ends so fast that he kicked his own hat off en-route.

Almanz Rose painted his fence again last week. He says that on account of the cool weather he was putting on an extra coat.

COURT NEWS

Sheriff Willis arrested Sam Maloof last week while he was repairing a pair of pants. Sam refused to be pinched without a kick, so the Sheriff gave him one—right in the pants. The Sheriff charged Sam with "cruelty to animals", and, after an explanation, Judge Hub. Millikin fined Sam 15c for "Sewing buttons on flies."

The Fly, 1917

The dominant newspaper of the Island's first journalistic era, 1885-1920, was:

The *Mid-Ocean* 1889-1906

Other lesser newspapers were:

Block Island Star 1875-1877
Block Island Weekly Budget .... 1885-1888?
(later became *Mid-Ocean*)
Block Island Surf .... 1894-1901?
Our Island Home .... 1895-1902?
Block Island Press 1903, 04
Block Island Wireless 1903
Block Island Topics .... 1913?
Block Island Fly 1917

The dominant newspaper of the Island's second era of printing (1964-1999) is:

The Block Island Times 1970-present

Other papers published recently:

Block Island News 1964
(later became *Hooter*)
Block Island Hooter 1965-1968
The Ocean View 1976, 77
The Reporter 1983
Island Crier 1992-1996
Block Island Beacon 1999-2000

After the *Mid-Ocean* ceased publishing at the end of the 1906 summer, Block Island was without a local paper until 1913 when the ***Block Island Topics*** was begun by J. S. Hammond, editor and publisher. The project was extremely short-lived.

Islanders then had a brief encounter, during the summer of 1917, with the ***Block Island Fly*** — a buoyant spoof printed by several young Island men who were quite full of themselves. The *Fly*, they announced, "endeavors to publish all the authentic news of the Old Harbor village and suburbs, including the Bandit Hills of the West Side."

Following that, Islanders had no local paper for nearly five decades.

For twenty of those years, however, resident Maizie Lewis reported the events of her town for mainland papers, notably the *Newport Sentinel*. In 1937 she was one of 10 nationwide "county correspondents" to receive awards for excellent local articles. As the *Sentinel* said: "She combines the personal and social type of reporting with human interest articles and straight news stories. Such qualities are rarely found in one correspondent."

In 1964, summer residents Marilyn and Brooks Scoville produced a mimeographed paper called the ***Block Island News***. Printed on a single 8 ½ x 14-inch sheet, the nine issues of the *News* managed to report, in its typewriter style, on history, fishing, movies, church schedules and the names of boats at Champlin's Marina — all on the front. On the back were two and three-line "ads" for some 20 Island businesses.

When the Scoville's did not return the next season, a similar newspaper was printed by Helen Cullinan and Edie Blane during the summers of 1966 and 1967. Within the boundaries of its small size and typewritten text, the paper — named the Block Island ***Hooter*** — was nevertheless an improvement over the *News*.

The Hooter, July 1, 1968

In 1968 the Hooter's new publisher, Lewis Gaffett, produced a bona fide newspaper. Although still only a single sheet, 11 x 17 inches, the paper was produced on a regular printing press and included photographs.

Lew's paper lasted only that summer, but the family's printing heritage has been furthered several times over by daughter Kim Gaffett, owner of the present-day Mid-Ocean Press on Chapel Street, and first warden of the town in the late 1990s.

THE BLOCK ISLAND

HOOTER

Week of July 1st, 1968 — Volume No. 1, Issue No. 1

Published by The Hooter — High St. — Tel. 466-2233, 466-5555, Block Island, Rhode Island

Prospects Look Good For This Season

CLEARING BLOCK ISLAND OF OLD AUTOS BEAUTIFIES LANDSCAPE, AND is a unique operation, since this is the only place removal must be accomplished by water.

Photo, Jill and Peter Stevens

In spite of its odd weather, last summer was good. This summer looks even better, as Island businessmen see it.

At the Chamber of Commerce, vice president James O'Malley reports that inquiries from prospective visitors are running 10% ahead of any previous year. Over 200 inquiries arrived in one recent week alone. Everyone has his own theory to explain the increased interest in Block Island, but O'Malley believes it has a lot to do with the growing number of boat owners.

Narragansett Hotel and Spring House owner Sam Mott has a different theory. He speculates that many people who were put off by last summer's weather reports intend to make up for it this year. He says reservations are running ahead of last year's. Mrs. Cyr, of the Surf Hotel and Gables says the summer looks at least as good as last year. The hotels figure that about 50% of their guests are first-time visitors to the Island.

Perhaps the most dramatic example of the interest in the Island is in the real estate picture. Most realtors say land prices have increased significantly even since last summer. Waterfront acreage averages as high as $5,000, inland property $2,000.

One curious fact is that many rental cottages go begging for tenants during the first two beautiful weeks of July. Rental agent Dorothy Sullivan says she can't figure it out. From the middle of July on, though, the demand seems greater than ever.

Whatever the reasons for the prosperous outlook, Block Island is glad to have it.

Construction is up too. Building inspector Harold Wescott has issued eighteen building and renovation permits this year. He estimates that about forty new houses have gone up on the island since last summer.

Reviews Favorable For Island Author

Anthony Towne, author of The Bishop Pike Affair and The Death of the Living God, and year round resident of this Island, recently received exceptionally favorable reviews including one in Times magazine) for his latest novel Excerpts from the Diary of the Late God.

When he finished writing the book, Towne grew a beard and felt like Hemingway. When he finished reading the reviews, he kept the beard and now feels like God.

Island Winter Not Like a July Day

It got cold, all right. On January 9, the mercury slid to -2°, it hardly got above freezing for eight days and both harbors froze over. As for the January thaw, there just wasn't one.

It wasn't so bad, really. The snow-covered bluffs made a fine sight when the winter sun turned them golden as it sets toward Montauk. Sometimes, too, you could see Ken Rose and Al Northup, among

Sandra Swan

VOL. I, NO. 4 SERVING BLOCK ISLAND, RHODE ISLAND APRIL 1976

The Ocean View, 1976

On June 26, 1970, the first issue of ***The Block Island Times*** was published — with a headline decrying the attempt by a West Warwick legislator to build gambling casinos on Block Island to make it the "Las Vegas of the East." (That sorry fate was soon to befall the seaside resort of Atlantic City in New Jersey — and then, in the 1990s, the nearby woods of Connecticut.)

The Times was begun by summer resident Margaret Cabel Self — also a writer of equestrian books — as an affiliate of Dan's Papers, the conglomerate of small-town newspapers based on Long Island, 15 miles away.

The paper flourished in a multi-page format similar in size to the present version, with the indefatigable Mrs. Self being a one-person operation: writer, editor, photographer, darkroom developer, and distributor (see her photo, page 75, bottom).

A notable change came after 1982 when the editorship, and later the ownership, was turned over to Peter and Shirley Wood, who soon transformed the operation into a multi-person effort by Block Island residents of all categories: winter, summer, young and old — photographers, artists and writers bold.

The paper grew during that decade: in number of pages, number of issues, circulation off-Island, and improved layout by production artist Alan Clarke, whose contributions were often listed under various *noms de plume*.

The success of *The Times* during summers of the 1970s, suggested a need for a year-round newspaper.

The ***Ocean View*** — coming out on January 31, 1976, smack in the middle of winter — sought to fill the vacuum. Publisher Charles Gale gave the Island an inside look at its own workings, which were then a mystery to residents, except the few who could regularly attend virtually all the various town council and zoning board meetings.

The monthly effort lasted only until that summer, but managed to report to residents that they had been duped by the town council and by sewer committee engineers into approving a sewer plant that would cost three times the operating cost announced to voters, and require three employees not the single "part-time employee" claimed by the designer, Fenton Keyes. Initial problems with the deer and the dump were reported as well — issues still haunting Block Island 25 years later, with high costs in both money and health.

The *Ocean View* made a one-issue comeback for the summer of 1977, then succumbed to the logistics of newspaper production and off-Island printing.

In January 1983 another attempt at a year-round newspaper was made by the twice-monthly ***Block Island Reporter***. Owner and editor Howell Conant II published his work at another crucial period when mopeds, contaminated town water, and state highway guardrails raised their ugly heads. During that spring, Howell's professionally produced paper spurred Island citizens into action.

A photograph in the March 28 issue of a worker dumping black sludge from dead

THE BLOCK ISLAND
REPORTER
Block Island's Year Round Newspaper
Volume I, Number VII March 28, 1983

THE WOODEN TANK, NEARLY 100 YEARS OLD, THE SOURCE OF BACTERIA.

Town Water;
Contradictions, Speculation, Accusations

The Block Island Reporter, 1983

Page 4 April 9, 1983 BI Reporter

DISPITE ASSURANCES FROM TOWN AND STATE AUTHORITIES WORK CONTINUED AS THIS PHOTO TAKEN APRIL 1st SHOWS.

birds out of the private water tank at Sands Pond that supplied Old Harbor's homes and hotels, said it all about that company, then owned by a group of Island businessmen.

Reporter Suzanne Wagner's hard-hitting story on April 9, showed the high-handed ways of the state's Department of Transportation, which arrived unannounced on Block Island and began installing over 11,000 feet (more than two miles) of metal guardrails next to historic stonewalls. Not only unsightly and unneeded, the hated railings were often placed a foot from the pavement, forcing pedestrians to walk on the road in front of cars, as they still must do two decades later. Howell's lobbying and intervention, as editor of the *Reporter*, saved a few sections of the Island's scenic roads from this fate.

But by July, advertisers had realigned themselves for another summer with the still-seasonal *Block Island Times*, and the *Reporter* ceased operations.

A new paper, the ***Island Crier,*** appeared in the summer of 1992. The *Crier's* eight free issues were distributed on weeks opposite the biweekly free editions of *The Times*, which charged 25 cents for its other issues. Publisher Kevin Weaver operated in the do-it-yourself manner of most previous papers. In 1993 a fee of 35 cents was charged, and in 1996, the last summer of production, the *Crier* became the first and only Block Island newspaper published in full color.

The Block Island Crier
August 2nd-16th, 1996 Block Island, R.I.

The Block Island Crier, 1996

Mitchell Farm

Where the cows are on Corn Neck Road.

The *Crier* often depicted the Island through the eyes of the youthful “summer help” who work at the Island’s many tourist hotels, restaurants, and stores — a memorable part of one’s life to which many year-round residents trace wistfully their arrival on the Island.

One poignant article, though, was a Fourth-of-July 1994 interview with 89-year-old Eugenia Beane as she was packing up the summer home owned for 44 years. The isolated 23-acre peninsula at the entrance to Great Salt Pond had been confiscated and sold by the federal government after discovery on the property of marijuana plants grown by a son.

On January 16, 1997, *The Block Island Times* was sold to Jeff McDonough, owner of the *Jamestown Press*, published in Jamestown, Rhode Island. Kevin Weaver, a logical choice to be *The Times’* new editor, became just that. But layout and production facilities were moved off Block Island.

As a partial community protest — of sorts — another paper arose from people’s minds. The preview issue of ***The Block Island Beacon*** appeared on November 10, 1999, under the leadership of Steve McQueeny. Almost simultaneously, however, ownership of *The Block Island Times* was sold to Bruce Montgomery, a longtime summer resident familiar with the publishing world, who had established a year-round home.

The *Beacon* and the *Times* battled through the summer of 2000, each introducing new formats, columns, and features to the benefit of readers. The effect to advertisers, however, was a double-edged sword. They could, for instance, express dissatisfaction with one paper or the other — by carrying ads in only one paper, or the other. But conversely, they could never be quite sure if advertising dollars were spent wisely. And those who generously, and graciously, supported both papers, wondered how long such a situation could continue.

The *Beacon* folded first, with a final issue on September 28, 2000, leaving a legacy of inspired photographic images by staff member Rosemary Tobin, and fine articles by Fran Migliaccio. Fran’s work has appeared in several local publications for the past decade, and her numerous biographies of Islanders will be read by future historians.

As shown by *The Block Island Times’* year-round demand — and large winter mailing list — people want to know the news.

And although not all of *The Times’* unabashed, longstanding prejudices — such as refusing advertisements for noisy, injurious rental mopeds — have continued intact into the 21st century, awareness perseveres that the more people writing, thinking, and being read, the better any town will be.

THE BLOCK ISLAND TIMES 25¢

25¢ Vol. XXVIII No. 51 Saturday, December 19, 1998 Call 401-466-2222 / 466-8804 FAX 25¢

On The Block

Holiday ferry-schedule changes

Travelers take note that there is a special holiday ferry-schedule that is in effect from Dec. 21 through Dec. 27, with no service on Christmas Day.

School music department offers holiday program

The Block Island School will present a music program that will begin at 9 a.m. on Dec. 22, in the school gym. A variety of musical offerings

Planned ordinance would ease strict Old Harbor zoning rules

By Neva Flaherty

The Planning Board has decided to draft an ordinance providing more flexible zoning and parking rules for the Old Harbor Commercial District.

At its Monday meeting, the board voted to develop an ordinance containing a point system, as recommended by planning consultant Phil Herr. Herr’s plan, called “Village Compatible Development,” would give proposed commercial buildings points for design elements — Chairman Norris Pike said.

If a building met the prescribed point total, it could be built on a lot as small as 5,000 square feet, compared to the 20,000-square-foot minimum in the Old Harbor Commercial zone. Additionally, maximum lot coverage could increase from the current 75 percent to 90 percent.

Historic District Commission approval would still be required.

Alterations and additions to existing buildings also could use the point system.

Islanders with a penchant for writing or for news reporting did not always have a local newspaper available — but their efforts might be printed by a mainland paper.

The article on the right appeared in ***Cooley's Weekly*** of Norwich, Connecticut. Although inland on a river, Norwich was a terminus for passenger steamers to New York City, for trains to most anywhere in the United States, and for summertime ferries to Block Island.

The wedding recounted was that of Nellie Smith, age 21, to Jeremiah Littlefield, Jr., age 25. Nellie was the sister of writer Addie Smith, a founder of the Island's first newspaper, the ***Block Island Star*** (see page 135).

Because Addie had died 15 years earlier, at the age of 19 — when her sister Nellie was a six-year-old — we may imagine this wedding had added significance for the Smith parents.

The house in the story, on a lane off Corn Neck Road (plat 4, lot 19), is still in the family — passed down from Nellie and Jeremiah's son, fisherman Byron Littlefield — to his daughter, longtime Block Island town clerk in the 1970s and 80s, and first warden, Edith Littlefield Blane — who helped publish the ***Hooter*** in the late 1960s.

The wedding account was probably written by John Ed Littlefield (1853-1907), the author of many other Block Island articles printed by *Cooley's Weekly* during the 1890s. He had command of the descriptive term "electric blue," a color which must have seemed even more so on a bleak winter's evening.

John Ed's Cape Cod style home off Old Mill Road (plat 12, lot 8), became the residence of Peter Wood, who in the 1980s recast ***The Block Island Times*** from a six-issue free summer handout, into the Island's first year-round weekly newspaper — a conduit for many writing endeavors, ranging from news stories; to occasional columns; to happy letters-to-the-editor; and to other letters-to-the-editor that lit up many an issue, their authors presumably electric-blue in the face when they wrote them.

A Block Island Winter Wedding — 1892

from ***Cooley's Weekly*** of Norwich, Connecticut, December 20, 1892

ANOTHER MAGNIFICENT AND FASHIONABLE WEDDING came off on Tuesday evening of last week. The happy participants were Miss Nellie Smith, daughter of Mrs. Elizabeth Smith, and Jeremiah M. Littlefield, Jr., both of this town.

The happy event took place at the home of the bride, and a large concourse of invited friends and relatives were present to witness the happy ceremony and take part in the festivities which followed.

The home of Mrs. Smith had been elegantly decorated, and when the curtain of night closed about the handsome cottage the many lamps made the interior the wonder and admiration of all who beheld it. The lights sent forth from every window sparkling rays on the snow clad hills of Block Island, and the stars too shed their brilliant December lustre o'er this gay and festive assembly.

During the night of Dec. 19, and the day following, a furious north wind had been blowing, accompanied by a blinding storm of snow, which, however, cleared off in the afternoon — and the evening, though cold and breezy, was clear.

No one thought of cold, snow or the twisting northwest wind which was blowing. Some no doubt would have braved the storms of Siberia rather than miss this gorgeous display of matrimonial splendor. All seemed to keenly realize that this was an event not liable to soon occur again.

Early in the evening the cottage was thronged with guests dressed expressly for this special event. The gentlemen were in evening dress and ladies elegantly attired for the occasion. Rev. L.S. Brown, with whose name all our readers are familiar, was among the happy throng. As the time drew near for the bridal party to appear the throng seemed as if about to say, 'Behold the bridegroom', etc.

The ushers were John R. Payne, Jr., Simon R. Sheffield, Albert Smith and Otis P. Mott, Jr.

At 8 o'clock sharp the nuptial party entered the northwest parlor and took their station on a chenille rug in the centre of the room, Miss Clarissa A. Mott the while playing a wedding march. The marriage ceremony was performed according to the Baptist church services by Pastor Brown.

The bride was elegantly attired in an imported suit of electric blue silk, trimmed with plush, same shade, and steel passementerie, with white satin front and white chiffon lace at the neck and sleeves. Her floral decorations were wondrous, composed of white pinks, white rose buds and smilax.

The presents were numerous, costly and useful. There was table ware, chamber furnishing, handsome pictures and knick-knacks, in both silver and gold.

A magnificent wedding supper was served by Mrs. Otis P. Mott, Jr., Mrs. Ezra Smith and Mrs. Albert Smith, who also acted as waiters, assisted by Otis P. Mott, Jr., Albert Smith and John R. Payne, Jr., all of whom were dressed in accordance with, and expressly for the occasion.

May this worthy pair have many years of joy and happiness.

Looking down Beacon Hill Road, at intersection with Center Road, from left to right:

- **Blacksmith shop** (long gone)
- **Town Hall / High School** (moved from cemetery; built 1814, burned 1923) — see pages 42, 98
- **First Baptist Church** (built 1857, burned 1908)
- **Alvin Sprague's store** (still exists, now an apartment building)

CHAPTER 15

Complaints of the distant past

and a word of warning about One-eyed Islanders and Promiscuous Houses

EVERY TWO YEARS when aspiring political office holders settle into formal face-offs for the November election, they point out what is wrong with the Island — attempting to convince voters which of the candidates are seemingly the most rational.

Usually these problems will have been around for years, unsolved by previous town council members, some of whom cater to the agendas of a minority, rather than serving the best interests of the general public.

Only the brave or innocent town council candidate will actually suggest how to fix a problem. If he is elected but is insincere, then he has no intention of following through on his promise — and is on the council for the next two years simply to preserve some hidden status quo. If he is elected and is honest, he knows that the less caring town council members will vote against him and — ironically — he will be the one blamed by the uninformed public for not delivering on a campaign promise.

If all goes as usual, the men or women who are elected will fail to correct most of the Island's problems — and other aspirants two years hence will repeat the cycle, complaining stridently once again. Who runs this town anyway?

Least we should run out of ideas for these complaints — or the general phrases to express them (just fill in the blank with an appropriate problem) — history can help. Note amongst the following examples the increasing stridency of those whose viewpoints are regularly ignored, as first they test their persuasive powers using logic and humor, then sarcasm, culminating in a futile casting to the wind of words when no one seems to listen or care.

The first complaint by Europeans about Block Island was that the Island did not have a natural harbor. As related in an account of 1669, just seven years after the Island was settled by 16 families from Massachusetts: "It wants a Harbour."

That complaint remained valid for 200 more years — probably the Island record for longevity and one not to inspire confidence that the town council will solve the current most pressing complaints: the two-fold danger to our health from deer and mopeds.

The most handy complaints in history — for no one really expected them to succeed — were the ancient "protests" filed by shipwrecked crew members, whose duty after losing their ship was to locate a local government official and lodge a complaint against the weather. So it was with the most famous shipwreck episode on Block Island, that began as a voyage to transport Palatine emigrants from Germany. After losing his vessel, the PRINCESS AUGUSTA, on the Island's shore in December 1737, the captain of that wrecked vessel sought out Island warden Simon Ray, who duly recorded:

"He came ashore and desired to protest timely which complaint I accordingly accepted."

Upon reaching Newport in January 1738, the captain was able to remonstrate once more in the required manner, with the aid of a notary public this time, who wrote:

"I the said Notary did & do Hereby solemnly & publicly protest against the Boisterous Winds & Seas, the thick Snow Storms & Extremity of Cold as the Cause of the said Ship PRINCESS AUGUSTA running a Shore upon said New Shoram alias Block Island ..."

Other problems existed on Block Island that were more easily remedied, for it was humans who had caused them. The respected scientist Charles T. Jackson in his *Report on the Geological and Agricultural Survey of the State of Rhode Island*, published in 1840, discussed one unfortunate town policy, that of shipping rounded beach stones to the mainland:

Beacon Hill Road leading to the old Center, 1877

The Island's infrastructure was ill-prepared when the town suddenly embraced tourism in the early 1870s. Roads in particular, suitable only for ox-carts during the previous two centuries, were heavily criticized by riders of horse-buggies.

This photo is one-half of a stereoview made by Thomas Lewis of Cambridgeport, Massachusetts. One building (extreme right) still survives of the four then visible at the town's old Center.

"They ... are much sought for to be used as paving stones, large cargoes being frequently taken away to furnish pavements for the streets of New York. The Town of New Shoreham owns the privilege and sells the right of obtaining them. I should, however, consider it ruinous policy to allow their removal, for they constitute an important barrier against the encroachments of the ocean."

Although the practice ceased, the mentality did not. The town council needed to pass an ordinance 130 years later, in the mid-1970s, to stop privately owned dump trucks on Block Island from audaciously removing vast quantities of the same beach stones from Scotch Beach for use in the septic systems of new summer houses. And the town council holding office in 1998 proposed selling the very beauty of Block Island — to various cellular telephone and radio companies, by letting them build another large tower, well over 200 feet high, on the Island — all to benefit mainland customers of these companies, despite promise after promise, and obligation after obligation, having been broken in the past.

Major opportunities for complaints — enough to base a political career on — came with the rise of tourism on Block Island in the 1870s. The breakwater was finally built creating a harbor, hotels were constructed, then enlarged each year to match the growing number of steamship arrivals, and Islanders and mainlanders got to know each other for the first time since the 1600s.

Sometimes the introductions could be awkward, as reflected in the comments of a noted writer of popular history, Samuel Drake, who described Block Island in 1875:

"The island, having no rock foundation, is constantly wasting away. Cottages of wood, whitewashed every spring, are scattered promiscuously over the island, with wretched roads or lanes to accommodate every dwelling. The total disappearance of the island has often been predicted, and I recollect when the impression prevailed to some extent on the main-land that the islanders had only an eye apiece."

Maybe Islanders had covered one eye over during the first few years that tourists came, so they would see them only half as much.

Mainlanders might have covered their eyes as well; they did need to hold their noses. In the *Block Island Handbook,* written in 1877 by Connecticut author Ben Mush, appears a remarkably honest section titled "First Impressions of the Island Unfavorable." The present-day Chamber of Commerce would cringe at such forthrightness, even though they could, if they wished, give visitors of today more important advisories than those felt necessary 120 years ago:

"Cottages of wood, whitewashed every spring, are scattered promiscuously over the island ...

"I recollect when the impression prevailed to some extent on the main-land that the islanders had only an eye apiece."
— 1875

The Block Island Handbook, 1877

"A word of warning may not be out of place. The landing is not an attractive looking neighborhood; and what with its appearance, odor emanating from the fish curing houses, the warmth and the dusty roads, one's first impression of the place ... is often unfavorable to the island ..."

But Block Island readers — the practical farmers and fisherman — undoubtedly discounted *all* of the author's comments as irrelevant after perusing his final list of suggestions:

"A Few Practical Hints:
"Bear in mind that the moist sea air will shrink your woolens perceptibly,
"Expect your scissors and other steel trinkets to rust somewhat,
"Unless you are particular, bring a lot of paper collars and cuffs; the dampness will take the starch out of your linen."

Although Block Island underwent great changes in the next twenty years, reaching at the turn-of-the-century the peak of prosperity and population (about 1,300 year-round residents in 1900, compared to 850 throughout the 1990s), gripes were still forthcoming.

When things are going well, people begin complaining more and more about the minutia of life --- usually a good sign. Not only do they have nothing worse to worry about, but there really are more things that go wrong in a complex society, even one that functions well in general.

These complaints from the Victorian age are mostly taken from the twice-weekly summer newspaper *Mid-Ocean* (see photos and text, pages 134, 136).

The Manisses Hotel and wooden sidewalk on Spring Street, ca. 1902

Wooden Sidewalks a Hazard

***Mid-Ocean*, August 4, 1897:**

"The old plank walks around Harbor Village are in a bad condition, in dangerous condition. They require constant care on the part of the solitary pedestrian even during the day. In the case of a group walking closely together, such care is impracticable; in the night it is impossible."

***Mid-Ocean*, July 13, 1901:**

"The plank walks here would be, perhaps, of some value as food for kitchen fires, though even that is doubtful."

***Mid-Ocean*, August 10, 1901:**

"The main street along the harbor front should be widened and a plank walk twenty feet wide built along its front ..."

[High-priced consultants have said the same in their reports of the 1970s, 1980s and 1990s, showing it might be cheaper to just make the improvements in the first place, instead of paying for recycled advice.]

***Mid-Ocean*, August 21, 1901:**

"If that sidewalk on High Street does not involve the town in a suit for damages it will be strange. Last Sunday, while going to breakfast, the editor saw a lady, one of a group of them, while coming down the street, fall off the walk, to which there is no railing. She landed on her head and shoulders in the ditch more than five feet below."

High Street.

High Street's wooden sidewalk, ca. 1910:

Citizens lobbied for decades in the late 1800s for wooden sidewalks — finally built up High Street, up Spring Street, and along Water Street — then spent years criticizing their upkeep. In 1903 a 1,320-foot concrete sidewalk was laid up Spring Street, paid for by three hotels — but that no longer exists.

There is still no sidewalk from Old Harbor to New Harbor — and Corn Neck Road has been reduced in the summer to a three-mile slalom course of zagging pedestrians and zigging vehicles, each fighting every foot of the way to create their own constantly changing pathway.

Meanwhile for 18 years the poorly placed metal guardrails installed by the state with no announcement in 1983, besides being unsightly, prevent pedestrians from walking on the road's shoulder, forcing them instead onto the pavement in the way of traffic (see photos, page 141). The town council does nothing.

Roads in Poor Shape

***A Guide to Narragansett Bay*, 1878:**

"The drives will not favorably impress the stranger, although they are far better than they were last year. In order to reach many of the points of interest, you are obliged to alight from your carriage and take bars down and open gate-ways, as the points you desire to reach are on private grounds. The roads are either hilly and stony or of soft sand, and as might be supposed are not watered save by the heavens."

***Providence Dispatch*, July 27, 1879:**

"The execrable roads have the advantage of forcing the pedestrian to strike out for himself in a bee-line for his point of destination, over walls and fences . . . The Islander evidently thinks that the roads are good enough for horses and oxen. Sidewalks are unknown, and one readily deserts the narrow dusty, crooked roads for the cool, dry turf above. One of the funniest sights can be seen here, we mean an ox harnessed singly to a cart. There is not much necessity of hurrying . . ."

***Mid-Ocean*, August 21, 1901:**

"There has been much unpleasant criticism by patrons of the hotels and cottagers over the condition of roads at a distance from Harbor Village. For some unknown reason the usual spring repairs were not made, or at least were made very imperfectly and the result is that nearly all the highways except the new macadam road are in a much worse condition than usual." [Ocean Avenue was made with macadam in 1895 to link Old Harbor with New Harbor, and for two decades was the only paved road.]

Steamship Passengers Harassed

A Providence Newspaper, 1878:

Block Island hackmen are getting noisy and turbulent and there is just cause of complaint. It was to be hoped that at least one landing place could be found where travelers could go on shore in peace, and that place should be here. It would add another to the many attractions of the island.

***Mid-Ocean*, July 9, 1895:**

The scene on the dock: passengers are hustled this way and that, while a perfect Babel of shouts greet their ears, the thirty or more hotels each having from one to half a dozen runners, until one wonders the visitors don't go back on board the boat, hire a stateroom and lock themselves in. Runners leap on board while the passengers are coming off if they can escape the eyes of the busy officers and solicit patronage, forcing their way into the crowd, stepping on ladies' dresses, pushing over little children and making a nuisance of themselves generally ... It simply has the effect of offending and disgusting visitors, and should be stopped."

Roads Dusty

***Mid-Ocean*, July 23, 1895:**

"The editor was a modest factor in pushing the business of securing a watering cart here early in the season ... Everybody supposed that the cart would be here ere this. Granted that the first half of July was so wet as not to need it, the next month will probably be so dry as to make it a necessity. It is needed badly today, will probably be needed worse tomorrow, and be one of the features that we badly need, but don't have, by the close of the week. Please order by telegraph wire, gentlemen of the committee."

***Mid-Ocean*, August 8, 1896:**

"It is dust, dust everywhere and not a sprinkling cart in sight. Are we so stuck on Block Island that we want it all stuck on us? Why, for the past week, whenever there was a breeze, and as everybody who has ever visited Block Island knows there generally is one here, one could scarcely breathe on Water street. Why not put on a sprinkling cart? We will all subscribe for it. Kind Heaven has been good to us in the way of storms buy we cannot expect them to come always at just the right time."

An artist's complaint

by J. Harris Knowles

Block Island, August 10, 1901

The crystal sea smiled at me
 As I tried to paint its tints;
Its vision of deed mystery,
 Its gleams and pearly glints.

"You cannot catch my beauty,"
 It seemed to say to me.
"I vary with each moment,
 E'en while you look and see.

"I change, and gleam, and glisten,
 Go, paint me in your heart,
The memory of my beauty,
 Will be better than all art."

Humbled, I tore my sketch to shreds,
 I looked upon the sea;
In thought the smiling, shining deep
 Will ever be with me.

Horses and buggies awaiting passengers at Old Harbor Dock, ca. 1900

Hackmen for hire, and from the Island's many hotels, invariably jostled for the attention of customers in the early decades of Block Island's tourism, creating an unfavorable first impression to visitors of Block Island.

A similar problem has occurred on Block Island since the early 1980s — the hucksterism of moped rental dealers. Standing on the sidewalks, imploring visitors who are straight-off-the-boat to rent the dangerous two-wheel vehicles, the moped dealers' carnival-like solicitations of complete strangers degrades the Island — and themselves.

The distant steamer is the side-wheel MOUNT HOPE from Providence. On the right is the much smaller GEORGE W. DANIELSON, running from Newport.

Cars awaiting* MOUNT HOPE *passengers at Old Harbor Dock, 1923

Meeting the steamer* BLOCK ISLAND *(later the* YANKEE*) at Old Harbor Dock, 1940

"Block Island Police Station and Prison"

Postcard, postmarked 1914

The act of viewing the old jail seems to have tapped into the part of observers' brains controlling humor — as happened to the writer of this purposely pompous postcard caption. Affected also were several of the men on the jail's porch, three of whom, in uniforms, appear to be lifesavers from the old life-saving station on the opposite side of Corn Neck Road (now site of Beachhead).

No one knows exactly when, around the turn-of-century, the jail was erected, but the first uniformed policeman was felt to be necessary in August 1901, as reported in the *Mid-Ocean*:

"By order of the town council Block Island now has a policeman, a uniformed officer whose duty it is to preserve order and look out for malefactors ... Mr. A. Chandler Littlefield has been appointed the police force and his first appearance in uniform upon the streets on Monday caused considerable staring. The police force wears a helmet and brass buttoned coat and carries a formidable 'billy.'"

Block Island needed a force of only one until the 1970s when the police department burgeoned — even making cars park all in one direction along the sides of roads.

Besides hiring numerous part-time summer policemen, the police department proceeded to transform itself into a year-round industry, with two permanent year-round officers — then an additional staff of year-round dispatchers, then three year-round officers, then in 1998 a request, granted, for a fourth permanent officer — even though the year-round population in 1900 was 1,300 people; and in the 1990s, only 850.

A derelict jail, July 1927

***Mid-Ocean*, July 20, 1901:**

"On nasty, rainy, foggy days, when there is no more need for a street sprinkler than Hades has for a powder-house, the man with his little squirt wagon persists in saturating our main thoroughfares with Sand's Pond juice to the discomfiture of pedestrians, teamsters and bicyclists. On the other hand when the day is dry and dusty, and the winds of Heaven threaten to blow the Island over to South Africa, bodily, this same street sprinkler is conspicuous for its absence."

Dangerous Ball Playing In Streets

***Mid-Ocean*, August 17, 1901:**

"There are many complaints of base ball playing in the public streets and reports of narrow escapes from serious injuries to pedestrians."

Garbage Dumped On Beach

***Mid-Ocean*, August 23, 1890:**

"We desire to protest in behalf of public health, and common decency against the dumping of swill and garbage on the beach between the sea and the Neck road. The stench from it on the beach with a westerly wind, or on the road with an easterly wind is almost unbearable. We don't know whom this hits, and we don't want to know, but we do hope that those who are innocent will create a public sentiment in the matter that will do away with such an abomination."

***Mid-Ocean*, July 6, 1895:**

"Would it not be wise for the hotels to take some concerted action regarding the dumping of tin cans, bottles, barrels, boxes etc., on the borders of the Neck road ...? Employees sent down after dark or early in the morning to dump this litter, drop it in the most convenient place, regardless of the regulations posted up ... Let us by all means have this nuisance abated."

***Mid-Ocean*, August 20, 1895:**

"It is probably useless to call attention to the fact that a few dollars expended in putting up an awning on Crescent Beach in front of the bath houses would be highly appreciated by spectators or to suggest that the dumping of garbage on the beach in the sight and smell of guests and citizens is in violation of an ordinance which could be and should be enforced."

***Mid-Ocean*, August 25, 1896:**

"We are again most unwillingly compelled to call the attention of the public to the fact that swill and offal from the hotels is being dumped on the beach and ... the stench is offensive to the bathers on Crescent Beach. It must be conceded that the usual heterogeneous collection of tin cans, barrels, bottles, broken crockery, glass ware, etc., which usually decorates the roadside, is not so conspicuous as in past years, but the fact is that, if the town is to allow kitchen refuse, etc., to be dumped upon its beaches it should insist upon its being properly covered up."

***Mid-Ocean*, August 4, 1897:**

"In the name of common decency, is there not some way to stop the dumping of refuse from the hotels, bandboxes, papers, bottles, broken dishes, etc., alongside the Neck road ... within ten feet of the roadway ... a nuisance which should be abated if it has to be done with a shotgun."

***Mid-Ocean*, August 14, 1897:**

"Once more, is that nuisance on the Neck road off Crescent Beach, to be abated or not ...? Is nobody but the *Mid-Ocean* interested in the case?"

Noise At Night

***Mid-Ocean*, July 4, 1896:**

"No more midnight orgies. No more drunken rows and ribald songs along the streets during the small hours of morning — we hope."

***Mid-Ocean*, August 21, 1901:**

"Fun is fun, but it can be carried too far. Few people except cranks object to young people having a good time, and at shore resorts the hours are somewhat elastic, but what particular pleasure a party of half drunken roysterers can find in singing and shouting on the street and keeping people, that need sleep, awake until 2:00 am or 3:00 am is one of those things which no feller of ordinary common sense can find out."

Ballard's Inn at Old Harbor dock, 1977

The Town of New Shoreham's dock, located next to Ballard's Inn, became an unsavory place for families during recent decades. Here, summer revelers with beers in hand carouse on the Inn's balcony, spilling over into the street, onto the dock and surrounding property.

A comparable problem exists today when bars — with the blessing of the police and town council who could stop the policy — play loud amplified music until closing time at 1:00 am (instead of stopping the music at 12:30 am) and then force all their patrons onto the street within a 5-minute period. The resulting yelling and boisterous antics by party-goers who had been drinking and dancing up to the very moment the bars close, wake up residents and hotel guests as the throngs pass through Old Harbor's streets.

Drugs and Medicines

Waiting in front of the old drugstore

The horse car was a viable means of transportation, from harbor to harbor, ferry to hotel, and hotel to beach — shown here next to the present-day *Inn at Old Harbor*. A portion of the horse is visible on the extreme left.

(Also see postcard, page 161; and photo, page 200.)

CHAPTER 16

The Block Island Horse Cars

More than just a ride

IN LESS THAN **20** YEARS, from 1898 to 1916, the horse cars on Block Island passed from luxury to novelty to oblivion — and 20 years after that, to perhaps an even worse fate in Spain.

So complete was the demise of the once popular vehicles, that at the time of the Spanish Civil War in 1937, one of the Island's two horse cars was shipped to the mainland as scrap metal — presumably to be sent overseas in the form of an artillery shell or two — causing Island philosophers of the Depression era to ponder which is more fatal, getting struck in the head by a bullet or an ancient transportation wagon.

Like a politician, the horse cars began with a promise and ended with a lie, but had a heck of a lot of fun along the way.

In the mid-1890s a mainland group of businessmen told Block Islanders they would build a rail line and run trolley cars in the summer from Old Harbor to New Harbor. Electricity would be supplied by overhead wires. When, instead, three horse-drawn cars were brought here for the initial year in 1898 — already worn out from years of duty on the streets of Providence — the ambitiously-named "Island Light and Transportation Company" proclaimed them as just a temporary solution for a problem they had encountered: the Island had no electricity.

There was, in fact, to be no Island-wide electricity for another 27 years.

Tracks were laid for about a mile and a half from the town dock in Old Harbor to what is now Payne's Dock in New Harbor, following the scenic route by the beach. The rails took up part of the right side of the road when viewed by passengers traveling from Old to New Harbor.

In 1899 the Island's first important newspaper — the semiweekly, summertime *Mid-Ocean* — reported on the new enterprise in its issue of July 5: "The cars of the street railway are now making regular trips and visitors find them a great convenience in passing between the two landings or in reaching Crescent Beach."

The horse cars took less than 15 minutes from harbor to harbor — depending on whether passengers disembarked to push the car up the hill from New Harbor. About halfway between the harbors a switch let the two cars pass, since one car was usually coming from Old Harbor as another approached from New Harbor. From 9:20 a.m. to 11:00 p.m. each summer day the system operated.

When asked about the electric trolleys that were planned to replace the horse-drawn cars, the Island Light & Transportation Company would respond "wait until next year." As late as July 20, 1901, the *Mid-Ocean* foretold the car line was "soon to be operated by electricity."

Was Block Island behind the times? Yes. In mainland Rhode Island towns, horse cars had been used since 1864, a year before the Civil War ended — and electric trolleys had operated since 1889. But no one on Block Island seemed to mind not having the very latest system.

On August 7, 1901, the *Mid-Ocean* reported: "The horse cars are running full a large part of the day and during the evening it is difficult to secure standing room."

Said the *Mid-Ocean* on August 21. "If the cars are not making money this summer, the route had better be abandoned, as the cars are crowded most of the time from 9 a.m. to 11 p.m.."

After the 1901 season, there were no more aspirations announced in public to electrify the route. The daytime popularity of the beaches, the necessity of humans to wish always to see the "other" — in this case the "other harbor" — and the nightlife engendered by the several hotels that featured orchestras had made the horse cars extremely successful.

And then there was the amusement of just riding the cars for themselves. A succinct message written on the back of a postcard depicting an Island horse car, implied the excitement and informality of taking a ride: "You should ask for a job as conductor down here. You don't even have to wear a suit and when you go round corners you have to hang on with two hands."

On July 25, 1903, the *Mid-Ocean* remarked with a sense of pique: "Beginning next week the three cars will be on and will run on schedule time instead of according to the driver's convenience."

Whatever was the local problem, and no matter how great might be any future improvement to the horse cars, their ultimate doom was spelled out within another article just inches higher in the same column. The future would proffer a way of life so different — so unneedful of horse cars, or horses at all — that few who read it would have guessed the extent of the change underway:

"Mrs. Hattie S. Osborne, of New York City, a guest at the Ocean View, has made an application for a license to run an automobile and hers is expected at the Island in a few days."

Hers was not the first automobile on the Island. Another had been brought here previously by an Island store owner, as explained in the *Mid-Ocean* article:

"Mr. C. C. Ball has not been using his auto lately and is hoping that another one will come to the Island that the horses may become accustomed to it before he takes his out. Mr. Ball did not buy his auto for use on the Island, however, but is contemplating taking an automobile trip through the country after the season closes."

There were a lot of horses that needed to be "accustomed" to the new future, and the process would be a lengthy one — the use of horse cars continued for a dozen more years. A more immediate acclimatizing was needed by the Block Island tourist — just to figure out when the next horse car would come and take him or her away. The *Mid-Ocean* obliged them with an explanation on August 1, 1903:

"The two horse cars went on duty last Saturday and have been running ever since. While the summer visitors here have never doubted that the cars run on schedule time, still, according to the inquires made at the *Mid-Ocean* office, they have never been able to find out what the schedule is."

A sequence of daily times then followed, listing when the horse cars theoretically departed from New Harbor and Old Harbor. Looking like a mathematical puzzle for an IQ test, the *Mid-Ocean* attempted to spare readers from pondering the logic behind the listings by explaining:

"The cause of the irregular intervals of first 15 then 25 minutes between cars is caused by the necessity of their passing on certain switches. Twelve horses are used on these two cars. A span is used for two hours, then taken off and allowed to rest four, before being used again. The cars leaving from 9:20 a.m. to 12 noon, and from 3:35 to 4:15 p.m., stop at the bathing beach."

The horse cars were a success. They were never electrified. They were just too much fun as they were — for riders and onlookers, as one viewer noted in 1905:

"While looking out our office window the other day, we saw a woman get off a street car in the proper manner. We often wonder why it is that so few women know how to get off a car. We suppose it is just about as sensible as asking 'Why is a hen?' and as little likely to receive an answer.

"The average woman in getting off a car, grasps the rail, wheels around in a semi-circle until she faces the rear platform, and steps off. If the car happens to be at a complete standstill, all is serene; but if it has not quite come to a full stop, the

"You should ask for a job as conductor down here.
"You don't even have to wear a suit and when you go round corners you have to hang on with two hands."

— Aug. 13, 1909

"'Why is a hen?"

— 1905

New Harbor Pavilion,

Restaurant and Wine Room,

End of Car Track==New Harbor,

EMILE SONTAG, Proprietor.

Shore Dinner Served, Beginning at 12:30 p. m.

A Special Feature will be our Evening Lunches of BROILED LIVE LOBSTER and other delicacies, ICE CREAM, FRUIT, ETC.

Special attention paid to orders of private parties.

FEW CAN RIVAL, NONE CAN SURPASS THE

WINE SERVICE either in quality or in the methods of serving.

Imported and Domestic Cigars, kept dry and fit to smoke.

A pleasant evening ride from East Harbor Village.

A LA CARTE at all hours.

Ad for New Harbor Pavilion, 1901

The New Harbor Pavilion was replaced in the 1930s by the Dead Eye Dick's building. The ad noted that this was the "End of Car Track" and "A pleasant evening ride from East Harbor Village" — which came to be known as Old Harbor.

woman receives a jerk backward which lands her in a heap in the street. The only wonder is that this does not happen more frequently."

"Occasionally an athletic girl comes along and swings off the car as dexterously as a man. When this occurs it is sure to attract comment, while the other form of exit is too common to cause more than a passing smile."

The summer of 1916 was the last the horse cars ran. Automobiles were everywhere.

Over the next two decades many of the tracks were recycled, some in dock construction and some to reinforce the vault in the town hall. One small section could be seen next to the Beach Avenue bridge until 1997 when the bridge was replaced.

In 1925, more than a quarter-century after Island Light and Transportation Company promised to do so, someone else strung wires and erected poles — and the Island went electric, a decade after the last horse car had stopped running.

During the winter of 1936-37, scrap metal prices rose on the mainland. Germany had been arming itself for several years and was now practicing on Spain for the second World War, which many European countries suspected would soon come.

Day after day during that winter, and week after week, piles of old metal appeared on the Old Harbor dock waiting to be shipped off: broken mowing machines, harrows, boilers, rusty parts of condemned cars, the metal parts of vessels wrecked on the beaches in previous decades — everything imaginable. More than 100 tons of scrap were shipped off by January 1937.

It was said if you drove an older car down to meet the ferry and left it for a few minutes, off it would go with the junk.

The metal was sent to a Providence dealer who separated the iron from the steel. Islanders said steel was just iron with a college education because it had been refined so to speak.

After several weeks of such activity the ferry captain claimed the Island rose six inches out of the ocean and could be seen 15 minutes quicker than ever before.

But the horse cars would never be seen here again.

A good story, though, like a good ride, should not end so soon:

In the late 1930s the great Spanish painter Picasso produced one of history's well-known works of art, a massive abstract image named for the bombed town of Guernica in Spain. When the painting was brought to New York several years ago to fill an entire wall at the Museum of Modern Art, curators touching up the surface noticed a sub-image, apparently painted over during Picasso's early stages of work. Removing the superficial top layer, they were in awe to discover amongst the braying heads of terrified horses and the ruins of the town, what was later identified as a rendition of a Block Island horse car, just tumbled from the sky, sitting harmlessly and intact in the road.

The Picasso story is actually not true, of course.

But it is factual that the horse cars were a good ride. And unlike today's notorious moped rental dealers, who have literally bled more than 1,000 tourists and broken many a bone, the horse cars never had a reputation for hurting people.

A postcard tour from New Harbor to Old Harbor by horse car, ca. 1907

One end of the horse car line — the New Harbor dock

During summers just after 1900, in one of the Island's busiest decades, four ferries berthed in New Harbor at the present-day Payne's Dock. Approaching on the left of this view is the steamer **BLOCK ISLAND**, arriving from Norwich, Connecticut, via New London and Watch Hill.

Already at the dock, from left to right, are the small steamer **GEORGE W. DANIELSON**, from Newport; the **NEW SHOREHAM**, from Providence via Newport; and the **SHINNECOCK**, an overnight steamer from New York City. Lined up, ready to take the disembarking tourists on the mile-and-a-half trip to Old Harbor, were horse-drawn buggies, some sent by hotels, and some for hire as cabs. Just out of view on the right, where the dock met Ocean Avenue, were the rails of the horse car line.

The New Harbor Pavilion

The building pictured here — with two full stories facing Ocean Avenue — was later torn down, and the now familiar, but smaller, Dead Eye Dick's restaurant erected in its place in the mid-1930s.

Mid-Ocean newspaper, August 19, 1903:

"Last Sunday afternoon as the car was going down the hill in front of the Hygeia [to the New Harbor dock] at a moderate pace, one of the horses stumbled and fell. In spite of the fact that the car was heavily loaded, having 63 passengers at the time, the driver brought it to a stand-still before it had gone more than half its length. Before it could be stopped, however, it pushed the horse a few feet along the track and cut one of his legs.

"He was removed from the track and taken up to the barn while a fresh one was put in his place. As there were six minutes left in which to catch the boat, the passengers had plenty of time and suffered no inconvenience. This is the first accident of the kind that has occurred since the cars have been running here."

Looking down Ocean Ave., back toward the New Harbor dock

The rails for the horse car ran on the far right-hand side of the road. A wide sidewalk now occupies this space. Sometimes passengers would have to alight coming up this hill, and give a helping hand to the horses with a good push on the back of the horse car. If a viewer turned around while standing on this spot, the Hygeia Hotel would have been visible — as in the next postcard of this series.

The Hygeia Hotel, with a horse car turning left on Beach Avenue, heading toward Crescent Beach

The Hygeia Hotel — which burned to the ground in 1916, the same year the horse cars stopped running — was a grand landmark for tourists proceeding up or down the hill to New Harbor. The present-day fire/police station was built on the site in 1970.

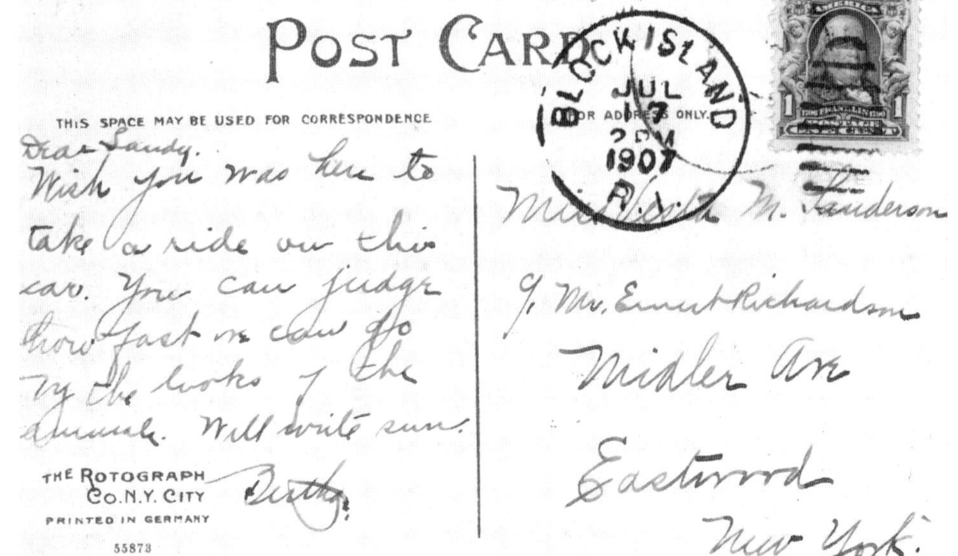
POST CARD

THIS SPACE MAY BE USED FOR CORRESPONDENCE

Dear Sandy.
Wish you was here to
take a ride on this
car. You can judge
how fast we can go
by the looks of the
animals. Will write soon.
Bertha

THE ROTOGRAPH
CO. N.Y. CITY
PRINTED IN GERMANY
55873

FOR ADDRESS ONLY

BLOCK ISLAND JUL 17 2 PM 1907 R.I.

Miss [illegible] M. Sanderson
c/o Mr. Ernest Richardson
Midler Ave
Eastwood
New York.

The old bathing pavilion on Corn Neck Road, opposite the intersection with Beach Avenue

The postcard's title "Rapid Transit at Block Island" is in jest. The true nature of the horse cars is revealed by the handwritten message on the back, dated July 17, 1907:

"Dear Sandy, wish you was here to take a ride on this car. You can judge how fast we can go by the looks of the animals."

A short spur of tracks led from the main horse car line into the midst of the bath houses, where a turnaround area was provided. This bathing pavilion was located a few hundred yards south of the present State Beach building, and was removed when the state made plans to build their facility shortly after World War II.

Rolling along by the sand dunes at Crescent Beach, a perfect sunset

Horse car at Yellow Kittens

More than just a few passengers have disembarked for long stretches at the famous Yellow Kittens — shown here with a rooftop advertisement for "Beer" and "Ale"

To allow the horse cars to pass each other while going in different directions, a switch and siding were built in the tracks at the Yellow Kittens.

Another siding was located in front of the Hygeia Hotel at New Harbor.

Horse car on Dodge Street

On Dodge Street, pedestrians coming down the steps of the former John Rose & Co. Hardware Store (in the left foreground, for the past decade the home of Juice & Java coffee shop), could almost hop onto the horse car without touching the sidewalk .

The horse car is visible on the left side of the road, with the cupola-topped National Hotel in the distance on the right.

The rails on Dodge Street, approaching corner by the Surf and National hotels

The horse car rails are on the left, passing in front of a corner of the Public Market's porch, which was given its now familiar brick facade about 1930. The white building is the Blue Dory Inn, built in 1897.

On the right, a horse and buggy wait in front of the porch of Darius Dodge's drug store, built in 1889 — the open porch was filled in with partitions in the 1980s when the building was turned into apartments called Gables II. Just beyond the buggy, and on its right, is the dark roof of Lester Dodge's house, which was torn down in the early 1970s to build the Island Free Library with funds he left to the town.

Block Island, R. I. - Surf Hotel

The Surf Hotel

For the final sweep onto the main street of Old Harbor, horse cars arriving from New Harbor and the beach would come from the left around this curve, passing in front of the multi-gabled Surf Hotel. The glorious Surf achieved its spectacular look in segments — the two-story gambrel roofed section was built in 1873; the three-story center section with the cupola, in 1884; and the four-story left section, in 1888. If the viewer of this scene turned around, the image on the next postcard would be visible.

View from Surf Hotel, Block Island, R. I.

Sidewalk and twin rails of the horse car, leading down Old Harbor's Water Street

On the left, the Ocean View Hotel — with a length more than twice that of the Spring House — looms over Old Harbor. In the distant center, the tower of the Adrian House pokes skyward, one appropriate reason the hotel is now the First Baptist Church. And on the extreme right is the porch corner of the National Hotel, whose massive bulk casts an even larger shadow across Water Street.

The vacant lot next to the National was created by the disastrous fire of the summer of 1902, when five structures were destroyed, two of them hotels: the first National and the Narragansett House (see photo, page 111). The New National was built during the next winter, opening for the summer of 1903.

The vacant lot was filled-in with the present-day Water Street Inn (built in 1910 as the Mechanics Building), and the building that now houses Phelan Real Estate and the Book Nook (built in 1912 as a post office) — see photos page 113.

The three-story mansard-roofed building visible just beyond the vacant lot was erected as the Ocean Cottage in 1887, but has been known since the 1960s as the New Shoreham House.

Front Street, Block Island, R. I.

"Front Street" — now called Water Street, Old Harbor

Present-day names of the buildings, from left to right, are (1) the Seaside Market, which now resembles a huge box, (2) Star Department Store, (3) the Ice Cream Place, (4) Harborside Inn, (5) New Shoreham House, (6) National Hotel, and at the very end of the street (7) the Surf Hotel.

If the viewer turned around, the image on the following postcard would be seen.

Waiting for the return trip to New Harbor, passengers pose in front of Old Harbor's drug store

Having just come up the hill from the town dock, where ferries from Providence and Newport landed, a horse car waits in front of the present-day *Inn at Old Harbor*.

More than 60 passengers could fit aboard the horse car — either hanging on outside or squeezed inside — for the open-air trip to Crescent Beach and New Harbor. Note that tourists of the Victorian era were consistently well-dressed — no tee-shirts, casual shorts, or their equivalent (also see photos, pages, 152, 200).

• *For another image of a horse car — see page 121*

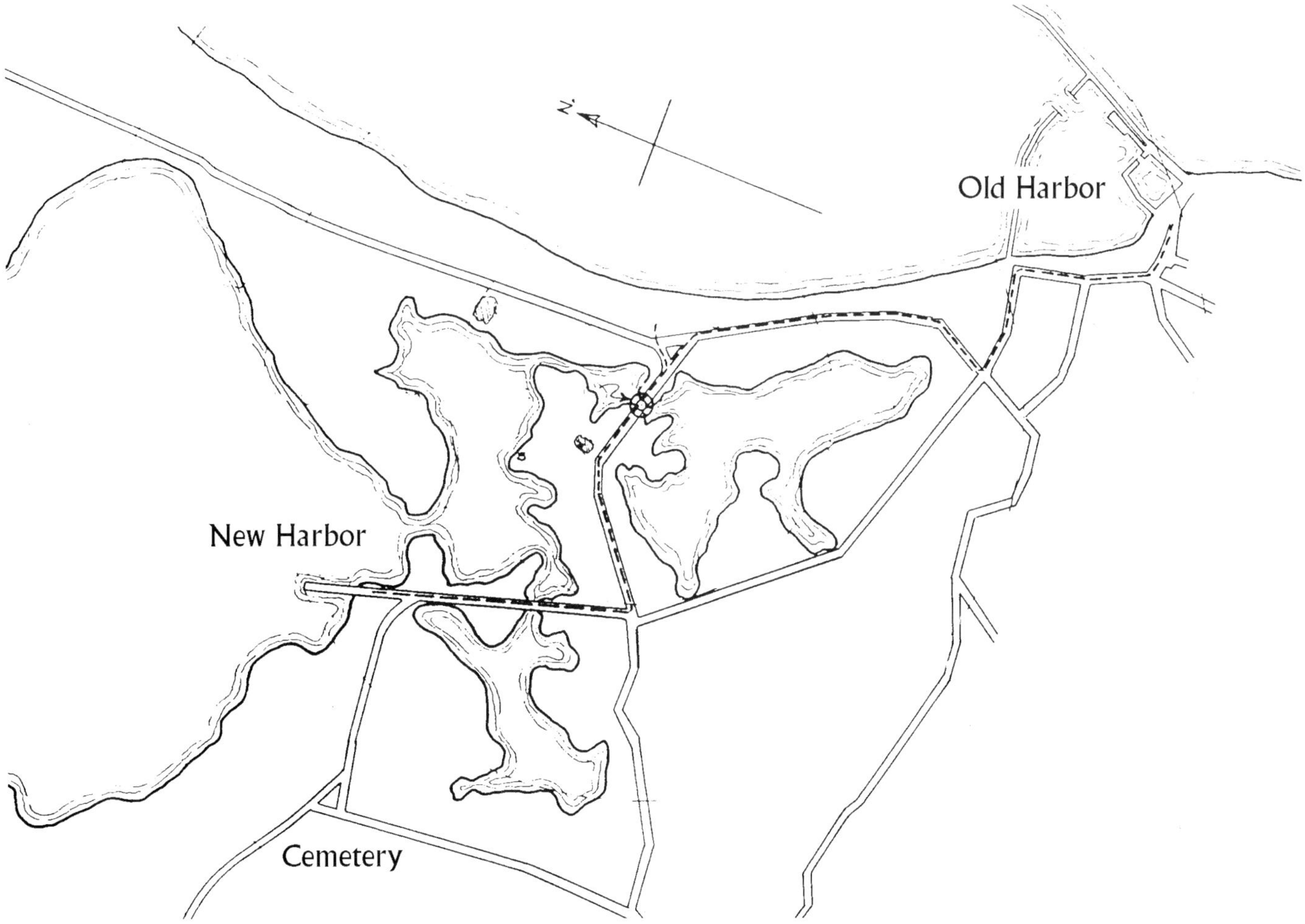

N.

Old Harbor

New Harbor

Cemetery

Horse car route 1898-1916

Wooden tower on Beacon Hill — elevation 211 feet — ca. 1895

In the latter part of the 1800s, a wooden observation tower beckoned walkers and carriage riders to the top of Beacon Hill. The tower that stood earlier, in the 1870s and 80s, lacked the second-story addition shown in this image (compare to photo, page 164).

CHAPTER 17

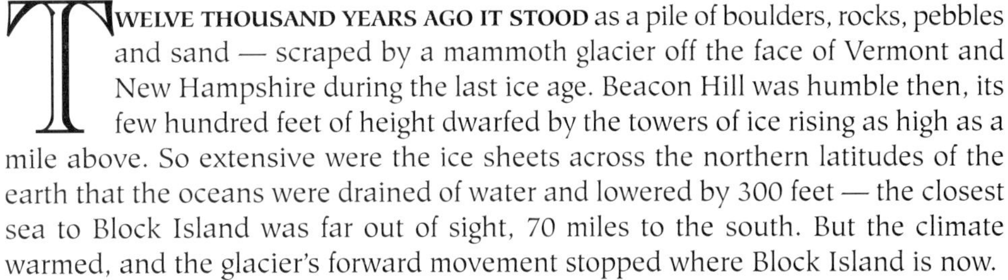

Beacon Hill

The aptly named high point of Block Island

TWELVE THOUSAND YEARS AGO IT STOOD as a pile of boulders, rocks, pebbles and sand — scraped by a mammoth glacier off the face of Vermont and New Hampshire during the last ice age. Beacon Hill was humble then, its few hundred feet of height dwarfed by the towers of ice rising as high as a mile above. So extensive were the ice sheets across the northern latitudes of the earth that the oceans were drained of water and lowered by 300 feet — the closest sea to Block Island was far out of sight, 70 miles to the south. But the climate warmed, and the glacier's forward movement stopped where Block Island is now.

Over the next several hundred years, Beacon Hill's height shrank from erosion, but gained in relative stature as the melting mass of ice disappeared over the northern horizon. To its utter astonishment — if Beacon Hill could think — the mound of glacial debris was now lord of the land, the tallest spot in an undulating plain stretching to the horizon in all directions. *Mount Long Island* was visible to the southwest, and, on the clearest of days, *Mount Martha's Vineyard* could be seen off to the east.

One year a vast flatness glistening in the sun appeared to the south, growing closer as the centuries passed. The ocean was coming back, fed by the shrinking glaciers now far from view in the opposite direction. On a definitive day some eight or nine thousand years ago, this highest hill in the area was surrounded by the sea, becoming part of an Island. Yet no parade, not even a bumper sticker, celebrates the event. Nor does any T-shirt declare: "Glacier Day — think big, remember the day the glacier stopped."

Humans migrating between the receding glacier and the sea would have seen Beacon Hill, and seeing it, been beckoned there as to all heights. Not known is when the first people arrived on Block Island, but artifacts more than 3,000 years old have been uncovered.

The names earlier groups may have had for Beacon Hill — and the sights, the travelers, and the adventures witnessed from that hilltop for thousands of years — are each-and-everyone lost forever in time. Not until the white settlers came in the 1660s did the name "Beacon Hill" stick and a written record begin.

The first mention of a beacon on Block Island came in 1705 during one of the numerous wars between France and England in their struggle to control the New World. On April 13, Fitz-John Winthrop, the governor of Connecticut (from 1698 to 1707), wrote from his home in nearby New London to Samuel Cranston, the governor of Rhode Island (from 1697 to 1727):

"The certaine intelligence you have ... of the enemye's designe to infest these parts, obliges to all methods necessary for the prevention of their designe, and tis thought if a good beacon were set up at Block Island, it would be of spetiall service to give notice of ye enemy, both at that island and to these parts."

And the French certainly came, as they had been for the previous 15 years of warfare. In 1706 the *Boston News-letter* — a newspaper that was the public's primary source of information — reported how an English captain returning from the Caribbean on May 23 had passed Block Island, been mistaken for a French privateer, and had thus inadvertently made "the People of Block-Island fire the Beacon."

The alarm of the Islanders was understandable. They had been attacked and overrun by the French three times between 1690 and 1693. In 1705 and 1706, Governor

Wooden tower on Beacon Hill, 1880s

Cranston had stationed "a quota of men at Block Island for the defence of Her Majesty's interest there."

The fear was widespread. During that spring of 1706, more than 200 men were at work each day in New York City building a protective stockade across the entire width of Manhattan "with several Block-Houses at convenient places." More than 50 cannon faced the harbor, and 4,000 men were on call in outlying communities, ready to rush to the city within 24 hours for its defense.

In the first week of June, to the north of Block Island, a French sloop chased and captured a Connecticut vessel bound for Boston. The English captain and his crew succeeded in escaping by small boat and reached Watch Hill. Soon 1,000 armed men were lining the shores of southern Rhode Island, as far west as Stonington, Connecticut. At Newport, Rhode Island, where the governor resided in that era, 100 volunteers manned two sloops, and four hours later — just south of Block Island and within sight of its shores — they seized the French sloop, together with a crew of 37, without a fight.

Proprietor.

HAVE YOU BEEN TO

BEACON HILL OBSERVATORY,

Positively the Highest Point on the Island, commanding a View of

Four States, and of the Ocean Completely Around the Island.

Advertisement from tourist booklet, 1893

No one would have ever disputed that Beacon Hill is the Island's highest point of land, but this advertisement sought to assure tourists that such a fact was "positively" true. Nevertheless, truth in advertising failed, because the ocean cannot be seen "Completely Around the Island" from the top of the tower on Beacon Hill — a small portion of the horizon is obscured by Mohegan Bluffs near the Southeast Light.

When seen from the mainland, the Block Island beacon was not taken lightly — it was the equivalent of pulling a modern-day fire alarm or dialing 911. On April 6, 1707, an express messenger from Narragansett rushed to the governor again with news that "the Beacon at Block-Island was on fire" and that several guns had been heard. The *News-letter* described the result of what proved to be a false alarm:

"The Governor immediately caused the Drum to beat up for Volunteers to go ... in a Sloop and Briganteen, and in 2 hours time there was 200 men compleat in Arms on Board; the Brigt. came up with Block-Island in the Evening, where they saw a small Sloop that came from New-York who had surrounded the Island 3 times, as tho' on purpose to alarm them."

In 1740 when England was at war again, this time with Spain, the Rhode Island legislature voted to station up to 60 men, and six cannon, on Block Island to assist the inhabitants. To communicate warnings throughout the state, a network

View from Beacon Hill, looking southeast, ca. 1890

The Island's rolling fields, criss-crossed with stone walls, were laid out before viewers of the past. But thick growths of bayberry and shad bushes — and summer houses — now obscure the Island's landscape.

The mansard-roofed home in the middle of the photograph still stands next to Beacon Hill Road (on plat 18, lot 24).

Also currently in existance is the smaller white house just to the left (plat 16, lot 83), shown next to Beacon Hill Road as the road crests a hill (see photo, page 70) — but the classic, tiny white house across the street was torn down in the fall of 1998.

Between these two houses can be seen the white-steepled Baptist Church that dominated the Old Center, near the bottom of the hill leading to today's airport (see photo, page 144) — the church burned in 1908 and is commemorated on a nearby granite marker.

of beacons was in place, including one at Block Island and five more on the mainland: at Watch Hill, Point Judith, Newport, Portsmouth, and Beavertail Point in Jamestown.

Twenty-five years later during the Revolutionary War, when each citizen had to choose one loyalty — either to the king in England or to the new United States — Block Island by geographic necessity clung to neutrality. A barrel of tar was kept on Beacon Hill not, this time, to warn the mainland of surprise visitors, but ready to be lit as a signal to Islanders that desperate men of suspect intent were coming from America, fleeing their own woes there. When the flames were seen, watchful residents picketed the shoreline.

Although the British frequently visited Block Island — to purchase goods, refill their ships' water casks at ponds, and exchange prisoners of war — the Islanders welcomed opportunities to assist the colonists on the mainland. In the spring of 1780 an enormous French fleet of 44 vessels was being readied to sail to America's aid. Because the landing was to be made at Newport — which the British had recently evacuated after several years' occupation — the great General Lafayette sought the help of Block Islanders. In 1780, orders sent to Lafayette by the French minister of war — written on March 5 at the king's opulent palace in Versailles — instructed:

"The British may have changed their minds and returned there [to Newport], we wish M. le Marquis de Lafayette to obtain authorization from General Washington to send a few of the French officers attached to him to Rhode Island, and even to Block Island if it is inhabited and the inhabitants are dependable, in order to prevent the French squadron's being taken by surprise."

If the French fleet could safely enter Narragansett Bay and proceed to Newport, the following signal was to be raised at Block Island, at Point Judith on the west side of the bay's entrance, and at Sakonnet Point on the east side:

"The white French flag and, below it on the same pole, the red flag."

If the French saw the following signal — meaning the British had returned to Newport — then they would depart the area:

"The American flag, with a blue flag below it on the same pole."

After a voyage of 69 days, the French, led by Admiral de Ternay and General

Rochambeau, passed Block Island in darkness and fog on the morning of July 11, 1780, and, as the fog lifted, they saw the French fleur-de-lis flying at Point Judith. The 6,700 crewmen and 5,000 soldiers proceeded safely toward Newport — to help change the history of the world.

Sixty years after the end of the Revolution, in the mid-1800s, Beacon Hill was used for more peaceful signals by a young federal government eager to map its coastline accurately — the project was called the Coastal Survey (see part of the resultant map on pages 62-63). Because Block Island was situated 'off to the side' of the continent, Beacon Hill was a convenient corner for the imaginary triangles surveyors made to determine the distance between points of land. Other prime corners for measurements were Montauk Point, 14 miles to the southwest, and Newport, 23 miles to the northeast.

Over the next four decades — as measurements were undertaken with increasing detail — the Island continued to be an important triangulation point. Brass geodetic survey markers are still maintained on Beacon Hill and elsewhere on the Island.

When tourism overtook Block Island in the 1870s, the hill was taken as well. Owned by farmer William Dodge, whose fields swept gracefully over the crest, Beacon Hill became a popular destination by foot and by carriage. Although at first freely open to the public, a fee was soon charged. By the 1890s local newspaper advertisements were used to lure sightseers, with a promise that Beacon Hill was "positively the Highest Point on the Island" (see ad on page 164).

Eventually the observation building the government survey team had erected was extended upward one floor for tourists, with a flagpole positioned on top (page 162).

A tourist from Connecticut described the scene in 1877, letting his male imagination wander to the extreme:

"The great attraction of Beacon Hill is the magnificent view it affords on a clear day ... the winding roads, the network of stone fences, the brown and treeless meadows with here and there a dark green field of waving corn, a haystack or a picturesque windmill, the various sized ponds, the almost solitary farm-house, the church and the clump of hotels and dwellings over near the harbor ... the undulating surface of the

A Beacon Hill stone, ca. 1900

Smiling demurely, a Victorian-era woman wiles away a mysterious moment with her partner and a Beacon Hill rock — which, to her hesitant friend, seems to have all the appeal of a hot potato.

The smoothly rounded granite stone, proferred by one woman to the other, is a remnant of glaciers — as are all the materials in the distant walls, all of Beacon Hill, and all of Block Island.

William Doggett, on top of the world, 1920s

The magnificent panorama from the Island's highest point lets one's cares fall away, as William Doggett (center) and two friends demonstrate.

island, the languid but constant heaving of whose broad bosom is suggestive of a usually calm soul, mildly agitated with pleasure."

He might have found the cafe at the top.

An observer in 1882 wrote more dispassionately of the view from Beacon Hill:

"On its summit some enterprising genius has erected a tower, from which in summer floats the American flag, and where for a pittance one may have the use of a good glass and an outlook of miles over sea and land ... It is simply a mass of sand-hills thrown up in every conceivable shape, but every suggestion of barrenness hidden by green pastures and smiling meadow. In every hollow glimmers a pond ...

"The hills are treeless, bare, and cut into squares and parallelograms by numerous stone walls — a form of rural architecture almost universal on the Island — and on their summits, rarely at their bases, are set the farmhouses — isolated, whitewashed structures, each surrounded by its cluster of out-buildings and communicating with the highway by a grassy lane, which often winds through the fields for a mile before reaching its destination."

In 1885 the observatory, and with it the cafe maintained inside, was sold to local Islanders: A. D. Mitchell and Abraham Milliken. By then Beacon Hill had a dubious popularity, as recorded in the *Providence Journal* that July 3:

"It will be under the charge of the latter gentleman, who will conduct it on strictly temperance principles, greatly to the satisfaction of neighboring householders, who have been annoyed much in former years by revels at the observatory and in its vicinity."

For the next 35 years Beacon Hill catered only to the curious.

The casual walk or drive to the top began the relaxation process, whereby the sightseer wandered quite secure in the knowledge that nothing would intrude on his life more pressing than to view a 360-degree panorama of the ocean — except for the one small spot where the bluff by the Southeast Lighthouse obscures the Atlantic from view.

The next greatest change to happen at Beacon Hill — a mild second to the presence of the glacier 12,000 years earlier — was the coming to Block Island of William H. Doggett of Dedham, Massachusetts. As a young man in his twenties — and a 1916 graduate in engineering from Cornell, William Doggett visited the Island in 1922 at the invitation of the Manisses Hotel's manager. Beacon Hill, then vacant of structures and available for sale, was one of the sights that intrigued him.

After returning home, William soon made arrangements to purchase the property. Six years later he and his father, Thomas T. Doggett, resolved to build a stone tower. Architect Roger Bullard, a neighbor in Dedham — who often worked in New York and in the Hamptons on Long Island — fashioned a structure reminiscent of a very small castle: a two-story tower attached to the end of a single-story house, with a wooden entrance portico at the juncture. From simplicity, elegance can flow (see page 168).

The Doggetts' stone tower

William Doggett and his father, Thomas, purchased Beacon Hill in 1922, erecting their stone tower in 1928 for use as a summer cottage.

From a series of postcards made for William Doggett.

According to a 1970 article, whose writer spoke with William Doggett, the material for the building was dragged from two nearby stone walls (a violation of current town ordinances). The natural contours of the stones were meshed together without cutting the edges, and both the interior and exterior sides of the building's walls were faced smooth. Work was done with the help of mainland masons, who used an Islander's stone-boat to haul the rocks to the site. A block-and-tackle, gin-pole, and slanting boards were used to hoist the stones — the largest of which, at the bottom of the walls, weigh from 800-1000 pounds.

Having saved up his vacations, William stayed with the masonry part of the project from beginning to end: July to December 1, 1928.

The next summer the interior was finished and the vacation home was occupied. From his hilltop eyrie, for the next several decades, William Doggett eagerly dispensed the Island's history to his many equally enthusiastic visitors. As many as four or five hundred people might sign the guest book in a season.

In 1933 the small white wooden cottage — a few hundred feet to the east, and lower down the hill — was built for William's sister, Agnes G. Ruddy. During the remainder of the decade, Agnes, an accomplished cook, and her husband, a singer, operated a tea room on Beacon Hill. During those immensely more quiet and relaxed years, several such tea rooms were scattered about the Island offering lunches, desserts and entertainment — such as the A-and-A Tea Room (plat 19, lot 66) on West Side Road, and next to Frank Mott's house on Corn Neck Road, just north of the Mansion Road.

To commemorate their achievement a bronze tablet was dedicated by the Doggetts in 1936 for Rhode Island's Tercentenary celebration. Located over the brick and fieldstone fireplace, the plaque declares:

"On this spot was flown the royal flag of France as a signal to Admiral de Ternay to enter Newport Harbor in July 1780. This building erected in 1928 by Thomas T. Doggett of Dedham, Massachusetts as a perpetual beacon for the guidance of mariners. Roger H. Bullard, Architect"

Interior of the Doggetts' stone tower

This postcard, made for William Doggett, is titled "View of fireplace in living room of the Doggett Beacon, Beacon Hill, Block Island, Rhode Island."

A small trap door in the center of the room preserves the stump of a post discovered when the hill was cleared in 1928. The Doggetts believed the rotting wood to be the bottom of the flagpole used to send a signal to the French fleet during the Revolution — but testing might determine if the fragment were instead a surveyor's pole erected in the mid-1800s, or part of the wooden lookout tower of the late 1800s.

Beacon Hill's life was changing rapidly in the 1920s and 30s, and the upheaval was not to stop soon. The souvenirs of war would again mark the hill, and for the same purpose it had always been used: as a lookout and signaling platform. This time the form and mass would not fade so easily.

On December 8, 1941 — the day after the Japanese attacked Pearl Harbor — William Doggett was visited by an Army officer in Dedham and informed that his Block Island property had been commandeered for the duration. After removing personal belongings, six years would pass before the Doggetts again visited their beloved stone home. They were paid a rental fee — but one based on the low rates then prevailing on the Island.

The Army had chosen six locations on Block Island for the construction of eight lookout posts to assist with the firing of mainland guns used for coastal defense. These 16-inch naval weapons — the largest caliber cannons ever produced by the United States — could fire projectiles weighing as much as an automobile toward distant enemies 25 miles at sea (see map, page 11). If desired, the shells could arch high over Block Island. To house the guns, massive concrete emplacements were hidden around Narragansett Bay, at Fishers Island near Connecticut, and at Montauk Point on Long Island.

Two 16-inch guns, designated Battery Hamilton, were located near Point Judith at Fort Greene — part of which is now a state camping area, passed by automobile drivers just a mile before reaching the ferry dock at Galilee.

On Beacon Hill, the lookout tower — called a "Fire Control structure" by the government — was built into the westerly slope of the hillside, next to Doggett's stone house. The new building was disguised as a summer cottage, with the cottage section built of wood, and the tower — protruding unobtrusively from the western end — made of concrete. The army's goal was to protect, on the west, the Long Island Sound entrance, and to the northeast, the great naval installations of Narragansett Bay.

Fire Control structures were outfitted with Depression Position Finders — sophisticated telescopes that would allow the distance and compass angle of any sighted ships to be communicated to the mainland gun batteries. The Beacon Hill Fire Control used two DPF's — both faced westward, one on each of the top two levels of the cement tower.

Although the Island's Fire Control structures may have helped in test firings, no shots were ever fired at enemies.

Block Island's facilities were already in a caretaker status when, in May 1945 — on the morning World War II ended — the German submarine U-853 was sunk by Navy and Coast Guard ships seven miles east of the Island. The lookout towers did not participate — sonar, a new invention carried aboard the American vessels, had located the submerged U-boat.

After the war, the Doggetts made a swap with the federal government. Rather than have the new Fire Control building removed, or have the damage and vandalism to the stone tower repaired, each party just called it even.

Today the three structures remain: the wooden cottage, the Fire Control cottage, and — literally above all else — the stone tower.

The Doggetts' monument is a fitting Block Island crown of rock and masonry, a gesture of mankind's resistance, token though it may be, against the crumbling of the Island's sand and gravel base by the sea.

Corrected to August 1944

STRUCTURE: x 90,027.49
Location (by coordinates) y 61,812.82
Location (by site description) Beacon Hill
Date of transfer 26 February 1944
Cost to that date $17,344
Type (for observing stat.--tower, dug-in, cottage, etc.) Cottage
Type of construction Wood frame and reinforced concrete
(a) Roof Wood frame and roll roofing
(b) Remainder of bldg. Wood frame and reinf. conc.
How concealed To simulate cottage
How protected F.C. Stas. by reinforced concrete
Height above concealment Not applicable
Height above protection " "
Conspicuous at ______ yards Not conspicuous

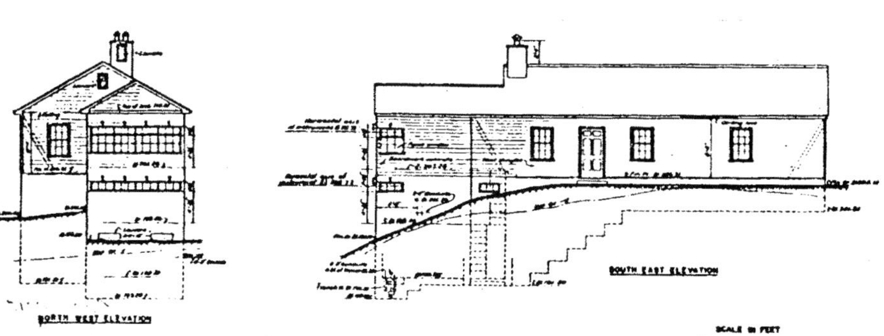

SECRET

F. C. STRUCTURE I-A
B^7_1 S^7_1 B^9_2 S^9_2
BLOCK ISLAND, RHODE ISLAND
HARBOR DEFENSES OF NARRAGANSETT BAY

Secret World War II report — lookout tower on Beacon Hill, 1944

The shorter end of the building shown on these once "SECRET" plans, is a concrete tower where lookouts were posted during the early years of World War II.

This war report of 1944 describes the building as a "Fire Control Structure" built with "wood frame and reinforced concrete." Because it was "concealed" — and disguised "to simulate cottage" — the three-story tower was considered to be "not conspicuous."

Eight concrete lookout towers were built on Block Island, designed according to various styles. In addition to this tower at Beacon Hill, three others still exist: on Spring Street (plat 8, lot 23), Pilot Hill Road (plat 9, lot 87), and Corn Neck Road (plat 2, lot 31). All four are now private homes.

See diagram of Spring St. tower — page 8.

See photos of towers torn down — pages 7,11

"Souvenir of Block Island" — ca. 1905

Six views of Block Island were depicted on this plate sold by the store of John Rose & Co. on Dodge Street.

All six scenes, etched in blue, were adapted from postcard images sold on the Island at the time (for an example, see page 223).

For tourists who could not decide why they were buying this item — which they would never consider purchasing if the plate were found in any other town or city in the entire world — the plate itself provided the answer: "Souvenir of Block Island."

CHAPTER 18

The China Connection 1890-1910

Souvenir china dishes

A HUNDRED YEARS AGO **Block Island** stores competed with each other selling custom-designed souvenir china dishes to tourists of the Victorian era. In one of those lingering misnomers of history, the china came from Germany and England.

These filigreed dust-collectors of great-grandma's are now considered either fancy enough to display, or just too plain junky to keep — diverse opinions deciding whether the dishes are cherished beyond reason by a zealous collector, or tossed away after an unsuccessful garage sale.

It was emotion that caused people to buy these knickknacks in the first place.

At most tourist attractions such as Block Island, visitors contemplate, often unconsciously, questions such as:

"Why am I here?"

"What is the essence of this place and how do I savor it?"

"Are other people finding more enjoyment than I am?"

"How do I prove that I was here and have inside information about this place only visitors are privy to?"

For such a thinker, souvenirs were made.

During the last two decades of the 1900s, the favored mementoes have been T-shirts with a logo, making the wearer look like a walking old-time sandwich board advertisement.

For the forty years before that, travelers brought back felt pennants to hang on juvenile walls, or bumper stickers and decals for dad's car — mom didn't have a car then (see bumper stickers on pages 130-131, and 226-229).

But a hundred years ago, our ancestors returned from vacation trips with souvenir china.

The cachet of intriguing towns has a particular attraction and souvenir china that survived attic shelves and boxes — and bears the name ***Block Island*** — is now a kind of "Everyman's" treasure.

Properly speaking, china is a type of ceramic distinguished from porcelain by being fired twice — the heat turning the raw material of clay, feldspar, and flint into glass that has the hardness, but not the translucence, of porcelain. Underneath the glossy surface, china is not porous — as is earthenware, which is fired at a lower temperature.

But "souvenir china," being a loose modern term, can be any of the above: china, porcelain, or earthenware.

These keepsakes were first sold on Block Island in the early 1890s, a few years before the even more popular craze of "picture postcards" erupted in 1898. Traveling salesmen from intermediary American firms — such as ***C. E. Wheelock Co.*** and ***Jones, McDuffee and Stratton*** in Boston — visited resort merchants urging them to order souvenir dishes in any of a multitude of styles, colors, and sizes. The

MADE IN GERMANY
C. C. BALL
BLOCK ISLAND, R.I.

MADE IN GERMANY FOR
IRVING M. BALL,
BLOCK ISLAND. R. I.
274

MADE IN GERMANY FOR
SURF HOTEL BAZAR
BLOCK ISLAND. R. I.

store owner who had been "sold" would provide a pictorial scene — often a photograph or a picture postcard — to be applied to the blank dish chosen from the catalog.

At least nine Block Island businesses sold souvenir china, importing their wares from England, where earthenware was a specialty — or more often, from Germany and Austria, where great quantities of porcelain were manufactured.

The shapes were of enormous variety, nearly surpassing the ability to categorize them: vases, plates, cups, saucers, tumblers, bowls, creamers, candy dishes, ash trays, pitchers, crescent-shaped fish bone containers, and more.

In Europe the store-owners' images were made into steel engravings. The design was then printed with oxides on paper transfers, and applied wet to each dish. The paper burned away when fired. But the design was retained in the clay, which was left black-and-white, or hand-colored in pastels, usually combinations of pink, blue, orange or green.

A year might pass before the finished product made the return voyage across the Atlantic.

Cassius Clay Ball's general store in Old Harbor, called ***C. C. Ball's***, was the Island's largest merchandiser and — judging from what has survived the decades — the seller of the greatest amount of Block Island souvenir china. The building, which now houses Ernie's Restaurant, was moved from the other side of Water Street in the late 1920s (see page 174).

Another prolific supplier — judged by the same method — was the ***John Rose & Co.*** hardware store on Dodge Street (see pages 176, 177), now the site of the Juice & Java coffee shop and the Été clothing store.

J. Eugene Littlefield's — still functioning as a grocery store but now called the Seaside Market — sold souvenir china as well (see page 180), as did five smaller business owners: ***Mrs. Emma G. Ball***, the ***Surfside Bazaar***, the ***Surf Hotel Bazaar***, ***Ray S. Littlefield***, and ***Irving M. Ball*** (owner of the Pequot Hotel, now the Harborside Inn). All had their names stamped on the dishes' bottom, establishing their immortality, perhaps.

Other than the actual present-day existence of the china pieces, there is scant knowledge about the selling of these items on Block Island.

On July 20, 1901, the local summer newspaper *Mid-Ocean*, reported: "Call at C. C. Ball's and examine his new line of souvenir crockery imported from Germany."

A price for some of these objects was given in the *Mid-Ocean* on August 15, 1903: "Mr. C. C. Ball has a special line of 10-cent Block Island souvenirs. These include china trays, toilet bottles, etc."

Although souvenir china from the turn-of-the-century was not intended to be manufactured in the most careful manner, a blue and white plate made by the prominent Wedgwood company of England was sold at C. C. Ball's store. The front depicts the Southeast Lighthouse, while the back notes: "The European steamers take their departure from this light."

About the time of World War I, the fad of souvenir china collecting in America waned, as did the great initial popularity of postcards.

The only comparable Block Island item sold since — similar in concept to the early custom-decorated souvenir china — is a four-piece set of white and brown Wedgwood plates made in the 1960s for the former Esta's Gift Shop, located at the corner of Water Street and Chapel Street.

Now most of the Island's generic souvenirs are — in a great irony — imported from the real China but are truly of cheap manufacture and design, much inferior to the souvenir dishes of 100 years ago.

Today, however, explorers of Block Island can also discover locally made crafts by the Island's many artisans. These are the collectible mementos future generations may cherish.

Enlarged underside of souvenir dishes

▲
C.C. Ball's store on Water Street, now Ernie's Restaurant, ca. 1905

Built in 1879, C. C. Ball's store was the most well-stocked on the Island for several decades. Nearby in 1882 — also on Water Street — Cassius Clay Ball constructed directly across from each other the *Empire Theatre* and the gingerbread-festooned Drug Store (now the *Inn at Old Harbor*).

C. C. Ball's store was moved across the street, toward the viewer, in the late 1920s — this postcard shows what is now the rear of today's Ernie's Restaurant. (For another view of the building in this location, see page 111 — for views of the building in its present-day location, see pages 106 and 114.)

Behind C.C. Ball's store is the gargantuan Ocean View Hotel that belonged to C.C.'s father, Nicholas Ball. That venerable hotel burned to the ground in 1966 (see photo, page 20).

C. C. BALL,

At his General Store, OLD P. O. SQUARE,

Carries thousands of kinds of merchandise, but he makes claim to three specialties only,

CLOSE, CAREFUL BUYING,
SELLING FOR CASH AT MODERATE PROFITS,
PROMPT, COURTEOUS ATTENDANCE.

Headquarters

—FOR—

Dry and Fancy Goods,
Gents' Furnishing and Outing Goods,
Summer Books,
Block Island Souvenirs, in China, White Wood and Silver,
Tennis and Bicycle Sundries,
Bathing Outfits, for both Ladies and Gentlemen,
Fine California Fruit, Confectionery and Cigars,
Livermore's Guide Book and Map of the Island.

But it is impossible to specify.

DO NOT FAIL TO CALL ON US BEFORE YOU LEAVE, and if you don't see what you want ASK FOR IT; the chances are ten to one that we have it in stock.

AGENT FOR Adams Express Company

AND FOR

Butman & Tucker's Laundry.

Souvenir china advertisement — C. C. Ball's store, 1895

An 1895 advertisement for C.C. Ball's eclectic general store mentions "Block Island Souvenirs, in China ..."

The description of the diverse inventory ends with the lament, in fine print: "But it is impossible to specify" everything (see bottom of dish, on page 178).

The "White Wood" is now called "Mauchline ware" and is highly popular with collectors.

The Ocean View Hotel — three dishes, each trimmed in gold

The pitcher on the top shows a black and white view of the Old Harbor breakwater and the distant Ocean View Hotel, once the summer home of the Island's most distinguished visitors.

In the middle is another pitcher, with a closer view of the 360-foot long structure. And on the bottom is a pink rimmed plate from Germany with the exact same scene.

B. F. H. S.
CHINA
MADE IN AUSRTIA
for John Rose & Co.
Block Island R. I.

Vase of New Harbor dock, with pink band on top and bottom

The John Rose & Co. hardware store was second only to C.C. Ball's store as the largest seller of souvenir china. The black-and-white etching on this pitcher is surrounded by pink highlighting and gold trim. That these ceramic items were not of the highest quality is evident by misspellings, as in *"AUSRTIA."*

John Rose & Co. Hardware, Dodge Street, ca. 1910

The Island's longtime hardware store — on the right above — fulfilled that function from its construction in 1896, until the 1970s. The building is now best known as the site of Juice & Java coffee shop.

On the left is the Gables Inn — built in 1880 as the home of Capt. Burton Dodge (1854-1883) but called for all of the 1900s by its present name.

The white building in the middle is a small hotel, the Woonsocket House, that became the Block Island Historical Society in the 1940s (see photo, bottom of page 115).

Block Island Souvenirs

New and Exclusive Designs.

Novelties and Whist Prizes.

Fishing Gear FOR

Fresh or Salt Water Fishing.

OUR SPECIAL LINE OF

FANCY CROCKERY

is worth an examination.

Hardware, Cutlery and Glassware.

A FULL STOCK TO SELECT FROM.

JOHN ROSE & CO., Main Street.

"Block Island Souvenirs" advertisement — John Rose & Co., 1903

Southeast Light and bluffs, ca. 1900

Southeast Lighthouse and bluffs — five dishes, each trimmed in gold

The image most frequently used to depict the Island at the turn-of-the-century was the same one favored today: the Southeast Lighthouse atop Mohegan Bluffs.

The dish with the woven body on the left and the small circular bowl on the right, have pastel skies of blue and pink.

The bowl was *"Made in Germany"* for store owner *"C.C. Ball, Block Island, R. J."* — as the large red imprint on the bottom declares, with a typographical error.

The oval bowl on the left and the pitcher on the right feature black-and-white etchings of the lighthouse and bluffs.

A dark green border on a plate from Germany, with gold filigree accents, rings a color depiction of the "South Light" atop the bluffs.

J. Eugene Littlefield's store, now the box-like Seaside Market, ca. 1900

Island politician J. Eugene Littlefield built his store in 1887 with graceful curved dormers and decorative ornamentation. What would have been considered now to be one of the Island's choicest historical buildings, was literally boxed-in by an owner in the early 1950s, becoming the cube we see today.

On the right is the present-day Star Department Store built in 1883 for photographer H. Q. Morton. The Star's altered upper facade can still be seen, above an addition built in 1903 that extended the lower floor toward the street (compare to photos, pages 112, 239).

J. Eugene Littlefield, welcomed at New Harbor dock, ca. 1920

Store owner John Eugene Littlefield (1858-1927), a state legislator and one of the Island's most popular politicians, is welcomed back from Providence at the New Harbor steamer dock, now known as Payne's Dock. The present-day Sullivan House on Indian Head Neck — built in 1904 for summer resident L. U. Maltby of Philadelphia — appears, as it seems to in most pictures of New Harbor, in the background.

The Island lost its two positions in the state legislature — both representative and senator — when the town was lumped in with various mainland districts in the 1960s.

Because it no longer had a vote to make, or to trade, Block Island also lost nearly all influence in determining its own fate, as has been amply demonstrated by the rental moped accidents of the past 20 years, all allowed to continue solely because of leverage brought to bear on the state legislature by five rental dealers.

If you can't comprehend that, then you probably also won't figure out which of the men in this photo is J. Eugene Littlefield.

Plates, with Harbor windmill design

The second most popular Block Island image was of a windmill located off Old Town Road near the old Center. Neither of the Island's two Dutch-type windmills survived. (For photos of this windmill, called the Harbor Mill, see pages 208-213.)

Pequot House, now the Harborside Inn on Water Street

Cobalt blue vase, showing New Harbor dock

A subclass of china pieces were those made with dark bodies in lustrous "cobalt blue " usually trimmed with gold. Scenes were tinted in contrasting pastel colors, such as the light orange and blue sky in this view of present-day Payne's Dock.

The pitcher was manufactured for Block Islander "Emma G. Ball" in "Dresden" Germany, and imported here through the middleman firm of C.E. "Wheelock" of Boston.

Wedgwood plate — 1960s

Although the popular era of souvenir china ended in the 1920s, a resurrection of the genre was made on Block Island in the 1960s by the famous Esta's Gift Shop on Water Street.

Jack and Esta Gray commissioned a special set of four different Block Island plates from the Wedgwood company of England — producers of fine, carefully crafted pottery. All that remains of that time are the plates — and a small park overlooking the harbor, given to the town as a memorial by Jack, named by him Esta's Park.

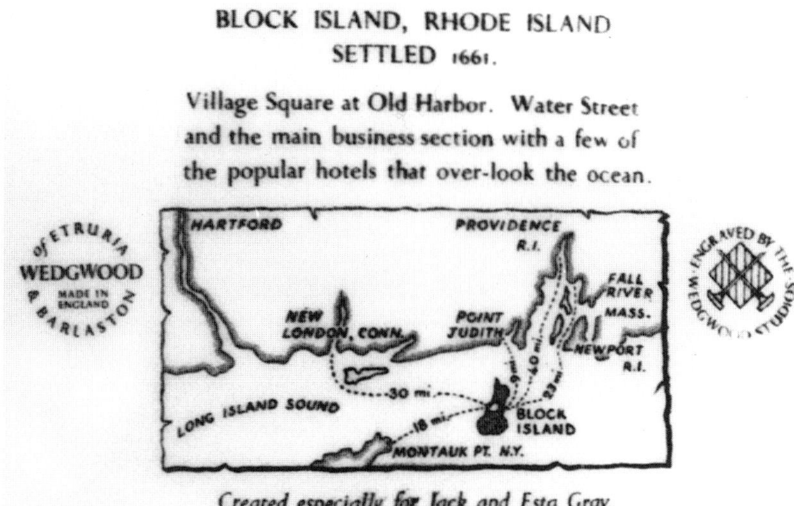

BLOCK ISLAND, R. I., JUNE 15th, 1875.

TO THE PUBLIC.

In issuing this circular I w
to this island, which, to the casual seel
pleasure, is comparatively little known,
sive works erected by the U. S. Gove
water, Light Houses and Life Saving St
some attention to it.

There is a very large and respect
who need two or three months of quiet
from the trials and vexations of busines
a certain extent, be untrammeled by
great highway of travel, yet not so far
reached in two hours, where they may
extent, Nature's three great restorative
Sea. To such, Block Island offers indu
those of any resort upon our coast.

The OCEAN VIEW HOTEL — 4-page brochure, 1875

This earliest example of a promotional brochure set the tone for all such later Island publications. As the Ocean View grew to a colossus four times larger than the small hotel pictured in this engraving — becoming the largest hotel in southern New England — so did its circulars grow from this four-page handout, to 50-page booklets with colored covers (see page 125).

BLOCK ISLAND

R. I.

OCEAN

VIEW

HOTEL.

Fine bass and blue fishing; superb bathing; 500 guests; electric lights; elegant music hall; fine orchestra; cable office; stock reports. Send for handbook.

O. S. Marden

Fifth Avenue Hotel

New York City.

CHAPTER 19

"I wish to call attention to this Island"

Old Hotel Booklets

The OCEAN VIEW HOTEL — envelope, 1878

By 1878 the Ocean View had extended the facade to the left — and hired a professional manager, Mr. Orison S. Marden, to handle reservations and promotional materials on a year-round basis. After his Block Island career ended, Marden wrote some three-dozen inspirational books, each of which served as a pep-talk to life.

Final length of the OCEAN VIEW HOTEL — letterhead, ca. 1890

See Chapter 3 for photographs showing the Ocean View Hotel's growth in size.

Although a few sightseers had wandered Block Island's way before the late 1800s, the Island's tourism boom occurred only after construction of the granite breakwater at Old Harbor in the early 1870s allowed ship passengers to land easily. Each successive year for the next three decades, Old Harbor blossomed with new buildings catering to summertime visitors.

The tourists asked for directions.

The earliest Block Island brochure is an 8 x 11 inch sheet of paper — folded once to make four pages — that advertised the Ocean View Hotel in 1875, the first summer that grandest of the Island's hotels was open. During the next quarter century, the Ocean View was not only the most prolific issuer of informative brochures but also the producer of the largest, and often the best, examples.

Setting the format for the future, the 1875 brochure began — supposedly in the words of the hotel's proprietor Nicholas Ball — with the mundane sentence:

"In issuing this circular I wish to call attention to this island ..."

That was, and still is, the main function of the Island's hotel owners, who, for the last 15 years have issued an ever increasing flow of colorful glossy brochures, some disseminated by the individual hotels, and some by two organizations, the Chamber of Commerce and the Block Island Tourism Council, that have themselves become small businesses.

None of the recent efforts, however, have surpassed the size of the hotel booklets from the 1880s, which had first to convince readers that vacations should indeed be taken, and second induce them through a series of logical steps to do their vacationing on Block Island.

And so the old booklets initially stressed the healthful qualities of the Island. Nicholas Ball tried it this way:

"The casual seeker after health and pleasure ... may enjoy to the fullest extent, Nature's three great restoratives, Air, Sunshine and Sea."

The theme was elaborated on with amateur medical advice and the inclusion of air temperature charts.

Statements were also made informing prospective tourists that *other* worthy people had preceded them to the Island:

"There is a very large and respectable class of people who need two or three months of quiet summer rest; away from the trials and vexations of business ..."

Then a bit of Block Island hocus-pocus was added:

"Those who frequent the sea side resorts upon the numerous Headlands and Inlets of our New England coast, know from experience, how grateful and invigorating is the pure sea breeze, and are painfully aware of the colds and influenzas which are sure to attack whenever the breeze changes and blows from the land."

You surely knew how dangerous land was — didn't you? Well, if not, this brochure implied you may be beneath contempt and must be of that lowly class who are less than "frequent" travelers.

A lengthy description of Block Island was then offered, recounting scenic spots (the beach and cliffs) and various diversions (the beach and fishing), followed — now that you are hooked on the place — with details of the particular hotel that printed the pamphlet.

Each year the Ocean View Hotel published a new brochure, which peaked during the 1880s at more than 50, 5½ x 8 inch pages, filled with advice, maps, hotel floor plans, scenic engravings, comments by famous visitors next to their autographs, and both local and national advertisements. The contents were altered gradually as the summers progressed. Each year a new cover was designed to catch the eye, leaving us fine examples of the typographers' art.

And the booklets worked, luring to Block Island senators, Supreme Court justices, and ambassadors from Washington, D.C.; governors from around the country; robber barons of industry; and famous public figures — several dozen men and women you will still find in today's encyclopedias — plus the hundreds of thousands of others who sought fun, health, and even, perhaps, the celebrity of being known as a frequent traveler.

The MANISSES — ►
36-page booklet, 1886

In the 1880s the Manisses Hotel proudly stated in italics that "Great care has been exercised in the plumbing and drainage ... all waste empties into the ocean." Such sewage pipes, from other hotels, can still be seen — now unused — extending onto Crescent Beach next to the breakwater.

• *For other tourist-oriented paper items — see color section, pages 124-125*

PEQUOT HOUSE,

BLOCK ISLAND, R. I.

Thaddeus A. Ball, - Proprietor.

SEASON OF 1886.

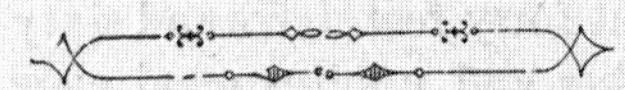

BLOCK ISLAND.

The health giving isle, Block Island, is steadily gaining in popularity as a resort that restores health to the sick, vitality and energy to the brain worker and those confiined within doors, and enjoyment and pleasure to all who seek it for recreation, or to escape the heat, sultry breezes and mosquitoes of the main land. It is a refuge for those suffering from malaria, or wishing to escape from infected districts.

Being situated in the Ocean, fifteen miles from the nearest point of land, exhilarating breezes, (from whichever point of compass,) filled with the salt spray of the Atlantic give elasticity to the step and bouyancy to the spirits; and visitors get all the benefits of an ocean voyage without its discomforts.

Hills, ravines, numerous ponds, bluffs, beaches, and light-houses are objects of interest and curiosity, and lend variety and beauty to the walks and drives of the Island.

The Bathing Beach, which is hard sand and free from stones and seaweed, is one of the best on the Atlantic coast it is also one of the safest, there being no undertow.

The PEQUOT HOUSE —
4-page brochure, 1886

Known as the Royal for most of the 1900s, the hotel has been called the Harborside Inn since 1980.

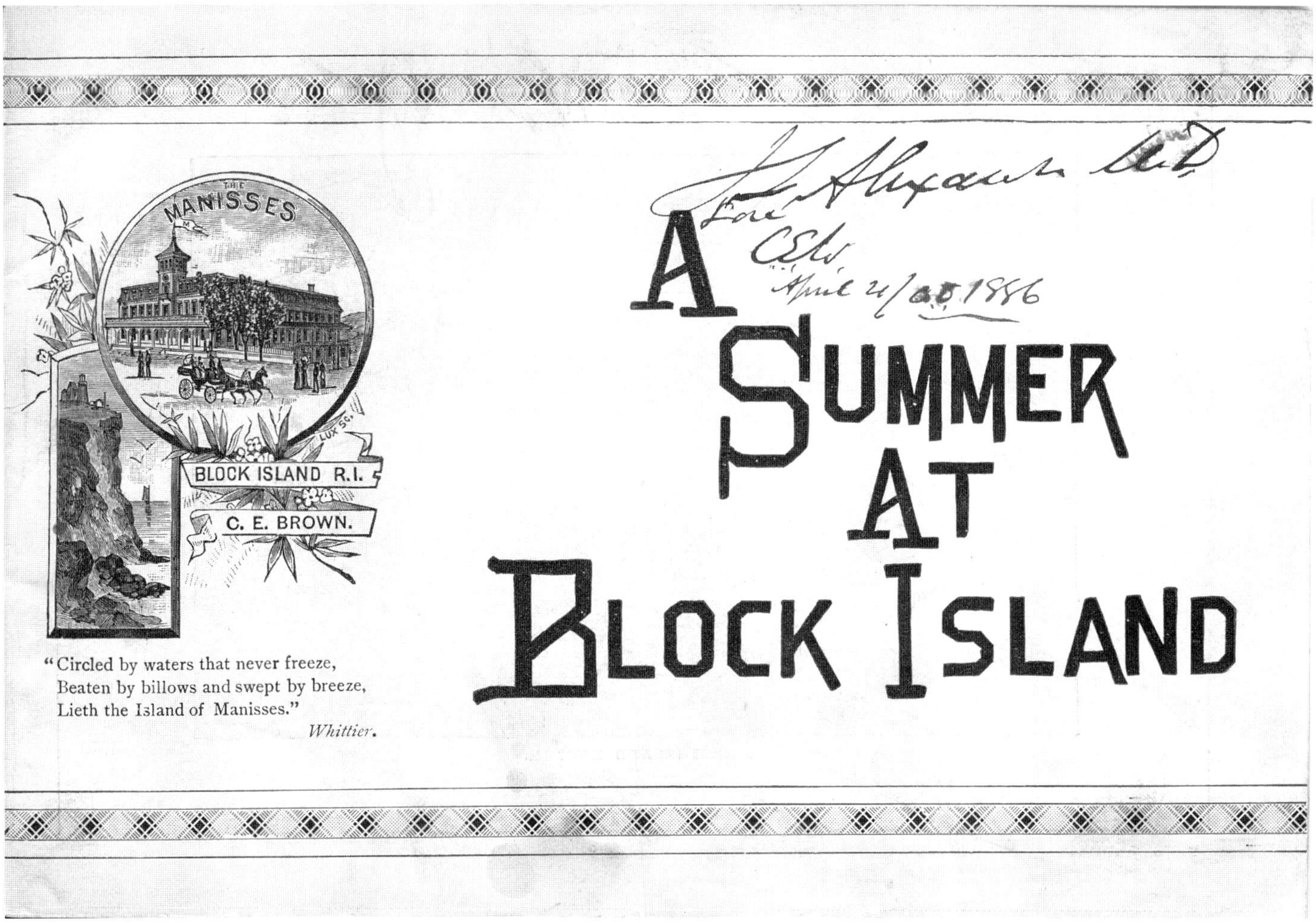
THE MANISSES
BLOCK ISLAND R.I.
C. E. BROWN.
"Circled by waters that never freeze,
Beaten by billows and swept by breeze,
Lieth the Island of Manisses."
Whittier.
A SUMMER AT BLOCK ISLAND

HIGHLAND HOUSE
BLOCK ISLAND

The HIGHLAND HOUSE — 16-page booklet, ca. 1889

The Highland House, built in 1877 by Delorin A. Mitchell, stood off High Street a few hundred feet west of the Atlantic Inn. The building was abandoned in the mid-1900s, and torn down in 1968 by the town.

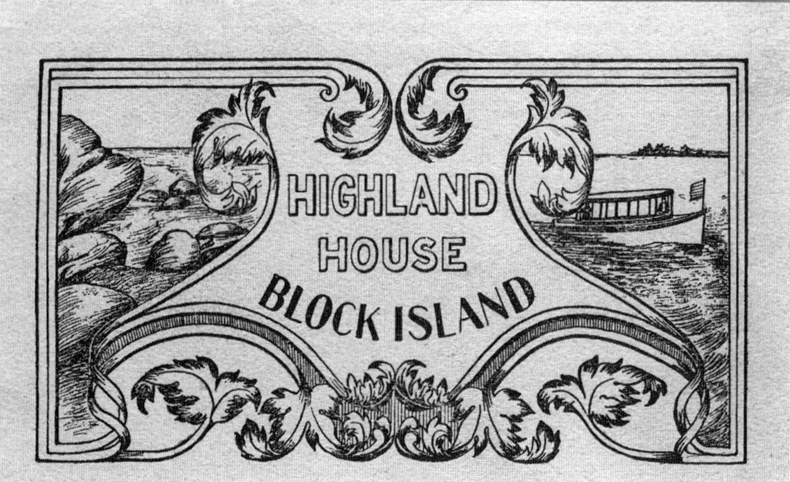

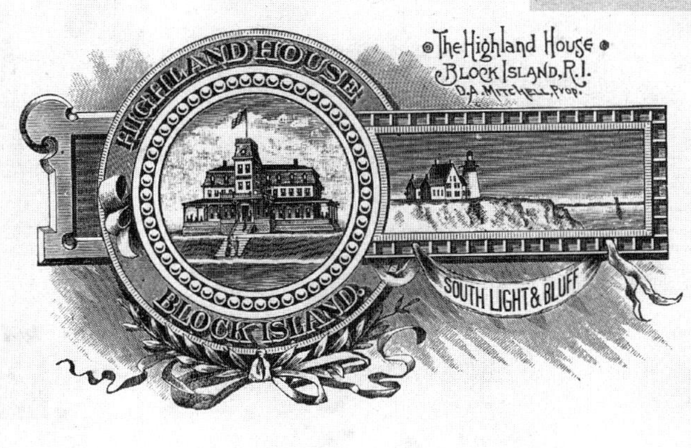

The Highland House
Block Island, R.I.
D.A. Mitchell, Prop.
HIGHLAND HOUSE
BLOCK ISLAND
SOUTH LIGHT & BLUFF

The HIGHLAND HOUSE — with Southeast Lighthouse, 16-page booklet, ca. 1890

The SPRING HOUSE — booklets, 1894 (top) and 1920s (bottom).

The typography of these two brochures reveals changes in society during the intervening four decades, as the fanciness of the Victorian age was supplanted by the clean lines of the modern age — a transformation that occurred also in the fields of architecture, fashion, industrial design, and furniture styles.

The NATIONAL HOTEL — 16-page booklet, ca. 1910

The CROWN — brochure, late 1930s

The Crown Inn, located in New Harbor near the Narragansett Inn, which it strongly resembled, burned in 1940. The site was subdivided in the late1970s, by the longtime family owners, to build condominiums called Trim's Ridge (see photo, page 61).

The SURF HOTEL — 16-page booklet, 1890s

This 10-page effort stressed that at the Surf: "hot salt water baths" were free to the guests — and the rooms came with "celebrated Bliss springs and good hair mattresses on every bed."

The SURF HOTEL — brochure, 1950s

The importance of Block Island to the Surf's owners, the Cyr family, was made clear in their brochure map of the 1950s, with the Island rendered larger than all the rest of the state — an attitude unconsciously adopted by any visitors who stay longer than a few days.

The "hunting" was for pheasants or ducks — there were no deer on the Island until the regretable day a few were purposely released by the town council in the mid-1960s.

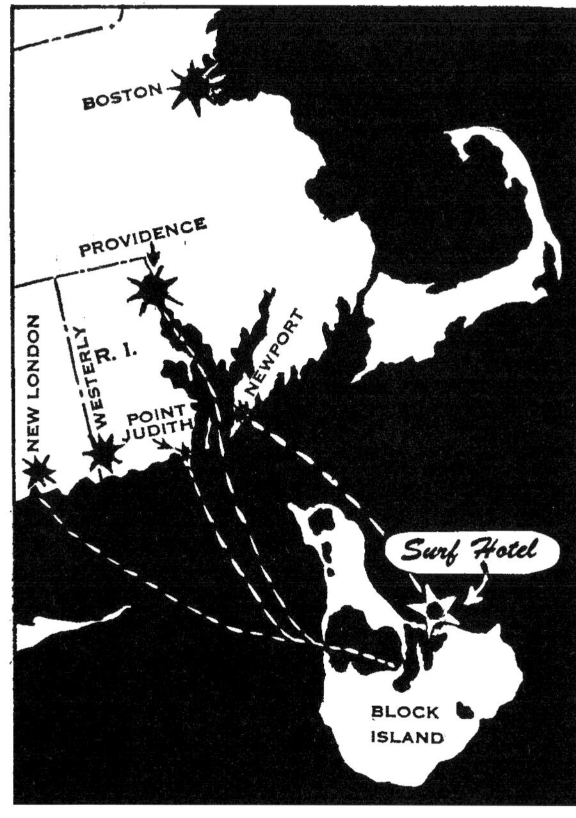

FOR A WONDERFUL VACATION . . . .

. . . . THE BERMUDA OF THE NORTH

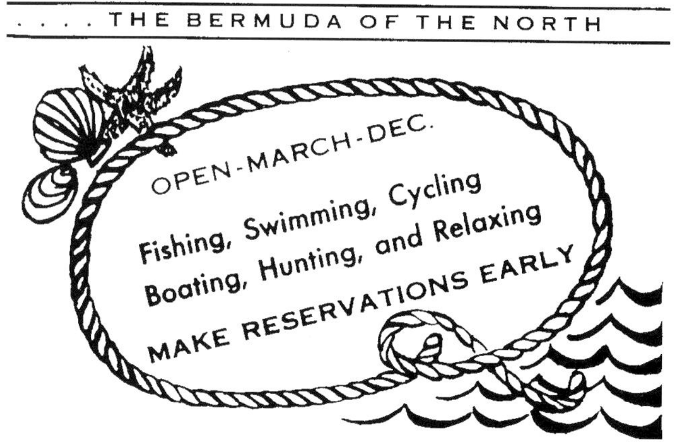

CHAPTER 20

Island photographers

and their lasting pictures of the early 1900s

A companion story to Chapter Two:
The First Photographs of Block Island from the 1800s

ALTHOUGH HORDES OF TOURISTS visited Block Island during the early 1900s, only a few carried the small compact cameras first popularized by Kodak at the turn-of-the-century. The preservers of posterity for us were instead a half-dozen or so professionals who for decades labored to make detailed images of the Island's architecture, streets, harbors, and people.

There were but three photographic giants here in the first half of this century: — Byram Woodhead, who worked from 1896 to 1922 — R. Adelbert Negus, from 1915 to 1925 — and Robert Geer, from 1923 to 1959.

Other photographers whose efforts were less extensive on Block Island, and whose work is not shown on these pages, were: — H. Ladd Walford of Westerly, who photographed Island scenes from about 1905 to 1920, but is most remembered for his views of the LARCHMONT sinking, published as post cards, dead bodies and all — Harold West and Elmer F. West, of the "Sunny Jim" studio which specialized in developing the film of others in the late 1920s and 1930s (see page 195) — and Clarence Lewis, a native Island farmer, with photography as a sideline, whose views of the damage wrought by the 1938 hurricane, together with those taken by his 20-year-old son Rob, left an accurate record of the force of 150 mph winds.

Setting up shop each summer with their tripod-mounted cameras and black cloth head-coverings, the early professionals would solicit customers to their studios — or traipse off to the beach in search of likely paying subjects — or create thoughtfully composed 'set-shot' images of the Island's land and architecture, to sell later as souvenirs. The work of the summertime commercial photographers — using large-format negatives — captured precise detail to a far greater extent than did the mass-produced postcards sold at Island stores by national distributors from 1900 to the 1970s, and by local and regional photographers in the 1980s and 90s.

We cannot readily visualize how Block Islanders fished and farmed in the 1700s and early 1800s — before the invention of photography. But we can conjure in our mind's eye the attributes of the 1910s, 1930s, and 1950s, even distinguishing with great accuracy the architectural, fashion, or automotive characteristics of one decade from another — and that is due almost solely to photographs, and their offshoot, the movies.

Known to many, unknown to us, ca. 1900

The identity of this lovely woman has vanished in time, but was surely not lost to her peers. She is indoors, standing in front of a painted backdrop of the sea at the Woodhead studio on Water Street. The child shown standing in the photo on page 192, which was taken at a later date, stood in precisely the same spot — the waves and canvas blemishes on the immediate right of both individuals are identical .

But, for the photo of the child seated in a play cart on page 192, the photographer chose for a background a portion of the canvas much further to the right.

This image is a positive "contact print" made in a darkroom by laying photographic paper directly against the negative. The original print (3½ x 5 inches) is therefore the same size as the negative. The negative's wide tab, used to slide the film from its camera holder, is visible along the bottom.

The Woodhead brothers

WILLIAM AND BYRAM WOODHEAD BEGAN PRACTICING photography on Block Island in 1896. Byram returned summers to Block Island until 1922.

One of their specialties for visiting tourists was the posed beach photograph, with family members and friends arranged on the sand in spirited postures, or piled to overflowing atop one of the photographer's popular props: a donkey carriage or ox-cart.

The resulting images were unlike the staid photographic portraits of the late 1800s — when slow shutter speeds necessitated unnaturally frozen facial expressions.

Woodhead customers nearly always smiled — particularly when encouraged by their arrangement in precarious positions. These willing participants might be grouped in long train-like lines, hands on the shoulders of the person in front — or stacked like a pyramid, balanced on the knees or shoulders of companions (see page 194).

This presented — as may well have been the underlying reason for many photographs — an excellent opportunity for members of the opposite sex to hold each other without raising too many nearby eyebrows. An attractive person to one's left, for instance, might receive a meaningful message sent via a tight grasp — while the person on one's right would be held more pragmatically. The process of taking the photograph was a hugely successful adventure for all involved — some groups of visitors finding a need to pose often.

The Woodheads' summer business — called the Block Island Photo Co. — was housed in a small building that no longer exists, located on Water Street on the left side of the present-day Seaside Market (2nd building from left, page 239). In 1923 the building and the photographic business were transferred to an assistant — the even more prolific photographer, summertime resident Robert Geer.

Teddy bear and child at Woodhead studio, ca. 1905

Compare this image to the two other studio photographs made in front of the same painted backdrop, page 190 and below. The rugged beach 'stones' were made from hollow boxes, but the seaweed — readily available on the other side of Water Street — looks real enough.

Photo Post Card by Woodhead — against painted studio backdrop, 1905

Some Island studios posed their subjects against painted backdrops depicting Block Island's shoreline. The backdrop shown here extended on each side beyond this view, allowing the photographer to compose his picture with waves only, or a "Block Island cliff" on either the right or the left.

Photo by Woodhead, 5" x 7"
— donkey cart and Emmett family at Crescent Beach, 1905

The pleasure derived by the participants during the photographic session was as much reason to hire one of the wandering photographers, as was the actual receiving of the finished image the next day. Here a donkey cart is overwhelmed — which was the photographer's plan — with a man peering between the creature's ears, a woman mounted on the donkey's back with a dog sitting in her lap, and others posed jauntily in the cart itself.

The man in the middle, standing on one leg, is aiming his own, much smaller, box camera at the photographer.

Photo by Woodhead, 5" x 7"
— ox cart and Emmett family at Crescent Beach, 1905

On another day at the beach, multi-generations of Emmetts pose with another photographer's helper, a single-yoke ox-cart, which, before the advent of motor trucks, really did perform most of the hard labor on Block Island.

Here the man atop the cart and the two men behind the ox — all with hands on hips and elbows spread wide — seem to be challenging the ox in a primitive test of whose the biggest. This time the dog wants no part of the front of the rig and is securely sequestered over the wheel. Other photographers' props, less frequently employed on Crescent Beach, were a monkey and a camel.

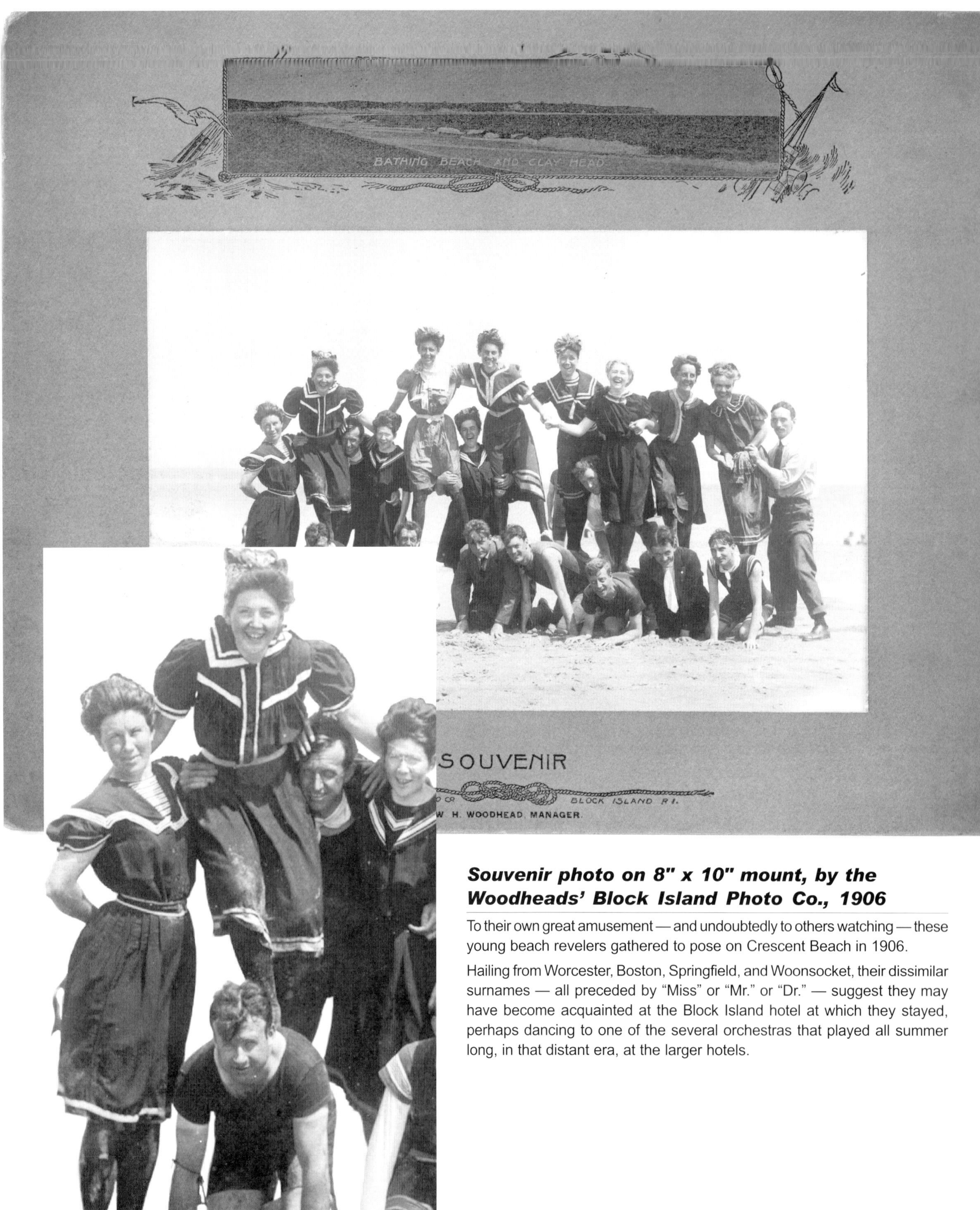

Souvenir photo on 8" x 10" mount, by the Woodheads' Block Island Photo Co., 1906

To their own great amusement — and undoubtedly to others watching — these young beach revelers gathered to pose on Crescent Beach in 1906.

Hailing from Worcester, Boston, Springfield, and Woonsocket, their dissimilar surnames — all preceded by "Miss" or "Mr." or "Dr." — suggest they may have become acquainted at the Block Island hotel at which they stayed, perhaps dancing to one of the several orchestras that played all summer long, in that distant era, at the larger hotels.

Sunny Jim's Studio on Chapel Street, ca. 1926

Sunny Jim's Studio, on the extreme right, developed the ubiquitous snapshots taken by Brownie cameras and others in the 1920s and 30s — although a few images of Block Island were also sold by the shop as souvenirs.

The studio was initially located on Chapel Street in the building now housing Eli's restaurant. That is just a camera-throw from the latest Block Island photographic store, Photo Dog, which also develops film on the premises. In the late 1920s, Elmer West moved the photo shop to a space inside the building that is today's Seaside Market.

A large shopping center was built at this location in the mid-1990s, but familiar buildings remain. The area is overrun with rental mopeds and is the least attractive part of Block Island to visit.

Photo envelope for Sunny Jim's Studio, 1930s

Sunny Jim's Studio

Next to Island Dept. Store

E. F. West, Prop.

R. Adelbert Negus

AMONGST YEAR-ROUND ISLANDERS in the early 1900s, R. Adelbert Negus was the most extensive practitioner of commercial photography. Owning what is now the Star Department Store, Negus specialized in drygoods but competed also, from about 1905 to 1925, with the Woodheads' photography business, which was located just two doors away.

Negus' building, which Adelbert purchased in 1903, already had a long photographic association, having been built in 1883 by the Providence photographer Hosea Q. Morton (see top of page 180). Numerous mounted photographs and stereoviews were sold by Morton to tourists in the 1880s and 90s — and their reverse side, stamped "H. Q. Morton," always listed the other Block Island titles in the series, a feature no other photographer after Morton practiced.

By 1914 Negus had enlarged his building outward toward the street and combined it with an adjacent structure, forming the large-windowed storefront that we now admire as the Star Department Store. Negus also festooned his building with 20 signs, 12 of them promoting his photography business, which included: *tintypes, group photographs, developing, and printing* (see photos: top of opposite page, and on page 112). Although his large store hosted enough signage to have completely covered the front of the Woodheads' nearby smaller building, it was in the latter structure that photography on Block Island prevailed the longest.

Negus, from living on the Island year-round, became involved with Block Island in other ways — perhaps the reason for his departure from photography in the mid-1920s — organizing the Volunteer Fire Department in 1924 (housed in the building on Weldon's Way that is now Aldo's bakery) and holding the position of first warden of the five-member town council (the equivalent of mayor) from 1928 until his death in 1938. Amongst the accomplishments mentioned in his obituary were: "one of ten men who originally stocked the island with pheasants" and "the official town photographer."

Photographs by Negus were mounted on 8" x 10" cardboard stock, with a logo — "Negus Studio" or "Island Studio" — embossed on the front. More readily found are his sepia-toned postcards with white-borders, with the telltale words "Pub. by A. NEGUS, Block Island, R.I." on the back. He did not, however, always make his postcards from new negatives — some were manufactured from negatives of H. Q. Morton that were 20 or 30 years old (such as the photograph of the old windmill, top of page 212).

For other photographs by R. Adelbert Negus, see:

- *Ice at Old Harbor dock — page 91, top photo*

The present-day Star Department Store, when owned by R. Adelbert Negus, ca. 1910

Active in photography from 1905 to 1925, year-round resident Del Negus was designated the official Island photographer.

At the time of the photograph on the right, 20 signs covered the front and side of his building, 12 of them proclaiming the abilities of his Island Studio photography business to produce portraits of people and scenic views of Block Island (see a view of entire building, page 112.)

Swordfish caught off Block Island by K. P. Lincoln Party.

Postcard by Negus — swordfish on Old Harbor dock, 1924

The day's catch — unloaded each afternoon at Old Harbor from the Island's dozens of fishing work boats — was always an attraction for children and adults, forming as well the subject of numerous postcards made by Island photographers.

In the old days, the average weight of a swordfish was more than 200 pounds, with individuals twice that size not unusual.

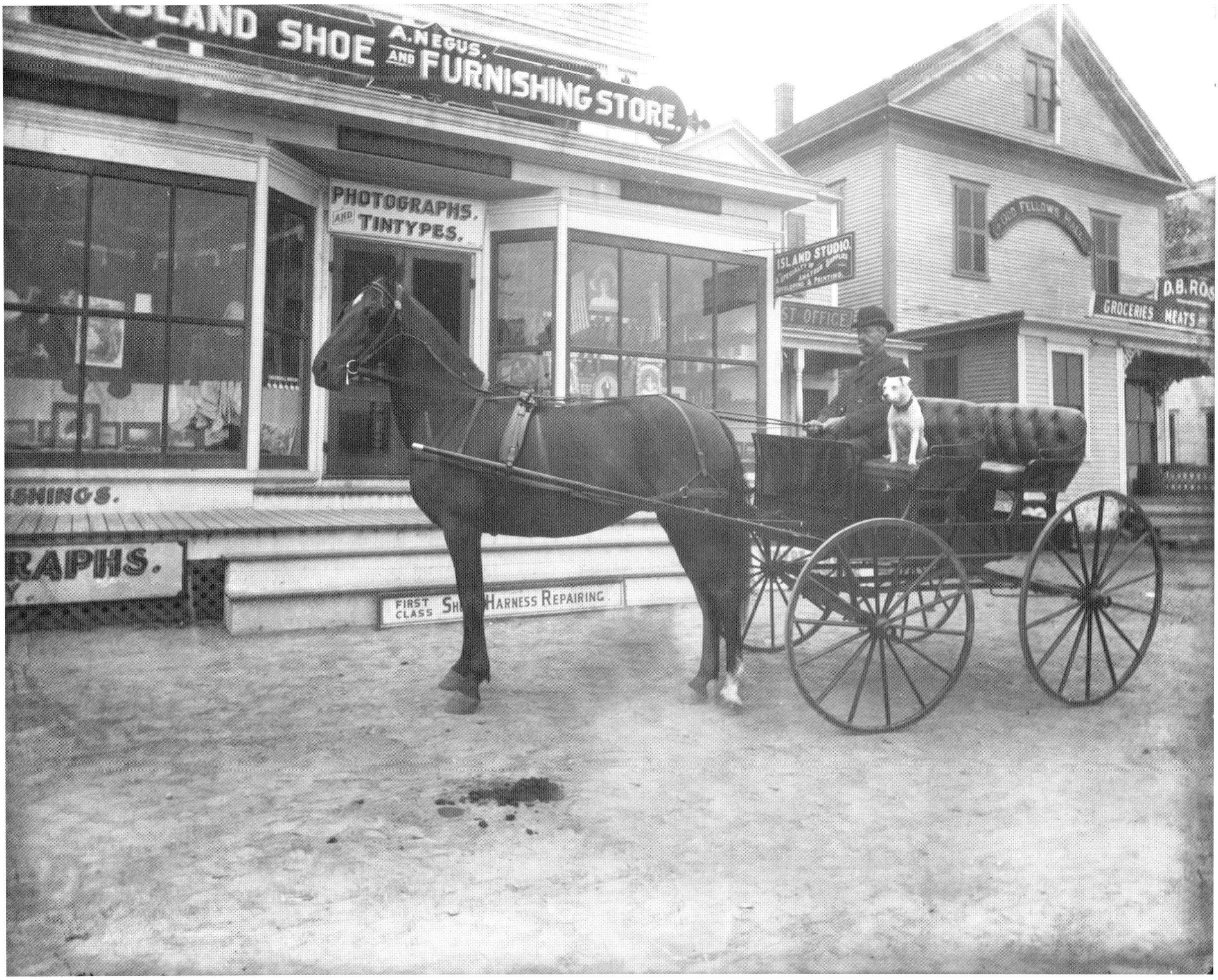

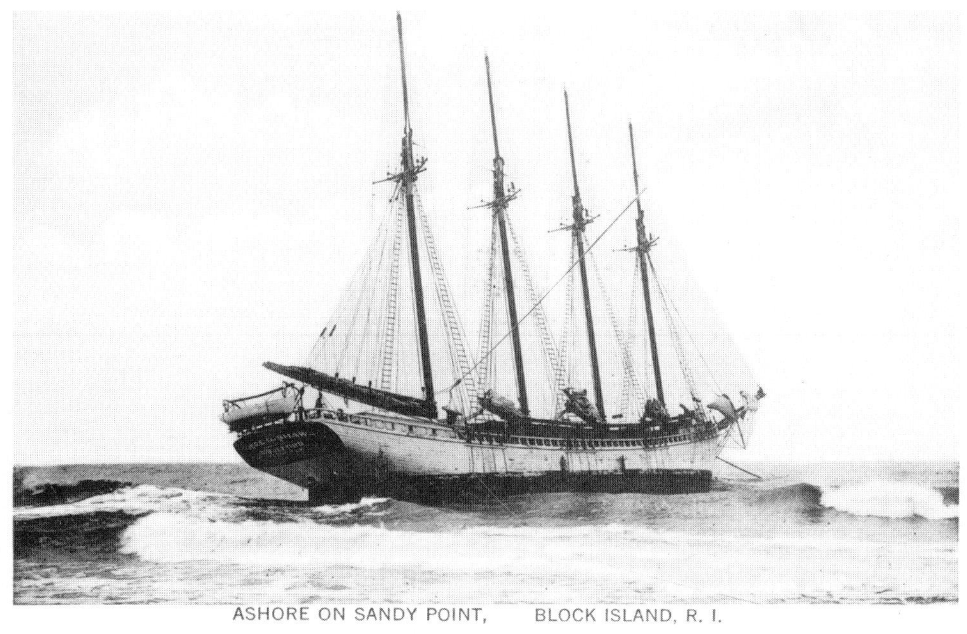

Postcard by Negus — schooner aground, Jere G. Shaw, 1920

R. Adelbert Negus photographed the grounding of the four-masted schooner **Jere G. Shaw** in March 1920 with his large box-style camera. The size of the negative was 5" x 7" — about 20 times the area of today's common 35 mm film.

The schooner struck the beach adjacent to the east side of the North Lighthouse, and was safely towed off after removal of the cargo.

ASHORE ON SANDY POINT, BLOCK ISLAND, R. I.

Robert L. Geer

ABOUT 1920, TWO DOORS DOWN AT THE WOODHEAD STORE, Byram Woodhead hired a young man from Three Rivers, Massachusetts — a town located near Byram's own home in Palmer.

The new assistant, Robert L. Geer, purchased the business from Woodhead in 1923, and returned each summer, eventually creating the longest photographic record ever made of Block Island — some 40 years of effort. His thousands of negatives usually depict outdoor scenes and activities, but occasionally he utilized the Woodheads' decades-old painted canvas backdrop — inside his Star Photo Shop — that depicted the beach, the waves and the Island's bluffs.

To view his achievement in the highest quality form, you must search for Geer's well-produced *Photo Post Cards*. These images are actual photographs developed on photographic paper, but with a reverse side partitioned for an address similar to a regular postcard. Sometimes Geer stamped the back with an oval bearing the words "Geer's Star Photo." He perpetuated the skills of the Woodhead's, who had also manufactured their own photo post cards, printed on various earlier styles of photo card stock.

Geer's work is more easily seen today in the less distinct, ordinary post cards produced on a printing press and sold in the late 1940s and throughout the 1950s by Brayton White, a year-round Islander to whom Geer released some of his negatives for reproduction. These black & white images have the words "Published by the Bob White Shop, Block Island, R.I." printed on the back. White's store stood on a lot just to the right of the Empire Theatre. In August 2000 the small structure — which had fuctioned for the previous 25 years as a gift shop known as The Figurehead, and then as The Hurricane — was moved to the rear of the same lot, facing Chapel Street. Built in 1890 as the office of the *Mid-Ocean* summer newspaper (see photo, page 134), the building also had housed the Island's first high school at the turn-of-the-century.

Unmounted photographs of Block Island were sold by Robert Geer on 5" x 7" paper, sometimes stamped on the back: "Geer's Star Photo Shop, Block Island, R.I."

"Bob White" post card; based on photo by Geer — ferry leaving Old Harbor, late 1940s

The grand years of leisurely and more personal ferry travel were such that people waving on the dock were nearly face-to-face with people leaving on the ferry.

That was the case just moments before Robert Geer took this photograph of the departure of the Island's tiny ferry, the World War I sub-chaser **ELIZABETH ANN**.

The end of this casualness came in the 1980s when — for travel to both Pt. Judith and New London — large stern-loading ferries were built, replacing all the old boats that had character.

Robert Geer's Photo Post Card — wreck of the LIGHTBURNE, 1941

The last great ship to wreck on Block Island was the 416-foot tanker LIGHTBURNE, which struck rocks and sank directly in front of the Southeast Lighthouse in February 1941.

A red navigation buoy marks the spot — a popular site for scuba divers now, on days with no swells.

For other photographs by Geer, see:

- *Old Harbor;* p.149, center & bottom
- *Smilin' Through;* p. 224, bottom

With the demise of the Star Photo Shop when Robert Geer died in 1959, no organized photography of Block Island occurred until the *Block Island Times* began publication as a summer weekly in 1970 — but the *Times'* 35 mm negatives were only seen as poorly reproduced newspaper photos.

For 60 years the Star Photo Shop on Water Street — through both Woodhead and Geer — served longer than any other location in preserving our conception of 20th century Block Island. The building was demolished in the 1960's. A rental moped dealer now uses the site, next to the Seaside Market's driveway, to park his equipment.

Since the mid-1970s, the defacto Island photographer has been Malcolm Greenaway, whose painting-size images are larger and more colorful than any Island views published previously. Less known to visitors are Malcolm's news-type photos of Island events (see photos on pages 246, 247), long used by local publications — and sometimes credited, but sometimes not. The photographer, being a philosopher, seems resolved to this fact, Malcolm instead focusing on discovering by his own longevity whether or not the state-of-the-art processing used for his color images will indeed last for centuries, as planned.

Robert Geer's Star Photo Shop on Water St., ca. 1940

This small, two-story store had a flat-topped "Western" style front, as can be seen near the left side of the aerial photo on page 239. The building was removed from the site in the 1960s.

Capt. Cornelius W. "Connie" Rose, who retired from the sea to his farm and taxi cab, appears to be in command of this part of Water Street.

The car is one of the few made by the American Austin Co. (later the American Bantam Co.) during the 1930s. If the vehicle looks oddly familiar, it is because this mini-auto was transformed shortly afterward into World War II's famous "jeep."

Man and beast admiring the statue of Rebecca, ca. 1910

The statue of Rebecca at the Well was erected in 1896 by the Women's Christian Temperance Union — temperance being the operative intention of the multi-orifice, three-level water fountain meant to satiate the thirsts of horses, people and dogs — all of which appear in this photograph.

CHAPTER 21

"For God and Home and Every Land"

Rebecca, a 100-year-old young lady, and the woman who put Rebecca in her place, and us in ours — Lucretia Mott Ball

GIVING DIRECTIONS TO A TOURIST, an Islander might say "Go to Rebecca, the fountain, and take a sharp left"not only helping the visitor find a store or a road but also the heart of Block Island.

For if a heart is the place where one's blood cells leave but always return after a trip around the body, then so has the statue of Rebecca been Block Island's heart. At the center of the Island's road system — at Block Island's only rotary — we are pumped out from Rebecca along four roads, always to return.

More than a century of events have passed since the Woman's Christian Temperance Union — the stalwart WCTU — erected the statue on July 22, 1896, atop a seven-basin water fountain in hopes of curbing the imbibing of alcoholic beverages.

"Water" — the fountain proclaimed obviously, with its three levels of basins for horses, people and dogs — was the healthiest, most preferred drink for both man and beast. And there was no mincing semantics in the 1890s, just as there is none today amongst feminists, about the meaning of the word 'man' — it referred solely to human beings of the male gender, many of whom undisputedly had a penchant to drink alcohol, and too much of it.

An inscription at the top of the pedestal's north side declared the WCTU's universal aspirations: "For God and Home and Every Land."

It was not a new concept, to raise one's ideals at the urging of others. The State of Maine passed the first liquor prohibition law in 1851. Four years later 13 of the 31 states had a similar law. Rhode Island — always late or early in national affairs and definitely different — waited until 1886 before enacting a prohibition amendment to its constitution, then quickly repealed it in 1888 and allowed each of the 39 towns and cities to decide for themselves.

On Block Island, sentiment against liquor remained strong, particularly through the resolve of the WCTU. Its very name says it all, each and every word carrying the weight of a sledgehammer — or, in the hands of a famous WCTU contemporary on the mainland, Carry Nation, a saloon-smashing hatchet. The WCTU chapter on Block Island was founded by a woman less radical, but nevertheless formidable, Lucretia Mott Ball, who, over a stretch of five decades until her death intervened, was its first and only president.

Some younger family members say there has been no one like her since, thank God. Or, as a dedicated drunk might suggest in a polite moment: that Lucretia Mott Ball was a tough nut to crack.

To achieve this distinction four items were in her favor, the first being she was a woman the drunk would obviously be a man, and ultimately we all know our place.

Secondly, she was descended from just about every early family on the Island from the 1600s and 1700s — from John Rathbun, one of the original Block Island settlers in 1661, and from whom every "Rathbun," "Rathburn," and "Rathbone" in the United States is also descended; from Walter Rathbun, perennial town clerk for 60 years in the 1700s and early 1800s; and from a vast array of others with quintessential Block Island names such as: Ball, Champlin, Dickens, Dodge, and Mott.

Thirdly, Lucretia married Cassius Clay Ball, a Block Islander who inherited from his father, Nicholas, the Ocean View Hotel — the largest hotel ever built on Block Island, and once the largest in southern New England (see Chapter 3) — where President Grant paid homage one day in 1875, and where United States Supreme Court Justices and the wealthy power brokers of industry and politics spent their vacations in the 1880s and 90s.

The fourth intimidating factor for alcohol imbibers on the Island was, of course, that Lucretia was the president of the local 20-member chapter of the WCTU — and not just any old president. As a state vice-president of the WCTU, and often as state representative to national conventions, Lucretia was associated with Frances Willard, a nationally renown educator who enlarged the WCTU into a worldwide organization and was an early crusader for women's rights — her life is still studied in the 1990s. So influential was Willard in Lucretia's eyes that funds were raised on Block Island for a Frances Willard memorial window at the Baptist Church — the fine colonial-style church at the old town Center, at the bottom of the hill to the airport, that burned in 1908 (see photo, page 144).

Lucretia Mott Ball at age 19, in 1885

Late in her long life, in 1941, Lucretia bequeathed to her fellow citizens three of Block Island's most valuable assets:

— the building for the First Baptist Church,

— the contents of the Historical Society,

— and the first conservation land preserved during the 1900s: Nathan Mott Park, otherwise known as "The Enchanted Forest" (see text on page 206, and map on page 57).

As a civic-minded citizen, Lucretia's interests were not limited to temperance. Born on the Island in 1866, she was writing lengthy stories for the *Christian Messenger* as early as 1884 — at the age of 18 — on behalf of the welfare of the country's Indians: "Long and bravely did the red man fight for their native soil ..." After a hurricane struck the southern Atlantic coast in 1893, Lucretia organized the transportation of barrels of provisions to Beaufort, South Carolina, containing clothing, food, and garden seeds for the citizens, both "white and colored."

And how tough could she be? The year 1895 was one in which the local Block Island populace had voted to be a "dry" town, meaning no alcohol would be sold here. Instead, however, to the consternation of many citizens, liquor was openly available that summer at numerous Island businesses.

In August the WCTU of Block Island employed two detectives from Connecticut to buy liquor on the Island in a 'sting' operation. That evidence was enough for a Newport court to convict four Islanders who received 10-to-30-day jail terms and $20-to-$60 fines. The court case was well publicized at the time in newspaper articles in the *Newport Journal,* which prominently named the convicted men: Darius Dodge, a long-time representative to the State Legislature from Block Island; Aaron W. Mitchell, the Island's Sealer of Weights and Measures; John L. Macomber, an Island constable; and Winfield S. Dodge, keeper of the Yellow Kittens restaurant.

It is no wonder that any citizen, never mind the WCTU, would be offended by the blatancy of the convicted men, particularly town officials. Their only defense — and not one which would hold up in court — was that others on the Island were just as contemptuous of the law.

The *Newport Journal* of December 21, 1895, told how it was on Block Island:

"During the summer the liquor trade is as open as in Newport [a legally 'wet' town], and some very well equipped bars are in operation for the accommodation of the summer visitors. There has been no attempt made to hide this trade, or to disguise the fact that large quantities of liquor are in summer daily sent to the island to be sold. In winter, when there are no visitors, the dealers can sell only to the natives, and it is said that their customers are those least able to waste their substance in buying rum or whiskey. There appeared, however, to be no objections to the summer visitors spending all they wished for beer and other liquors."

The same philosophy has been at work in the late 1900s as tourism has risen above and beyond the popularity of the 1890s. The number of liquor licenses issued each year, once capped at a maximum of nine in the 1960s, has grown to more than thirty in the 1990s — the highest per capita number of bars in the state. Every restaurant, new or old, whether large or small, pleads they must sell liquor in order to compete with other places, "and please raise the quota by one just for me." It's been done more than 20 times.

Lucretia Mott Ball's WCTU might have been adamant but they were not heartless. Her article in the *Christian Herald* a few weeks after the trial, explained:

"It is not pleasure for us to see our fellow men go to prison, but they all know we were willing to settle the case before it went to trial were they willing to sign an agreement to sell no more intoxicants."

The men, it seems, could be just as stubborn as the WCTU, but not as smart.

Seven months after this victory, the fountain and statue were erected by the WCTU, but it is not known now if the effort was in response to the Newport trial, or whether the statue had been ordered before the great saloon sting of August 1895.

The statue of Rebecca at the Well

THE WCTU ORDERED REBECCA from the J. W. Fiske Iron Works of Park Place, New York. A catalog of the period offers a nearly identical fountain and statue for $1,400, listing the item as "Drinking Fountain With Statue of Water Nymph / For Man and Beast." The granite base — particularly necessary because the main street was dirt in that era — came from the Dixon Granite Works of Westerly. During her early decades, Rebecca was always painted bronze — but during the past several, she has alternated colors, shifting every now and then to white.

The name "Rebecca" is not engraved on the statue or pedestal but has been associated with the statue from the beginning, first appearing in a newspaper account in September 1896 titled "Rebecca at the Well." The funds for the "thousand dollar fountain," the story reported, had been raised by the women during the previous year, by way of "a charity quilt, birthday party, concert at the Adrian, a musicale at the Ocean View, and money received by subscription." The Adrian House hotel belonged to Lucretia's father, Nathan Mott, and is now the First Baptist Church. And the charity quilt — with each square containing donors' signatures written in thread — still exists. As with present-day Island projects, much of the statue's cost was contributed by summer visitors who wished to help a worthy Block Island cause.

Rebecca serving her purpose, ca. 1908

A horse drinks from one of the two large basins intended for equine use on Rebecca's pedestal. The small lower basins, one in each corner near ground level, were for dogs.

A spigot on the front side emptied into a medium size basin for humans. This postcard image is titled "W. C. T. U. Drinking Fountain, Block Island, R.I."

Rebecca sports her paradoxical grapes, a cluster at each ear, 1999

Close observers over the decades have noted that Rebecca's full-length cloak seemed to become more sheer during repairs by crafty local craftsmen in 1977.

The tiny amount of land for the statue, although in the center of the busiest intersection on the Island, was privately owned — but fortuitously by Lucretia's husband, C. C. Ball, who donated the property to the WCTU. In 1939, two years before Lucretia died, the fountain was deeded to the town — and was described once again as "Rebecca at the Well."

Rebecca, if spelled Rebekah, would refer to the obliging woman in Genesis 24 of whom Abraham's servant says: "She quickly let down her jar from her shoulder, and said, 'drink, and I will give your camels drink also.'" From this gesture the servant deemed Rebekah worthy of marrying Abraham's son Isaac. But this story does not explain the grapes tantalizingly framing the face of Block Island's Rebecca.

The fountain is similar in style to many others erected near the turn-of-the-century in towns across America. The motif is an eclectic mix of Classical, Renaissance, and Rococo designs with — according to a report prepared in April 1996 for the Block Island Conservancy — "egg and dart molding, acanthus, fish scale, cartousche medallions with relief busts, palmettes, waves, and scrolled foliage."

Once fed with water piped down from Continental Pond on High Street, and later from Sands Pond further south, the fountain is no longer functioning, and the water basins have been filled since the 1960s with potted flowers.

Did the statue of Rebecca have its intended effect after being erected on July 22, 1896?

Although the single water basin meant for humans, was pointedly facing Old Harbor's steamboat dock — so visitors walking up the hill to town would encounter it — and although men and beasts did drink water from the fountain for several decades, the temperance concept did not soak in. It didn't during the Prohibition years of the 1920s when Block Island was a central staging area for rumrunning boats, and didn't during the past 30 years when the number of liquor licenses tripled, and didn't any other time.

So the story goes that Rebecca is not "Rebecca at the Well" at all, but rather, the good Victorian ladies at the turn-of-the-century somehow purchased a handmaiden to Bacchus, the Greek and Roman god of wine, or some other nymph with qualities different from the crystal-clear pureness of the water that the WCTU intended to flow forever from their statue's base.

There have been many a toast to such theories in the last 100 years. And, as plain as day, those are GRAPES hanging from each side of her wide adorable face, with a smile as enigmatic as the Mona Lisa's.

National PROHIBITION 1920 — 1933

THE TEMPERANCE MOVEMENT receded briefly then swelled once more across the United States. By1916 anti-saloon laws had been adopted by 23 of the 48 states. On December 22,1917, Congress submitted to the states for ratification the 18th Amendment to the Constitution, prohibiting alcohol sales throughout the country.

Rhode Island fought this amendment so hard that it was the only state whose legislature in both the House of Representatives and the Senate, refused to ratify Prohibition. Rhode Island even took the extraordinary step of appropriating $25,000 for the state's attorney general to challenge the constitutionality of adding such an amendment to the United States constitution.

When the amendment took effect on January 16, 1920 — passed by the required two-thirds majority of states — the law was flouted across the entire nation, and the wondrous Roaring Twenties was born.

It was no particular surprise then that during the next 13 years — before Prohibition was repealed in December 1933 by ratification of the 21st amendment — the largest rum fleet of bootlegging ships on the East Coast sometimes happened to be off Rhode Island, and, as geography would have it, directly off Block Island.

At first the legal offshore limit for these vessels — that brought liquor from foreign countries and waited for smaller boats to smuggle the cases ashore — was only three miles. Even when increased to 12 miles in May 1924, the distance was not enough to keep the Island from being in the thick of things, instead making Block Island an ideal place to layover in the day, preparing for the nightly games with the Coast Guard.

And so bootleggers from the mainland brought their long sleek craft into Old Harbor in the morning. Tourists could see the mechanics changing the spark plugs of the Liberty airplane engines — surplus motors from World War I converted to marine use — producing enough discarded spark plugs from the two to four 12-cylinder engines to fill a bucket.

Walking past Rebecca's beckoning vase, the rumrunners would come — some no doubt mentioning the grapes in her hair — to Maloof's department store on Water Street, where they would discard their dirty clothes from the previous night's outing, and simply order a new set of white flannel trousers, flannel shirt and shoes. A complete outfit every time they came in.

So central was Block Island for everyone involved, that by the mid-1920s the Coast Guard from New London had set up an advance base at the Narragansett Inn — in the building across from Dead Eye Dick's Restaurant. But the rumrunning boats kept coming in.

Everyone knew who everyone was, the catch being the Coast Guard had to apprehend the rumboats while evidence was aboard. Each year for more than a decade the cat-and-mouse game was played out off the Island as the fast contact boats dashed

The WCTU's worst nightmare, ca. 1900

This is the type of behavior the WCTU sought to curb, but anyone familiar with Block Island will realize the photo is clearly of another place.

back and forth to the rum fleet bringing their wares to the great throngs of customers waiting up Narragansett Bay or down Long Island Sound.

The Coast Guard did not bother the local speakeasies, and — as was widely the case across the United States — there were a few.

Rebecca on her perch, 1999

Lucretia's real legacy — 1941

On **March 11, 1941**, Lucretia Mott Ball passed away at the age of 74.

She was born the daughter of a Block Island farmer and hotel keeper, and became one of the Island's two most influential women of the 20th century, the second being Elizabeth Dickens (see pages 254-261). Only two other women, both born in the 1700s, have been as noteworthy in Block Island's history: Catharine Ray and her niece Catharine Littlefield, intimate friends of national figures such as Benjamin Franklin, General Lafayette, George and Martha Washington, and Eli Whitney.

But, while the two Catharines moved within the tapestry of mainland events that created the United States, Lucretia Mott Ball — as did Miss Dickens — wove threads permanently into Block Island's fabric, forever affecting future residents and visitors here.

Three bequests of Lucretia's will perpetuated her life's influence (also see page 55).

She bequeathed the Adrian hotel, overlooking Old Harbor, to the Island's First Baptist Church. When the main Baptist church building burned tragically in 1944, the Adrian became the center of church affairs. The sanctuary, protruding from the front, was added in 1952 to create the present-day building, which has ever since hosted ecumenical activities and community events, and been Block Island's focal point of year-round church services (see page 129 for photo of church, Rebecca and President Clinton).

Secondly, she arranged for her family farm, named for Lucretia's father Nathan Mott, to be converted into a public park "for the use, enjoyment and benefit of the residents of Block Island and visitors." Lucretia was thus the first individual to leave land on the Island for her fellow citizens to enjoy as open space — foreseeing this need more than 30 years, an entire generation, before the next land conservation efforts occurred in the 1970s (see Chapter 26 about the Block Island Conservancy).

But Nathan Mott Park — a part of which is commonly referred to as the Enchanted Forest — has been whittled away. Twice the state condemned large tracts of land — in 1949 to create the airport; and in 1961 to erect light poles in the vacant land at the end of the runway, on the west side of Center Road. Then in the early 1990s the First Baptist Church — paradoxically — attempted to seize a good 10-acre portion of the park next to Old Mill Road, ignoring, amongst a host of things, the obvious maple trees that had been planted 40 years earlier by the park's trustees at 20-foot intervals — the church did succeed in acquiring a 3.35-acre lot from the park's northeast corner, later to be sold. Because of these activities, of the 77 acres that initially were left to the public as Nathan Mott Park, only 39 acres remain (see map, page 57).

Thirdly, Lucretia ordered that all her personal property "of historical or genealogical interest or shall be of value as antiques and art objects" would be given to the most appropriate museum. Since no museum existed on Block Island at the time of Lucretia's death, the Islanders decided to create one — which was done in 1942 with the formation of the Block Island Historical Society, where her collection of heirlooms and Island furniture can be seen today (see photo, bottom of page 115).

A New Head for Rebecca — 1959

The **Islanders continued** living out the century — the rush of excitement of the 1920s — the depression of the 30s — the war — and the quiet, stagnant 50s.

A 1939 deed — another of Lucretia's preparations for the future — transferred Rebecca from the WCTU to the town on the condition that Rebecca must continue functioning as a fountain and must be painted "biannually." The town took ownership but met neither condition.

The noticeable decay of Rebecca can be said to have begun dramatically on Halloween night 1959 when the weight of a tin-can decorated line strung by Island kids around the statue — across the road to the drug store in one direction, and to the Empire Theatre in the other — swung in strong winds pulling the statue off the base and smashing Rebecca's head and vase on the pavement. It was enough of a tragedy to warrant two *Providence Journal* articles, including photographs — one in November 1959, and another in March 1961 when the statue was re-erected with a new, professionally cast pot metal head and a repaired vase.

By 1976, corrosion was evident from a more relentless culprit — the weather. Before the town could devise a restoration scheme for Rebecca, fate again took a swift turn at the hands of humans, this time the hands being at the wheel of a skidding tow truck that slammed into the fountain pedestal in January 1977, dislodging it. Well-meaning Islanders spent the next year and a half — some paid by a $1,000 insurance settlement, some volunteers — removing the statue to retouch the effects of time with epoxy and fiberglass. The previously hollow cast iron base was filled with concrete and, for the third time in Rebecca's life, she was mounted atop her fountain bottom.

Other repairs were made locally in the late 1980s replacing missing sections of the vase, and volunteers continued painting Rebecca and planting flowers in her former water basins.

With her 100th birthday pending, a study was commissioned by the Block Island Conservancy to give Rebecca a checkup. The resulting report of April 1996, states emphatically that the informal, homemade Island remedies of the past two decades have ironically hastened the dissolution of Rebecca's metal, both of the cast iron in the fountain's base and of the pot metal in the statue.

For instance, not only does the cement inside the pedestal attract moisture from the ground, keeping the interior of the fountain in an ever-corroding condition, but the embedded wire-reinforcement prevents easy dismantling of the fountain's four sections to make corrections.

Estimates for Rebecca's repair range from $11,700 for short-range preservation, to $140,000 for an entirely new fountain and statue cast in a modern alloy.

Apart from financial considerations is the emotional choice of keeping the original Rebecca. With defects and limitations, yes — but a statue we know is really she.

If there is a new, younger replica — it will not at all be the same Rebecca we grew up with. Not the Rebecca that Lucretia touched. Not the one the rumrunners did a shuffle around. Not the statue so many high schoolers embraced, climbing her Halloween night with a bucket of paint in the other hand.

If Rebecca is replaced, Rebecca will be gone.

A vacant pedestal, winter 1977

Even with Rebecca absent from her pedestal — after damage by a sliding truck — the slow pace of winter life on Block Island continued as usual, with these travelers obediently following the customary counter-clockwise direction of the Island's only rotary.

View from edge of Beacon Hill Road, showing two windmills, 1884

Looking east toward Old Harbor in the distance, the two dominant windmills in Block Island's history are visible in this view. The Littlefield Mill, on the left next to Center Road, was moved to Old Mill Road in 1888. The Harbor Mill, near the middle of the photograph, was located north of Old Town Road. Both mills disappeared from the landscape in the early 1900s.

Note how the stonewalls have a foot-high layer of smaller stones along the top. Most of the Island's walls have lost this layer, usually fallen off — or, although the walls are presumably protected by town ordinance, used in some cases to build the cement foundations of modern houses.

The house in the foreground, often considered one of the oldest on Block Island, has been extensively remodeled — many of the original timbers, as in the roof, have been replaced with modern lumber, and original handhewn beams placed in new locations. During the War of 1812, when the Island was considered neutral by reason of its location, the commanders of the British 74-gun ship **POICTIERS** and the war-sloop **MEDSTONE** were entertained at dinner by the homeowner, Samuel Ball.

CHAPTER 22

Air Motors

Nearly 200 years of non-stop motion on Block Island

YOU CANNOT MISS THEM. They move by themselves — recent ones looking like spindly Martian invaders in H. G. Wells' *The War of the Worlds*. They fascinate. They make the wind on your face seem visible, and they do work for 'nothing.' They are windmills, first devised untold thousands of years ago.

Like an impressionable kid, you are enthralled to see them, unless one looms above your backyard bayberries, malfunctions, and makes noise with everlasting relentlessness.

They have been going around on Block Island for nearly 200 hundred years.

The Dutch-type windmill — for grinding food

WHEN THE FIRST BREED OF WINDMILL on Block Island — the familiar Dutch-type — approached a hundred years in age, they were appreciated for more than the fact they ground grain.

An ode to the two Island windmills was printed by the local newspaper in 1891 — the mills were loved then for their mere existence:

"The two windmills, one on the road to the Center and the other on the West side, form a unique and striking figure in the landscape.

"Not that there is anything peculiar or uncommon in the use of wind as a motor, but simply that the odd, fantastic appearance of the mills themselves, their heavy oak frames, the moss covered shingles, and the very air with which, with their long vanes that nearly sweep the ground, they mount guard over the surrounding country, seems to imply a consciousness of superiority over the neighboring edifices, based upon an old age following a life of unchallenged usefulness.

"Generations have come and gone, children have grown up to manhood and descended the hill of life, some tarrying until perchance, their own grandchildren were gray-headed men, and still the tireless vanes go round.

"But Father Time, who also goes his rounds with the same tireless persistence, and whose sickle, first or last, falls on all created things, animate or inanimate, has for some time had his eye upon the old mill. Verily, they have nearly fallen into a state of 'innocuous desuetude.'"

A POST MILL AT FRESH POND — THE FIRST DUTCH WINDMILL: In the very early 1800s the north end of Fresh Pond, east of the small cemetery, was a center of Island life — with a school, a meeting house, and a small 12-foot windmill of the 'post' type. To turn the vanes of a post mill into the wind, the entire building was rotated around a vertical pole fixed firmly in the ground. Because of the weight involved, the design prevented such mills from being large or of great use.

A ROTATING CAP MILL AT FRESH POND — THE SECOND DUTCH WINDMILL: A larger windmill, capable of generating greater power, could be erected if the entire structure did not need turning toward the oncoming wind — if, for instance, only the top portion supporting the vanes could be swung around.

Harbor Mill and former house of the mayor of Leavenworth, Kansas, ca. 1895

Looking north.

Neither building in this view exists today. The house was built in the mid-1800s for Joshua F. Dodge (1816-1891).

Shortly after Joshua's wife, Lucretia, died in July 1887, the property was purchased by Capt. W. M. Fortescue, the former mayor of Leavenworth, Kansas — who was to enjoy many summers admiring the fine view of Harbor Mill on the adjoining property.

In 1888 the old farmhouse, now called "Kansas Cottage," was remodeled with the addition of 100-feet of piazza, eight feet wide — visible in this photograph.

Three windmills of that type, with rotating caps, were built on Block Island. The first, named the Honeywell Mill for the owner, was also located at the northeastern corner of Fresh Pond. Although not well regarded for its workmanship, the mill was superior to its predecessor.

This was the only windmill on the Island whose cap was rotated by a long pole extending at an angle from the rear of the cap, down to the ground. By grasping the pole's lower end — which was attached to a wagon wheel that rolled on the ground — the miller could push the cap around to the proper position facing the wind.

The approximate location of this mill is shown on maps of Block Island made in 1831, 1838, and 1850. But no photographs exist of the first two windmills.

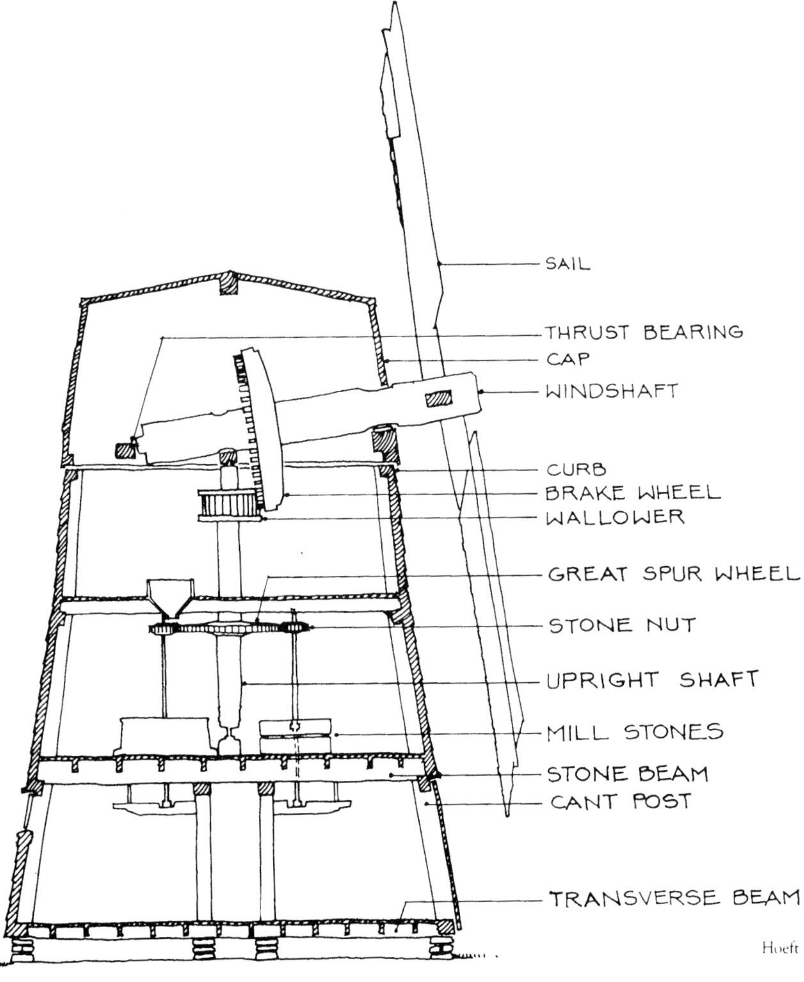

Cross-section of a typical 1800s windmill with a rotating cap

Although no photograph, sketch, or description exists of the interior workings of Block Island's two Dutch-type windmills, they functioned in a manner similar to this drawing. Variations existed according to geographical area. Preserved windmills from the 1800s can be found on Long Island, Cape Cod, and the mainland part of Rhode Island — most are now historic sites that welcome visitors.

The windmill design in this diagram does not incorporate the large vertical wheel at the rear of the cap, as was used on each of Block Island's windmills (see photos, pages 213, 215). The upright wheel allowed the miller to stand outside on the ground and turn the cap by pulling an endless rope.

The drawing shows two grinding stations on the second floor, one on either side of the "upright shaft." Each station ground with a different degree of coarseness. Fine stones, often imported from France, were used to grind wheat. Coarse granite was used to grind corn.

Each set of stones comprised an upper millstone that revolved against a stationary lower millstone. It is not known if Block Island's mills had two sets of stones or one — but the millstones still in evidence around the Island are coarse granite, except for a small, smooth stone at the Block Island Historical Society.

Cross-section of typical windmill interior of the 1800s, with two sets of millstones

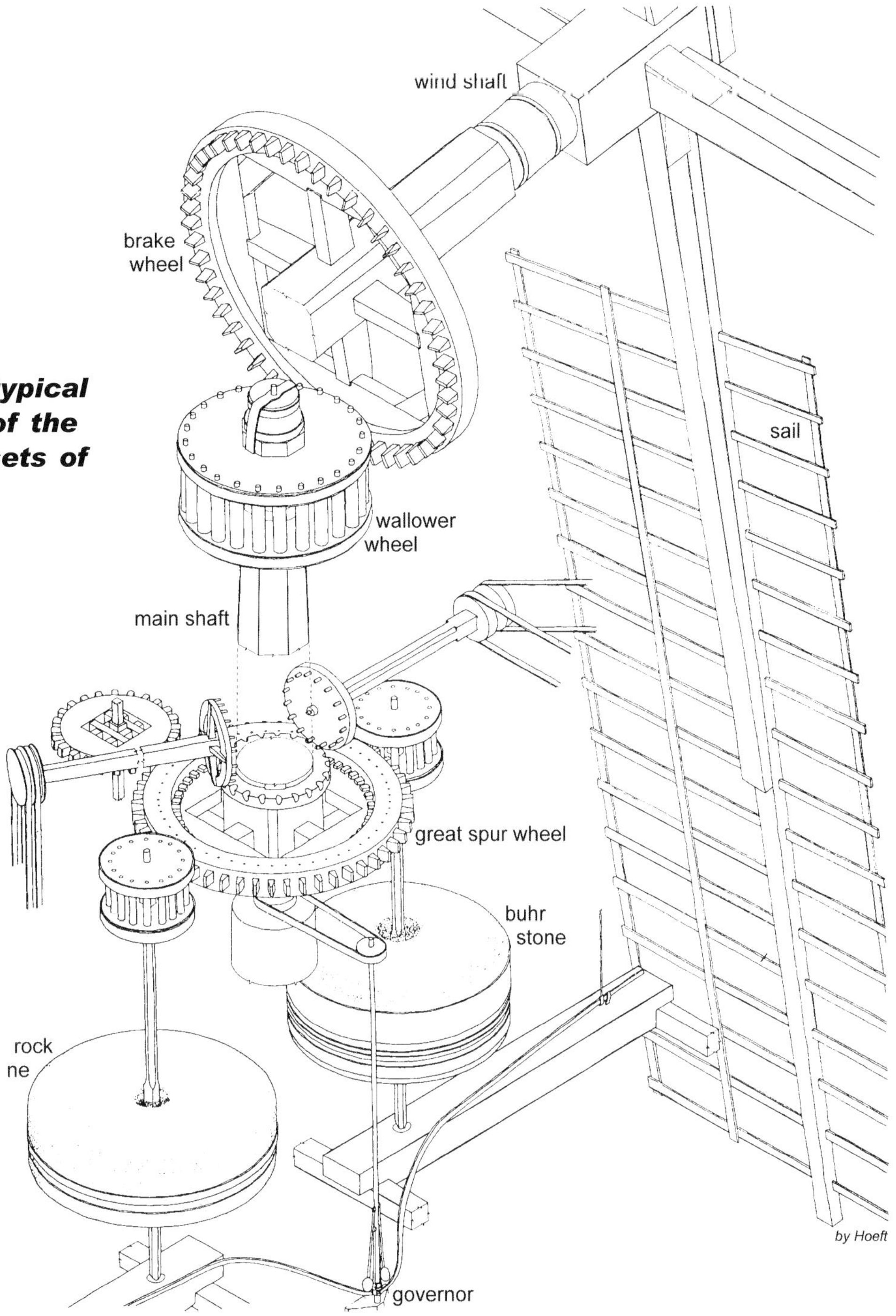

Millstone grooves

The two patterns of furrows to the right are from *The American Miller and Millwright's Assistant* of 1850.

As the grain was ground, the resulting flour or corn meal followed the grooves toward the center hole, eventually falling into the miller's bag. Periodically, the grooves needed rechiseling, a process called "dressing."

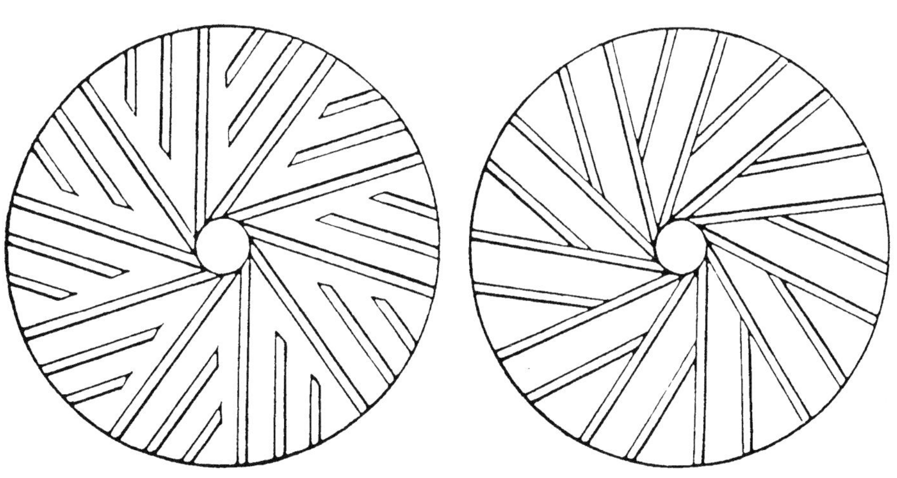

Harbor Mill, north of Old Town Road, ca. 1886

Looking northwest.

The site of the Harbor Mill is on a ridge, now pine covered, just north of a dirt lane off Old Town Road.

The house in the foreground still exists (plat 17, lot 51), as does the house just to the left of the windmill (on Beach Ave., plat 17, lot 31).

In the distance is Great Salt Pond.

The Harbor Mill, erected at two different locations — the third Dutch windmill

THE TWO MOST IMPORTANT WINDMILLS on Block Island — the Harbor Mill and the Littlefield Mill — spent portions of their lives at four Island locations. Each was erected, then, after many years service, dismantled and re-erected elsewhere on the Island.

The 38-foot high Harbor Mill — dating from the 1770s, but brought to Block Island about 1810 — was first located at a site just behind the present-day National Hotel. Excavation work underneath the hotel in the mid-1980s unearthed a broken mill stone that had served as part of the foundation. That rescued artifact is now displayed upright on the National's rear lawn.

In the mid-1850s the Harbor Mill was moved to a ridge (plat 17, lot 55) on the north side of Old Town Road. The location is now pine-covered and no trace of the mill exists. But the original dirt lane — on the left side of the mansard-roofed home that a decade ago was the Island's funeral parlor — will still lead the curious walker two hundred yards to the site, where the ridge rises abruptly on the left.

A decade after the windmill ceased operating in 1891, a preservation group led by summer residents purchased the mill and two surrounding acres. Two years later hopes were still high that the deteriorating structure would soon be a museum, as described in the local newspaper:

"The top, which had blown off, has been preserved and is ready to be put in place again. It is the intent ... to put the mill in perfect repair, and have it grind corn again ... to make it an educational example of what was done in more primitive times. The mill is to be used as a sort of museum, where curios of all kinds, Indian relics, interesting souvenirs of the boats which have been wrecked on the Island, relics of old sea-captains, etc., will be kept.

"It is part of the plan to transform the land into the most attractive park, where trees, rare flowers, lotuses and aquatic plants shall grow luxuriously ... The committee is now at a standstill for the lack of funds, and it has decided to hold a fair ..."

The effort failed — local residents did not rally to the cause — and the property was sold back to the original family in 1910. Three decades later the remaining portion of the abandoned mill was demolished by the 1938 hurricane. A museum was not created on the Island until 1942 when the Block Island Historical Society was formed.

Postcard of the abandoned Harbor Mill, postmarked 1909 ►

Looking south.

Shortly after the turn of the century, the Harbor Mill lost its cap.

Exposed to view is the wheel (on left) that allowed the miller, standing on the ground, to revolve the cap by pulling on an endless rope looped over the wheel.

This photograph is the only 'interior' view of a Block Island windmill.

The building on the left (plat 17, lot 50), on Old Town Road, was built as a Baptist parsonage in 1887, serving as the Island's funeral home in recent decades, until the 1980s.

Harbor Mill, north of Old Town Road, ◄ ca. 1900

Looking northeast.

The Harbor Mill was about 38 feet high from the ground to the top of an upright vane. The four arms — shown here without the sail-like cloth tied to the lattice framework — were each 18 feet long and four feet wide.

The foundation of the house is still visible, dug into the south base of the ridge, but no trace of the windmill is evident. At about the time this photograph was taken, an effort was made to restore the abandoned windmill as a museum of the Island's history — the project failed.

Of the four Dutch-type windmills built on Block Island, photographs exist only of the Harbor Mill (shown on these two pages) and the Littlefield Mill.

The Harbor Mill had a triangular box at the rear of its cap, and the vanes were composed of two rows of lattice — the Littlefield Mill had a rectangular box, and vanes composed of three rows of lattice (see page 215).

Littlefield Mill, on Center Road, mid-1880s

From the 1870s until it was moved in 1888, the Littlefield Mill shared its site with the Central House, a small hotel with a cupola directly opposite the intersection of Beach Avenue and Center Road.

Standing at the photographer's location today — with the airport off to the left, and the cemetery to the right — a viewer would see only the middle structure: the Central House annex, constructed in 1883 and now a summer residence.

The Central House — on the right — was built in 1876 for Ray S. Littlefield, and burned about 1910 (see map 88).

The Littlefield Mill, erected at two different locations — the fourth Dutch windmill

The other important Dutch-type windmill on Block Island — the Littlefield Mill — was erected in 1815 on Center Road, directly opposite the intersection with Beach Avenue. The meal produced for corn-cakes was so superior that farmers on the mainland shipped their corn here to be ground. The Reverend Samuel Livermore of the Island's First Baptist Church, writing in 1877, spoke of the status this mill held in the community — beyond the grinding of corn:

"This mill, owned by Hon. Ray S. Littlefield, is capable of grinding one hundred bushels of excellent corn-meal in a day when the wind is favorable. The quantity ground in it annually may be estimated at from nine to ten thousand bushels. A large amount of grain is brought from abroad and ground here, in addition to the corn raised on the Island …

"Many [summer visitors] will remember with pleasure the Littlefield mill, so near the Central House, and in and around which the children have played in summer, and within whose dusty walls some of them have been gathered for an hour's Sabbath-school, where they have sung their familiar hymns and recited their lessons …

"This mill, on the street through which most of the funeral processions of the Island pass, has always been stopped while they have been passing."

But 11 years later, in February 1888, the *Providence Journal* reported:

"Considerable difficulty is experienced by people here in getting table meal ground from the Island corn. Both the old wind-mills are badly out of repair and practically worthless, and it does not pay Mr. John F. Hayes, who put in steam power for the purpose of grinding corn, sawing lumber, etc., enough to make it an object for him to grind, so the citizens are in a dilemma. Hon. Ray S. Littlefield, who owns one of the old windmills, thinks of putting in a modern wind motor."

The modern wind motor for grinding corn was *not* brought to the Island. Instead, that same year, the old windmill was moved

Littlefield Mill with pond, next to north side of Old Mill Road, ca. 1900

The pond, as well as the hill where the windmill once stood, is now part of the Island's conservation land.

The network of public paths called The Greenway passes by the mill's low, circular stone foundation.

Only the sunken stone cellar remains of the house at left — the former home of John R. Dodge (1808-1874) whose heirs owned the hill in this view, where the Littlefield Mill was moved and rebuilt in 1888.

to the West Side by Gilbert Sprague and John Edward Littlefield, and rebuilt near the home of John Rose Dodge, whose family owned the hill the mill sat upon. John Littlefield, who would be the new miller and coax a last gasp of productivity from the grindstones, lived in a Cape Cod style house (plat 12, lot 8) just to the south, on the other side of a dirt lane.

Littlefield urged the town to improve the dirt lane and designate it as a public road, creating a shortcut across the West Side — and a shortcut to the mill. The new road, initially called Littlefield Avenue, is now known as Old Mill Road. The mill began operating at the new location in 1890 and was in use throughout the decade, becoming the last working Dutch windmill on Block Island.

By then a completely new style of windmill was a common sight on the American landscape — a skeletal tower built of wood or steel, with thin metal rotating blades, and used for pumping well water.

In 1894 a writer compared the latest style American mill with the old Littlefield Mill, offering, as other observers had, his adulation for things ancient — but with a warning:

"In this age of air-motors, with their slender framework, surmounted by small and graceful vanes, a visit to this old mill, with its massive oak timbers, and cumbrous shaft revolving under the pressure of the wind against four immense sails spread upon vanes over thirty feet in length, affords a striking comparison of old with new methods.

"If one intends visiting the mill, he should select a day when there is a good breeze of wind, otherwise the mill will not be likely to be running. When there is a movement of from fifteen to twenty-five miles an hour, the jar and tremble of the mill, and the groaning, creaking, and straining of its timbers, produce a sensation slightly trying to the nerves of a timid person."

Littlefield Mill, after move to Old Mill Road, 1890s

The Littlefield Mill, shown here after being moved to Old Mill Road in 1888, is easily distinguishable from the Harbor Mill by its square back at the rear of the cap, and its three rows of lattice, as opposed to the Harbor Mill's two.

Note the wooden cleats at the mill's corners for securing the cap-turning rope.

After 1900, the Littlefield Mill was abandoned also, but the circumstances of the mill's disappearance are entirely forgotten.

Two of its millstones are preserved at the bottom of the hill that leads to the airport — part of a memorial to the Island's old Center. The millstone on the left, with a circular hole in the center, was the fixed 'bed stone' — used at the mill in the lower position. The millstone on the right, with a partly rectangular hole in the center, was the rotating 'runner stone' — used in the upper position at the mill.

Besides these two stones, and the one behind the National Hotel, three other millstones have found alternative uses on Block Island — but from which Island mill they originated is unknown. In the southernmost corner of the cemetery, a millstone stands upright as a private memorial. Another is preserved on the grounds of a home off Black Rock Road (plat 11, lot 22). And at the house near Fresh Pond called Smilin' Through, a millstone is in use as a stepping stone to the side door — but two other Block Island millstones, once displayed on the lawn of this home, were taken to Cape Cod in the late 1980s by the landowner.

At the Littlefield Mill's last location, a circle of foundation stones one layer high can easily be seen (plat 16, lot 21). The hilltop site can be found along a Greenway path leading north off Old Mill Road, near the small pond (see photo at bottom of opposite page) donated in the late 1980s to the Nature Conservancy by Peter and Shirley Wood, who happened also to be owners of John E. Littlefield's former house across the road.

North Lighthouse and windmill, 1930s

Barely perceptible in this photograph is the girder-type windmill that stood on the shed just behind the North Light.

The town now maintains the still-functioning lighthouse as a museum, open during summer. The shed no longer exists.

Windmill advertisement from Sears Roebuck catalog, 1908

As with other isolated American communities, Block Islanders found an easy way to purchase the nation's products when the Sears Roebuck Company in Chicago began issuing their nearly all-inclusive catalogs.

A windmill 90-feet high, with attached water tower, stood behind the Ocean View Hotel in the early 1900s — a similar model is featured in the Sears catalog. Other smaller windmills for pumping water, also like those sold by Sears, were scattered about Block Island.

At least one Islander, Rufus D. Willis, bought his entire house from Sears — as a mail-order kit. The cottage, erected in 1914, still stands (plat 18, lot 47-1) on a dirt lane south off Center Road.

Steel girder windmills — for pumping well water

THE MODERN AIR-MOTORS mentioned in 1894 spread across Block Island, just as they had across the nation, taking on in their own right the status of an American icon — a nostalgic conjurer of bucolic rural life and family values.

On Block Island the largest of these water-pumping windmills was erected about 1920 behind the Ocean View Hotel. It rose like a mammoth creature above Old Harbor, 90 feet high — and surely would have impressed H. G. Wells, or even, perhaps, Martians. The dual-purpose tower held a 30,000-gallon tank 60 feet aloft, surmounted by a smaller tower on which the spinning metal vanes of the windmill drew water upwards from underground.

At least eight other air-motor windmill, all without raised tanks, were scattered about the Island in the early and mid-1900s:

(1) near the Neptune Hotel at the west end of Mill Tail Swamp Pond; (2) at a farm where the Block Island Power Company was later built; (3) at the North Lighthouse; (4) at Champlin's Marina until the 1970s; (5) on Harbor Pond behind the Hygeia Hotel; (6) at the Sands Pond reservoir; (7) behind the Gothic Inn on Dodge Street; and (8) for generating electricity, at Lewis Farm off Cooneymus Road.

The Champlin's Marina windmill, perched next to Great Salt Pond, pumped water from Dick's Spring. So aesthetically pleasing was the short tower, that various images of this scene were printed as postcards and published in books. Mainland artist Paule Loring sketched the windmill for his 1964 booklet, and views were included in the hardbound books of two noted marine photographers: Morris Rosenfeld, in 1947; and Peter Barlow, in 1972.

NASA's electricity generating windmill, 1979

Looking east at the Block Island Power Company on Ocean Avenue.

In the background is Harbor Pond — and in the distance, Crescent Beach and the Atlantic Ocean.

NASA windmill — for generating electricity

THE ULTIMATE EVOLUTION of Block Island windmills, in size at least, was the wind turbine erected by the Department of Energy (DOE) for a proposed two-year experiment in 1979 (see photo, page 217). Although conceived and funded by the DOE, another federal government agency — NASA — tackled the design of the turbine and blades. NASA is the very same "National Aeronautics and Space Administration" that brought us the moon landing on TV in 1969.

If H. G. Wells had not died by then, he may have been inspired — upon viewing this gargantuan alien-looking erector set — to re-write his book, with the Martians winning this time. The blade itself was 125 feet across. For comparison, that is 20 feet longer than the Harborside Inn on Water Street. Think of that next time you're savoring a drink on the hotel's porch.

Constructed on the grounds of the Block Island Power Company to generate electricity, this largest of Island windmills was described in the smallest of newsletters, the ***Wind Turbine News***. The seven-inch by seven-inch sheet of paper, printed on both sides, was published monthly in 1981 by the Wind Energy Project Office of NASA's Lewis Research Center.

During the winter and spring of that year, the engine produced 30,000 to 45,000 kilowatt hours monthly, or about 18% of the Island's electricity. As one of only four such 200-kilowatt windmills in the United States, the experiment was a success in gaining new information. The $2.3 million unit was sold to the Block Island Power Company in 1984 for $1. The privately owned power company — which charges the highest rates in the continental United States, and was making extra money for the owner by assessing customers a double markup on diesel oil — then sold the windmill as scrap for $2,000.

That same year, 1984, the NASA windmill was dismantled — it had been built to last 30 years

But the wind is always high on Block Island, and the giant's smaller, commercially produced cousins have multiplied. As long as the power company's electric bills stay as outrageously lofty as the wind's speed, independent women and men will continue plucking power from the sky with their own air motors.

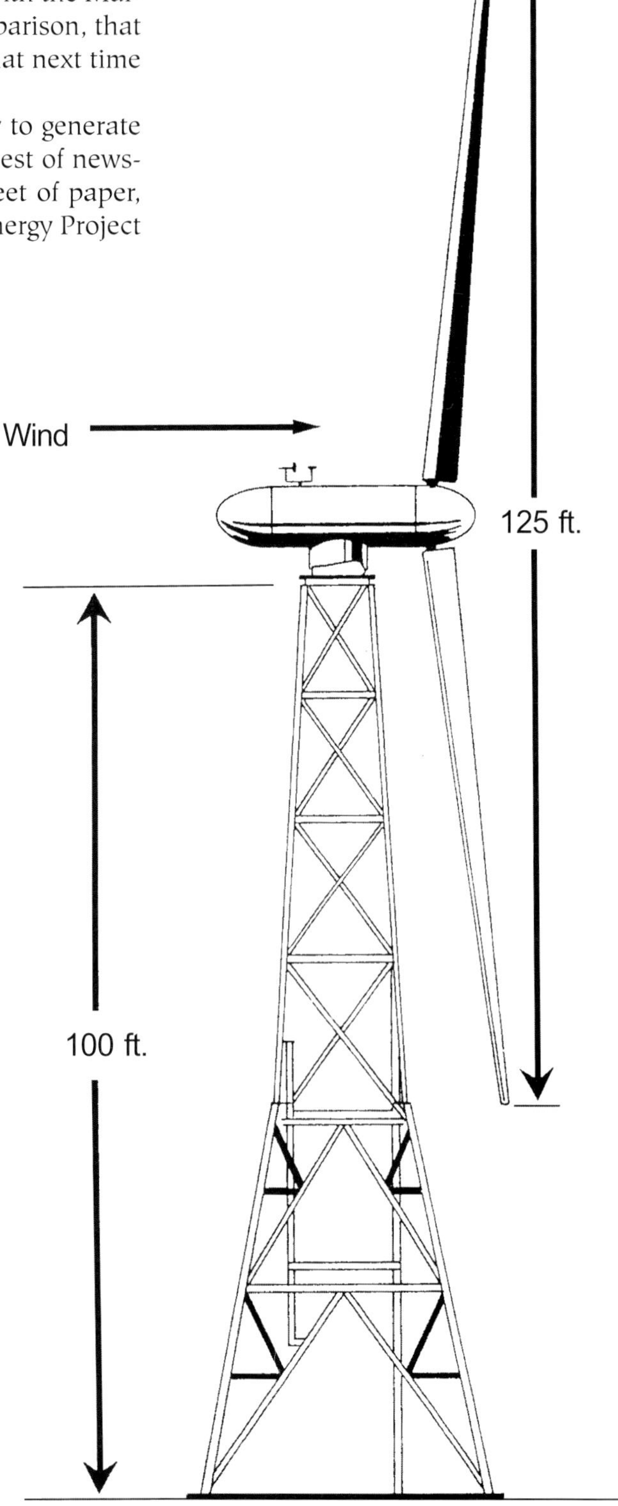

Drawing of NASA tower

The federal Department of Energy's windmill, designed by NASA, towered over the Block Island Power Company from 1979 until 1984.

The wood composite blade was 125 feet in diameter, weighed 2,600 pounds (as much as an automobile) and rotated 40 times per minute. The amount of power could be altered by varying the pitch of the blades.

Block Island Power Co.

WIND TURBINE NEWS

Vol. 1, No. 3 May 1981

Current Events

In March, the wind turbine ran for 494 hours. It generated 45,970 kilowatt hours of electricity. This was 18.4 percent of the Islands total electricity generated.

If you recall, last month we told you about our town meeting at the New Shoreham Town Hall. Part of the meeting agenda was devoted to answering a series of questions about the wind turbine submitted by Larry Shaw, President of the Block Island Economic Development Foundation. As space permits, we'd like to devote the remainder of this page to re-printing the questions and answers. The answers that don't fit here will be included in next month's issue of the News.

Q8: Has the cable TV contract been fully implemented, inspected and accepted by DOE?

A8: Since the cable TV is being installed under a BI Power Company subcontract, authorized by DOE, Block Island Power has a primary responsibility for implementing, inspecting and accepting the cable TV system.

DECAS in Boston is the Federal agency responsible for inspecting and accepting the cable TV contract. They have examined the contract and have not issued their findings as yet. As soon as an answer is obtained, that information will be forwarded to the cable TV committee.

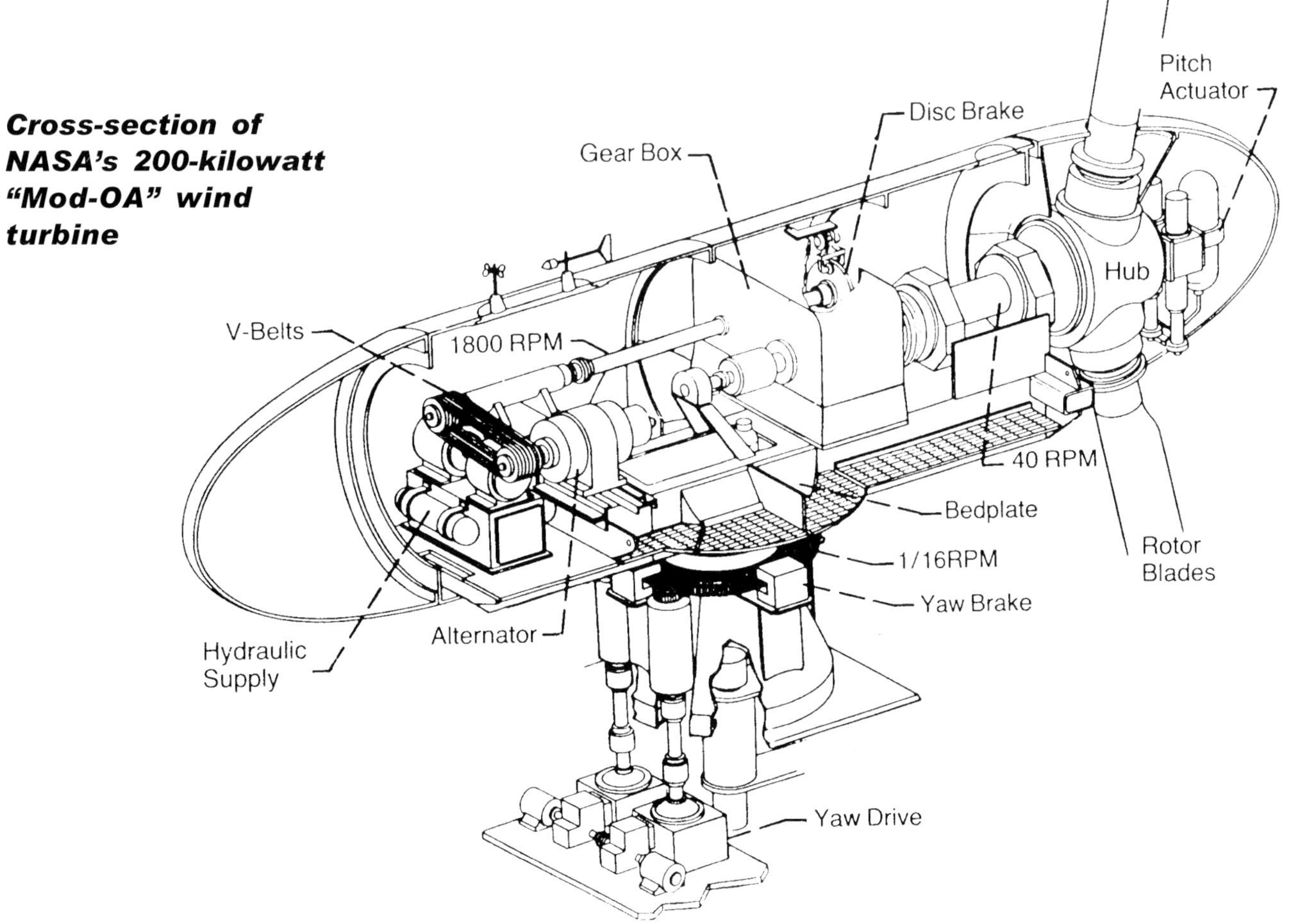

Cross-section of NASA's 200-kilowatt "Mod-OA" wind turbine

Souvenir Edition

Smilin' Through

Introduced in
Joseph M. Schenck's
Motion Picture Version
of the
Fantastic Play
"Smilin' Through"
featuring
Norma Talmadge

A First National Attraction

SOLO – FIVE KEYS
C (c to d); D, (d to e); Eb, (eb to f); F, (f to g); G, (g to a);
DUET – TWO KEYS, C and Eb

Lyric and Music by
Arthur A. Penn

M. Witmark & Sons
New York

60¢ net

Printed in U. S. A.

CHAPTER 23

Smilin' Through

A house, three movies, and a play — all named for a song;

but the original house no longer exists, and the movies haven't been seen for 50 years

Smilin' Through was written for a 1919 Broadway play starring Jane Cowl

There's a little brown road windin' over the hill
To a little white cot by the sea . . .

So begins the once popular song written in 1919 by the then famous songwriter Arthur A. Penn. In 1922 he purchased an old Block Island cottage — "cot" to him — fitting the description of his lyrics so perfectly that years later Islanders mistakenly believed the song was named for the cottage, instead of the other way round.

The gambrel-roofed home in the center of the Island next to Fresh Pond was used only in summers by Penn, his wife Nell, and her mother. It was, indeed, on a brown dirt road that wound over a hill — but of course most Block Island houses were on unpaved roads then. To match the song even more, though, Penn painted the wood shingled structure white.

There's a little green gate
At whose trellis I wait . . .

And he added a gate and trellis too.

What most people do not know is the meaning of "Smilin' Through." The two words seem to act as a noun — just the name of an old house. But Penn's message had a deeper purpose:

While two eyes o' blue
Come smilin' through
At me!

The words were a verb, and the music and lyrics formed a love song. Not the love-at-first-sight of the young, but the true, faithful love of the older:

There's a gray lock or two in the brown of the hair,
There's some silver in mine, too, I see;
But in all the long years
When the clouds brought their tears,
Those two eyes o' blue
Kept smilin' through
At me!

Sheet music, copyright 1919 — advertising first Smilin' Through movie, made in 1922

Norma Talmadge — one the silent era's heroines of tearful melodramas — starred in the 1922 movie based on Arthur Penn's song of the same name, *Smilin' Through*. She was married to the film's producer, Joseph M. Schenck, who co-founded 20th-Century film company in 1933 and was awarded a special Oscar in 1952 "for long and distinguished service to the motion picture industry."

THE HOUSE WAS ALREADY FAMOUS before the Penns began living there. A 1907 postcard features a view of the tidy cottage, and a small lake stretching beyond, with the caption "Great Fresh Pond & oldest house on Island, Block Island, RI." (see page 223).

The building had been built approximately 200 hundred years earlier — the date is not known — perhaps by one of the first Island settlers of 1661, Trustrum Dodge. In 1914 Mary Mott Hull, a lifelong resident of the house, died at the age of 70. Her obituary mentions that even then the house was still known for her father, not her — still called the "Old gambuled roofed house of Mr. Rathbone Mott," who had died in 1882.

In Mary's youth the house was called "The Cherry Trees" — not to be confused with Cherry Tree Hill which is further to the west, where Cooneymus Road sweeps down toward its juncture with West Side Road. (And, for the record, there never was a

road called Cherry Tree Hill Road, or Cherry Hill Road, or anything of the sort. That is a misnomer created by an errant Chamber of Commerce map in the 1970s — the name then finding its way, within parentheses, onto town tax maps.)

Arthur A. Penn came to America from England in 1903 at the age of 28, writing dozens of comic operas and sentimental songs before his death in 1941. There is no relation between Arthur A. Penn, the English-born songwriter of the early 1900s, and Arthur Penn, the American movie director of the 1960s and 70s.

Although he owned his summer home, Smilin' Through, only from 1922 to1925, Penn continued visiting Block Island for many years afterward. The nationwide fame of his song, together with the resultant movies, made the cottage on Block Island a significant landmark for tourists during the 1940s and 50s.

Smilin' Through was written for a play, of the same name, that opened at the Broadhurst Theater in New York City on December 30, 1919, running for 175 performances and continuing on the road as a great success.

In 1922 Sidney Franklin directed a silent movie — also with the very bankable name *Smilin' Through* — starring 25-year-old Norma Talmadge, a Hollywood superstar then at the peak of her fame.

After a way was devised for sound to be added to film tracks, the movie was reshot as a "talkie" for MGM in 1932 by the same director, featuring three accomplished stars: Norma Shearer, Frederic March, and Leslie Howard.

The final movie version, filmed in color by MGM, was released in October 1941 — two months before the United States entered World War II. Although another superstar — singer Jeanette MacDonald — played the leading role, the tearjerker production received a "thumbs-down" from reviewers. A 78 RPM record was also recorded at the time by MacDonald.

By the middle part of the 1900s, the house on Block Island had a double significance — as the oldest on the Island, and as the summer home of the

Smilin' Through

Arthur A. Penn

There's a little brown road
  windin' over the hill
To a little white cot by the sea;
There's a little green gate
At whose trellis I wait,
While two eyes o' blue
Come smilin' through
    At me!

There's a gray lock or two
  in the brown of the hair,
There's some silver in mine, too, I see;
But in all the long years
When the clouds brought their tears,
Those two eyes o' blue
Kept smilin' through
    At me!

Fresh Pond & oldest house on Block Island — ca. 1905

Even before being purchased by the famous songwriter Arthur A. Penn in 1922, the house he named Smilin' Through was already celebrated on the Island as the oldest home.

At the edge of the pond are two large icehouses: at left, and near the right.

Island's most famous resident. Yet in 1953 Smilin' Through underwent repairs by dedicated new owners from New Jersey that replaced the old building with a new one.

After realizing the extent of termite damage and powder post beetle rot, a decision was made to replicate the building with new lumber and some of the original interior wood. The venerable structure was completely razed — except for the brick chimney, and the two fireplaces and beehive oven at its base (see page 225). Floorboards and old chestnut beams were carefully numbered to be placed back in their original locations, and many of the handmade nails were straightened to be hammered back in.

In the spring of 1954 a new frame was built. The foundation sills, floor joists, wall studs, and roof rafters were new, 2x4's, 2x6's, etc. — the smooth-planed lumber of the post-World War II era — purchased through the local John Rose & Company Hardware store. After a diligent search of New England by the owners, old barn boards and new hand-split shakes were brought to Block Island and incorporated into the structure. A writer for the *Providence Journal* enthusiastically endorsed the effort, which at the time was considered by some to be a valid restoration:

"Responsible for the reconstruction, which may give one of the island's most famous houses another two centuries of life, were the owners, Mr. and Mrs. Richard Mazzur of Oradel, N.J."

Throughout the 1950s and 60s, Smilin' Through's new owners acquired antiques from many old Island homes and in 1967 opened their new building as a private museum. The local newspaper, the *Hooter*, wrote in July 1967:

"Many of the Islanders, who wouldn't lend or sell historical items that have been saved and handed down for generations, simply donated them to this unique museum."

There were ship models, a four-poster bed, paintings, children's toys, Island-made violins, two goose yokes, the Lewis Farm's spinning wheel, and much more.

Smilin' Through's owners also acquired the nearby Peckham Farm, whose vacant acreage gazed down upon Rodman's Hollow to the west and Fresh Pond to the east. In the mid-1980s the Island's conservation groups sought to purchase Peckham Farm but were rebuffed. The ancient farmlands were instead sold to a developer, Donald Huggins, Jr. — the same person who, with partner David Henderson, transformed the small Cutting Cottages on Corn Neck into the giant, highly visible structures renamed the Crescent Beach Cottages. Both developers were soon revealed to be two of the state's most nefarious real estate wheelers-and-dealers, costing taxpayers throughout Rhode Island millions of dollars in losses.

Today Peckham Farm is subdivided and boasts a well-wrought "PRIVATE" keep out sign at the entrance. New houses protrude prominently along the eastern ridge of the otherwise pristine Rodman's Hollow, but some home owners have aided the cause of conservation by helping purchase empty subdivision lots, preventing further building.

Fresh Pond & the replica of Smilin' Through — 2000

The once-clear farm fields have grown to bayberry bushes and briars, with many summer houses visible everywhere.

The scenic hill on which the photographer stands, however, was preserved for the public in 2000 through the extraordinary efforts of a neighbor, Louise England.

The original land that Smilin' Through rested on — stretching for hundreds of feet around the northern and western sides of Fresh Pond — also were threatened by development. Redoubling their efforts, the Island's conservation groups, led by the town's newly formed Land Trust, sought help from the state to purchase and preserve this land as well as the replica of Smilin' Through.

The $3 million purchase price to save 27 acres of meadows and scrub bushes — and rights to 16 acres of Fresh Pond — was obtained in 1988. But when Smilin' Through's owners packed up to move to Cape Cod, many of Block Island's antiques left as well — even several massive granite mill stones that had ground the Islanders' corn throughout the 1800s and in more recent decades had graced the yard of Smilin' Through.

In 1990 — to recoup part of the purchase price to preserve other areas of the Island — voters decided to sell Smilin' Through, along with three surrounding acres, allowing the building to once again serve as a private dwelling.

The roughly boarded up house, with new owners Mr. & Mrs. Penn, 1922

When Arthur Penn purchased the old closed-up house, he described its condition as "a dirty, tumble-down wreck."

WHAT DOES THE PHRASE "SMILIN' THROUGH" mean now? A song that can be played but seldom is, except at High School graduations. Three movies, not likely to be seen again, and the memory of a house.

The best use of the name, though, is for the human spirit described by Arthur Penn. His meaning would be the same no matter where he wrote the words:

But in all the long years
When the clouds brought their tears,
Those two eyes o' blue
Kept smilin' through
At me!

And then there is the land and the surroundings. Being a place that must necessarily be passed on all tours of the Island — and Islanders take many "an Island tour" — Fresh Pond never escapes attention from passersby. The land surrounding much of the pond — below, that is, the ridge where the PRIVATE "Peckham Farm" sign stands — is a summer green of undisturbed rolling hills.

Battles have been won and lost here — for the Island's landscape and heritage. But sunny skies are still mirrored in the valley's pond, the combination forming many a day "two eyes o' blue" that keep smilin' through.

Arthur Penn and wife at his new "green gate and trellis," ca. 1923

To match reality to fiction, songwriter Arthur Penn painted white his newly purchased ancient farmhouse, adding a green gate and trellis, as in the lyrics of his hit song of the post-World War I years *Smilin' Through*.

Smilin' Through and haystack, ca. 1930s

This classic view of Smilin' Through was captured by the Island photographer of the era, Robert L. Geer.

The image was reproduced throughout the 1940s and 50s — as a black and white postcard — as a colorized postcard (with telephone poles removed) — in the Chamber of Commerce's early 1950s brochures — and in the 1955 booklet *Lore and Legends*.

Providence Journal, June 1954

When Block Island's oldest house was demolished, the building of a replica was chronicled by the state's leading newspaper.

Replica Rises On the Site of Razed Cottage

By ROBERT N. COOL

BLOCK ISLAND this year has a new "Smilin' Through Cottage" on Cherry Hill Road overlooking Fresh Pond, but the new landmark is just like its predecessor.

During the winter workmen completely razed the original gambrel-roofed colonial house that was named for a song and then reconstructed it with solid new timbers. To help achieve the effect of age, expensive irregular shingles—first weathered and then covered with a protective coating of what looks like plastic—were used. They have the "loosened" appearance of those on an old house.

Responsible for the reconstruction, which may give one of the island's most famous houses another two centuries of life, were the owners, Mr. and Mrs. Richard Mazzur of Oradel, N.J.

Was Composer's Home

The house was famous as the onetime home of Arthur Penn, an English composer who came to America in 1903 when he was 23 years old. He spent several years upon the island during the period when he achieved renown as the composer of several comic operas and such sentimental songs as "Smilin' Through," "Sunrise and You," and "The Lamp-lit Hour."

Originally a farm house, the old structure stood on rock foundations next to the road amid the stone walls and ponds of Block Island's central plateau.

August, 1953: The famed Block Island 'Smilin' Through' house looked as it had for a century or more, like this.

January, 1954: Only a chimney and foundations remained of the original as reconstruction started on landmark.

Four examples of Smilin' Through sheet music 1919 - 1950s

Even as Arthur Penn's famous house was being torn down, sheet music of his song was still being published. The music has been recorded by major singers for more than 90 years, and is available on every type of recordable media, from the old cylinder records to modern CD's.

1919 sheet music

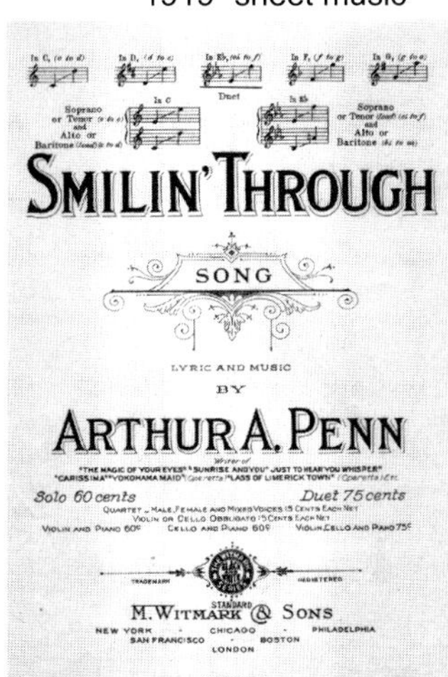

1932 movie, Norma Shearer

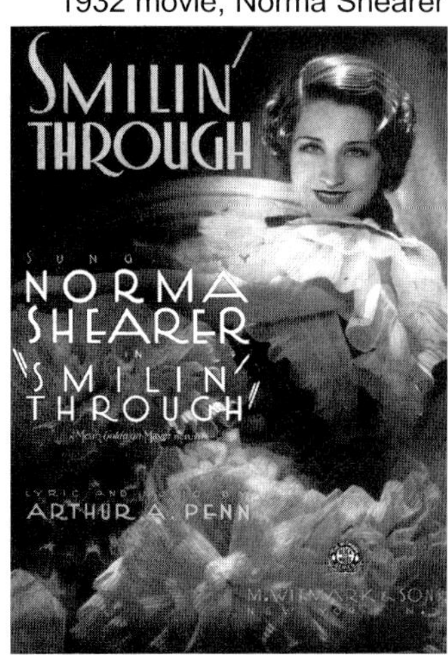

1941 movie, Jeanette MacDonald

1953 sheet music

Rear of typical Block Island car, summer 1997

Decals and bumper stickers often express the concern that lovers of the Island have had for their home in the 1970s, 80s and 90s — concern about deer ticks which cause the dangerous Lyme disease, making it unsafe for children or adults to cross fields, leave paths, or have picnics on private land or in public conservation areas — concern for protection of the ecology and scenic landscape from developers who have run rampant Block Island — concern about the needless and very bloody moped accidents caused by the five rental moped dealers.

***I'd Rather Be On Block Island* — 1980s**

These words may have been inspired by a 1920s song titled:

I'd Rather Be at Block Island than Any Place I Know

The music is still played occasionally at school graduations. The first line states an appropriate truism around which Block Island life revolves:

"Summer's the time that we all like best cause vacation time is here."

CHAPTER 24

The Bumper Sticker Museum 1961-1990s

SOUVENIR BUMPER STICKERS of the long rectangular type, traditionally displayed by tourists in the past, have become passe on Block Island. With the demise of Esta's Gift Shop in Old Harbor after the summer season of 1995, these mementos of the Island were no longer available at stores.

In the 1950s and 60s American tourists — traveling ever more easily on the new interstate highways to savor the country's scenic sights — announced their past destinations, trophy-like, in two different ways: with bumper stickers pasted on the front and rear of the family car, or with small transparent decals plastered on the inside of the side or rear windows. The fad was a great way for the kids to remember where they'd been, or for grown-ups to recognize fellow vacationers at rest stops and strike up a conversation to find out what attractions may be on the road ahead.

Now the trend is to buy small stickers about the size of those older decals, but not transparent — just small enough to be applied to a window or a bumper, take your pick. One common form of small sticker available now at Block Island's shops features an outline map of the Island — another consists of just the two letters "BI" centered in a white paper oval, mimicking the metal medallions long popular in European countries.

The traditional horizontal bumper sticker is not quite dead on Block Island though — at least six different ones can still be procured from conservancy groups or as advertising from a few businesses.

And of course every couple of years at election time, one or two new bumper sticker designs are printed by Island politicians. A favorite of the 1998 campaign, sporting irrefutable logic, proclaimed "Do more with Les." But political stickers are not covered here.

- *To view color images of eight other bumper stickers — including Block Island's earliest bumper sticker (from 1961) and the Town of New Shoreham's coat-of-arms — see the color section, pages 130-131.*

BLOCK ISLAND
A NO WAR TOY ZONE

No WAR TOY zone — 1990s

This bumper sticker appeared in 1993 after some Block Islanders realized children in war-torn Bosnia were playing with toy guns made in the U.S.A. It is not a reference to real missiles and tanks — the form of toy that grown-ups often graduate to.

Help Us Save The Land and Environment — 1990s

H.U.S.T.L.E. was formed when Judge Thomas Calderone of the Rhode Island Superior Court ignored Block Island's zoning ordinance and allowed developers Donald Huggins Jr. and David Henderson to tear down 21 small one-story rental cottages and construct 21 three-story condos with twice the footprint and six times the size of the originals. During construction in the summer of 1989, Islanders picketed the site — the first time in the Island's history. The battle had been lost in court, but the *Providence Journal* declared the Cutting Cottages property one -of the five worst atrocities in the state's coastal history.

ENOUGH ! — 1990s

As large-scale development proposals threatened to turn Block Island into a "Warwick, RI," or a "New Jersey shore town," H.U.S.T.L.E issued a single-word bumper sticker to sum up most Islanders' feelings. After successfully negotiating in 1993 to prevent construction by the owner of the Spring House hotel of 12 houses — on the magnificent lawn of the hotel itself — the group became part of other Island organizations such as *Scenic Block Island.*

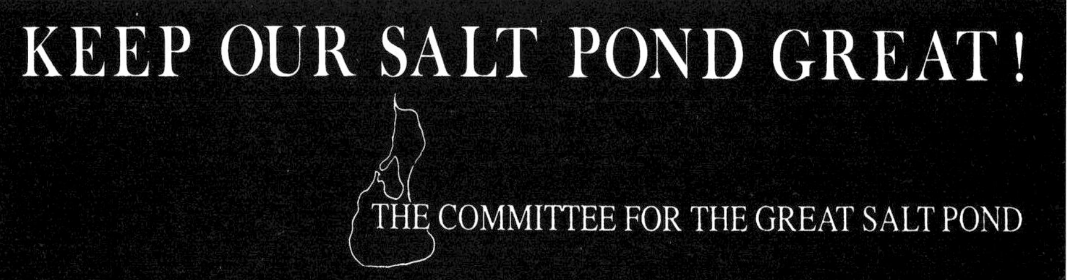

Keep Our Salt Pond Great! The Committee for the Great Salt Pond

In 1987, Island residents formed the *Committee for the Great Salt Pond* in response to the polluting effects of the more than 1,000 boats that often visited the harbor daily, and to fight — in court when needed — against several large condominium projects grossly inappropriate for the Island. Only one such project was built — on Ocean Avenue — in a scaled down form. In 1996, summertime clamming was again allowed in Great Salt Pond for the first time in ten years.

New England Airlines "Since 1970" — 1980s

Although New England Airlines is still going strongly at the Block Island Airport, the bumper stickers are not. The occasional souvenir collector will have to be content with books of matches.

(For the history of NEA, see pages 235-39.)

New Harbor Circus — Summer of 1993

The New Harbor Circus was a one-time show at the Samuel Peckham Inn in New Harbor, featuring the usually acrobats and clowns — and a human zebra, the first on Block Island.

Preserve like the Dickens — Early 1980s

The effort by several conservation groups to save the Dickens and Lewis farm properties along the Island's southwest shore was begun in earnest in 1982.

To purchase the more than 200 acres of diverse plant, bird and insect life — which was also the largest undeveloped tract of coastal land left on Block Island — $1.1 million was needed. The goal was met in 1984 through the hard work of many individuals (see pages 245, 246), this bumper sticker being one humble part.

See Chapter 27 to read of Elizabeth Dickens (1878-1963), the Islander whose life and memory inspired the project.

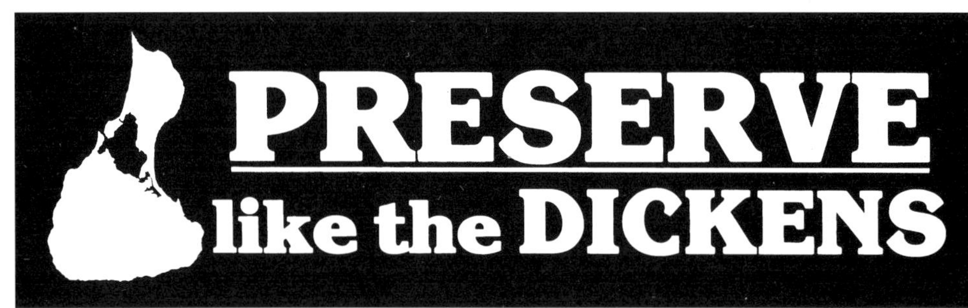

Bethany's Airport Diner "Real Food For Real People!"

For several decades the intimate restaurant at the airport has been a refuge for visitors who arrive by plane, as well as for year-round Islanders. Named "Bethany's" since the early 90s, the diner fulfills its motto: "Real Food For Real People."

BETHANY'S AIRPORT DINER
"Real Food For Real People!"
Block Island, RI (401) 466-3100 Open Year Round

NOPEDS — 1980s

Not only has the tranquility of the last 20 summers on Block Island been disturbed by the noisy rental mopeds, but more than 1,000 people have been injured seriously enough to require medical attention. From the start of this calamity, Islanders protested to the state legislature to reinstate the motorcycle license requirement that had formerly been needed to operate mopeds — but to no avail.

The total number of resulting injuries is greater than the entire population of Block Island. When you hear a siren, watch out for the ambulance soon to come, followed by a representative from one of the five rental dealers, eager to put the moped back on the road with another renter aboard.

Year 2000 — 1998

The "Year 2000" campaign was a private endeavor to raise $2,000,000 by the turn-of-the-millennium for the preservation of Block Island's landscape — for all to enjoy, evermore.

K-R Challenger airplane, at the Minister's Lot on Corn Neck Road, 1928

Landings on Block Island from the 1920s to the late 40s often took place in a pasture at the Minister's Lot on Corn Neck. In the mid-1960s, the Minister's Lot — which had been set aside by the first settlers in 1661 to provide rental fees to support a minister — became the Island's first housing development, called locally Salt Box City for its non-traditional impact on the landscape (see photo, page 244).

This group is posed next to a *K-R Challenger* C-2 (KR-31), powered by a 90-horsepower OX-5 engine. With an open cockpit — and the pilot seated in the *rear* —- the two passengers riding side-by-side in front were afforded a splendid view of scenery, and the propeller (see page 232 for a view of this plane taking off).

The plane is probably the Challenger flown at the time by Robert A. Kamm, a popular barnstorming pilot from Glastonbury, Connecticut. After clearing a field in 1925 next to Post Road in Charlestown — on the mainland shore of Rhode Island — he staged aerobatic shows and flew sightseers to Block Island. During summer months, Bob Kamm also delivered the *Providence Sunday Journal* to the Island, a special service begun by that newspaper in 1928 (see photos on page 234).

CHAPTER 25

Air Wars

Commercial airlines to Block Island

TO INITIATE REGULAR COMMERCIAL AIRPLANE FLIGHTS to Block Island — and to begin the local air wars — the first airline was quite appropriately formed by four veterans of World War II who named their company ***Veterans' Airways, Inc.*** Initial flights from their base at the Westerly State Airport were scheduled for a Saturday in December 1949, but — setting the tone for the next fifty years — plans and planes ran afoul of government regulations. Just a few days before the inaugural trip, *Veterans* discovered they must have a license as a *common carrier* from the state public utilities administrator.

When the government was finally satisfied, *Veterans* began service to and from Block Island and Westerly, and between Block Island and the main state airport in Warwick. Using a four-passenger plane that carried cargo as well, two departures left daily from Westerly, five days a week. Landings were made in the northern part of the Island on Corn Neck, at a meadow used by planes for at least 25 years, and known since the 1660s as the Minister's Lot.

Six months later, on July 15, 1950, another Block Island pasture — near the center of the Island and also used as a landing field from the 1920s to the 40s — was dedicated as a full-fledged Rhode Island State Airport, boasting a terminal building with a ticket office, a paved runway 2,000 feet long by 100 feet wide, and an automatic switch to turn runway lights on by sensing the sound of planes approaching within 800 feet. To help Governor Pastore dedicate the new $250,000 facility, forty airplanes arrived on Block Island, ten times the daily average.

The small terminal — the same one in use today — also managed to find room for a small snack bar, known in these beginning years as the Airport Luncheonette and run by Babe and Jimmie Rachels. Starting the continuing tradition of a little place that packs a big wallop, they featured Maine's "I Scream," lobster rolls, clam cakes, chowder, and home made pastries — and were open from "0800-2100." Somehow, the seemingly unlikely setting of the airport restaurant has been, for nearly fifty years, winter and summer, a stalwart refuge for Islanders hungry for food and perhaps a little human contact.

Veterans' Airways soon lost out to ***Howard Airways***, also based in Westerly, whose owner, Colonel Raymond Howard, had flown to Block Island occasionally since 1947. Howard, who had served in both World Wars, cemented his ties to the Island in 1949 by acquiring vacant land here — the land was still unbuilt upon when he relinquished it in the late 1950s.

During that decade, pilots who flew to the Island were dependent on their own vision rather than outside navigation equipment. If the Island was foggy, then you returned, thwarted, to the mainland.

But the unsophisticated nature of the era also had benefits. One of *Howard's* pilots, Don Monaco, wished to placate a grumbling storekeeper who complained that newspapers had not been arriving in a timely fashion. Flying over Water Street one day while en route to land at the airport, Monaco tossed out two rolled up *New York Times*. After

striking the statue of Rebecca, the bundles ricocheted, landing nearly at the store owner's doorstep — he was the first Islander to receive the papers that day..

Competition grew to cutthroat dimensions on the Westerly to Block Island run, especially in the mid-1950s when another newcomer appeared, ***Travel Air Service, Inc.*** Launched by Mel Frazier, a former Connecticut printer, the Westerly-based company began service to the Island with a Cessna four-seater and a three-place super cruiser. Shortly afterward, in 1955, Frazier was equipped with a five-seat 165 m.p.h. Cessna 195 Executive Liner. His air fleet outclassed Col. Howard's planes, which ranged from two-seat Cessna 120s and 140s, to a four-passenger Cessna 170.

Frazier soon followed the majority of his customers and moved south across the sound, making *Travel Air* Block Island's first resident airline company.

That year of 1955 the Airport Luncheonette was operated by Norma Lewis. She was, according to advertising, "formerly of Norma's Garden Gate," and offered breakfasts, lunches, and fountain service — with chowder and lobster salad being "our specialty."

Infringement on the territory of *Howard Airways* by upstart *Travel Air* was not taken lightly. As remembered by pilot Monaco, whenever a phone call requesting a flight was received by one of the companies, those passengers might be "stolen" by the competition — sort of an unwritten part of the business plan for both Colonel Howard and Mel Frazier, the outcome to be discussed later in "heated arguments" over the FAA radio.

Perhaps Monaco's experience in the 'wild' skies over Block Island prepared him a little for the future — he later flew 60 combat missions in Vietnam and spent 22 years piloting commercial airliners across the Pacific. In 1993 he returned to Block Island to fly, once more, small one-prop planes back-and-forth to Westerly, this time for ***New England Airlines***, which had become Block Island's resident air service in 1970.

In 1958 *Howard Airways*, also known as *Howard Aviation*, was absorbed by ***Coastal Airways*** of Westerly, but *Coastal* would never have a significant part of the Block Island market. Mel Frazier and his *Travel Air* pilots found themselves with the field, as it were, to themselves, providing round-the-clock service that would — as described in a newspaper article that December — "fetch the mail, newspapers and milk, pick up gifts and groceries, and guests, and run errands of all descriptions."

Once when the ferries were unable to operate for several days, Frazier trans-

K-R Challenger taking off from Minister's Lot, 1928

The plane shown on the previous page takes off into the southwest wind.

This view looks toward the south; the plane passed over Corn Neck Road a few seconds later.

Burned frame of airplane wreck, at Minister's Lot, August 1931

The Island's first flying fatality occurred on August 27, 1931. The pilot, Gottfred Lundberg, died after his airplane crashed and burned at the Minister's Lot.

While the loss of life on Block Island's shores from shipwrecks has been reduced to nearly zero by modern technology, plane accidents in the last quarter of the 1900s hit hard and unexpectedly — and likely always will due to the great speeds involved.

Recent tragedies are as daunting as mythical tales of old, and are, for now, best passed down by that ancient storytelling method: word-of-mouth.

ported three and a half tons of groceries, in an "air lift operation worthy of Berlin." With no doctor on the Island during most of 1958, his pilots arranged a "stork schedule," ensuring that at least one pilot would be present on the Island at all times so expectant mothers could reach a mainland hospital.

And at Christmastime, Santa Claus now arrived by plane. Santa may or may not have been the real one, but the presents — for each child on the Island — were definitely provided by Mel Frazier. With a pencil-thin mustache, and a seat cushion to prop him up high enough to see over the instrument panel, Mel Frazier was a colorful character.

Airplanes had become firmly woven into Island life, complimenting the ferries.

IN MID-**1961** THE STATE CONSTRUCTED its second building at the Block Island airport: a hanger resembling an extra large garage with a small ell the size of a home garage. In response, Henry Hutchinson, owner of the Island Light & Power Co., formed a new air service, ***Blair***, and bought a new two-engine Aero Commander considerably larger than any of *Travel Air's* five planes. *Blair* provided the Island's first regularly scheduled flights.

When Hutchinson put his plane inside the hanger — wedging the hefty craft in after 45 minutes with the use of jacks — no room was left for any of *Travel Air's* craft. Mel Frazier felt the situation was unfair, since his company had 97 percent of the air business, his service was on Block Island first, and he was paying half the hanger's $170 monthly rent. In 1963 Frazier notified the state he would not pay rent. The state notified Block Island that no one could use the hanger.

But that didn't keep the planes, or the storks, from flying. At 4:10 a.m. one Sunday morning in August 1966, the Island's physician, Dr. Wade Ortel, called Mel Frazier's home from the Southeast Light. The wife of a coastguardsman was expecting soon. By 4:30 a.m. a plane flown by pilot Charley Melot left the Island with Seaman Wallace Dana and his wife Janice aboard. At 6:15 a.m., a baby boy was born in Westerly Hospital.

Times can change quickly in unexpected ways, and one year later Mel Frazier's *Travel Air* was out of business, and ***Viking Airways***, which purchased Hutchinson's *Blair*, became the new service with bigger and better equipment — a twin-engine Aztec — and two Cessna Skywagons, each able to act as an air-ambulance, carrying a horizontal stretcher to the mainland in any weather. In the summer of 1967 — to speed the evacuation process further — two-way radios were supplied to the Island's rescue, fire, and police personnel.

Three planes over Old Harbor, July 22, 1928

An aerial view of Old Harbor was printed in the *Providence Sunday Journal* on the occasion of that company's first airplane delivery of the *Sunday Journal* to Block Island. For this publicity photo, three planes were used — the other two are visible over the fishing docks.

"The Journal Plane Ready For Block Island Trip" — February 21, 1937

So great was the allure of flying in the golden decades of aviation — the 1920s and 30s — that every stride forward was highly touted to a public with an insatiable appetite for planes, progress and heros. In 1928, to great self-acclaim, the *Providence Sunday Journal* began flying their paper during summer months to Block Island. Nine years later when the service became year-round, the *Journal* thought the effort to be also worthy of significant note, as shown above.

The special airplane — decked out in this newspaper photograph with a banner announcing its purpose — left the Warwick state airport at 8:00 a.m., landing "approximately 20 minutes" later on a grass field at Block Island. The papers were distributed to most subscribers by 9:00 a.m. — beating the ferry's delivery by five hours.

Zeppelin dirigible* Los Angeles, *over Block Island, ca. 1930

Although the 658-foot long **Los Angeles** never landed at Block Island, viewers from the level of land would, nevertheless, have been duly impressed by both her length and the 90-foot diameter. (From a Block Islander's point of reference, if you laid the Los Angeles along Water Street, it would be twice as high as the roof of the National Hotel.)

Acquired from Germany in 1924 as part of World War I reparations, the Navy dirigible was christened by President Coolidge's wife, and in the next few years made more than 300 successful flights, until finally scrapped in 1939. Many trips were flown from her base at Lakehurst, New Jersey, to participate in Naval operations off Newport, Rhode Island — the direction she is coming from in this postcard view sold on Block Island in the 1930s.

The country's initial euphoria for such behemoths — which were designed to carry passengers on regularly scheduled trans-Atlantic crossings — gave way to reality as disaster after disaster befell them, culminating with the cataclysmic explosion of the **Hindenburg** in 1937.

Viking was begun by 25-year-old Thomas Corwin of Long Island, who entered the aircraft business three years earlier by forming an airplane leasing company. By 1968, *Viking* had 10 aircraft including four twin-engine planes, amongst them a 10-seat Britten-Norman Islander developed on the Isle of Wright off England's southern coast. The ultra stable, well-regarded Islanders have since been a fundamental ingredient of life on Block Island, an airplane flight in them being as familiar to many residents as a trip in the venerable family auto.

With Charley Melot signed on as a pilot, and the addition of Vera Sprague behind the desk at the Block Island terminal, *Viking* continued in the pattern of *Travel Air* a decade before — in the words of one account, hauling "everything from diapers to fresh flowers and newspapers ... flying off dirty linens, among other things, and as a free public service for sick or injured residents."

As far back as 1969 there was a public cry to enlarge the much frequented airport snack bar — known then as Sky King's after the popular TV show, as well as for the owner King Odell. The diner is still too small, but perhaps that's why people like it.

In 1970, for the first time, two commercial airlines provided regularly scheduled flights from Block Island. *Viking* flew to Westerly and Providence, and a short-lived newcomer, ***Montauk-Caribbean***, offered daily flights to Flushing airport near New York City, with stops closer by at Montauk and East Hampton on eastern Long Island.

Then, late in the summer of 1970, came dramatic change again. *Viking Airways* was the one out — and ***New England Airlines*** the one in, started by a young,

Looking southeast over airport, 1950s

Very much has changed since this photograph of the Block Island airport and surrounding landscape was made in the 1950s — most notably the construction of dozens of summer homes.

Visible across the grass on either side of the runway is the old route of Center Road, which once ran nearly straight from Fresh Pond (upper right) to the location of the airport entrance (lower left). The semicircular road on the right was created in 1950 when the state built the airport.

In 1961 a hanger was erected just to the right of the terminal, and shortly afterward the runaway was lengthened from the original 2,000 feet, to 2,500 feet.

former *Viking* pilot, and certified instructor, Bill Bendokas. Beginning with two planes — a six-seat Cherokee 6 and a four-seat Cessna 172 Skyhawk — *New England Airlines* has been far and away the dominant air carrier ever since, bringing the first of their own Britten-Norman Islanders into service in 1971. That is not to say, though, that others have not tried storming the walls.

Usually the competition came from mainland-based carriers, such as ***Yankee Airways*** which flew out of Westerly airport by special charter for more than a dozen years in the 1970s and 80s. Rivalry with *Yankee* remained constant but relatively benign.

Other regional charter airlines periodically entered the Block Island market. ***Air Ventures Inc***., operating from the Griswold Airport in Madison, Connecticut, solicited passengers in 1977 via an Island-wide mailing offering "special Madison-Block Island commuter tickets."

North Central Airways, of northern Rhode Island, proposed opening regular service between Warwick's Green State Airport and Block Island on April 2, 1979. So *New England* followed suit with the same proposal, set to begin May 1. *North Central* scheduled two round trip flights daily, from Monday to Friday. So *New England,* which two years earlier had found the route to be unprofitable, nevertheless upped the ante, scheduling three daily flights, seven days a week. *North Central* then matched, changing their two daily flights to three.

So *New England Airlines* advertised specials, such as, in 1980: a student fare, child's fare, 10 % commuter discount, and the Christmas "Shoppers Special Week" with round trip tickets to Westerly for $20. Regular fares were $16 each way.

The walls held.

In 1982 ***Quonset Airways***, of Wickford, Rhode Island, tried a new advertising approach: round trip air fare from Quonset to Block Island for $35. The proposed "luncheon special" flight would stop at the Block Island airport diner to give passengers "the best grilled-cheese sandwich on the East Coast." Airline owner Carl Dworman said: "A flight to Block Island—I'm not kidding about this—can be better than a flight to Bermuda."

Action Air, of Groton, Connecticut, boasted in a full-page newspaper ad during the summer of 1983: "We are the best, we are on time, we have the lowest rates." But they catered mostly to the lesser air travel between Block Island and Connecticut. In 1987 their ads in the local paper were a half page in size, and by 1997 one eighth page.

Not only did *New England Airlines* stay in business, but, to honor 15 years of outstanding service provided by owners Bill and Lois Bendokas, Governor Edward DiPrete proclaimed Saturday, August 3, 1985, as *New England Airlines* Day.

More than one million pounds of freight had been carried by *New England*, including goats and lambs; more than 500,000 passengers had been ferried between Block Island and the mainland; and more than 1,000 medical cases evacuated. Pilots had flown a total of 54,000 hours, most of them on the 15-minute journey to Westerly but also on charters as distant as Miami and Nova Scotia. *New England Airlines* was, in fact, the only commuter airline headquartered in the State of Rhode Island.

At a ceremony with officials in attendance from the FAA, the state, and the town — and red roses being proffered in all directions — the Bendokas's presented Vera Sprague with a new watch "for her untiring efforts to keep Bill on time." Vera stayed at her post, ever-faithful to travelers and her fellow Islanders, until 1995.

To outside observers the governor's proclamation belied true circumstances — because by this time the walls had been topped.

An ambitious company, ***Watch Hill Air Charter***, was formed in July 1983 at the Westerly Airport as part of Helms Aviation. The president, Jeff Helms, had operated a flight school at that location for 15 years. *Watch Hill's* co-owner was Charles Taylor. Non-scheduled flights were begun to Block Island in 1984 for only $17 each way. *New England* then slashed its $22 fare to meet the competition — and capitalism took over with a vengeance.

Watch Hill's 1984 brochure, mailed to every Block Islander, advertised "You Now Have A Choice Of Air Carriers To And From The Island ... low time aircraft ... at a time most convenient to you."

Yankee Airways, which had been calmly flying charters out of Westerly for 10 years, fled a bit further away to Waterford, Connecticut — and in the late 1980s ceased operations.

Terminal building and plane landing, early-1950s

The airport's terminal building has changed little since this postcard view was made nearly fifty years ago.

Watch Hill began with one aircraft and two pilots in 1983. By August 3, 1985 — the day proclaimed as *New England Airlines Day* by the governor — *Watch Hill* had nine aircraft and seven pilots and, on the other side of the runway from the traditional Westerly terminal, had plans for a new $750,000 operations center, enormous in size, with 20,000 square feet of space.

Now under attack was the very headquarters of *New England Airlines*: the old Navy control tower building that dated from World War II, when Naval fighter pilots trained at the then new airfield. (This building burned in 1998 —- the state constructed a new facility.)

Earlier in 1985, *Watch Hill* had even installed and manned their own tiny counter at the small Block Island terminal, just a few feet across from and directly facing New England Airlines' 15-year-old counter — and Block Island residents were hired to staff the booth. Competition was elbow close. *Watch Hill* might have lost that day of August 3, but they were ready to take the rest of the century.

The 1985 version of *Watch Hill's* promotional mailing declared "Now you have an alternative — 24-hour emergency service — Island-based aircraft & pilot."

Taylor claimed that by operating non-scheduled flights to Block Island, "We give the people a choice. Whether there's one person or six, we're gonna go." Just show up at the airport and fly —that was the idea — no reservations, no waiting.

Bendokas filed complaints with the U.S. Department of Transportation claiming *Watch Hill Air Charter*, despite its name, was a disguise for a "scheduled commuter service," for which *Watch Hill* was not licensed.

Then in October 1985 another charter business was formed offering service to Block Island, this one based at the Newport State Airport. ***Sakonnet Air Charter's*** president, 27-year-old Kimberly Dunn, had simply borrowed two seldom-used planes from her husband's company: a six-passenger, twin-engine Piper Navajo, and a three-passenger, single-engine Cessna Skylane. The idea didn't get off the ground.

In early 1986, *Watch Hill's* rate had climbed to $19 each way and New England's were at $18 --- but for the last 12 days of days of March *New England* welcomed the coming of spring with a special rate of $12 — which was extended to April 14, with another special offer to fly for $14 if you wanted a free Chinese dinner in Westerly. Block Islanders were partial to Chinese food as a treat, since none was available at Island restaurants.

Ground for *Watch Hill's* new terminal was broken by Governor DiPrete on April 17.

Watch Hill now had 12 aircraft (versus *New England's* nine), 18 employees, and plans for further expansion. But lesser competitors mused neither of the two Block Island air services could be making money.

For passengers who had flown with *New England Airlines* during the previous 15 years, group dynamics at the Block Island terminal could now be awkward. Each of the two opposing ticket counters might be manned by friends — and everyone could literally bump into everyone else in the small room, or when exiting through the only door to the runway.

Once you were in Westerly, problems were not over. If, for instance, you flew to Block Island on *New England,* you left your car on one side of the airfield. But if you went back to the mainland on *Watch Hill,* you were dropped off at their new terminal on the other side. You might see your car parked straight across the runway, but to get to it required a lengthy circumnavigation by road.

By the summer of 1988 *Watch Hill Air Charter's* fleet included two helicopters and two jets — which, if they had ever been used on the short 15-minute hop to Block Island, would have been serious overkill. But *Watch Hill* now claimed to cover the entire United States and Canada.

Taylor was quoted in the *Providence Journal* of July 27, 1988: "We can get the job done when no one else can." And as partial proof, if pizza arrived at the Westerly airport as a flight was leaving to Block Island, it was delivered for free.

WITH ONE OR TWO EXCEPTIONS, it is difficult to imagine an entity falling flatter and faster than did *Watch Hill.*

Three months later, the company's mailing of September 20, 1988, stated: "The cost to properly maintain the aircraft fleet ... has escalated at a pace faster than we could justifiably increase our fares ... we plan to reduce our charter activity to and from the island."

Watch Hill Air Charter had folded. Ten years later, one of the co-founders was working at a nearby, newly opened Indian gambling casino.

But others kept trying on the Block Island air route.

In 1990 a Groton-based company, ***Coastal Air Services***, decided to expand further by opening an office on Block Island. *Coastal* had been in operation since 1955, maintained a fleet of 20 aircraft and had other offices at the state airports in Westerly and Warwick, and on the resort islands of Martha's Vineyard and Nantucket. *Coastal* no longer exists — *New England Airlines* does.

In the mid-1990s, two new air charter services were formed locally.

Resident Rick Vila, a commercial airline captain, established ***Resort Air***, which features a twin-engine Piper Seneca III, with weather radar, de-icing, and full instrumentation. The company thrives.

On April 1, 1996, ***Block Island Airlines*** *(BIA)* was created, co-owned by a Block Island moped rental operator and a commercial airline pilot. Two years later, both had dropped out — but the name was acquired by new owners operating out of Long Island's Farmingdale airport — well away from Block Island, near New York City.

Two aspects of flying from Block Island, though, remain consistent.

The Island's airport luncheonette became Bethany's Airport Diner in 1992, with the refuge remaining as down-to-earth as ever.

And in Westerly, planes do not disembark passengers on the *other* side of the runway. *New England Airlines* commands the skies.

Also see bumper stickers:
- *for New England Airlines — page 228*
- *for Bethany's Airport Diner — pages 131, 229*

Water Street, Old Harbor, ca. 1960

The big benefit of flying off the Island, as everyone notices, is checking things out below. This view will never be seen again — from the mid-1960s to mid-1970s most of the sand dunes were paved for parking.

Paths for pedestrians cross the dunes. The wooden boxes on the shore are lobster cars, anchored in the harbor by fishermen to store their live lobsters.

Compare to other photos of Water Street buildings, pages 112, 128, 160, 207.

Fighting the bad guys without calling them names

Looking west to Black Rock Point, 1977

Block Island's greatest conservation lands converge in the southwest corner of the Island: Rodman's Hollow falls to the sea beyond the first point of land, nearly joining with the Lewis-Dickens Farm at Black Rock Point in the distance. See maps: pages 250, 253

CHAPTER 26

The Block Island Conservancy: the early years

THE ISLAND WAS DOWN-AND-OUT, the sanctum sanctorum had been invaded, the most holiest of sites where the last great glacier 12,000 years ago had left a plunging inland ravine that swooped from the plains above, down to within three feet of sea level, then rose briefly before dropping in a defeated cliff face of eroded gravel, clay and boulders, down to the sea itself.

It was, as happens to virginal landscapes, and as living things had long ago learned to fear the most, an invasion by humans, and rather heathen ones at that, or so those people who had lived on Block Island for decades, and for generations, and even for centuries, had decided.

The *Providence Journal* summed up the onslaught in November 1972 with an article titled "Last Chance for Block Island?" and a lead paragraph that pulsed with all the alarm felt for the previous 5,000 years when eyes scanning seaward had spotted unfamiliar vessels, prows aimed here:

"Land-hungry developers ranging up and down the East Coast have backed the remaining unspoiled, rural areas into a tenuous corner."

Twenty-nine years ago that was written — and for twenty-nine years the message has been reworded, re-cried out, against a generation of professional speculators and mom-and-pop subdividers who have continued spoiling the unspoiled, until even the land's greatest lovers must admit it is gone and recognize the logic of the pro-developers who say "well the landscape is GONE, and much as we might have liked to do things differently, it's gone, quit living in the past and help us develop it some more since now it really doesn't matter, does it."

The November 1972 article continued:

"And nowhere is there a real estate plum riper for picking than the scrub-grown acres of Block Island, its sea breezes and magnificent ocean views only a long stone's throw from the escape-seeking city dwellers of New York and Boston."

The invaders in this case were professionals from New York City: Alan Rudolph, a developer, and Harold Edleman, an architectural planner. They had bought 37 acres in the heart of Rodman's Hollow two years earlier for $75,000 and they wanted money. As Block Island has seen many times since: land planners, architects and lawyers do not make for good development.

Their plans for Rodman's Hollow were later described by a *Yankee Magazine* writer: "It was something like a butcher's chart for cutting up beef, that you see in the markets."

The kernel of a grassroots effort to save the Hollow — and, in the long-term, the Island — was hatched in the fall of 1971. A year later, on September 9, 1972, the Block Island Conservancy was incorporated with a retired merchant marine captain as president: Block Islander **Captain John 'Rob' Lewis**. By the end of the next month, a real estate appraiser hired by the Conservancy declared the threatened Hollow's fair market value to be $109,000 — 45% higher than the $75,000 the developers paid for the property two years earlier — and an offer was made to purchase the 37 acres.

A commitment for $27,500, to be matched by Block Islanders, was won from the state's

Green Acres program — a conservation fund begun a short time earlier by Governor John Chafee. If those funds were secured, they would then be matched with a grant from the Federal Bureau of Outdoor Recreation, quadrupling the Conservancy's commitment.

For the acquisition there was no cost to taxpayers, only to those individuals who chose to make an outright contribution or to purchase the bright orange bumper stickers that proclaimed S O S — an Island cry to "Save Open Space," echoing the nautical "Save Our Souls." But the developers were recalcitrant to sell. For a year and a half, nearly every car displayed the large florescent rectangle.

Rodman's Hollow was saved only by utilizing a state law that allowed municipalities to condemn land for recreational purposes — and finally, in April 1974, a deed for Rodman's Hollow was recorded giving the town ownership.

An additional $28,000 was raised by the Conservancy and paid in 1976 to the developers, who threatened court action in the belief they had not made enough profit — even with those S O S bumper stickers, bought with tiny contributions from hundreds of people, staring them in the face wherever they went on the Island.

Through the succeeding years, members of the Block Island Conservancy continued to work, the greatest influence of the group ultimately being not the amount of land the Conservancy itself acquired, but rather the remarkable number of larger organizations that rallied to the Conservancy's cause, acquiring considerable properties in their own names, to be preserved for all.

The Conservancy nibbled away here and there, slowly at first, forming a large base of goodwill and a legacy of environmental awareness, the fruits realized admirably in the 1990s as the organization came to be perceived as the beloved patriarch of Block Island's conservation groups.

In December 1975 the Conservancy received an unexpected, unsolicited gift from **Richard and Sallie Mazzur**, 6.4 acres abutting the eastern side of Rodman's Hollow. Captain Lewis appreciated that the land encompassed a ridge top: "Upon seeing it for the first time, one is immediately awe-struck by the comprehensive, wide-ranging, 360-degree view from this splendid overlook, which is nothing less than spectacular!" But the Conservancy president also knew of the site's other future value: "It is of special strategic importance to the well-being of wildlife inasmuch as it brings wildlife closer to the availability of a protected source of fresh water in Peckham Pond."

To establish that link between Rodman's Hollow and Peckham Pond, a commitment was made in 1976 to purchase 3.6 acres of intervening land for the appraised market value of $35,000. The Captain's announcement of the new fundraising effort in December 1976 reminded the Conservancy's friends:

"It is important to remember that 'Peace On Earth' means peace to all the earth, and to all the creatures thereof — 'Human, Creature, and Plant alike' — each one a magnificent creation."

Rob Lewis at one of many meetings, Aug. 1993

Saving land means attending meetings. Listening to the always carefully prepared Rob speak, are two fellow Block Islanders — **Chris Littlefield**, manager of the Block Island office of the international conservation organization, the Nature Conservancy — and **Keith Lang**, the Nature Conservancy's director for all of Rhode Island.

One of the initial directors of the Block Island Conservancy was **Elise S. Lapham**, who with her **husband David**, forever altered the history and way of life on Block Island in 1978. They arranged for 135 acres of their land along Clay Head — on which they had planted trees, created paths, and welcomed the public for more than a decade — to be permanently protected from development by transferring the conservation rights to the State of Rhode Island. The winding paths are commonly called "The Maze," although the more formal name is "Bluestone."

The Lathams wanted nothing in return.

Not only is the Lapham land highly visible from Old Harbor and from any spot along the entire two-mile length of Crescent Beach, but these 100-foot high cliffs are also the first part of the Island to be seen by travelers approaching from

YANKEE

MARCH • 1975

TOWN MEETING '75/the Land

LAST CHANCE FOR BLOCK ISLAND

You can't compromise with zoning when all you've got to work with is ten and three-quarter square miles of land. So out on Block Island they've taken the matter into their own hands . . .

by Deborah Stone

☐ Bright fluorescent orange bumper stickers, with bold black print proclaiming SOS – those bumper stickers appeared everywhere on Block Island last summer. I saw them on bumpers, fenders, windows, or in stores and other public places, stacked in neat piles beside cans provided for donations.

Bumper stickers mean causes, and causes are what we summer people go to Block Island to get away from for a while. Removed 12 miles from the Rhode Island coastline, this tiny, tear-shaped, three-by-six-mile island provides a perfect summer escape. If you don't mind a schedule of beaching, sailing, a little clamming, a little fishing, then life on the Island is not too hard to take. Who wants to think about causes?

But those pesky bumper stickers stuck in my head, the way the image of the sun sticks in your eyelids when you've looked at it too long. On closer look, I found the SOS stood for Save Open Space. Not the traditional maritime distress signal, but a call for help just the same.

How to save its open space is Block Island's biggest problem, according to Herbert Whitman, First Warden and President of the Town Council. Not so long ago, Block Island had plenty of open space. It belonged to a few families, most of them descendants of the first Block

From atop 150' Mohegan Bluffs, Southeast Lighthouse on Block Island flashes its green beacon visible for 21 miles. Below: *This view of the U.S. Coast Guard station at Harbor Neck, across Great Salt Pond, exemplifies the openness of Block Island.*

The saving of Rodman's Hollow

Yankee magazine article, March 1975

Point Judith on the ferry — this first impression of Block Island is a grand one, indeed, whereas now many other overly-built portions of the coast do not at all put the Island's best foot forward.

As was to happen with several other generous gifts made to the public, the appraised value of $1,000,000 was used as a match to obtain another $1,000,000 (from the federal government this time) that could be used to protect still more land on Block Island.

In this manner during the 1970s, major efforts were begun by several groups — both private and governmental, and at the local, state, and national levels — to expand Block Island's two large conservation areas: Rodman's Hollow in the south, and Clay Head in the north.

Also in this manner, as exemplified so well by the family of Block Island Conservancy director Elise Lapham, was begun the trend of absolute allegiance — of putting one's heart where one's name on the stationary is — of the BIC members, directors, and officers, setting examples as however they might be able.

For the next two decades from amongst those initial officers of 1972 were to come gifts of the land itself, back to the people, to the plants, to the animals of the world:

- from director **Helen Cullinan**: near Grace's Cove,
- from the family of directors **Cliff Payne** and **Blake Phelan**: near Mohegan Bluffs, and near Sands Pond,
- from director **John Gray**: south of the dump and at Esta's Park in Old Harbor,
- from director **F. Albert Starr's** family: along Great Salt Pond, at both Andy's Way and Indian Head Neck,
- from president **Rob Lewis's** family: in the southwest and on Old Town Road,
- from treasurer **Luella Ball's** family: on Corn Neck, near Clay Head,
- and from assistant treasurer **Adrian Mitchell**: the land where the cows are, halfway down Corn Neck Road (see photos, page 3 and bottom of page 141).

Looking west at Salt Box City, in the Minister's Lot on Corn Neck, 1977

The lesson of Salt Box City, a cheaply made mass-development created in the mid-1960s on Corn Neck Road, reaffirmed the need for Block Island to create a zoning ordinance — or the "anything goes to make a profit" mentality of developers would degrade the Island's rural landscape completely. The mainland speculators who built the housing development — although one was a Connecticut lumber yard owner — used the poorest quality construction possible, such as #3 grade wood shingles for siding. The knots of #3 grade fall out exposing the interior framing to Block Island's moisture and high winds — Islanders traditionally use clear #1 shingles which are knot-free. These houses are inland, but across Corn Neck Road (the horizontal roadway visible in the upper right corner) and directly on Great Salt Pond, the developers built for themselves a waterfront home, manorial by comparison to the houses offered for sale to the public.

By the time a two-acre zoning law was established in 1967 — grossly inadequate compared to the minimum five-acres required by the Island's closest mainland towns — everyone had learned from the example of Salt Box City that the easy way to make money on Block Island was to buy four or more acres, and subdivide it into two or more lots, then build a house on one and sell the remaining land to get your money back.

The simple math was not lost on anyone, and subdividing was the way of the next 30 years — by Islanders, by mainland contractors, by bored housewives of summer homeowners, and by summer visitors whose mainland professions left them with discretionary income: college professors, architects, ex-governors, lawyers, and others.

The 9th annual meeting of the Block Island Conservancy on September 4, 1981, was held "at the height of a raging Easterly storm" that lasted several days. But nevertheless, as Captain Lewis noted proudly, the Conservancy had been so successful that officials managed to attend from several regional groups, such as the Audubon Society of Rhode Island, the Rhode Island Department of Management, and the charitable Rhode Island Foundation — as well as representatives of nationwide organizations: the Nature Conservancy, the Natural Resources Defense Council, and the Environmental Defense Fund.

As the Block Island Conservancy's 10-year anniversary approached in 1982, the pace of acquisitions was increasing. In August 1981, 2.9 acres of meadow in the southwest corner of the Island — on the south side of Cooneymus Road "about two-thirds of the way up Cherry Tree Hill" — were given by **Dr. Alvin Goodman, Susanna Goodman, Carl Panero**, and **Ann Shipley**; for which those individuals had paid the full market price.

Adjoining the Coast Guard Road, 1.5 acres of beach land were donated in December 1981 by **Richard and Rosalie Sorenson**. Captain Lewis, still guiding as president, noted "we see here an opportunity to preserve a valuable habitat area and possible nesting area for a variety of shore birds."

At the northern end of Great Salt Pond, bordering on the ocean, 4.3 acres were given, also in December, by **Sidney Pinney, Jr. and Sarah Pinney**. Captain Lewis wrote "this parcel contains a widely varied wildlife habitat area which includes meadow land, brush land, beach land, a pond, fresh water wetland, and it borders on salt water wetland."

On August 7, 1982, **William Murray and his sister Georgette Murray McIntire** gave 1.7 acres in the southern part of the Island, at the corner of Lakeside Drive across from the popular painted rock (see photo of rock, page 129). Called a "most beautiful natural garden" by Captain Lewis, and featuring a roadside pond famous for its water lilies, the corner was designated the Murray Nature Sanctuary to the memory of other family members who had lived in the area for generations.

Inspired by the Block Island Conservancy's activities, the larger groups were tackling the preservation of 194 acres of the **Dickens and Lewis Farms** in the southwestern part of the Island — a $1,100,000 program, even though some acreage was an outright gift by the Lewis family and the rest acquired at less than 1/2 of market value. Elizabeth Dickens (see Chapter 27) was the revered teacher of bird studies at the Block Island school, and a neighbor fondly remembered by generations of the Lewis family. She passed away in 1963 at the age of 85, leaving a 50-year diary of her daily bird sightings.

As part of that effort, the BIC was able to pledge $53,000, to help match $100,000 given to the Nature Conservancy by the M&M Foundation of New York. If the BIC is considered as a platoon rushed to the front to plug a gap that the enemy was pouring through, then now the rest of the battalion had arrived. Again John Chafee — risen from governor, to Secretary of the Navy, and then to senator, and, appropriately enough, a Marine captain during World War II — had pledged his aid, together with that of Rhode Island's other longtime distinguished senator and Block Island benefactor, Clairborne Pell.

With the motto "Save like the Dickens," the state Department of Environmental Management (DEM), the Audubon Society, and the Nature Conservancy succeeded — dedicating the Lewis-Dickens nature preserve on July 28, 1984.

Negotiations of a more tedious nature were begun in 1982 — overshadowed always by heartrending thoughts of a potentially nightmarish future — to connect the Rodman's Hollow land with the Lewis-Dickens farm. The conservancy groups were dealing once more with two outright developers — from Westport, Connecticut — who had plans to build 36 houses along Black Rock Road, a winding rutted dirt lane that passed through moor-like meadows, swales, and knobs parallel to the nearby ravine in Rodman's Hollow.

With only $400,000 available to thwart the project, the state DEM and the town's planning board had even considered agreeing that 'only' 25 houses would be built on the northern half of the Black Rock land, saving the area near the sea — a compromise by some standards — a 'Sophie's Choice' by others.

Dedication of the Lewis-Dickens Farm, July 28, 1984

From left to right:

Senator John F. Chafee, Hob Calhoun (Audubon Society), Keith Lewis, Robert Bendict (state DEM), and Keith Lang.

John Chafee — as Rhode Island's former governor, and during his long tenor as senator in the 1980s and 90s — often supported the cause of the environment nationwide, worldwide, and on Block Island.

The two Keiths, each a Block Islander, have led the way since the 1980s in preserving the Island's landscape.

The titled roles — for Keith Lewis, as head of the Land Trust and Block Island Conservancy — and for Keith Lang, as head of the state chapter of the Nature Conservancy — are easily stated, but the constant roles behind-the-scenes are the award winners.

There were blockbuster donations such as $500,000 raised by the town's selling of bonds (the taxpayers were taxing themselves to save the Island); $437,500 given by the National Park Service (from taxpayers nationwide); and $350,000 from the mainland-based Champlin Foundations. But to reach the full price being asked for the land, new mailings were still being sent out as late as August 1985, bringing in gifts ranging from $5 to $2,500. The BIC scraped together $45,000 (gifts from the same people whose taxes were comprising other monies). Keith Lewis made a substantial donation. And William Penn — a mainland banker, and chairman of Island preservation committees such as the successful campaign to save the Lewis-Dickens farm — pledged $12,500 as a memorial.

Finally — to end this particular bad dream — in late 1985 the entire 114-acre Black Rock parcel was acquired for $1.675 million dollars in the name of the Nature Conservancy, the rights to be apportioned to the town and to the state DEM.

Meanwhile, amidst the multifaceted struggles occurring simultaneously on various Island fronts, the BIC made their greatest effort since the initial Rodman's Hollow struggle of 1972: helping to save Mansion Beach.

For decades Mansion Beach, at the extreme northern end of Crescent Beach, had been used by Islanders and visitors alike, many of whom considered the remote site with its spectacular view of Old Harbor two miles distant, to be the loveliest sandy spot on the Island's shore. For families who lived and summered here, this was essentially an heirloom to be shared with young ones and passed down to them.

But the undeveloped site was in private hands. In this case, however, the owner sought not to build nor to threaten, only to sell the property to the public for a fair appraised value. The town had available $527,500 of the $630,000 needed ($500,000 of that amount pledged again by Island taxpayers through the selling of bonds).

Into this breach, to the rescue, came the Block Island Conservancy with a commitment of $102,500 — at the time the largest amount to be raised by the group for any project.

The thorough Captain Lewis has been noted since his merchant marine days — and perhaps from teenage years working on Island fishing boats — for leaving no stone overturned in his labors. Possibly that last $500 donation, small but necessary for the purchase, came from an appreciative donor who read these exacting words at the end of the Captain's letter extolling the many virtues of Mansion Beach: "... and no coral!"

Dedication of the Lewis-Dickens Farm, July 28, 1984

Other private individuals continued to support the BIC in extraordinary ways. In December 1984 **Mrs. Avery Rogers Brooke** donated 6.7 acres in the southwest that linked the Lewis-Dickens conservation area with the previous private donation of the Goodman-Panero-Shipley land.

Also in December, **Jonathan Murphy** pledged 1.6 acres next to the earlier donation of the Pinneys at the northern end of Great Salt Pond, to be given incrementally during the following five years.

Captain Lewis's letter in August 1985 — addressed that year, as always, "Dear Friend of Block Island" — thanked four youngsters for their $19.91 contribution, 10% of the net proceeds from their lemonade stand: **Suzanne Ellis, age 7; Anna Koopman, age 7; Amy Lewis, age 6; and John Ellis, age 12.**

During the next 12 months, 20 acres of land were pledged to the BIC: 10.2 acres from **Ted and Lucy Martin** on Old Mill Road; an additional lot by the Goodman-Shipley-Panero families (adjacent to their previous gift), given with other neighbors **Arthur Stisel, Eugene Nesic, and Richard Foote**; a pine grove near Settler's Rock from **Sim and Bill Attwood**; 1.5 acres near Mohegan Bluffs from **David Slattery**; and the nearly 1-acre Sisal Bog near Franklin Swamp from developer **Richard Rizzo**, as part of his agreement with the Planning Board for a subdivision.

In 1987 there were four substantial gifts of land: 4.7 acres from **Dorothy and Don McCluskey** at the north end of Great Salt Pond; 2.3 acres near the West Side Church from **Dr. Mary Pettit**; a 2-acre easement at Franklin Swamp from **Mary Bernadette Ryan and Dermott Ryan**; and from **Adrian Mitchell** an easement on 19 acres of grassland at Mitchell Farm, where the cows are on Corn Neck Road — protecting the groundwater of all of the Neck, and providing nesting habitat for birds such as the upland sandpiper and the grasshopper sparrow.

Participants in the first 16 years of the Block Island Conservancy's history will realize how inadequate a short rendition of that time period can be. During the next dozen years, the Conservancy's ever-escalating activities affected many parts of the Island — not to mention the enormous efforts of other private landowners and more than a half-dozen Island, state, and national conservation groups.

"the earth is the list"

Rather than reading a list of land donations, it is indeed more pleasurable to move instead about the Island, seeing the good deeds in nearly any direction you look — the earth is the list.

Captain Lewis's leadership spread amongst his fellow Islanders, moved outwardly to the shores of America, and passed even more so amongst his own family. In 1986, son Keith led a group of Block Islanders who sought to establish the town's Land Trust — to preserve open space through a three percent real estate tax on Island land transfers — winning over the Island's voters, the local real estate businesses, and, with more difficulty, the state legislators of other towns, who do business within the ill-defined corridors of the Capitol building in Providence, a journey Keith took daily for many months — maneuvering with the aplomb and directness of a master mariner. During the last years of the 1980s, Keith also accepted the presidency of the BIC from his father.

Following the tenures of **Robert Ellis Smith** and **Connie LaRue** from 1989 into the early 1990s, **Captain Lewis's other son, David**, was given the helm of the Block Island Conservancy. David's advice was threefold: open space costs lots of money, the government cannot do it all, everyone must participate. And to demonstrate his commitment to those beliefs, **Read Kingsbury** is the current president.

Now maps are made showing the scores of open space sites — they appear as variously colored darker areas on a white background. The conservation land seems to spread — at just three percent of Block Island in 1972, to 30% by some accounts in 1999. But that figure is misleading because it includes large areas of beach, sand dunes, and bluffs that never would have been built on — the actual percentage of the Island saved from being developed by conservancy groups is closer to 20%.

No land, though, has been gained.

No acreage has been added to the total area of Block Island. Open space is preserved, but no open space is ever created over what previously existed here. When land is acquired by a conservation group, there are no barges that bring thousands of loads of 'open space earth' to attach to the shore and make new land.

"A Community Unites to Turn Back a Tide of Development"

The international Nature Conservancy Magazine, Jan./Feb. 1992

Instead, the rural landscape that was viewed by people who were here 25 years ago, or even last year, is constantly destroyed — most often through the building of vacation houses that remain vacant during the off-season, and may even be used as rental businesses in the summer by mainland owners who hardly inhabit the space at all — their choice of location and size of house often hurting everyone.

And when a conservation area is established, the nearby land becomes even more built up, nullifying much of the original good efforts and intent. Look at the Cutting Cottages next to Mitchell Farm, or the large new houses overlooking Rodman's Hollow, or the mega-structures that peer across the Lewis-Dickens Farm from as high a perch as they can find. And then there are real estate dealers who offer land for sale "bordering on conservation land."

For information about other efforts to preserve Block Island, see remainder of this chapter as well as:

- *page 57 — map of Nathan Mott Park; the first open space land donated to public;*
- *pages 223-224 — Smilin' Through and land around Fresh Pond;*
- *pages 130-131 and 228-234 — for history of seven conservation-oriented groups (and their bumper stickers)*
- *page 261 — a lesson of this Island*

A People's Revolution of 1973

By the summer of 1973 the first annual meeting of the Block Island Conservancy was being planned. Capt. John R. Lewis, the president, wrote an annual report starting off "Dear Friends" that listed many of the people who had contributed time and talent, some of them being:

- the Land Conservation Trust of New Canaan, Connecticut, for providing a model for the bylaws;
- for adapting that model to Block Island: **Merrill Slate** (bird study teacher at the school), **John Gray** (past first warden of the town council), and **Herbert Whitman** (then first warden);
- for bringing legal scrutiny to the bylaws: Commander **Joseph Wadsworth** (summer resident at Cormorant Point);
- for legal help to incorporate and obtain tax exempt status: **F. Albert Starr** (then town solicitor);
- for typing: **Mary Nelson** (Starr's secretary);
- for creating an official seal: **George and Connie LaRue** (who later made the gilded, carved sign at Rodman's Hollow);
- for making "eye-catching" contribution boxes placed about town next to stacks of bumper stickers: **Marianne Loferski** and **Keith Lewis**;
- for making advertising posters: artist **Gillian Stevens Gordon**;
- for mailing membership cards: **Helen Cullinan**, **Kathleen McKnight**, **John F. Ryan**, and **Beatrice Stiefer**;
- and several "young people" who addressed fifteen hundred envelopes: **Richard Batchelder**, **Christopher Blane**, **Mary Ann Donnelly**, **Gay Ann Hall**, **Marianne Loferski**, **Patricia McQuade**, **Adrian Mitchell**, **Michael Riley**, and **Catherine Sprague**.

Rob Lewis, the hero of Rodman's Hollow — and Block Island

It was a people's revolution. Captain Lewis, usually conservative, also noted:

"Finally ... I believe that anyone who cares about Block Island does not want to see it despoiled and bled by speculators, developers, fast-buck operators, and the like who, in the last analysis, care nothing about Block Island or its people, and whose only interest is personal profit ...

"I dare say that those who have contributed financially to the Block Island Conservancy, Inc. have done so at considerable personal sacrifice; we are not an affluent people, and this island means much to us. We are a small island fighting for our life."

And lastly the seafarer — who during World War II, as chief mate of an ammunition ship, stood and slept atop multi-ton loads of bombs being ferried into northern Africa on a route known by U-boats, daring the Germans would not blow he and his crew into atoms — and in the middle of the war, at age 25 became the youngest merchant marine captain with an unlimited master's license in American history — was to beg 30 years later of his fellow countrymen:

"Herewith, I earnestly plead with those who are relentlessly pursuing the courses of development and speculation to spare this lovely spot."

And they did not.

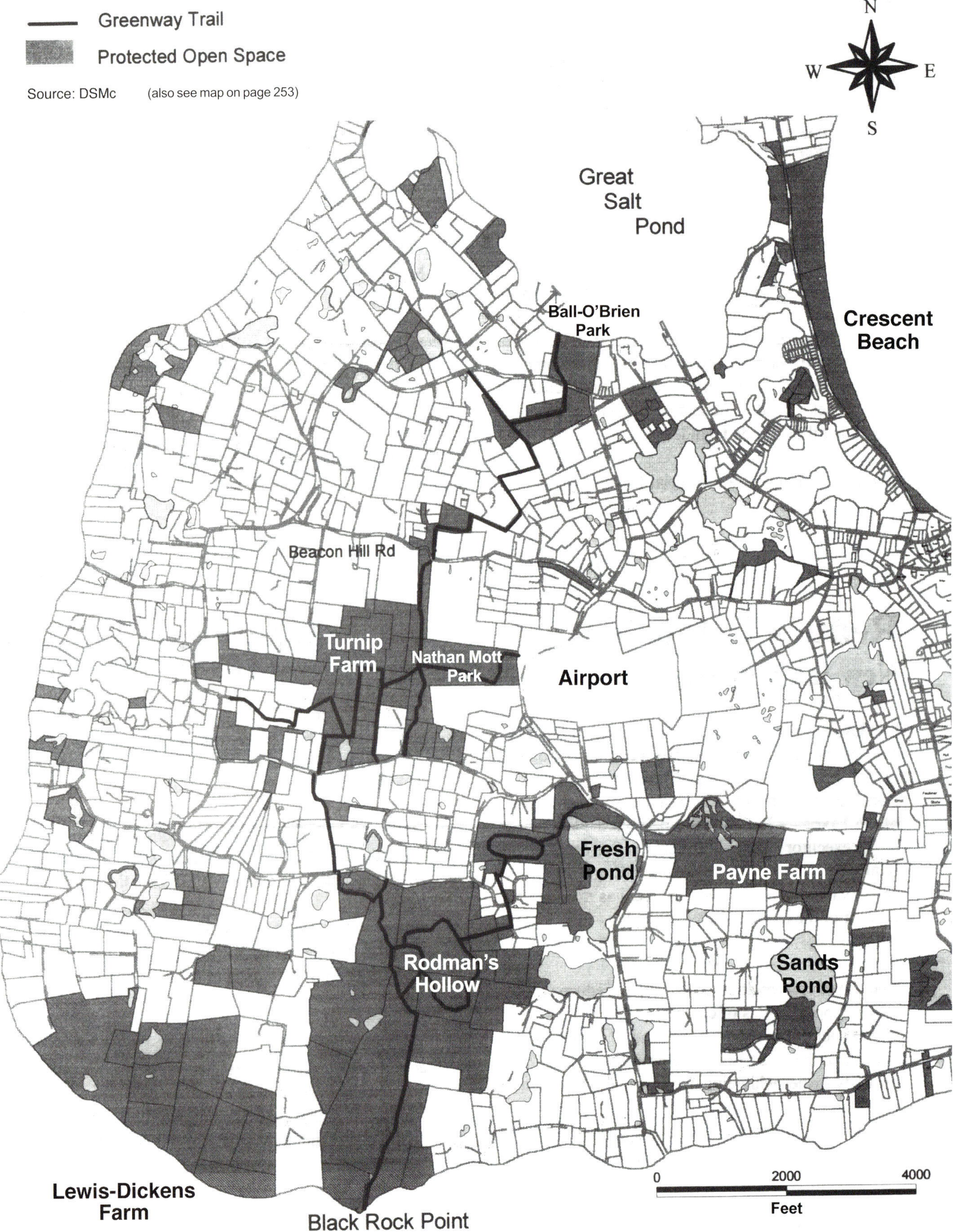

Southwest part of
Block Island Greenway — 1999
Greenway Trail
Protected Open Space
Source: DSMc
(also see map on page 253)
N
W
E
S
Great Salt Pond
Crescent Beach
Ball-O'Brien Park
Beacon Hill Rd
Turnip Farm
Nathan Mott Park
Airport
Fresh Pond
Payne Farm
Rodman's Hollow
Sands Pond
Lewis-Dickens Farm
Black Rock Point
0
2000
4000
Feet

The Greenway

A little bit of England on Block Island

In Great Britain, paths have long allowed travelers to pass by foot throughout nearly the whole of the country. The series of similar walkways in the northern and southern portions of Block Island — collectively called the Greenway — may seem as though they have been a part of Block Island nearly forever too, but that is not so. The concept may seem so good — so obviously beneficial to everyone — that no particular person could be credited with originating the scheme, but that is also not the case.

The first segment of the Greenway was dedicated on August 18, 1990, and grew from an idea proffered — then acted upon — by Shirley and Peter Wood. As explained by Keith Lang, then the director of the Rhode Island office of the Nature Conservancy:

"During the Christmas season of 1988 I went to see Peter and Shirley Wood on Old Mill Road and they walked me over the hill from Turnip Farm to Rodman's Hollow, describing their dream of a walking trail connecting the two preserves and eventually reaching New Harbor. They made a very generous offer of land and easements to get the project started. Bob Smith, who was president of the Block Island Conservancy then, did a huge amount of work on the project. We did a fund-raiser and got people excited. But it was the Woods who deserve the credit. It wouldn't have been done without them."

A tribute delivered by Peter Wood, at the dedication of the first Block Island Greenway, Old Mill Road, August 18, 1990

The day at the pond by the Greenway entrance on Old Mill Road was one of general congratulations for a well-conceived task: to leave a fitting legacy to future generations. Plaques were presented to Robert Bendict, former head of the state's Department of Environmental Management; and to Martha Ball and Bill Ball, for a recent conservation easement north of Mansion Beach.

◀ *The Greenway in the southwest of the Island*

The initial Greenway portion dedicated in 1990 began at the Nathan Mott Park, near the airport; ran across the large expanse of the adjacent Turnip Farm land, saved from development earlier by Burt King; and crossed several other properties before completing the southward journey to the sea along the seldom-used dirt track called Black Rock Road.

Paths do not come easily — many people enjoy walking on other land, but not everyone allows public walkways in their own backyard; and the Greenway paths run through many properties.

Nevertheless, a northward extension, dedicated on May 30, 1998, continued the Greenway to Great Salt Pond, completing a 10-year dream. A half-dozen organizations and town groups participated, led by Keith Lang (who switched hats from the Nature Conservancy and had become a board member of the Block Island Conservancy) and Dorothy McCluskey, vice president of the BIC, and a member of the town's planning board.

The last segment near Beacon Hill that brought all the pieces together was supplied by Kurt and Erica Tonner.

Once again people could traverse across the earth's landscape from the sea to the Great Salt Pond — as humans had done for thousands of years, until the 1960s when the then knee-high bayberry meshed together in the old farm fields taking over the pastures, and owners of new summer homes began their own concerted campaign of erecting "private" or "keep out" signs on ancient lanes that once welcomed the traveler.

Block Island CONSERVANCY
Newsletter
Block Island, Rhode Island 02807

May 1998

Trail open from Pond to Sea

Final Greenway seqment completes 10-year vision

See Map Page 3

A 10-year-old vision has been realized with the opening of the last link in the Greenway that now reaches from Black Rock to the Great Salt Pond.

The segment from Beacon Hill Road to the pond will be thrown open to the public on **Saturday, May 30**, with an inaugural walk starting at the Ball-O'Brien Park at 10 a.m. Leading the walk will be Keith Lang, who as an original trustee of the Block Island Land Trust, as the founding state director of The Nature Conservancy and now as a Block Island Conservancy director has seen the Greenway through every stage since birth. The Land Trust, The Nature Conservancy and the Town of New Shoreham, all involved in putting together this last piece of trail, are co-sponsoring the event.

"During the Christmas season of 1988 I went to see Peter and Shirley Wood on Old Mill Road and they walked me over the hill from Turnip Farm to Rodman's Hollow, describing their dream of a walking trail connecting the two preserves and eventually reaching New Harbor," he recalled. "They made a very generous offer of land and easements to get the project started."

Lang quickly brought the Block Island Conservancy and The Nature Conservancy together to negotiate easements, purchase land and cut the route. "Bob Smith, who was president of the Block Island Conservancy then, did a huge amount of work on the project," Lang said. "We did a fund-raiser and got people excited. But it was the Woods who deserve the credit. It wouldn't have been done without them."

The trail from Black Rock to Beacon Hill was opened in 1991 but the path onward to the pond proved more difficult to complete. Lang and Dorothy McCluskey, vice president of the Block Island Conservancy and a member of the town Planning Board, have played key roles as the path has been pieced together through the years.

(turn to page 2)

Winter Light — Mohegan Bluffs, 1978

The complexity of the clay and gravel Mohegan Bluffs is revealed with the help of light, shadow and snow. In 1993 the Southeast Lighthouse was moved to safety, relocated next to the former Coast Guard house on the left.

Parcels of land along the bluffs' edge in this photo were preserved for the public, beginning with donation of the **Edward S. Payne Overlook** (in the middle distance) by the **Payne and Phelan families**.

Winter Beach — Mansion Beach, 1976

Two conservation areas at the north end of Crescent Beach are widely used by the public. **Mansion Beach**, purchased by the town in the mid-1980s, is in the foreground — shown at low tide in its winter form, with most of the sand washed out to sea by storms.

Behind the Littlefield farm, its stonewalls lined with snow, is the beginning of the **Clay Head Nature Trail**, given to the public by the **Lapham family** in 1978. For another mile, paths — commonly called the Maze — wind along the cliffs for all to enjoy.

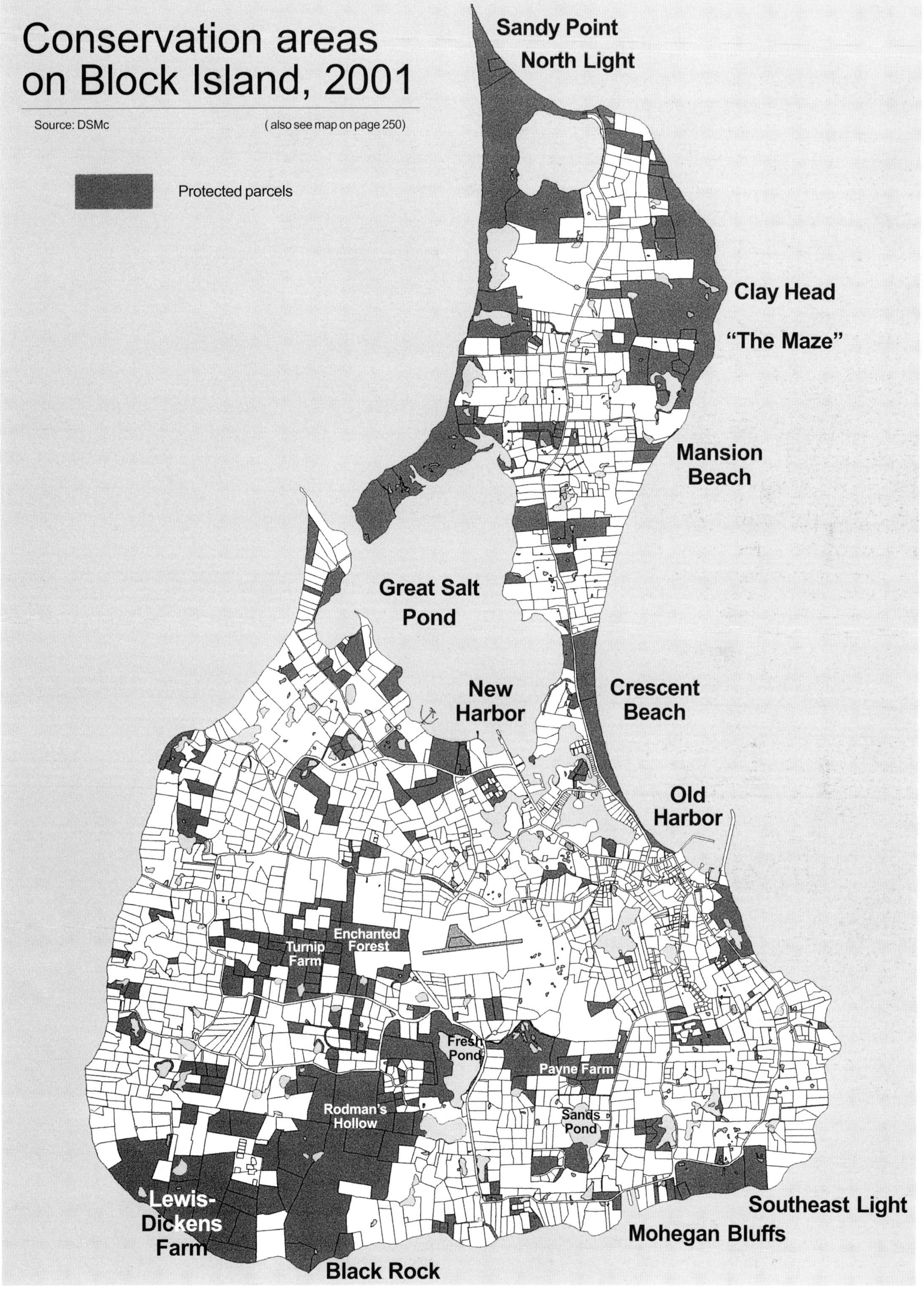
Conservation areas on Block Island, 2001
Source: DSMc
(also see map on page 250)
Protected parcels
Sandy Point
North Light
Clay Head
"The Maze"
Mansion Beach
Great Salt Pond
New Harbor
Crescent Beach
Old Harbor
Enchanted Forest
Turnip Farm
Fresh Pond
Payne Farm
Rodman's Hollow
Sands Pond
Lewis-Dickens Farm
Black Rock
Southeast Light
Mohegan Bluffs

Perched on the porch of her cottage in 1960, the profile of 82-year-old Miss Dickens was as imposing as the life she led

During one eight-year stretch, Elizabeth noticed that a pair of banded barn swallows returning from South America did not vary by more than three days from April 19 in finding her fields: "Sometimes he would come first, then she would. They were like folks. They were glad to get back, and they would talk to you."

CHAPTER 27

Miss Dickens

Block Island's Grande Dame of the 20th Century

ONE OF THE THREE BEST PLACES to see birds in America is Block Island — it has been said — and the fall is the greatest time to see them.

The birds have been tracked for most of this century: since the 1920s in a Christmas census; in the spring during the northward migration; and in the reverse spectacle, the southward migration of late September and early October. One person amongst all others noticed the birds.

Passing through her years like a steady vessel at sea, Elizabeth Dickens emerged in the last half of her life as the Island's ship-of-state — the most well-known, beloved, written-about person of her lifetime — all because of birds. Due to her, binoculars replaced on Block Island the gun barrels of turn-of-the-century bird hunters, and the Island's fame as a welcoming mat for both the birds and their watchers spread.

Living at the end of a dirt road, facing the sea and the setting sun, Elizabeth Dickens must have led one of the last pure Island lives. Surrounded by silence — cut off by that rutted lane from the noises of cars and trucks, and by time from the din of planes or summertime rental mopeds — her world was the sound of wind changes, barnyard animals, and the singsong of a bird or whoosh of an entire flight.

In the fields around her, she could bask in the sun warmth of a cool fall day. No soap opera on TV in the afternoon for her. No romance novel or courtroom paperback filled her time. Outside, the book of nature was spread open, its pages turning magically by themselves — from morning to evening, from winter to summer. And she recorded that world by listing on the empty pages of notebooks the sights around her: each bird noticed each day, each notebook becoming five years' worth of days. She started her bird diaries in 1912 at the late age of 34. Two years later she began teaching classes in bird lore to the Island's school children. Both endeavors would last another 50 years.

An entry from her diary's first year, for August 13, 1912, reads:

"2 Bartram's Tattlers, 4 Black-billed Cuckoos, 1 Yellowlegs, 5 Least Sandpipers, 2 Spotted Sandpipers, 1 Semipalmated Plover, 150 Wilson's Terns, 1 Ruddy Turnstone, 25 White-rumped Sandpipers."

Miss Dickens' listings were not solely for her own knowledge — many sightings were sent to the U.S. Fish and Wildlife Service where they helped divulge the migratory habits of North American birds. Her reports were used for the preparation of two standard works: the American Ornithologist's Union's *Checklist of North American Birds*, and the *Life Histories of North American Birds* by A. C. Bent.

On Elizabeth Dickens' brief trips off the Island, her widowed father would keep the record. Somehow during the early decades, she missed a day. For one day — inadvertently — nothing was written. Not bad, considering that each 24-hours most of us see little of note, and write absolutely nothing about it.

The five-year diaries piled up, eventually becoming 11 volumes of sightings and terse comments on other happenings. In 1942 she noted "Dog Susan is 5. The best dog in the world." Living alone she let the southwest corner of the Island fill her life. But she reached out too — the monthly teaching of the children, both in the classroom and in the fields, became a window for them to life they may not have seen.

In 1932 she wrote for the American Ornithologist's Union:

"Rare Birds on Block Island —

"*Fregata magnificens* [magnificent frigate-bird] — November 16, two of my former bird study pupils brought me a beautiful female man o war which had been shot and left on one of the fishing wharves at Old Harbor.

"*Vanellus vanellus* [northern lapwing] — On Nov. 20 one of my high school girls brought me a fine specimen of a lapwing which had been shot on Block Island. It had passed through many hands before it was salvaged by my little friend.

"*Chen hyperus atlanticus* [*C.C. atlantica*] — A greater snow goose was shot on the morning of Oct. 27 and was secured by a high school boy for the School Collection."

Writing to famed ornithologist Edward Forbush, she described a flight of herons in November 1910:

"I'll never forget. In the early morning I was attempting to feed my flock of 75 turkeys when they suddenly all became sky-gazers. Of course, I did likewise and beheld 12 great blue herons circling above the flock. Round and round and round they flew until I was almost dizzy trying to follow their motion with my eyes. At last they seemed to have had enough of this and flew away to the southeast. A little later another dozen came from the west and alighted in a row along the edge of the bluff. 'Twas interesting to see the difference in heights and sizes.

"Then there came groups of threes and fives and nines and so it continued at intervals all day. In the afternoon came one great flock of just a hundred birds. As they reached land a life-saving crew fired into them and the flock became two bunches of 40 and 60 birds each. I don't know how many herons I saw that day but there must have been several hundred."

Elizabeth Dickens and parents, late 1880s

As a young girl, Elizabeth Dickens traveled to Providence with her parents, Lovell and Nancy, to pose for this formal portrait at the studio of photographer H. Q. Morton.

Her father was also a lifesaver, assigned to one of the Island's three stations — and perhaps had a few thoughts to relay the next day to his brethren about the beauty of birds.

To the Island's children, Elizabeth issued many such words. They eagerly joined her conspiracy of appreciation — bringing her dead specimens they had found — killed usually by encounters with cats, automobiles, lighthouses, or telephone wires. These were sent to the mainland to be stuffed — but if the birds had been shot for that purpose, Elizabeth would refuse acceptance. The collection of mounted birds grew to 175, and were moved by sheer necessity from her home in 1936 to the Island's newly built school, where they can still be seen.

One of her earliest students was a boy named Eddie of whom she later wrote:

"Many of our boys who were 'real boys' were proud possessors of air guns and some of them were accurate shots. In fact, one of our old neighbors said of his grandson, 'Eddie is a good shot. Yesterday he shot enough of them little fall birds to cover a double page of the *Providence Journal* when he laid 'em out.'"

But forty years later — after being in Miss Dickens' classes in his youth — the young Eddie had grown up in more ways than one, and now helped *his* grandson in the spring to have "bird houses ready for first arrivals, and woe betide cat or starling that interferes with their guests."

Beginning in 1924 Elizabeth conducted school children on an annual Christmas bird census — one year leading them 10 miles in 36-mph winds, another year 11 miles with two inches of sleet on the ground. She missed only the tally of the last December before she died, but that count was nevertheless made, led by one of her former students.

Like a mother's face constantly over the crib of a child, "Miss Dickens" im-

Ruby-throated hummingbird and Elizabeth Dickens

Miss Dickens and one of the 175 mounted specimens from her collection, displayed since 1936 at the Block Island School.

planted herself onto the Island's young — and through her photographs, seems to do the same to us.

There is a photographers' adage that because children are inherently full of life and beauty "you can't take a bad picture of a child." So it was also with this woman in her last thirty years, when ornithologists, newspaper reporters, and magazine writers from *Life* and the *Saturday Evening Post*, increasingly found their way to the door of her remote Cape Cod style cottage, grasping at what for them, even while there, was an unusual life to capture — and which for us, now, will always be unreachable.

One reporter visited her in September 1962 — she had by that time in her life seen over 300 species of birds on Block Island — and wrote later:

"She was 84 then, a little regretful at the thought of not teaching in the coming winter, but still just as interested in everything around her island and in the outside world. She noted they were looking for a new superintendent of schools, talked about the water problem and other topics of current interest.

"And there were her birds. Stacks of diaries listing daily counts, lay in piles about the small living room which was filled with mementos of her full life. The diaries will be of great value to ornithologists ... She was responsible for making the island known to bird watchers throughout the country.

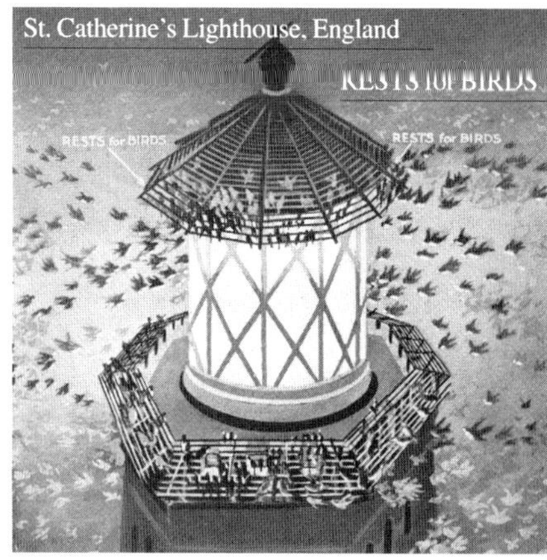

Lighthouse with bird trellis

In England, trellises were built around tops of lighthouses for birds to rest at night. Once, in the mid-1930s, 252 black-polled warblers were found dead from exhaustion on the lawn around the Southeast Light.

Miss Dickens and Susan live in this cottage at Dickens Point, remote from the town.

Providence Journal photograph, 1948 — Miss Dickens and her dog Susan

Elizabeth Dickens' rich life unfolded in a traditional farmhouse, one of 300 or so that once defined Block Island's graceful landscape. Many recent summer houses are so overwhelmingly large that Miss Dickens' home would constitute just one room. In the last 30 years over 1,000 new houses have been built, most for summer use, and many of those for summer rental only, destroying the beauty those mainland people had come here for in the first place. So now, houses are built, or bought, purely for business reasons, to function like 100s of miniature hotels, the owners having no interest in living on Block Island.

Postcard, 1934 — "Carting coal from wrecked barge"

Elizabeth Dickens sent this postcard on March 28, 1934, to a friend in Providence — not to describe the dramatic image of Islanders gathering coal with ox-carts from one of the several shipwrecks near her home, but to write on the back something more important, the birds she had recently seen:

Just to say our first Robin since Dec. 26 arrived March 2. Two more since.

Fox Sparrow — March 4 — stayed 2 days.

March 5 — Killdeers were reported from various points of the Island.

Our own pair were the first to report themselves that morning.

Hastily, Elizabeth Dickens

(Many dead waterfowl)

"Miss Dickens lived all her life on the family homestead, but not in the same house. Her original home burned in 1894 with everything in it. 'I went to sleep that night with some of the best prospects of any girl on the island,' she recalled. 'The next morning I had nothing.' But there was no sense of loss in her voice and her real meaning seemed to be that she had long ago put a realistic value on materialistic things …

"On that bright, sunny day last fall, Miss Dickens noted that changes come, even to an isolated island. 'The farms are going and the meadowlark is disappearing,' she remarked."

On June 12, 1963, at the age of 85, Elizabeth Dickens entered as usual the temperature in her diary "55," followed by the birds sighted: "1 Barn Owl, 1 Crow, 1 Pheasant, 6 Barn Swallows, 5 Redwings, 2 Song Sparrow, 1 Northern Yellow Throat, and 1 Robin."

On June 13 she listed the temperature: again "55."

There were no entries for June 14 and 15.

Her home was visited by friends on the morning of June 16, after Elizabeth had been missed at the High School graduation she attended annually. As related in Herbert Whitman's biographical booklet *Elizabeth Dickens, the bird lady of Block Island*, published in 1982:

"They found her lying in the long grass between her house and the barn with a soup can in her hand. The back door of the house was open and the lamps, their chimneys standing beside them, were ready to be lit … Elizabeth was barely alive. Her arm was broken."

She was scarcely able to talk. The next day, after transportation to Westerly on the mainland, Miss Dickens died. Islanders would no longer hear her familiar phone

call: "Run to the window, and look at the sunset!"

The obituary and medical records from 1963 read "Miss Dickens had suffered a cerebral hemorrhage and fractured an arm when she fell. She later contracted pneumonia."

Her stature has grown since her death. In the 1986 book *A World of Watchers* by Joseph Kastner, she is featured in a chapter titled "The Imbuers: Elizabeth Dickens and the Woman Writers."

The literary company — to be found on the pages around her — would have pleased Miss Dickens: from Audubon in the 1800s, to Forbush in the early 1900s, to Roger Tory Peterson of the late 1900s — but not so much, not ever as much, as the world around her on Block Island.

• *To read how the Lewis-Dickens Farm was saved — see Chapter 26, pages 245-246*
• *For the location of her farm — see maps pages 250, 253*

Elizabeth Dickens at school, 1948

In 1948 a *Providence Sunday Journal* article pictured Miss Dickens displaying a sparrow hawk to youngsters Larry Rose and Lester Littlefield.

On the left is a mounted snow owl, on the right a horned grebe.

The example she set was so strong that the Rhode Island Audubon Society established the Elizabeth Dickens Education Fund in 1956 to assist financing all of the Audubon's various teaching projects. That fund has since been merged with others.

And in October 2000 at the University of Rhode Island — 37 years after her death — Elizabeth Dickens received a posthumous award at the Rhode Island Natural History Survey conference.

She is still a tough act to follow.

AS THESE CHILDREN WENT from the Block Island School in 1950, across the empty fields, diverging to their various homes, then so diverged in adulthood all the Island children of the 1950s — each and everyone a bird studies student of Elizabeth Dickens.

Some left the Island for good, or for bad.

Some remembered the joy of walking unfettered across Block Island's barren landscape, remembered their walks with Elizabeth Dickens and the simple pleasure of enjoying what they could see and were shown. As adults they labored to preserve the fields for themselves and for all others who would come just to see. They sacrificed. They gave up some leisure. They gave up money they had earned — and a lot more that could have been made.

Others took a different path, burning their bridges as it were, so they could never go back, so no person could go back, so no one would ever walk the fields that had stayed empty in the 1700s, the 1800s and into the 1950s. They became land developers. They took what is the easy route on Block Island, building summer houses on their inherited property, or scouring the town's plat maps for someone else's vacant lots that could be built on.

The developers' victories in life were enjoyed in the committee rooms and back-slapping taverns that formed their environment, a Block Island closed to the sky.

During the building boom of the last 35 years of the 20th century, a new social order was formed on Block Island that did not mind — despite loud protests — replacing the Island of Miss Dickens with their own, one gone so far in the wrong direction that most of the house builders did not care to stay here and live with what they had done — while others remained, blind to it all.

The neighbors of Elizabeth Dickens, with great struggle, saved most of her land.

If *YOU* wish to see, you may.

PHOTO CREDITS & OTHER IMAGES

Many thanks to those individuals and institutions whose photographs and other graphic material appear in this book. Of the 354 images in ***Block Island–The Land***, more than three-quarters, or 268, are from the author. The Block Island Historical Society contributed 44 photographs, while several other sources supplied the remaining 42. The book — and the enjoyment of readers — would be lessened by excluding any. All copyright restrictions apply to the reproduction of any image in ***Block Island–The Land***.

Title page & p. 263 .... *Photographs by Robert M. Downie*
viii-xi .... *Robert M. Downie Collection*

Chapter 1 World War II — The Furthest Island
2, 9 .... *Photographs by Chuck McMellon*
4 .... *Providence Evening Bulletin*
5, 6 .... *Providence Journal*
7 .... *Robert M. Downie Collection*
8, 11 (bottom) .... *United States Army*
10, 11 (top) .... *Photographs by Robert M. Downie*

Chapter 2 First Photographs of Block Island
12, 14, 16-19 .... *Robert M. Downie Collection*

Chapter 3 The Ghost of a Grand Hotel
20, 27 (top) .... *Photographs by Robert M. Downie*
22 .... *from* Voyages of Nicholas Ball, *1895*
23-26 .... *Robert M. Downie Collection*
27 (bottom) .... *Chart by Robert M. Downie*

Chapter 4 Ume Tsuda
28 .... *from* The White Plum, *1991*
30 .... *Robert M. Downie Collection*
31 .... *BI Historical Society Collection*

Chapter 5 We Discovered an Island ...
32-36 .... *Robert M. Downie Collection*

Chapter 6 The Cemetery
40, 41, 43-51 .... *Photographs by Robert M. Downie*
42 .... *Robert M. Downie Collection*

Chapter 7 Rathbun Family & Early Settlers
52, 61-63 .... *Robert M. Downie Collection*
54, 56 .... *Rathbun Family Association*
57 (map), 58 (chart) .... *map & chart by Robert M. Downie*
59 .... *Photograph by Robert M. Downie*
60 .... *map from Rhode Island Historical Society*: Collections, January 1923

Chapter 8 Farming of the Past
64-66, 67 (top), 68, 72 (bottom) .... *BI Historical Society Collection*
67 (bottom), 72 (top), 73 (top) .... *BI Historical Society's Mansfield Collection*
73 (bottom), 75 (top) .... *BI Historical Society Collection*
70, 71, 75 (bottom) .... *Robert M. Downie Collection*
74 .... *Robert M. Downie Collection — Courtesy of Arnold Flaig*

Chapter 9 Burning Peat
76 .... *BI Historical Society's Mansfield Collection*
78, 80 .... *BI Historical Society Collection*
79 .... *from* Block Island Scrapbook, *by Maizie, 1957*
80 .... *Photograph by Robert M. Downie*
80-81 .... *diagram from* Peat Resources of Block Island, *1979*

Chapter 10 Block Island Ice
82, 84-86, 88, 90 (top), 91 .... *Robert M. Downie Collection*
87, 89, 90 (bottom) .... *BI Historical Society Collection*

Chapter 11 School Days
92, 95, 101, 105 (top) .... *BI Historical Society's Mansfield Collection*
94 (top), 96, 98, 103, 104 .... *Robert M. Downie Collection*
99, 100 .... *BI Historical Society Collection*
105 (bottom) .... *Photograph by Robert M. Downie*

Chapter 12 Post Offices
106 .... *courtesy of Martha Bodington and Jean Scott*
109-10, 111 (bottom), 113-14, 115 (top two) .... *Robert M. Downie Collection*
111 (top), 112 .... *BI Historical Society's Mansfield Collection*
115 (bottom) .... *Photograph by Robert M. Downie*

Chapter 13 Postcard Messages
116-123 .... *Robert M. Downie Collection*

COLOR SECTION
124-127, 130-131 .... *Robert M. Downie Collection*
128-129, 132-133 .... *Photographs by Robert M. Downie*

Chapter 14 Newspapers — People Want to Know
134-135, 136, 137, 138 (bottom), 139-142 .... *Robert M. Downie Collection*
136 (bottom), 137 (bottom), 138 (top) .... *BI Historical Society Collection*

Chapter 15 Complaints of the Distant Past
144, 147, 149-151 .... *Robert M. Downie Collection*

Chapter 16 Block Island Horse Cars
152 .... *BI Historical Society Collection*
155-161 .... *Robert M. Downie Collection*

Chapter 17 Beacon Hill
162, 164 (top), 165 .... *BI Historical Society Collection*
164 (bottom), 166-168 .... *Robert M. Downie Collection*
169 .... *U.S. Army*

Chapter 18 Souvenir China
170-183 .... *Robert M. Downie Collection*

Chapter 19 Old Hotel Booklets
184-189 .... *Robert M. Downie Collection*

Chapter 20 Island Photographers of the 1900s
190, 192 (bottom), 193-96, 197 (bottom), 198 .... *Robert M. Downie Collection*
192 (top), 197 (top), 199 .... *BI Historical Society Collection*

Chapter 21 Statue of Rebecca
200 .... *BI Historical Society's Mansfield Collection*
202 .... *courtesy of Martha Ball*
203 .... *Robert M. Downie Collection*
204, 206, 207 .... *Photographs by Robert M. Downie*
205 .... *BI Historical Society Collection*

Chapter 22 Windmills — Air Motors
208, 212 (top), 213-216 .... *Robert M. Downie Collection*
210 (top), 212 (bottom) .... *BI Historical Society's Mansfield Collection*
210 (bottom) .... Historic American Engineering Record *(HAER)*
211 (top) .... *HAER* (Hook Mill in East Hampton, NY)
211 (bottom) .... *from* American Miller and Millwright's Assistant, *1850*
217-219 .... *NASA*

Chapter 23 Smilin' Through
220, 221, 223-225 .... *Robert M. Downie Collection*
223 .... *Photograph by Robert M. Downie*

Chapter 24 The Bumper Sticker Museum
226 .... *Photograph by Robert M. Downie*
227-229 .... *Robert M. Downie Collection*

Chapter 25 Airlines — Air Wars
230, 232, 235-237 .... *Robert M. Downie Collection*
233, 239 .... *BI Historical Society Collection*

Chapter 26 The Block Island Conservancy
240, 244, 249, 252 .... *Photographs by Robert M. Downie*
242, 251 .... *Robert M. Downie Collection*
246, 247 .... *Photographs by Malcolm G. Greenaway*
250, 253 .... *adapted from maps by Donald S. McCluskey*

Chapter 27 Elizabeth Dickens
254 .... *Saturday Evening Post, 1960*
256, 257 .... *BI Historical Society Collection*
258 (top), 259 .... *Robert M. Downie Collection*
258 (bottom), 260, 261 .... *Providence Journal, 1948, 1950*

The landslide, 2001

John and Pam Gasner, with two-month Julia, stand atop the 30-foot high landslide, a primordial jumble of earthern stalagmites, deep fissures, icy-slick clay slabs, and wooded debris.

The sharp-tipped pyramids of earth formed when the mound sank approximately three feet, leaving behind these sturdier remnants of the former height. Half of the landslide, including everything visible here, was washed away by the sea within three days.

(See full view on title page.)

Source Material

Research material for ***Block Island–The Land*** came primarily from the author's collection of original Block Island items: more than two-dozen old maps (dating back to the 1600s); 200 hardbound books, 250 pamphlets, 1,500 newspaper articles (each category beginning in the 1700s); and more than 1,000 historic photographs (dating to the Island's first, in 1873). Additional research was undertaken by the author during the past 25 years at libraries and archives from New England to Washington, D.C.

Footnotes are not used, since the result — with one or more superscript numbers above most sentences — would be extremely distracting.

Nor is a bibliography attached, since those entries would need to be extensively annotated, so as not to direct the public to misleading publications, or parts of them. A complete bibliography of Block Island deserves a book of its own.

For additional information about the Island, read the companion volume ***Block Island–The Sea***, containing completely different photographs and stories — about pirates such as Captain Kidd, hurricanes, lighthouses, shipwrecks, ferries, Prohibition and rumrunning, some famous visitors, swordfishing, World War II, a nearby sunken U-boat, two BLOCK ISLAND aircraft carriers, and other subjects.

The author, Robert M. Downie, has lived on Block Island for a third of a century, serving on various community committees, writing for newspapers and publications, and following the voices of the sea toward many tasks and pleasures.

INDEX

A

B

C

D

E

F

M

N

O

P

Q

R

T

U

V

W

—0—